WELCOME to the Racing Post's latest guide to the jumps which not only looks at the new season but gives everything you need to enter the new-look Ten to Follow.

Inside these pages there is an in-depth look at the firepower from eight British trainers, while our experts look at the scene in Britain and Ireland and highlight the horses they believe can score plenty of points in racing's biggest competition.

As well as that we have pen portraits of the 400 horses in this season's Ten to Follow, which will prove invaluable in selecting your squad.

Please be aware there are various changes to this year's competition – full details can be found on pages 103-104 and at racingpost.com/ttf. And there is also a helping hand with some strategy advice on pages 86-87.

I hope you find the information in these pages useful – and maybe you might just use it to become our next big winner.

Enjoy reading and I wish you a happy and profitable season.

David Dew
Editor

Contributors

Colin Boag
Dave Edwards
Dylan Hill
James Hill
Paul Kealy
Steve Mason
Brian Morgan
Kevin Morley
Johnny Ward
Nicholas Watts

Published in 2012 by Racing Post Books
Raceform, High Street, Compton, Newbury, Berkshire, RG20 6NL

Copyright © Raceform Ltd 2012

The Racing Post specifies that post-press changes may occur to any information given in this publication.

A catalogue record for this book is available from the British Library.

ISBN: 978-1908216298

Edited and designed by **David Dew**
Printed by Buxton Press, Palace Road Buxton, Derbyshire SK17 6AE

Lowdown from the trainers

Ten to Follow

Statistics

Huge firepower can see Henderson finally reclaim trainers' championship

FOR the past four seasons, **Nicky Henderson has played bridesmaid to Paul Nicholls' bride in the trainers' table. Last season despite training 167 winners at a strike-rate of 27 per cent, earning his owners £2.7 million in prize-money, the success of Neptune Collonges in the Grand National yet again swung the championship Ditcheat's way. However, there are good reasons to believe that 2012-13 might be Henderson's year – no less an authority than Nicholls himself believes his rival has a favourite's chance. As will become apparent, the quality and strength in depth of his team this season is awesome.**

Frankel has shown us on the Flat that every so often a special one comes along, and it could just be that **Sprinter Sacre** is such a horse. Last season was perfect for the six-year-old, with wins coming at Doncaster in a novice chase, where he immediately flagged he was going to be very good over fences, and in the Wayward Lad at Kempton's Christmas meeting.

The Game Spirit came next, where he won on the bridle, before a staggeringly good performance in the Arkle. He didn't need to run up to that mark at Aintree as Barry

Geraghty never asked the question, but his win was still deeply impressive. The question is: just how good can this horse be?

"Well, he has to do it all again, and there are sure to be some young pretenders out there, but at six you'd like to think he could still be improving," Henderson says.

"He's a pure two-miler and that makes his targets straightforward to plan: races like the Tingle Creek, the Victor Chandler, the Game Spirit, and then the Champion Chase. He looks really well."

Finian's Rainbow was three from four last season, winning the Desert Orchid, the Champion Chase and the Melling Chase and becoming the first horse to do that Cheltenham-Aintree double since the great Moscow Flyer back in 2005. The Melling win was over two and a half miles, which opens up a new avenue for Finian's Rainbow, and might help his trainer.

"The fact he did it so well over the longer trip was good, as I'd obviously like to avoid him clashing with Sprinter Sacre. I might well step him up again and think about the King George. It seems odd to be thinking about doing this with the reigning two-mile champion before the season has even started, but he was very good at Aintree and it looked like it really suited him. As for next March: there's the Ryanair at two and a half, but if he proved he stays three miles then who knows? He's another who has done really well over the summer and is looking fantastic."

Long Run went into last season as the reigning Gold Cup winner but things didn't pan out as connections would have hoped,

Sprinter Sacre: will have all the top two-mile races on his agenda

with him being beaten twice by a rejuvenated Kauto Star and then finishing third behind the ill-fated Synchronised and outsider The Giant Bolster.

"He's still a young horse and we start the new season afresh with him – I think he's matured physically. He had a very hard race first time out last season and perhaps he never quite got over that, although he broke the course record in the Denman Chase at Newbury. Anyway, it will be a similar campaign again, with the King George and the Gold Cup as the big targets."

It's amazing to think that the 2011 Gold Cup winner is something of a forgotten horse for some people, but I have a hunch that come next March his name will again be on everyone's lips.

Henderson seems sure to have another Gold Cup contender if things continue to go well for **Bob's Worth**, winner of last season's RSA Chase. After he was beaten by Grands Crus in the Feltham he had a breathing operation and it seems to have worked a treat. He ran well enough at Ascot in the Reynoldstown, where he needed the run, but then, back on a left-handed track at Cheltenham, he was magnificent.

"Barry Geraghty was always concerned about Bob's Worth's wind, and then after Kempton he said we had to do something about it. It worked, although I was worried it hadn't at the start as he looked a wreck after the operation, and in mid-January I was worried we wouldn't get him to Cheltenham. He's probably better going left-handed, but he just loves Cheltenham – he's unbeaten there – with the uphill finish, and he stays

really well. We have to be thinking Gold Cup with him after his performance in the RSA, and he might well start off in the Hennessy."

Riverside Theatre was another Cheltenham Festival winner for Seven Barrows when he landed the two-and-a-half-mile chasing championship by winning the Ryanair. He wasn't seen out until February when he repeated his win of 12 months earlier in the Ascot Chase, and he then won at Cheltenham due in no small part to a truly wonderful ride from Barry Geraghty.

"He never looked like winning, but Barry persevered and somehow got him home – it was amazing. He went to Liverpool after that but he was never going and I think we have to put a line through that one. It looks as though he wants three miles, and the King George looks like his race, as the trip is right and Kempton's a flat track suits – he was second to Long Run in the 2010-11 running."

Connections adopted a bold strategy with **Oscar Whisky** last season, opting to step up in trip and take on Big Buck's in the World Hurdle. That didn't work out as he didn't seem to stay the three-mile trip, and the 2011 Champion Hurdle suggested he needs further than two miles against the best. The World Hurdle apart, the seven-year-old was excellent, winning the Aintree Hurdle for the second year running on his final start.

"Our current thinking is that we'll stay over hurdles, and there are plenty of races for him. However, we desperately need a hurdles version of the Ryanair, a two-and-a-half-mile championship for horses who fall in between two and three miles – that would be his ideal race. He will race at two miles, I'm sure, as I fancy he'll go to the Welsh Champion Hurdle again, but two and a half is his trip.

"**Burton Port** was second to Long Run in the Denman Chase, fourth in the Gold Cup and then second in the Betfred Bowl at Aintree – I suspect it will be a similar campaign this season. Although he's not the biggest horse he's a great little jumper, as tough as teak, and we might consider the National for him.

"**Master Of The Hall** is a very good horse in small fields but I'm not convinced he really likes Cheltenham. So we'll just play around and find the right races for him, but he's a good horse on his day.

"**Tanks For That** has been very consistent.

I felt sorry for him when he finished second in the Grand Annual because he did everything bar win, just being caught by one of ours, Bellvano, who's sadly no longer with us. Can he progress beyond handicaps? I don't know – he's not a Champion Chase horse, and he's best at around two miles. He might be worth a crack at a race like the Peterborough.

"I think there's more to come from **Triolo D'Alene**. I thought he was one of my bankers for Cheltenham, but then things didn't go quite right. He's had a little wind operation since then and I hope that will help him. He's only five, so he's still young, and I think he's all right."

Henderson always has an impressive team who are going novice chasing – following the Henderson novices is a good strategy – and this time around is no exception. The most eagerly awaited among them must be **Simonsig**, who had a spectacular novice hurdling campaign.

He won the 2m5f Neptune at the festival, and followed up in the Mersey Novices' Hurdle at Aintree, winning both races pretty much as he pleased.

"He had a fantastic season and will probably be going chasing. Assuming that's how we go, we'll bring him back to two miles and aim him at the Arkle. Although we've only ever run him at beyond two miles, we've never felt it would be a problem stepping back in trip as he has plenty of speed.

"**Punjabi** is back following a year off. He deserved a rest and it looks like it's done him the world of good. Although he's nine, he's going novice chasing.

"**Cash And Go** is a new arrival from Ireland. He won three times over hurdles, including a Leopardstown Grade 1. He's only a five-year-old but he'll be going chasing.

"**Open Hearted** will be chasing too. He's had a great summer and has really grown and strengthened again, although he's only five.

"**Captain Conan** is exciting and he'd be one of the better novice chasing prospects. He won the Tolworth on his British debut, and we decided to bypass Cheltenham this year. He finished his season with two fine seconds, including behind Darlan at Aintree. I'd imagine he'll start out at two miles, and he wouldn't want to be going beyond two and a half.

"**Broadback Bob** is quite talented and we

could go either way with him. Unfortunately he chipped a bone in his hock at Cheltenham in January which curtailed his season – I'd hoped he'd be my horse for the Neptune. He'll certainly make a chaser but I'd quite like to see whether he progresses over hurdles – on balance I think chasing is probably the way we'll go.

"I like **Hadrian's Approach**. He's an Irish point-to-point winner, so I think we'll probably go chasing with him. We think he would have won the race at Ascot in January had he not tipped over at the second-last. He wasn't out again but he wouldn't have been mature enough for Cheltenham or Aintree anyway.

"**Kells Belle** is lovely. She won a mares' race at Cheltenham in April but I think we'll head down the chasing route with her – she's big enough to jump fences. She was probably the highest-rated mare in Britain by the end of the season and life would be tough off that mark, and with Quevega around she'd struggle in the better mares' races.

"I took a while to understand **Master Of The Game** but I like him. His first two runs were over two and a half miles but when we brought him back in trip at Bangor he was impressive. He's talented, bred to be a chaser, and that's the route we'll take.

"**Molotof** won his first three hurdle races in fine style. We gave him a break and he finished down the field in the Martin Pipe, and then fifth behind Simonsig at Aintree. He's done really well over the summer and was always going to be a chaser – I hope he'll be pretty good at it.

"**Oscara Dara** beat Malt Master in a novice event at Punchestown and I think they'll both go over fences. Oscara Dara has run only over two miles so far, but you'd have to think he'll be even better going a bit further. He could be very good.

"**Malt Master** won at Newcastle in November and we then held him back for the winners of one race at Punchestown which was a good plan until the other one of ours beat him. I like him and I think he'll do well over fences.

"**Seven Woods** won at Ffos Las in April but was very babyish last season. He'll go chasing and will stay well – three miles-plus will be his trip and he handles soft ground very well.

"**Oscar Nominee** is progressive and I think he'll be novice chasing too – it's not certain, but that's my current thinking. He could develop into a very good horse as he matures."

Moving to the hurdlers, **Binocular** is a favourite of his trainer. The 2010 Champion Hurdle winner was second in the Fighting Fifth last season and then won the Christmas Hurdle before being really impressive in the Kingwell at Wincanton. He was sent off second favourite for the Champion but could finish only fourth which, considering how he'd run in his previous race, had to be disappointing.

"After Wincanton both AP [McCoy] and I thought he was back to his best, but for some reason Cheltenham wasn't his day. He was lame after the race so that might have been a factor. At Wincanton his hurdling was very good and very quick, so I'm convinced there's another Champion Hurdle in him if we can get him right on the day. He's a bit behind some of the others so won't be out as early as some. He won the Christmas Hurdle last year and I think that's where we'll start. With him, all roads lead to Cheltenham."

Darlan won his first three races last season but then fell in the Betfair Hurdle at Newbury when still cruising at the second-last. I'm not talking though my pocket when I say I think he would have won but for falling. Second to Cinders And Ashes is no disgrace, but he might have won had Tony McCoy started his run sooner. His win in the Grade 2 Top Novices' Hurdle at Aintree was a good performance.

"We think Darlan will stay over hurdles because we hope he might prove good enough to go for the Champion Hurdle. The only time he was beaten over hurdles was when he was second in the Supreme Novices' and he came back to win well at Liverpool. He's going to be a chaser but I hope there's

Darlan: long-term chasing prospect, but could be aimed at the Champion Hurdle this season

still plenty more to come from him over hurdles. If he shows that he's up to it then either the Greatwood or the Fighting Fifth would come into consideration.

"**Grandouet** is over the leg infection he had before Cheltenham and he'll stay over hurdles this season. He's very, very good and the Champion Hurdle will be the aim again – his win in the International Hurdle at Cheltenham in December was very impressive. He's a genuine two-miler but, as he showed, he genuinely gets up the hill there. Where Darlan doesn't run, he will, and where he doesn't then Binocular will – it's a nice problem to have."

As always, there were a lot of bumper winners from Seven Barrows last season and Henderson has singled out a few of the better hurdling prospects.

"The best of them would probably include **Close Touch**, Open Hearted's half-brother

– he won well at Market Rasen; **Makari** is a gorgeous new arrival; there is **My Tent Or Your**, who was second in the Aintree Champion Bumper; **River Maigue** won a point-to-point in Ireland and then a bumper for us at Ayr, and the filly **Seaham Hall** was very good at Ffos Las.

"**Snake Eyes** was one of our best last year, and he might have a run or two in bumpers before going over hurdles. We bought **Tistory** in France and he won at Ludlow, and **Whisper**, who won at Ffos Las, I think can be high-class over hurdles."

The strength at Seven Barrows is staggering. Reigning champion Paul Nicholls won't roll over easily but you have to think that with only average luck, Henderson has a great chance of winning his first trainers' title since 1986-87. [Colin Boag]

HENDERSON AND THE STATS

After breaking the century barrier for the first time in 2008-09 with 115 winners, Henderson has had an influx in quality and quantity each season since. His tallies since that campaign have totalled 136, 153 and, last season, 167. His strike-rate in 2011-12 was 27 per cent, while a level-stakes loss of just -5.94 points is no mean feat considering his amount of runners and reputation, *writes Kevin Morley*.

After nearly wresting the trainers' championship from Paul Nicholls last season Henderson appears to have an excellent chance of achieving the feat this term, especially with so many high-class horses in his ranks. He will be well represented in most of the championship events and with a promising crop of novice talent, the future looks rosy at Seven Barrows.

Barry Geraghty became stable jockey in 2008-09 and he is one of the rare exceptions for that role in that he has been profitable to follow. He has maintained a 30 per cent strike-rate (+11.63pt) since taking up the job at Lambourn, although he may be hard pushed to keep that level-stakes column in the black. The bookmakers, already predicting Henderson will be champion trainer with quotes as short as 1-3, are likely to be on the defensive for the trainer-jockey combination.

Tony McCoy is often asked to ride for the yard and has an even better strike-rate than Geraghty over the last five seasons at 34 per cent, but he doesn't have such impressive level-stakes figures.

Henderson has an excellent win-to-run ratio but it's his runners over hurdles who hurt the layers most. His novices have struck at 30 per cent since 2008-09 (+14.56pt) and although his handicappers strike at a lower rate of 15 per cent, some oblige at massive prices highlighted by his mammoth level-stakes profit in that area (+114.77pt).

Henderson uses his conditional riders to good effect, particularly when it comes to handicaps, and those ridden by David Bass have been a good source of profit in recent years. However, now that promising pilot has lost his claim it might be the turn of Jeremiah McGrath to step into the limelight. His 11 winners from 41 rides for the stable in 2011-12 (27 per cent /+45.88pt) secured a handsome profit, which included a 40-1 winner at the Cheltenham Festival. His claim is now down to 5lb but he is well worth that, and more success should come his way this term.

Henderson has high strike-rates at quite a few tracks with his records at Market Rasen (43 per cent /+15.06pt) and Leicester (44 per cent /+21.40pt) standing out. He is also one to follow at tracks that stage higher quality racing. He has a 30 per cent strike-rate at Kempton (+37.74pt) and is renowned for sending out plenty of winners there over the Christmas period. He is also one of the few trainers who return a profit at Cheltenham. Given the competitiveness of the racing there, a strike-rate of 17 per cent with a level-stakes profit of +40.12pt is some achievement.

NICKY HENDERSON
UPPER LAMBOURN, BERKS

	No. of Hrs	Races Run	1st	2nd	3rd	Unpl	Per cent	£1 Level Stake
NH Flat	42	64	19	15	9	21	29.7	-18.81
Hurdles	123	375	95	63	35	182	25.3	+34.22
Chases	60	182	51	30	5	96	28.0	-17.28
Totals	192	621	165	108	49	299	26.6	-1.87
10-11	204	616	154	77	69	316	25.0	-90.15
09-10	170	516	137	77	54	248	26.6	-8.61

BY MONTH

NH Flat	W-R	Per cent	£1 Level Stake	Hurdles	W-R	Per cent	£1 Level Stake
May	2-10	20.0	-4.81	May	4-19	21.1	-0.75
June	2-4	50.0	+0.37	June	4-12	33.3	+0.83
July	0-1	0.0	-1.00	July	1-7	14.3	-5.64
August	0-0	0.0	0.00	August	1-6	16.7	-3.00
September	0-0	0.0	0.00	September	1-2	50.0	-0.67
October	0-0	0.0	0.00	October	1-20	5.0	-18.39
November	3-7	42.9	+1.22	November	17-43	39.5	-5.71
December	2-6	33.3	-2.42	December	21-67	31.3	+9.44
January	1-6	16.7	-2.75	January	14-53	26.4	-3.40
February	0-4	0.0	-4.00	February	7-36	19.4	-22.89
March	2-9	22.2	-5.55	March	11-59	18.6	+32.52
April	7-17	41.2	+0.12	April	13-51	25.5	+51.87

Chases	W-R	Per cent	£1 Level Stake	Totals	W-R	Per cent	£1 Level Stake
May	0-5	0.0	-5.00	May	6-34	17.6	-10.56
June	0-2	0.0	-2.00	June	6-18	33.3	-0.80
July	0-0	0.0	0.00	July	1-8	12.5	-6.64
August	0-0	0.0	0.00	August	1-6	16.7	-3.00
September	0-0	0.0	0.00	September	1-2	50.0	-0.67
October	1-2	50.0	+4.00	October	2-22	9.1	-14.39
November	10-32	31.3	-6.09	November	30-82	36.6	-10.58
December	13-38	34.2	-0.14	December	36-111	32.4	+6.88
January	8-28	28.6	-4.12	January	23-87	26.4	-10.27
February	9-21	42.9	+0.08	February	16-61	26.2	-26.81
March	7-32	21.9	+11.23	March	20-100	20.0	+38.20
April	3-22	13.6	-15.23	April	23-90	25.6	+36.76

DISTANCE

Hurdles	W-R	Per cent	£1 Level Stake	Chases	W-R	Per cent	£1 Level Stake
2m-2m3f	66-224	29.5	+82.14	2m-2m3f	22-64	34.4	+17.41
2m4f-2m7f	27-133	20.3	-35.92	2m4f-2m7f	19-66	28.8	-7.78
3m+	2-18	11.1	-12.00	3m+	10-52	19.2	-26.92

TYPE OF RACE

Non-Handicaps	W-R	Per cent	£1 Level Stake	Handicaps	W-R	Per cent	£1 Level Stake
Nov Hrdls	53-147	36.1	+22.61	Nov Hrdls	2-17	11.8	-10.25
Hrdls	26-85	30.6	-21.97	Hrdls	14-126	11.1	+43.83
Nov Chs	28-70	40.0	-10.00	Nov Chs	2-21	9.5	-14.25
Chases	15-31	48.4	+14.47	Chases	6-60	10.0	-7.50
Sell/Claim	0-0	0.0	0.00	Sell/Claim	0-0	0.0	0.00

RACE CLASS / FIRST TIME OUT

RACE CLASS	W-R	Per cent	£1 Level Stake	FIRST TIME OUT	W-R	Per cent	£1 Level Stake
Class 1	35-140	25.0	+39.18	Bumpers	12-42	28.6	-13.66
Class 2	15-71	21.1	+28.10	Hurdles	26-98	26.5	-6.47
Class 3	17-116	14.7	-65.10	Chases	20-52	38.5	+7.17
Class 4	73-207	35.3	+26.63				
Class 5	12-46	26.1	-18.94	Totals	58-192	30.2	-12.96
Class 6	13-41	31.7	-10.75				

Menorah leads the way with possible King George bid on the agenda

LAST season wasn't vintage for Philip Hobbs, but with 73 winners at a strike-rate of 14 per cent and just under a million pounds in prize-money, it was enough to get him into seventh place in the trainers' table. He also trained winners at each of the three great festivals: Cheltenham, Aintree and Punchestown.

Menorah, a 162-rated hurdler, unseated Richard Johnson at Exeter on his chasing debut when the race was at his mercy. He broke his duck over fences two months later at Taunton and followed that with a win in a better race at Kempton, but then fell in a Doncaster Grade 2 event. He finished third in the Arkle, again making mistakes, with some critics suggesting that he would be better off reverting to hurdling. However, he got it all together at Aintree, winning the Grade 1 novice event over two and a half miles. He rounded off his season at Punchestown where he was below his best on desperate ground, but again jumped well.

"Ignore Punchestown – he was over there anyway and the heavy ground was never going to be ideal. I'm not convinced it was the step up in trip that brought about the improvement at Aintree, but we now know he stays two miles and a half. Now he's got it together I hope that he'll continue to improve and we plan to start him off in the Haldon

Gold Cup. Having said that, it was such a good performance at Aintree that we maybe should be thinking of the Old Roan rather than Exeter, but we can sort that out nearer the time. I wouldn't rule out having a crack at the King George with him – we'll certainly give him an entry."

Captain Chris, the 2011 Arkle winner, looked sure to win last season's Haldon but, on a bad afternoon for Richard Johnson, unseated his rider at the last. After that it was third in the King George, then a poor effort in the Cotswold Chase at Cheltenham before a decent fourth in the Ryanair. Despite not managing to get his head in front last season, Captain Chris showed he retains his ability.

"He's definitely ground dependent – he doesn't want it too soft – and he's better going right-handed. I know that's an odd thing to say, because he handles a left-handed track, as his Arkle win and his good run in the Ryanair show, but he's always had a preference for going the other way round.

"He's in the same ownership as Menorah, so ideally we'd like to keep them apart, but the Haldon would also be a good place for him to start, and then races like the Amlin at Ascot, the Peterborough at Huntingdon, and the King George again will all come into consideration."

Memories are short in racing and **Cheltenian** is a forgotten horse. He won the Champion Bumper at Cheltenham in 2011, beating some good rivals – no less than 11 of those behind him have gone on to win. After his success he suffered a setback and when the news broke Hobbs said the horse had a

GILL & PUNTER RACING SUPPI
MANUFACTURERS OF JOCKEY CLUB APPROVED FENCES & ANCILLARY PI
TEL:01483 203044   FAX:01483 ?

minor tendon strain and would be given all the time he needed to get over it.

"He's not back yet but soon will be. Apparently his legs are good, and we hope he will be a high-class novice hurdler."

Fingal Bay had a great novice hurdling season, winning four good races, including the Persian War and the Challow, and being unlucky to be pipped in Aintree's Grade 1 John Smith's Sefton, where he was ridden very aggressively.

"He was brilliant and it's sad he lost at Aintree, but these things happen in racing – if Richard [Johnson] could ride the race again I'm sure he wouldn't have kicked on so early.

"Fingal Bay has always looked as though he would be even better over fences, and I hope that will be the case, so that's the route we'll be taking. There are novice events at Chepstow and Cheltenham in mid-October, and he'll probably start out in one of those. He copes very well with soft going so there's

absolutely no point in running him anywhere unless the ground is safe. We have to have the RSA Chase in mind for him, but the only time he has been beaten is over three miles. That said, he stays very well, but now there's a two-and-a-half-mile novice event at the festival that gives us another possible option."

Gauvain has good form from his days with Charlie Mann and Nick Williams, for whom he won last season's Peterborough. He was bought by Hobbs at Doncaster Sales for £46,000 and is in new ownership.

"With a high-class horse like him it's straightforward: if he wins he'll get a lot of his purchase price back in one hit, but it won't be easy to win with him because the races he'll be running in will be very competitive. The Old Roan Chase is the likely starting point."

Planet Of Sound is a grand old stager, and last season finished second in the Hennessy and third in the Racing Plus Chase, before running well for a long way in the

Grand National, fading only from three out.

"He's not getting any younger but I imagine we'll give him a run somewhere before the Hennessy. However, he doesn't want it too soft and this year's Hennessy is in December. He's shown he needs three miles at least but he took to the fences at Aintree, so I suppose the Topham might be worth thinking about."

Gauvain seems to run best when fresh, and seems fully effective at between two miles and 2m5f, so it will be fascinating to see how he does for his new connections.

"**Pateese** did very well last season, winning two handicap hurdles and we have plenty of options with him: he should be up to winning another handicap over hurdles, he has schooled very well over fences, and I think he could also win on the Flat. Realistically though, his future lies over fences, so I'm sure he'll be novice chasing at some point this season."

Snap Tie had been off the track since October 2009 before reappearing in a handicap hurdle at Punchestown in April. His win there provided a wonderful illustration of Hobbs's ability to get a horse ready at home, although Snap Tie has won first time out in each of the past four seasons in which he has raced.

"It was great to get him back. I would imagine he'll start out either in a conditions hurdle at Chepstow in mid-October, or perhaps in the Greatwood at Cheltenham. We have the option of going back over fences. He won his only chasing start but would be inexperienced in a handicap chase. There's the option of a graduation chase but that wouldn't be easy either, so my inclination is to stick over hurdles – Sea Pigeon won the Champion Hurdle as an 11-year-old, so why shouldn't Snap Tie do it? Realistically though, he's probably not quite in that league, but he's still high class.

"**Wishfull Thinking** has had wind

problems, but if we can manage them then he has the ability to win high-class chases. He was very good at Aintree when he finished second to Finian's Rainbow in the Melling Chase. I think two and a half miles is his best trip, and it might be that he's another possible for the Old Roan – although it's all about managing his breathing issues.

"**Village Vic** easily won a bumper at Chepstow on his first start for us and ran really well at Newbury on his next start, only just losing out, but things went a bit pear-shaped after that. He's had a really good summer, though, and has schooled well, so he'll be starting over hurdles. I think he should do well and his trip is likely to be around two and half miles.

"**Talkonthestreet** was progressive last season, winning twice over hurdles, at Exeter and Ludlow. He's very much a staying type and was well suited by the step up to three miles. He'll be going novice chasing although we'll probably start him out in a hurdle race."

Sadler's Risk, a former Mark Johnston horse, ran well in decent company last season, winning at Kempton and finishing sixth in the Triumph and third in Aintree's Grade 1 juvenile event. He was campaigned only over two miles but looked as though he would be well suited by further.

"Definitely. My worry is that he might be an in-between horse, not up to carrying big weights in handicaps off his mark of 148, and not quite good enough for conditions races. That will sort itself out as we campaign him, but he could be one who needs a longer trip. There is always the option of going chasing as he's big and strong, but you'd really rather they were five before going down that road.

"**Roalco De Farges** won two novice chases and ran a cracker on his final start, finishing second in the Bet365 Gold Cup at Sandown. He's a really strong stayer and has good form at Chepstow, so he'll be aimed at the Welsh National – the softer the ground the better it suits him. We'll need to get at least one run into him before then as he takes a bit of getting fit."

Colour Squadron now runs in the colours of JP McManus, having been bought by him just before Cheltenham, and he had a good first season over hurdles. After winning his bumper at Chepstow, he won a novice hurdle at Newbury, beating the useful Montbazon, and then was beaten a short head at Sandown where he lost the race through greenness. In the Supreme Novices' he was disappointing but he was running well when falling three out at Liverpool. On much softer ground at Punchestown he ran really well, beaten only by Dedigout.

"I don't know whether he'll stay over hurdles or go chasing, but he shows some speed, stays two and a half miles, and handles soft ground well. He's pretty good."

Ballygarvey has joined Hobbs following Henrietta Knight's decision to relinquish her licence. He has always looked like a chaser in the making and his Lingfield hurdles win on heavy ground was very much a bonus.

"I've had him only for a few weeks so I can't tell you much about him other than what you already know. Hen told me he has schooled very well over fences.

"**Fighting Flynn** is a big horse but he's been narrow and it took a while before he could be trained properly because he wasn't holding condition very well. However, chasing was always likely to be his game so I'm hopeful he can make his mark in races at the bigger tracks. We haven't yet schooled him over fences but I'd be surprised if he didn't take to them.

"**Bold Henry** could be much better over fences than he was over hurdles. Last season was his first and he was progressing very quickly. I was pleased with his hurdle win at Exeter in May.

"**Irish Buccaneer** is out of Supreme Serenade who I trained, and we were thrilled with his win in a Chepstow bumper. He'll be going over hurdles and two and a half miles should be his trip."

An intriguing addition to Hobbs's team is the ex-Charlie Brooks gelding **Tiqris**. A winning pointer, he finished second in the Chepstow bumper won by Irish Buccaneer.

"He hasn't actually been here yet – he's

Colour Squadron (right): ended last season by finishing second at the Punchestown festival and is well thought of by Philip Hobbs

owned by Roger Brookhouse and is still with him. However, I know Charlie was very keen on the horse, and we like Irish Buccaneer, so there are good reasons why he should do well over hurdles.

"**Persian Snow** is worth mentioning. His hurdles form last season was pretty moderate, but he was ill a lot of the time, whereas he seems really well now. He won a novice hurdle at Huntingdon despite the heavy ground being against him and his bumper form the previous season was good.

His handicap mark of 129 seems reasonable and we might give him a couple of runs before going novice chasing.

"**Princely Player** was a big improver last season and is still a novice until the end of October – he's still only five and there should be quite a bit more to come from him. He'll probably stay over hurdles this season."

Hobbs starts the new season with a typically strong team and his numbers have held up well despite the recession – another good year seems assured. [CB]

HOBBS AND THE STATS

Hobbs has been a regular fixture at the upper end of the trainers' championship for some years and managed a respectable seventh in the table last season. However, his figures have been on the slide and his seasonal tally of 73 with a 14 per cent strike-rate were his lowest numbers for quite some time, *writes Kevin Morley*.

With a trainer of Hobbs's standing it is hardly a surprise that following his string blind will almost certainly result in a substantial loss, just as it did last term (-145.80pt). The Withycombe handler is more renowned for his exploits with hurdlers and you can normally expect more than half of his winners to come in that area. Thirty eight of his 73 winners last season came over hurdles which was a standard representation of the ratio. The bookmakers are fully aware of Hobbs's expertise in this field, however, and price them up accordingly and it is difficult to find any consistent angle in that field.

Punters would have been better advised to side with his chasers last season. His runners over fences in handicaps (14 per cent /+10.13pt) and novices (31 per cent /+22.64pt) returned healthy level-stake profits, proving Hobbs is underrated more with his runners over fences.

Hobbs is also one of the better trainers to follow in bumpers. His figures were disappointing in this sphere last term with just five winners from 42 runners (12 per cent /-23.50pt) but his runners had returned profits in each of the three previous seasons.

When it comes to riding arrangements, the rare booking of Tony McCoy usually signals a big run is expected. The champion jockey was successful once on his three rides for Hobbs last term and the combination roughly break even with a 28 per cent strike-rate since 2008-09.

Stable jockey Richard Johnson rides the bulk of the yards winners but a level-stakes profit is almost assured. However, if concentrating on his rides for the stable's bumper runners over the last five seasons, Johnson turns over a big profit with a solid strike-rate (25 per cent /+39.52pt). If Hobbs has a winner in a bumper, it's more than likely that Johnson will be in the plate and it has a fair chance of obliging at decent odds.

The majority of the stable's success doesn't come at tracks far from Hobbs's West Country base. He sends out plenty of winners at Exeter, Wincanton and Newton Abbot, although the layers seem well guarded against his runners at those venues. Look a bit further north at those he sends to Chepstow and Bangor as the strike-rate and level-stakes columns read well.

Following the yard in the closing weeks of the jumps season has often proved a good money-spinner but figures last term, although far from disastrous, were below Hobbs's usual high standards. It highlights that he probably now lacks the strength in depth he once had, although there's no doubting he still possesses some high-quality sorts, most notably Fingal Bay, who should take high rank in novice chases this season.

PHILIP HOBBS
WITHYCOMBE, SOMERSET

	No. of Hrs	Races Run	1st	2nd	3rd	Unpl	Per cent	£1 Level Stake
NH Flat	27	42	5	9	2	26	11.9	-23.50
Hurdles	91	282	38	36	33	175	13.5	-105.81
Chases	53	188	30	29	22	107	16.0	-16.49
Totals	142	512	73	74	57	308	14.3	-145.80
10-11	153	560	86	76	80	318	15.4	-158.06
09-10	148	574	90	85	66	332	15.7	-72.60

BY MONTH

NH Flat	W-R	Per cent	£1 Level Stake	Hurdles	W-R	Per cent	£1 Level Stake
May	0-0	0.0	0.00	May	2-14	14.3	+1.50
June	1-2	50.0	+1.00	June	1-7	14.3	-4.63
July	0-0	0.0	0.00	July	0-6	0.0	-6.00
August	0-0	0.0	0.00	August	0-2	0.0	-2.00
September	0-0	0.0	0.00	September	1-4	25.0	-0.50
October	1-6	16.7	-2.25	October	4-26	15.4	-1.42
November	0-6	0.0	-6.00	November	8-44	18.2	+1.80
December	1-4	25.0	-1.75	December	5-31	16.1	-15.70
January	1-4	25.0	+1.00	January	4-37	10.8	-19.50
February	0-3	0.0	-3.00	February	3-32	9.4	-13.63
March	0-9	0.0	-9.00	March	5-41	12.2	-23.87
April	1-8	12.5	-3.50	April	5-38	13.2	-21.88

Chases	W-R	Per cent	£1 Level Stake	Totals	W-R	Per cent	£1 Level Stake
May	2-13	15.4	+3.91	May	4-27	14.8	+5.41
June	2-7	28.6	-0.30	June	4-16	25.0	-3.93
July	1-8	12.5	+5.00	July	1-14	7.1	-1.00
August	1-8	12.5	-2.00	August	1-10	10.0	-4.00
September	2-12	16.7	-6.92	September	3-16	18.8	-7.42
October	2-13	15.4	-7.81	October	7-45	15.6	-11.48
November	2-30	6.7	+6.00	November	10-80	12.5	+1.80
December	5-23	21.7	-3.00	December	11-58	19.0	-20.45
January	2-19	10.5	-11.93	January	7-60	11.7	-30.43
February	0-12	0.0	-12.00	February	3-47	6.4	-28.63
March	8-23	34.8	+23.25	March	13-73	17.8	-9.62
April	3-20	15.0	-10.70	April	9-66	13.6	-36.08

DISTANCE

Hurdles	W-R	Per cent	£1 Level Stake	Chases	W-R	Per cent	£1 Level Stake
2m-2m3f	13-133	9.8	-77.02	2m-2m3f	5-50	10.0	-30.68
2m4f-2m7f	21-100	21.0	-10.79	2m4f-2m7f	10-60	16.7	-0.40
3m+	4-49	8.2	-18.00	3m+	15-78	19.2	+14.58

TYPE OF RACE

Non-Handicaps	W-R	Per cent	£1 Level Stake	Handicaps	W-R	Per cent	£1 Level Stake
Nov Hrdls	16-91	17.6	-38.09	Nov Hrdls	1-12	8.3	-3.00
Hrdls	5-48	10.4	-34.97	Hrdls	16-128	12.5	-26.75
Nov Chs	11-36	30.6	-8.53	Nov Chs	4-16	25.0	+26.00
Chases	1-20	5.0	-18.09	Chases	14-116	12.1	-15.88
Sell/Claim	0-1	0.0	-1.00	Sell/Claim	0-3	0.0	-3.00

RACE CLASS / FIRST TIME OUT

	W-R	Per cent	£1 Level Stake		W-R	Per cent	£1 Level Stake
Class 1	6-78	7.7	-57.90	Bumpers	5-27	18.5	-8.50
Class 2	14-69	20.3	+13.32	Hurdles	12-75	16.0	-11.04
Class 3	15-128	11.7	-18.54	Chases	6-40	15.0	+9.91
Class 4	30-154	19.5	-29.39				
Class 5	5-53	9.4	-35.04	Totals	23-142	16.2	-9.63
Class 6	3-30	10.0	-18.25				

Quality team can help build on last season's prize-money breakthrough

ALAN KING last season cracked the £1m prize-money barrier for the first time since 2009 and his tally of 82 winners at an improved strike-rate of 16 per cent was highly respectable.

Raya Star earned more win prize-money than any other horse in the yard, largely down to his success in the Ladbroke at Ascot in December. After that he finished third in the Betfair Hurdle, was a bit below his best in the County, but rounded off his season with a career-best win in the Scottish Champion Hurdle at Ayr.

"He enjoyed a fabulous season. After Cheltenham we thought he'd had enough, and we were going to put him away but he came back from the race in such good form that we managed to get a Scottish Champion out of him. He's cantering and seems a lot more relaxed, which is lovely as he used to live on his nerves.

"He'll start over hurdles as I don't want to run him in a beginners' chase when he's very fresh, so he'll probably go for the Greatwood, and after that we can make a decision as to whether it will be hurdles or fences. I could see a step up in trip suiting him at some stage during the season."

Lovcen finished his campaign with a win in Aintree's Grade 1 Sefton Hurdle having previously finished fourth in the Albert Bartlett at the festival.

"He's a good, tough, honest horse who will have one or perhaps two runs over hurdles before we make the decision on whether he should go chasing. He'll be targeted at the three-mile Listed hurdle at the Paddy Power meeting as one of his owners sponsors that race."

Montbazon won two novice hurdles and finished fourth in the Supreme Novices', running an absolute blinder for a horse who King describes at not yet the finished article.

"He's seriously good. We always had to nurse him along last season, as he was plagued with sore shins – I think it was just immaturity. As he has only had four runs over hurdles he'll definitely stay hurdling this season. If we can get a good clear run with him, I think he's very exciting. We're not in a rush with him this season and he has done a lot of roadwork to try to harden up those shins. There's a lot more improvement to come from him."

Medermit flew the flag for Barbury Castle with great distinction last season, winning the Haldon Gold Cup, albeit somewhat luckily after the fall of Captain Chris, and he was placed on each of his other five starts, three of them in Grade 1 company. His performances were wonderfully consistent, with his third place in the Ryanair arguably the best of them.

"He did extremely well, with his rating going up after almost every run, and we're now up to 167. The plan is to start him out in the Old Roan Chase at Aintree, and if that was a week too soon then the Charlie Hall at Wetherby. I'd prefer to run him at Aintree over two and a half miles and then step him up to three for the Betfair Chase at Haydock – if he showed he was competitive at that level then we might think about the King George."

Smad Place, a decent juvenile the season before last, did really well in his most recent campaign. After winning a decent limited handicap at Ascot he was very consistent: second off a mark of 151 back at Ascot, a gallant third to Big Buck's in the World Hurdle and then likely to be second behind that same rival, had he not fallen, at Aintree.

"It was a good performance at Cheltenham, although Aintree was a huge disappointment as we learned nothing from the race. It hasn't been finally decided but I'd be inclined to stay over hurdles for the time being – without any disrespect to Big Buck's, he can't go on forever, can he? We'll certainly have a crack at him in the first part of the season and see where we are after that – if it looks like we've got no hope then we can go over fences. He'll be an exciting novice chaser but he's still only five, so there's no great rush."

Walkon started his chasing career in fine style, winning a decent novice event at Exeter but the rest of his form didn't fulfil that early promise.

"I don't know what went wrong. I was surprised by how well he won on his first run over fences, and maybe that flattered him, because he never seemed to be the same again. However, he's back and in good order, and we'll aim him at a graduation chase – he certainly wants a minimum of two and a half miles, and he'll easily get three."

Grumeti was trained on the Flat by Michael Bell and joined King for his novice hurdle season. He won on his debut at Taunton and also won Cheltenham's Triumph Hurdle Trial, and a Grade 2 at Kempton. In the Triumph he finished a decent third, and then went on to win a Grade 1 at Aintree.

"He improved quite substantially on the Flat in the spring, winning at Ascot and beaten just a short head at Goodwood. Because of that he was later getting his break so he's just coming back into work now. I hope he's a Champion Hurdle horse, and we'll train him

as such. The four-year-old hurdling season is notoriously tough and I don't yet know where I'll start him, but I feel he's the best juvenile hurdler I've trained – he needs to improve a fair bit, but I'm hopeful he will."

Vendor had decent hurdling form in France and won on his debut for King, landing a Newbury juvenile hurdle in good style. He didn't run again until Cheltenham, where he finished third in the Fred Winter, and he rounded off his season with an easy success at Towcester.

"I think he's very good. I didn't run him again after Newbury as I thought we were very well handicapped and didn't want to show my hand but in hindsight he could probably have done with a little more experience. He'd never been in a big field like the Fred Winter and at midway he looked like he might drop out the back, but he then stayed on really well up the hill.

"He'll stay hurdling and he'll probably have an entry in the Greatwood but we'll feel our way with him. I think he could get two and a half miles and we haven't yet seen the best of him."

Kumbeshwar is a tough sort and ran ten times last season, winning twice and being placed most other times. His wins were in novice chases at Hereford and Plumpton but he also finished third in the Grand Annual off 144 and fourth at Aintree.

"He's tough and consistent but fully exposed and won't be easy to place. That said, he'll go to the big meetings and we'll have a bit of fun with him – he might start off in the Haldon Gold Cup.

"**Bless The Wings** had a good season. He went up 8lb for winning at Cheltenham in January, so he's probably a little exposed now. However, now he's settling better – he used to be very free in his races – I think he'll get three miles and that will open a few extra doors for him. His final run was a good one, but two and a half miles round Market Rasen had him in top gear the whole way. He jumps very well and I think three miles will suit him – I think there's a decent prize in him.

"It was very disappointing that **Balder**

Grumeti: highly regarded and will be trained for a crack at the Champion Hurdle

Succes's season finished the way that it did with a fall in the Triumph, and then unseating Robert Thornton at Punchestown, because he'd been a very good jumper.

"I don't think the false start at Cheltenham helped him as he got very revved up and he probably wasn't focusing the way he should have been. At Punchestown he got unsighted going to the first. Before that he was three from three for us over hurdles. We still think he's very good – he'll most likely start back in a four-year-old hurdle.

"**Hold On Julio** seems to have come back in good form. He coughed in January and I could never get him back as I wanted, and deep down I probably knew my fate before he went for the three-mile handicap chase at Cheltenham – you can't go there 90 per cent. I had a look at a couple of races in the spring but I wasn't totally happy so we turned him out and he had a good summer. We might consider the Hennessy for him but I don't know where he'd go first – he's still a novice over hurdles so that's an option."

As with every jumps yard there are horses coming back from injury and there were some good horses among the list for King's stable.

"**Awesome Freddie** is back and I imagine he'll be novice chasing. **Bakbenscher** was here all last season but I couldn't get him on the track. I might give him a couple of outings over hurdles before he goes back over fences.

"**Bensalem** has been doing all of his roadwork at home in Ireland, so he'll be trained for the second half of the season.

"**Salden Licht** has just started cantering. I imagine he'll be novice chasing as he won't be well handicapped over hurdles. **Manyriverstocross** is back. He looks tremendously well and we might aim him at the Greatwood and then make a decision about staying over hurdles or going chasing. It's great to have him back.

"**Handazan** is a new arrival from John Oxx's yard – he was rated 94 on the Flat. He handled soft ground and stayed well and has had one little school so far. I'm very happy with him but I'm not in any great rush, and we'll try to ready him for around November.

"From last season's bumper horses, I think **Valdez** is lovely. He won two bumpers and was fourth at Newbury where he ran too freely. I think hurdles will settle him down.

"**Hollow Penny** was second in both of his bumpers but has made up into a proper horse this season – I think he's useful.

"**Letsby Avenue** stumbled badly when he won at Haydock and the second was well fancied – he's interesting.

"Of the fillies, **Call Me A Star** was very good and should be well up to winning a mares' novice hurdle."

King has a typically strong team for the new season and whether it's a good season or better is down to whether some of the younger horses coming through are able to step up and become stars. In any event, as always, this is a team to follow closely. [CB]

ALAN KING
BARBURY CASTLE, WILTS

	No. of Hrs	Races Run	1st	2nd	3rd	Unpl	Per cent	£1 Level Stake
NH Flat	32	52	7	7	3	35	13.5	-15.63
Hurdles	91	301	46	46	39	170	15.3	-85.50
Chases	44	163	28	27	28	80	17.2	-30.48
Totals	142	516	81	80	70	285	15.7	-131.61
10-11	171	600	87	103	80	329	14.5	-164.82
09-10	189	593	80	76	81	356	13.5	-151.05

BY MONTH

NH Flat	W-R	Per cent	£1 Level Stake	Hurdles	W-R	Per cent	£1 Level Stake
May	0-4	0.0	-4.00	May	2-17	11.8	-4.50
June	0-0	0.0	0.00	June	3-8	37.5	+2.95
July	0-0	0.0	0.00	July	0-4	0.0	-4.00
August	0-0	0.0	0.00	August	0-2	0.0	-2.00
September	0-0	0.0	0.00	September	0-2	0.0	-2.00
October	0-1	0.0	-1.00	October	2-10	20.0	-0.17
November	2-10	20.0	-2.13	November	2-45	4.4	-40.00
December	0-6	0.0	-6.00	December	8-49	16.3	-4.67
January	0-3	0.0	-3.00	January	9-51	17.6	+2.82
February	1-5	20.0	-0.50	February	5-30	16.7	-15.31
March	2-11	18.2	-1.50	March	5-49	10.2	-32.67
April	2-12	16.7	+2.50	April	10-34	29.4	+14.05

Chases	W-R	Per cent	£1 Level Stake	Totals	W-R	Per cent	£1 Level Stake
May	0-4	0.0	-4.00	May	2-25	8.0	-12.50
June	0-1	0.0	-1.00	June	3-9	33.3	+1.95
July	0-0	0.0	0.00	July	0-4	0.0	-4.00
August	0-0	0.0	0.00	August	0-2	0.0	-2.00
September	0-0	0.0	0.00	September	0-2	0.0	-2.00
October	2-8	25.0	-2.25	October	4-19	21.1	-3.42
November	9-36	25.0	+4.38	November	13-91	14.3	-37.75
December	5-33	15.2	-6.75	December	13-88	14.8	-17.42
January	4-23	17.4	-8.73	January	13-77	16.9	-8.91
February	3-16	18.8	+2.50	February	9-51	17.6	-13.31
March	3-23	13.0	-2.50	March	10-83	12.0	-36.67
April	2-19	10.5	-12.13	April	14-65	21.5	+4.42

DISTANCE

Hurdles	W-R	Per cent	£1 Level Stake	Chases	W-R	Per cent	£1 Level Stake
2m-2m3f	27-151	17.9	-44.52	2m-2m3f	9-50	18.0	-8.26
2m4f-2m7f	15-122	12.3	-34.98	2m4f-2m7f	9-62	14.5	-20.88
3m+	4-28	14.3	-6.00	3m+	10-51	19.6	-1.34

TYPE OF RACE

Non-Handicaps	W-R	Per cent	£1 Level Stake	Handicaps	W-R	Per cent	£1 Level Stake
Nov Hrdls	19-114	16.7	-41.48	Nov Hrdls	2-10	20.0	+8.00
Hrdls	15-65	23.1	-19.35	Hrdls	10-111	9.0	-31.67
Chases	10-51	19.6	-18.98	Nov Chs	5-25	20.0	+9.25
Chases	1-6	16.7	-1.00	Chases	12-81	14.8	-19.75
Sell/Claim	0-1	0.0	-1.00	Sell/Claim	0-0	0.0	0.00

RACE CLASS / FIRST TIME OUT

	W-R	Per cent	£1 Level Stake		W-R	Per cent	£1 Level Stake
Class 1	14-75	18.7	+20.94	Bumpers	6-32	18.8	+1.38
Class 2	6-44	13.6	-16.00	Hurdles	12-75	16.0	-21.77
Class 3	15-98	15.3	-34.20	Chases	8-35	22.9	-2.25
Class 4	34-221	15.4	-83.76				
Class 5	7-43	16.3	-11.95	Totals	26-142	18.3	-22.64
Class 6	5-35	14.3	-6.63				

KING AND THE STATS

In 2008-09 King sent out a record 136 winners but it was always going to be hard for him to maintain that level, particularly given he has had slightly fewer horses at his disposal. The rate of success hasn't dipped much in the last three seasons though, with a total of 82 winners last term (16 per cent strike-rate) a respectable tally given his ammunition, *writes Kevin Morley*.

King has lacked a top-quality Grade 1 performer in recent years and the likes of Voy Por Ustedes, Katchit and My Way De Solzen winning championship races at the festival seems a long time ago. Medermit did perform well in some of the top chases last term, picking up some valuable place money, while Grumeti and Lovcen landed Grade 1 novice hurdles at Aintree in April. Whether that trio are up to beating the best around this term is doubtful, though, and it's probable King will be relying on those further down the scale to provide him with the majority of his winners.

Most of King's success comes in novice races where he places his runners excellently. However, his representatives are given massive respect by the layers in run-of-the-mill handicaps and novices over both sets of obstacles, so backing him blind in these areas regularly incurs a loss. King also has a solid strike-rate in bumpers but, again, the bookmakers keep his runners in such races on their side.

Following stable jockey Robert Thornton returns a big negative figure and although Wayne Hutchinson deputised excellently when Thornton was sidelined through injury, King's back-up rider also recorded a loss, albeit the deficit was much smaller. Conditional Peter Hatton might be the one who catches the layers out. His five winners from 34 rides for the yard last term returned a healthy +18.75pt profit but it should be pointed that all of those victories were over hurdles. Hatton has yet to be entrusted with the chasers as he has only had two rides over fences for King. He still claims 7lb, though, and he's likely to have that lowered pretty quickly with the backing of King.

King has winners at most tracks but his figures at three stand out in particular. Strike-rates of 25 per cent at Towcester (+13.01pt) and 39 per cent at Plumpton (+20.11pt) are angles punters should explore. Ascot is where he has had most of his high-profile successes in recent seasons and it's the King hurdlers who have excelled at the Berkshire venue, striking at 18 per cent since the 2008-09 season (+34.42pt).

Arkle possible for Vulcanite as Longsdon bids to maintain momentum

LAST season was the best by far in Charlie Longsdon's short training career. His tally of 69 winners was his highest by some margin and a strike-rate of 20 per cent was admirable – little wonder blindly backing all of his runners would have shown a substantial level-stakes profit.

Vulcanite was a classy Flat handicapper for Ralph Beckett, rated as high as 103. He ran five times for Longsdon last season, winning at Southwell and running well on his other starts, most notably when down the field in the Supreme Novices' and when fifth at Aintree. He was very keen in his races and looked as though he needed further than the minimum trip over hurdles.

"Vulcanite has been purchased over the summer by JP McManus and I don't think he's badly handicapped off a mark of 134. The championship races he ran in at Cheltenham and Aintree weren't run at a strong gallop, and that didn't suit him. We might consider stepping him up in trip at some stage, although I'm not convinced that's essential.

"We haven't quite decided what he'll do this season – it could be decent handicap hurdles where they go a good gallop, or we could go chasing. I think the Arkle could suit him down to the ground. I think the key to him is a fast-run race."

Paintball gave the yard a big win when landing the Imperial Cup at Sandown in impressive style, powering up the hill.

"He loved the stiff two miles that day, and I think the problem in his two subsequent runs was that they were at sharper tracks. The first thing we'll do with him is to step up to two and a half miles, and the plan is to stay over hurdles this season as I think there's more to come from him."

Universal Soldier has had only eight runs but is on his third trainer. He ran twice for Longsdon, winning a beginners' chase at Towcester before finishing seventh, not beaten that far, in the four-mile National Hunt Chase at the Cheltenham Festival.

"It was an easy win at Towcester, it was a bad race. My worry at Cheltenham was always going to be the ground as he's a proper soft-ground horse. He got outpaced in the first half of the race but then stayed on really well and overall I thought he ran a decent race.

"He wants an extreme trip and loves the soft, so we'll be looking at decent races at places like Chepstow and Haydock – the Welsh National would be a possibility."

Grandad's Horse had a fantastic season, contributing four wins. He won two novice hurdles and then handicaps off 122 and 133. His final start was a gritty win over two and a half miles at Haydock.

"He won't be out until the spring as he injured himself at Haydock. Because of that he'll stay over hurdles this year as I'd want him to have a full season as a novice over fences. He's a lovely horse who loves his jumping and will make a nice chaser.

Wide Receiver: shot up the handicap last season but his trainer thinks he could show further improvement

"**Hildisvini** is another really tough horse who was thrown in at the deep end after two easy novice hurdle wins. When he came up against the experienced handicappers it took him a few months to find his feet, but at the end of the season he ran two great races, winning at Market Rasen and at Sandown. He'll be novice chasing this season at two and a half miles.

"**Wide Receiver** was a star for us last season, winning three times and going up in the ratings from 75 to 123. The big question is whether he can improve a bit more and his final two starts suggested that he could – he was collared on the line at Folkestone having been left in front and I think he came up against a very well-handicapped horse at Haydock.

"He's had a good summer and has come back in a lot better than he did last season. I'm hopeful there's another five to ten pounds

of improvement in him. He stays really well, and he slightly prefers going right-handed but he was so far ahead of the handicapper last season it didn't really matter.

"**Hazy Tom** started out well but I think they were two average novice hurdles he won. After that he had to rapidly learn a bit about racing and being headstrong probably didn't help his cause. I think fences will really help him – he'll back off them and as a result probably won't be so keen. We'll start him out over fences at two miles but look to step up to two and a half fairly quickly. He works nicely at home and jumps well.

"**Dawn Commander** also goes novice chasing. He was consistent last season and his only bad run was at Cheltenham in the Albert Bartlett. On his first start in a handicap he was second, giving the winner six pounds, but if they met again today we'd be receiving six pounds from him – that shows how well we ran there. I'd like to think Dawn Commander hasn't been too badly treated by the handicapper.

"**Cross Of Honour** is a really good fun horse who loves his racing. We should have won more than we did with him last year. I want to go chasing with him. Two and a half miles is his trip and while I'm not saying he's a superstar, he'll win his share of races.

"**West Brit** had a wind operation before he won at Musselburgh in February and he's had another one since then. Looking back I wish I'd gone for the Fred Winter at Cheltenham rather than the Triumph. Tom Scudamore said he jumped brilliantly and was going really well until his breathing caught him out at the top of the hill. There's no doubt he's a nice horse if we can manage his breathing."

There are several new arrivals in the yard, some from off the Flat and others with jumps form.

"**Ranthambore** will stick to bumpers for the time being. He's beautifully bred, being by Kayf Tara out of a hurdle-winning mare. He's got plenty of size and scope and comes from a nice family – he's the type who should be able to win a bumper."

Don't Take Me Alive won over a mile and a half on the Flat for Clive Cox and ran really well on a number of other occasions, while **Tidal Way** won as a juvenile for Mick Channon and ran well several times during his three-year-old career on the Flat.

"They're both nice horses and will be out early in juvenile hurdles. I like my juveniles and novices to be slick at their hurdles as that lets them get wins under their belts before things hot up."

Frisco Depot was bought out of Dessie Hughes's yard and has some good form over fences. He won a beginners' chase at Fairyhouse, was second in a Grade 3 novice Chase at Naas, won a Grade 2 at Limerick and would have been placed in Punchestown's Champion Novices' event had he not been brought down at the last.

"He's rated 141 and, while we've not had him for long, he has the look of a proper stayer. He's a lovely, big, strapping horse

and he'll start out in an intermediate or graduation chase.

"I'm pleased with **Joseph Lister** – he won for John Gosden on the Flat and for Nicky Henderson over hurdles. He goes nicely at home and I think he might benefit from being ridden by a professional rather than a conditional. It's no disrespect to the conditional who rode him, but some of these ex-Flat horses can be a bit lazy and only do what they have to do. Sometimes a senior jockey can persuade them to do a bit more and I think there might be a bit more improvement to come from him.

"**Sherwani Wolf** has obviously had a few problems but we've done a lot of work on his jumping. He'll be out when we get some softer ground."

Longsdon had a very strong team of bumper horses last season and hopes are high for them doing well over hurdles.

"**Pendra** won his bumper impressively at Huntingdon during Cheltenham week. He's by Old Vic and is from a lovely family. He has strengthened a lot over the summer and might go for the Listed bumper at the Paddy Power meeting in November, but he'll be hurdling later in the season. I think he's nice and he could be a smart horse.

"**Spirit Of Shankly** will run in one more bumper before going hurdling and we'll probably take the same route as Hazy Tom did last year: a Worcester bumper then novice events at Aintree and Wetherby. He shows a lot of speed whereas Pendra is a relentless galloper.

"**Up To Something** is from a staying family and not really bred to win bumpers, but he's won three, which takes some doing. He's a brilliant jumper who will start over two miles but he might want further midway through the season."

Success breeds success, and the plan is to increase stable numbers again for this season, and with some exciting new arrivals and young horses coming through, another progressive season looks very likely. [CB]

CHARLIE LONGSDON
OVER NORTON, OXON

	No. of Hrs	Races Run	1st	2nd	3rd	Unpl	Per cent	£1 Level Stake
NH Flat	34	58	16	6	4	32	27.6	+40.07
Hurdles	49	150	23	24	12	91	15.3	+29.70
Chases	38	138	29	20	15	74	21.0	-18.58
Totals	93	346	68	50	31	197	19.7	+51.19
10-11	62	242	46	40	28	128	19.0	+50.18
09-10	62	236	17	21	26	172	7.2	-119.40

BY MONTH

NH Flat	W-R	Per cent	£1 Level Stake
May	2-4	50.0	+5.57
June	0-0	0.0	0.00
July	0-1	0.0	-1.00
August	0-1	0.0	-1.00
September	2-5	40.0	-1.10
October	2-8	25.0	-2.00
November	1-4	25.0	+1.00
December	1-3	33.3	+6.00
January	2-5	40.0	+1.50
February	0-4	0.0	-4.00
March	5-15	33.3	+35.60
April	1-8	12.5	-0.50

Hurdles	W-R	Per cent	£1 Level Stake
May	0-3	0.0	-3.00
June	0-0	0.0	0.00
July	0-1	0.0	-1.00
August	0-0	0.0	0.00
September	2-9	22.2	+10.25
October	5-22	22.7	-11.34
November	2-19	10.5	-14.59
December	2-24	8.3	+45.25
January	3-13	23.1	+4.75
February	2-13	15.4	-2.33
March	4-25	16.0	+10.33
April	3-21	14.3	-8.63

Chases	W-R	Per cent	£1 Level Stake
May	2-6	33.3	-1.58
June	3-5	60.0	+8.75
July	0-3	0.0	-3.00
August	1-4	25.0	+4.00
September	4-8	50.0	+10.63
October	7-20	35.0	+0.88
November	1-19	5.3	-13.00
December	5-20	25.0	-1.50
January	2-12	16.7	-4.75
February	0-9	0.0	-9.00
March	0-17	0.0	-17.00
April	4-15	26.7	+7.00

Totals	W-R	Per cent	£1 Level Stake
May	4-13	30.8	+0.99
June	3-5	60.0	+8.75
July	0-5	0.0	-5.00
August	1-5	20.0	+3.00
September	8-22	36.4	+19.78
October	14-50	28.0	-12.46
November	4-42	9.5	-26.59
December	8-47	17.0	+49.75
January	7-30	23.3	+1.50
February	2-26	7.7	-15.33
March	9-57	15.8	+28.93
April	8-44	18.2	-2.13

DISTANCE

Hurdles	W-R	Per cent	£1 Level Stake	Chases	W-R	Per cent	£1 Level Stake
2m-2m3f	11-62	17.7	-6.75	2m-2m3f	8-33	24.2	+10.38
2m4f-2m7f	9-66	13.6	+47.86	2m4f-2m7f	13-48	27.1	-1.58
3m+	3-22	13.6	-11.42	3m+	8-57	14.0	-27.38

TYPE OF RACE

Non-Handicaps	W-R	Per cent	£1 Level Stake	Handicaps	W-R	Per cent	£1 Level Stake
Nov Hrdls	11-54	20.4	+52.73	Nov Hrdls	1-13	7.7	-7.00
Hrdls	4-18	22.2	-3.38	Hrdls	7-65	10.8	-12.65
Chases	9-21	42.9	+3.30	Chases	16-98	16.3	-24.38
Sell/Claim	0-0	0.0	0.00	Sell/Claim	0-0	0.0	0.00

RACE CLASS

	W-R	Per cent	£1 Level Stake
Class 1	1-27	3.7	-6.00
Class 2	1-20	5.0	-12.00
Class 3	15-89	16.9	-10.15
Class 4	31-126	24.6	+51.90
Class 5	6-38	15.8	-14.52
Class 6	14-46	30.4	+41.97

FIRST TIME OUT

	W-R	Per cent	£1 Level Stake
Bumpers	13-34	38.2	+45.82
Hurdles	4-33	12.1	+57.38
Chases	7-26	26.9	+0.38
Totals	24-93	25.8	+103.58

LONGSDON AND THE STATS

Longsdon is a trainer on the up and made a big step forward last season with a tally 69, which was a leap forward on his total of 44 in 2010-11. He was one of the biggest friends to punters in recording a level-stakes profit of +56.70pt (20 per cent). In fact, there has only been one season since taking out a licence in 2006 in which Longsdon hasn't kept his followers in the money. It will interesting to see how the layers react to his string this term.

The Oxfordshire handler is massively underrated in bumpers as his level-stakes profit of +50.23pt suggests. His hurdlers also did him proud last term returning a profit of +29.70pt. His chasers might have incurred followers a loss last term but in 2010-11 the figures were much more impressive (23 per cent /+19.81pt).

Longsdon is clearly an all-round trainer but his strengths over each set of obstacles lie in different areas. Over fences his handicappers have recorded the best figures since 2008-09 with a 16 per cent strike-rate and level-stakes profit of +7.71pt, while over hurdles it's the novices who have held sway, recording a profit of +22.24pt, striking at 12 per cent.

Felix de Giles rides the majority of the stable's winners and the victories come fairly frequent and often at decent prices (19 per cent / +93.41pt). The yard's conditional rider Kielan Woods also enjoys his fair share of success and his strike-rate and level stake profit is comparable to that of De Giles (23 per cent /+37.77pt).

Richard Johnson is a man in demand but when commitments allowed last term, Longsdon utilised his skills to good effect. Johnson rode six winners from 18 rides for the yard in 2011-12 (33 per cent /+7.93pt) and punters should take note.

There are several tracks at which Longsdon can be followed to good effect. Success comes often at Bangor, Market Rasen, Stratford and Worcester and there is a handsome profit at each course. He is seen less often at Wetherby but punters are advised to take the hint when he makes the trip to the Yorkshire venue as six of his 14 runners have obliged (43 per cent / +10.38pt).

His record at Cheltenham doesn't read so good with just one winner at the course from 45 runners. He has yet to train a festival winner and that will be high on his agenda in 2012-13. Every up-and-coming trainer needs a high-class horse to raise his profile and Longsdon will be hoping he has one in the novice ranks this term.

Abundance of quality should make for another successful campaign

DONALD McCAIN has come a long way in a short time. Every year has seen his number of winners increase and last season saw him turn out 153 at a strike-rate of 21, earning him third place in the trainers' table. Such has been his rise to prominence that no less an authority than reigning champion Paul Nicholls has said that McCain could be a live outsider to challenge both him and Henderson. It might be a year or two too early for McCain to mount a real threat to the big two but it will surely not take much longer than that.

Weird Al started last season in great style, winning Wetherby's Charlie Hall Chase on his debut for the yard and earning himself a 20-1 quote for the Gold Cup. Things continued on track when he was third behind Kauto Star and Long Run in the Betfair Chase, but in the Gold Cup he ran no sort of a race and was pulled up having bled from the nose, just as he had in the previous year's race. He ran well in the National on his final start of the season, but fell four out when he was seemingly weakening.

"He bled again and I have a theory that it's a nervous thing with him – there was a lot of noise, even in the pre-parade ring, and you could see him getting wound up. After that we put some earplugs in at Aintree, dropped him right in to get him to relax and he was running a nice race when he was brought down – still close enough if things had worked out for him. I think we're going to have to be conscious of his nervousness and work with it – I wouldn't be sure Cheltenham isn't the place for him, but we'll have to manage him carefully. He'll start out in the Charlie Hall again and I wouldn't rule out going to Aintree again as he took to the fences."

Overturn won the Scottish Summer Champion Hurdle, the Ascot Hurdle, and the Fighting Fifth on his first three starts of last season. He was then second to Grandouet in the International Hurdle at Cheltenham's December meeting, third to Binocular in the Christmas Hurdle, and second in the Champion.

"He's going over fences – I schooled him once before his break and he was very good. I tried to give him a longer break over the summer but he wouldn't have it – that's how he is. We're looking forward to going chasing and if he takes to it he could be very good."

One who didn't take to fences was **Peddlers Cross**, second to Hurricane Fly in the 2011 Champion Hurdle. He won his first two novice chases but his bubble was burst when he was put in his place by Sprinter Sacre – although there's no disgrace in that. He ran in the Jewson but it simply looked as though he'd not taken against fences.

"He'll start out in the Ascot Hurdle over two and a half miles and that will help us decide which route we take with him – there's a

Peddlers Cross: failed to spark over fences last season and will return over hurdles

possibility we might then step up to three miles. He's working as well as ever, and his work was no different last season – the only thing that changed was running over fences, so he's told us what we should be doing with him."

Cinders And Ashes is exciting. Beaten on his debut over hurdles he soon made amends, winning at Haydock and then going back there to land a Grade 2 contest in fine style. All of those runs were on slow ground and things were very different come the Supreme Novices'. However, he showed marked improvement under a superb ride from Jason Maguire to beat Darlan, on whom AP McCoy didn't have his finest hour.

"It's nice when your opinion of a horse is proved to be right. We'd said beforehand that we didn't want to hit the front until after the last – that maybe sounds cocky, but we knew how good he was. Although no-one believed us, we also knew he'd improve for better ground. When Jason got off, the first thing he said was: "He's bolted up and hasn't had a race", which is quite impressive considering he'd just won the Supreme Novices'. So, we'll head towards the Champion Hurdle, possibly starting off in the Fighting Fifth.

"**Any Given Day** had a setback in the spring but he's in pre-training and will be back. He's not very big and I can't see him jumping fences, but he's a grand little horse. He'll probably run in two-and-a-half-mile conditions hurdles but if we could sneak into a big handicap that would be nice – his handicap mark will decide that. He's a very solid, high-class handicapper.

"**Ballabriggs** will run more often this

season, but all roads will again lead to Aintree for the National. I'm generally not one for making excuses for a horse but the messing about at the start definitely didn't help him. He doesn't tend to get upset, but he was in a terrible state before the race – I've never seen him like that before. He arrived at the second-last with a chance but didn't see his race out and my belief is that was because of the pre-race antics. He'll be 12 by next April, but Amberleigh House was that age when he won and I can't see a reason this fellow should be any different – I think he'll have a great chance this season."

Ile De Re hasn't yet run over hurdles for McCain but he has done great things for him on the Flat, winning the 2012 Chester Cup and Northumberland Plate. For his previous trainer, Ile De Re won two novice hurdles and was rated in the mid-120s – on the basis of his Flat form surely he's a well-handicapped horse?

"He'll go hurdling again and when we find out whether he's well handicapped it will be in a decent race. The Betfair Greatwood, as it is this season, seems like an obvious race.

"**Our Mick** has never been the easiest to train but he improved throughout last season to become a very decent handicap chaser, winning three races. He was possibly being a bit unlucky at Cheltenham in the three-mile handicap, where he missed one going down the back when the pace was quickening – without that he might well have finished a bit closer. The Hennessy is an obvious possibility, although it's not a race I like as I think you can leave your whole season there."

Golden Call won three novice hurdles last season and started his novice chasing career in great style when an effortless winner at Bangor in May, which means he remains a novice over fences for this campaign. McCain thought him good enough to run in the Grade 1 Sefton Novices' Hurdle, but Golden Call fell early.

"I wish he'd stood up at Aintree as we'd then have a better idea of where we are with him. He's really tough and hard but we've never got to the bottom of him, so Aintree

would have been a big help – I expected him to run really well there. He's an eight-year-old but hasn't had a lot of racing. He jumped well at Bangor, so I think we might run him in a better novice chase quite soon and see how we stand.

"We'll start him at two miles but I think he'll need further and he's possibly better going left-handed – but I'll reserve judgement on that as he might be one who hangs whichever way he goes.

"**Desert Cry** needs a strong gallop in his races and every big handicap we ran him in was run at a steady pace, bar the County Hurdle. In that race he hit a hurdle and lost his place, but he then flew up the hill. After winning first time out he went up the weights and things were tough for him after that. I'm undecided about whether he stays over hurdles or goes chasing – I've schooled him. He's a two-miler over hurdles but fences might just help him get a bit further."

McCain had fairly high hopes for **Wymott** at the start of last season but the eight-year-old must have been a disappointment. After a promising sixth in the Hennessy he didn't show much in his other three runs.

"He illustrates what I said about the Hennessy. He ran with great credit, in some ways a really solid Grand National trial, but didn't perform for the rest of the season – in my opinion the hard race he had at Newbury was what did for him. I would think he'll run at Aintree at least once and possibly twice this season. I still think there's a good race in him.

"**Super Duty** is a grand horse and another we haven't yet got to the bottom of. The way he races suggests he's still immature but he always finds plenty off the bridle. We had no realistic chance of beating Simonsig at Aintree but I'd have loved Super Duty not to have made the mistake at the second-last so we could have seen how close he would have got. He'll be going chasing.

"**Hollow Tree** is a smashing little horse. Maybe I could have been a bit braver and run him in the two-and-a-half-mile novice race rather than the Triumph. He wants that

Ballabriggs: will be aimed at the Grand National again but will run more often than last season

longer trip but it probably wasn't the time to do it with his long-term future in mind. In the Triumph he ran well but just lacked the gears for the race – he's a galloper. He'd had a long season but with the benefit of hindsight I wish we'd sent him to Punchestown as he loves soft ground. It won't be easy to plan his season but there are a few four-year-old hurdles over two miles, so we'll start there and then step up in trip a bit later.

"**Lexi's Boy** had a great season and was going nicely in the Galway Hurdle when he got brought down. It's a similar story to Hollow Tree – it's a tough season for four-year-old hurdlers.

"**Bourne** won well at Ascot and it was our sponsor's race so it was the right day to do it. He was a novice last season and on occasion found decent handicap hurdles a bit much for him. However, with more experience and another summer behind him I expect him to be up to running well in those sort of races. He's suited by a galloping track as his Ascot win showed.

"**Real Milan** is a smashing horse and will go chasing. He copes well with soft going, but he didn't handle the desperate ground at Haydock on his final start. Although he finished fourth, in my opinion he was the second-best horse in the race behind Brindisi Breeze, who was very useful. He's big, he jumps, he stays and he relaxes in his races – he should be a very nice novice chaser.

"**Sydney Paget** will also go novice chasing. He's a lovely horse but was still immature last season. He'll start at two and a half miles but will get three okay.

"**Ubaltique** isn't over-big and I hadn't had him very long when he ran at Kelso – he'd won in France so had lost his novice status, so I wanted to run him in a decent race straight away. However, he didn't run well, so we had

him back and then managed to sneak in a win at Perth before the end of the season. As I say, he's not big, but when we schooled him the other day Jason Maguire was of the opinion he would jump fences, so we might do that, but I think we'll start him out in the Silver Trophy over two and a half at Chepstow.

"**Diocles** is talented and was a bit immature. He had a setback that curtailed his season – he's another who will go chasing.

"When we got **Rain Mac** from John Gosden we did his wind and we gelded him. Basically, he fell to pieces and I'd ignore his run at Doncaster. He's come back looking like a different horse and hopefully that will be how he runs – I still think he could be exciting.

"**Counsel** [ex-Sir Michael Stoute] and **Right To Rule** [ex-William Haggas] have come from the Flat and both have schooled well."

There are a number of ex-point-to-point horses that have joined McCain's team – which are the ones we should particularly look out for?

"There are loads of them. **Up And Go** is an obvious one as he comes with a fair reputation, having won in Ireland over two and a half miles – a lot of people wanted to buy him but he's ended up here. He's a nice and relaxed but you never really know that much until you race them. **Clondaw Kaempfer** was placed in two point-to-points and then won a very valuable Fairyhouse bumper. Again, I like him and he has decent form in the book. By Oscar, who is a sire I like, he's tough and genuine."

McCain has a superb squad and there are plenty of others we could have discussed. It will come as a major shock if this isn't another excellent campaign for the north's leading trainer. [CB]

DONALD McCAIN
CHOLMONDELEY, CHESHIRE

	No. of Hrs	Races Run	1st	2nd	3rd	Unpl	Per cent	£1 Level Stake
NH Flat	43	70	17	9	10	34	24.3	+22.62
Hurdles	126	481	104	85	56	236	21.6	+36.27
Chases	46	161	32	24	21	84	19.9	-36.24
Totals	168	712	153	118	87	354	21.5	+22.65
10-11	137	588	101	98	64	325	17.2	-165.76
09-10	135	546	91	75	62	318	16.7	-109.71

NH Flat	W-R	Per cent	£1 Level Stake	Hurdles	W-R	Per cent	£1 Level Stake
May	1-4	25.0	-2.33	May	5-29	17.2	-15.97
June	1-4	25.0	0.00	June	3-17	17.6	-4.38
July	0-0	0.0	0.00	July	8-18	44.4	+50.17
August	1-2	50.0	+10.00	August	9-21	42.9	+21.45
September	0-0	0.0	0.00	September	2-13	15.4	-6.93
October	1-6	16.7	-2.50	October	5-39	12.8	+10.20
November	1-10	10.0	-6.25	November	14-59	23.7	+0.36
December	4-10	40.0	+27.00	December	11-62	17.7	-15.28
January	3-9	33.3	+3.72	January	10-64	15.6	-24.46
February	0-7	0.0	-7.00	February	9-38	23.7	+20.21
March	3-8	37.5	+4.63	March	18-66	27.3	+20.90
April	2-10	20.0	-4.65	April	10-55	18.2	-20.01

Chases	W-R	Per cent	£1 Level Stake	Totals	W-R	Per cent	£1 Level Stake
May	4-13	30.8	-0.77	May	10-46	21.7	-19.07
June	1-6	16.7	-3.13	June	5-27	18.5	-7.51
July	1-7	14.3	-5.33	July	9-25	36.0	+44.84
August	1-5	20.0	-1.75	August	11-28	39.3	+29.70
September	0-4	0.0	-4.00	September	2-17	11.8	-10.93
October	3-10	30.0	+12.00	October	9-55	16.4	+19.70
November	5-19	26.3	-9.14	November	20-88	22.7	-15.03
December	4-28	14.3	-12.50	December	19-100	19.0	-0.78
January	4-25	16.0	-12.13	January	17-98	17.3	-32.87
February	5-10	50.0	+15.13	February	14-55	25.5	+28.34
March	0-19	0.0	-19.00	March	21-93	22.6	+6.53
April	4-15	26.7	+4.38	April	16-80	20.0	-20.28

Hurdles	W-R	Per cent	£1 Level Stake	Chases	W-R	Per cent	£1 Level Stake
2m-2m3f	61-275	22.2	-6.24	2m-2m3f	17-66	25.8	-6.33
2m4f-2m7f	32-141	22.7	+43.66	2m4f-2m7f	6-44	13.6	-16.25
3m+	11-65	16.9	-1.15	3m+	9-51	17.6	-13.67

Non-Handicaps	W-R	Per cent	£1 Level Stake	Handicaps	W-R	Per cent	£1 Level Stake
Nov Hrdls	42-164	25.6	-15.77	Nov Hrdls	4-29	13.8	-2.43
Hrdls	26-105	24.8	+17.24	Hrdls	25-156	16.0	+29.13
Nov Chs	17-66	25.8	-15.85	Nov Chs	5-25	20.0	-2.52
Chases	2-8	25.0	+5.00	Chases	8-62	12.9	-22.88
Sell/Claim	8-28	28.6	+8.90	Sell/Claim	0-1	0.0	-1.00

	W-R	Per cent	£1 Level Stake		W-R	Per cent	£1 Level Stake
Class 1	8-71	11.3	-22.01	Bumpers	12-43	27.9	+6.49
Class 2	10-59	16.9	+12.50	Hurdles	17-90	18.9	+30.60
Class 3	18-97	18.6	-5.56	Chases	8-35	22.9	-6.02
Class 4	72-310	23.2	-13.64				
Class 5	30-117	25.6	+32.74	Totals	37-168	22.0	+31.07
Class 6	15-58	25.9	+18.62				

McCAIN AND THE STATS

McCain has been on the up since taking out a licence and just about reached the century barrier for the first time in 2010-11 when sending out 100 winners. He hit overdrive last season with 153 winners and nobody else sent out more than his total of 717 runners. The extra horses in his armoury last term obviously caught out the layers as despite the sheer volume of runners he returned a level-stakes profit of +17.65pt – the first time he had done so since taking over from his father in 2006-07.

McCain sent out 32 chase winners last term, which was a similar total to those he had in each of the three previous campaigns, but he sent out 104 winners over hurdles (22 per cent /+36.27pt) for 2011-12 while his bumper runners also paid their way with 17 winners (23 per cent /+17.62pt).

Stable jockey Jason Maguire recorded a personal best with 144 winners for the season, 102 of which were for McCain, highlighting the advantages a rider who has the backing of a big, in-form stable. He recorded an impressive +37.33pt level-stakes profit on mounts for his employer last term (26 per cent) but it's likely he will find it tough to repeat that feat as he had previously returned significant losses for McCain.

With Maguire taking up the lions' share of McCain's winners, there wasn't a great deal left for the rest although conditional pilot Henry Brooke posted some decent figures last season. Brooke rode 22 winners from 92 mounts last season (24% /+23.15pt) and should put his 3lb claim to good effect in the coming months.

Bangor, near to his base in Cheshire, is a favourite track and he has significantly more runners there than anywhere else. It was surprising to see that he managed to secure a massive profit at the Welsh venue last term (30 per cent /+54.10pt) as the layers normally protect themselves better than that. McCain has broken even over a five-year period at Bangor and the figures from last season are unlikely to be repeated.

Elsewhere McCain has recorded steady profits and strike-rates at Ayr, Haydock and Wetherby and by targeting the northern tracks he has a better chance of avoiding horses trained by some of the bigger yards in the south.

February seems to be a month where the McCain horses go well. He has returned level-stake profits and healthy strike-rates in each of the last three Februarys and punters are best advised to keep a close eye on his stable during this period.

Given he was operating on the same level numbers-wise last season as Nicky Henderson and Paul Nicholls, the disappointment for McCain have been that he has failed to compete in the elite races on a regular basis. Cinders And Ashes winning the Supreme Novices' at the festival was a high point but Peddlers Cross was a letdown in his first season over fences. Unless he is reignited by a return to hurdles this term it is unlikely McCain will have much say in the championship events.

'Awesome' Sanctuaire leads the way over fences with big guns retired

IN 2005-06, Paul Nicholls ended a run of ten consecutive trainers' titles for Martin Pipe, and in the six seasons since he has made the title his own. Last season he trained 138 winners at a strike-rate of 23 per cent, earning almost £3.3 million in prize-money for his owners, a performance all the more remarkable as some of his string were unwell early in the new year.

Neptune Collonges's Grand National win sealed the trainers' title, but as Nicholls points out, he would have won by £9,000 in any event if the Aintree prize-money was excluded. By his own admission he faces a formidable task to retain his title but that's not because there is any shortage of high-class talent in the Ditcheat team. Rather it's that it would be difficult for any stable to lose a Champion Hurdle winner (to former assistant Harry Fry), a National winner (retired), Master Minded (retired), Denman (retired) and possibly Kauto Star, and still be as effective as before. One thing is for sure: Nicholls and his team will be giving it their best shot.

A decision was yet to be made on **Kauto Star's** future when we spoke but last season the great horse won the Betfair Chase and a record-breaking fifth King George. Connections will do what's right for the 12-year-old and, whether or not we see him racing again, he has left everyone with some great memories.

There are plenty of chasers within the team who will fly the flag this season. **Sanctuaire** leads the way and Nicholls is very bullish about him. Last season he started over hurdles but after Christmas was sent over fences and was a revelation. He started with a win at Taunton, stepped up again at Sandown but was fantastic back there in the Celebration Chase.

"You can't be anything but positive about the horse – to win at Sandown on ground that's probably soft enough for him, against seasoned older horses in the way that he did, was awesome. The handicapper rates him highly too, putting him just a couple of pounds behind Sprinter Sacre – that makes him the highest-rated novice chaser I've trained, higher even than Azertyuiop was after winning the Arkle in 2003. We think he's best fresh, so he'll have a light but aggressive campaign. He'll run in the Tingle Creek and then have one run somewhere before the Champion Chase, assuming that all goes well."

Nicholls has trained four Cheltenham Gold Cup winners and he fancies **Silviniaco Conti** to give him a fifth, but perhaps not until 2014. A useful hurdler the season before last, he went over fences and made a big impression. He won Wincanton's Rising Stars Chase and then split Grands Crus and Bob's Worth in the Feltham before rounding off his season with a fine win in an Aintree Grade 2.

"I'm open-minded about this season – if he improved and showed he was in the Gold Cup mix then he could go there, but he might equally show us he'd be better with more time, so I'm not going to rule anything out. We'll start him in the Charlie Hall and see where we go from there. He's only six and he's by Dom Alco so he should improve as he gets older – he's every bit as good as Neptune Collonges – in fact he has more pace than him and he won Grade 1s and was placed in Gold Cups. He's at that sort of level but just needs a bit more time to mature."

Al Ferof made a good start to his chasing career, winning a Cheltenham Grade 2 and then followed up in the Grade 1 Henry VIII at Sandown. He was third in the Victor Chandler behind Somersby and Finian's Rainbow before finishing fourth in the Arkle. He disappointed on his final start.

"Forget Aintree as he was over the top by then. In the Arkle he lost his chance when he hit the ditch just after halfway. We'll step him up in trip this season and we'll enter him in the King George.

"**Tidal Bay** was a new arrival last season and he won the Bet365 Gold Cup for us which was great. He'll be running in similar races again this season and I wouldn't rule out that he might go back to Aintree for the Grand National – he unseated his rider there a couple of years ago.

"**Harry The Viking** did well over hurdles and fences and was second in the four-miler at the festival. He was over the top in the Scottish National and this season we'll aim him at the Grand National.

"**Join Together** has had a breathing operation and will be aimed at the big long-distance handicaps like the Hennessy and Welsh National.

"Take out Hunt Ball, and **Edgardo Sol** must have been the most improved horse in training. He was a good second in the County Hurdle but then won an Aintree two-mile handicap chase in good style. He's higher in the handicap over both hurdles and fences, but I hope there's more to come from him. He could start out in the Haldon Gold Cup.

"**Kauto Stone** won impressively at Down Royal and was then second to Sizing Europe in the Tingle Creek. He didn't really fire after that and his French profile reads much the same as he never produced his top form in his spring campaign. He could go back to Down Royal for the three-mile Champion Chase, but we need him to start to relax and settle over that longer trip.

"**Cristal Bonus** loves soft ground and was progressive last season. He jumps well and will eventually be a three-mile chaser. He too could start out at Down Royal in the two-and-a-half-mile Grade 2 Chase.

"**Pacha Du Polder** did well and rounded off his season with a win in the Future Champions Novices' Chase at Ayr. He'll be going handicap chasing and there should be more to come from him as he's still only five.

"**Toubab** was unlucky to be brought down in the Grand Annual but was second to Sprinter Sacre at Aintree. He's still eligible for graduation chases but we might stick to the better handicaps for now as he likes a fast-run race."

Among the hurdlers the biggest name is the wonderful **Big Buck's**, now unbeaten in his last 17 starts. How does Nicholls cope

with the pressure of training such a great horse?

"I've had so much pressure training Kauto Star that it's made it easier training the others. He'll follow a similar route to last year: the Long Distance Hurdle at Newbury, the Long Walk at Ascot, the Cleeve at Cheltenham and then back there for the World Hurdle, and then the Liverpool Hurdle. One thing is certain now is that he'll never run in another chase – when he's great at what he does, why change?"

Zarkandar won Newbury's Betfair Hurdle on his seasonal debut and was then sixth to stablemate Rock On Ruby in the Champion, before falling at Aintree.

"He wasn't right last year but I'm delighted with the way he is now. It was just one of those years and I never had him the way I wanted – he coughed two days after his Betfair Hurdle win. I'm really looking forward to running him and we'll aim for the best races around at two miles, with a tilt at the Champion Hurdle the main aim. He might need further in time but I hope he'll be stronger this year as a five-year-old.

"**Ranjaan** won two hurdle races but it took him a while to come to himself after being gelded. He was impressive in his two wins but got a small injury that kept him from running in the Triumph. He still has great potential and we hope he'll develop into a top-level performer.

"**Brampour** did well for us and for his conditional jockey Harry Derham. Now off a handicap mark of 161, life won't be as easy but we can use Harry's 7lb claim and we might step him up in trip at some stage of the season.

"We had high hopes for **Dildar** in the juvenile ranks but he never properly got over being gelded. It's a fresh start with him and I hope he'll show improved form.

"**Pearl Swan** won't be out until mid-season as he sustained a little injury in the spring. He was one of the top juvenile hurdlers of last season. He was never travelling in the Triumph but was coming with a late run when he slipped and fell at

Kauto Stone: Down Royal winner needs to learn to settle better in his races

For Two (right) and Wonderful Charm are two new recruits expected to do well this season

57

the last – he still had a chance at that point. He's normally a good jumper so he remains a promising horse.

"**Dodging Bullets** is a really nice horse, and will probably start out in a four-year-old hurdle at Cheltenham's October meeting, and then revert to novice company at the Paddy Power meeting. There can't be a higher-rated maiden hurdler in training – he's off 148. He's exciting."

The novice chase division is always an inspiring one for the Nicholls team and this season looks like being no exception.

Poungach won a novice hurdle and a handicap off 137, before a fine run behind Oscar Whisky at Cheltenham on New Year's Day. He missed the festival and rounded off his season with a fine fifth behind Big Buck's at Aintree. Nicholls must think a fair bit of Poungach to have run him in the Liverpool Hurdle?

"I didn't know where else to run him. He wasn't right that day and he was one who'd been coughing when we had the problems early in the year. He'll go over fences this season – it had been the plan to do it 12 months ago but we opted to give him more experience over hurdles. He's still maturing so there's more to come from him and he'll eventually get three miles."

Hinterland had good hurdle form in France and this time last year was one of Nicholls' big hopes. He won at the Paddy Power meeting and the trainer didn't conceal how highly he regarded him. However, he didn't really progress on his next two starts and fell at Aintree having missed Cheltenham.

"We bought him as a chaser and that's what he'll be doing. He shows a lot of natural speed so he'll be out over two miles and we'll probably start him out at the Paddy Power meeting.

"**Rocky Creek** is a lovely chasing prospect for this season over staying trips. He won the three-mile Grade 2 at Doncaster but he was well below his best at the festival.

"**Empire Levant** was impressive in a conditional handicap hurdle at the Hennessy meeting and was second to Rock On Ruby two days later. He was never as good again but he's had a good break and will go novice chasing – we'll probably give him one more run over hurdles before then.

"**Merehead's** campaign was restricted due to injury but we've always considered him to be a chaser.

"**Sam Winner** was fourth behind Zarkander in the Triumph but fell on both chasing starts last season, picking up a little leg injury on the second occasion. We'll run him in a handicap hurdle before going back over fences – we know he's very good and we just need some luck with him."

As always, Manor Farm Stables has a stack of newcomers, either from the Flat, from France, or from between the flags. From this array of talent, who are the ones to look out for in the coming months?

Nicholls did well with the Graham Wylie horses last season and the owner has acquired **For Two**, winner of a newcomers' race worth £22,000 to the winner at Auteuil.

"He's a lovely juvenile and is a chaser in the making. I really like him. He could start out at the Paddy Power meeting.

"**Samtegal** will also be running in juvenile hurdles – the recent rule change means he'll still be a novice all season, despite winning at Enghien in April. Again, he'll eventually make a chaser.

"**Wonderful Charm** won over hurdles at Auteuil before he joined us. He's still a novice until the end of October, so we could run him in the Persian War at Chepstow before he goes chasing. His form in France is very good. Similar comments apply to **Funny Star**, who won his only start over hurdles at Auteuil in March.

"**Unioniste** won his only chase start at Auteuil in May and also has decent hurdles form. He'll be running in two-and-a-half-mile novice chases but should get further.

"**Elenika** is still a maiden over hurdles and fences but has some decent placed form in France. He could run over both hurdles and fences this season and should be fun."

Comeonginger is a name we'll be hearing more of. The ill-fated Brindisi Breeze's brother, he won both his point-to-points for Richard Barber, and is one to follow in novice hurdles. "I loved him when I first saw him, and he's going up our hill as though it wasn't there.

"We'll probably send **Buck's Bond** novice chasing – the winner of two point-to-points, he jumps well, stays three miles and handles soft ground. He's closely related to Big Buck's.

"**Nitrogen** is a half-brother to Best Mate and Cornish Rebel and won his only start in a point-to-point. He'll be novice hurdling but is a chaser in the making.

"**Fox Run** comes from Ireland, where he was an impressive winner of his only point-to-point. Still just four, he'll have a season novice hurdling."

The horses who didn't make the list would still comprise a decent stable by themselves, which is an indication of the strength Nicholls has in his team. This is a transitional season where the younger horses have to start to replace the established names who have moved on. By this time next year some of the up-and-comers could be household names. [CB]

NICHOLLS AND THE STATS

Nicholls retained the championship but the winning margin of around a half million can be attributed to Neptune Collonges' Grand National success and unless the trainer can land the Aintree marathon this term it is likely he will have his work cut out to deny Nicky Henderson again, particularly as his main rival beat him by 29 winners last season, *writes Kevin Morley*.

He'll still have the imperious Big Buck's at his disposal but Kauto Star's future and with Denman and Master Minded now retired, Nicholls looks short on championship contenders, particularly in the chasing department.

He still possesses enough quality to pick up some decent prizes and his string will still be given much respect by bookmakers. The market tends to keep his runners massively onside, suggested by a level-stakes column that shows Nicholls has returned a fairly heavy loss for each of the last ten seasons.

Expect his stable to gradually warm to the task in the early stages of the season before accelerating in November – a month which normally sees him at is busiest in terms of winners and runners. However, expect a few of those to start at short prices as he still usually returns a loss for that period despite the volume of success.

There are methods to exploit the Nicholls stable in punting terms, though, and looking at riding arrangements is one way. Unsurprisingly, backing all of those ridden by Ruby Walsh isn't a quick route to success. Aside from an anomaly in 2007-08 where the combination returned a 68.46pt profit, the loss returned in each of the last four seasons is the outcome that should be expected this term.

Noel Fehily had a good time for the stable in 2010-11 with 17 winners from 46 rides (37 per cent /+3.95pt). Last season he had one winner from six mounts for Nicholls – Rock On Ruby in the Champion Hurdle. Daryl Jacob was the man in demand as his total of 56 winners for the Ditcheat handler surpassed Walsh who rode 52. Jacob maintained a 26 per cent strike-rate for the yard in 2011-12 (+27.04pt) and was entrusted with some high-profile mounts, not least Neptune Collonges in the National.

Nicholls has his fair share of winners at most tracks but it is in lower grade events at some of the smaller tracks where he is most likely to keep his level-stakes column in the black. His figures at Stratford caught the eye last term. He sent out six winners from just 13 runners (46 per cent /+12.41pt) but his record at a couple of venues in the West Country have been more consistent over the past few seasons. Since 2008-09, his strike-rates at Taunton (37 per cent /+1.65pt) and Newton Abbot (32 per cent /+30.51pt) have impressed.

PAUL NICHOLLS
DITCHEAT, SOMERSET

	No. of Hrs	Races Run	1st	2nd	3rd	Unpl	Per cent	£1 Level Stake
NH Flat	28	39	7	3	5	24	17.9	-15.84
Hurdles	104	280	68	44	35	133	24.3	-18.44
Chases	93	279	63	50	35	131	22.6	-26.83
Totals	182	598	138	97	75	288	23.1	-61.11
10-11	188	582	132	87	81	282	22.7	-87.99
09-10	181	548	118	101	57	272	21.5	-137.28

BY MONTH

NH Flat	W-R	Per cent	£1 Level Stake	Hurdles	W-R	Per cent	£1 Level Stake
May	2-5	40.0	+0.08	May	3-6	50.0	+4.23
June	0-1	0.0	-1.00	June	2-8	25.0	-0.75
July	0-0	0.0	0.00	July	1-3	33.3	-1.00
August	0-0	0.0	0.00	August	0-0	0.0	0.00
September	0-0	0.0	0.00	September	0-0	0.0	0.00
October	0-3	0.0	-3.00	October	9-29	31.0	+9.56
November	0-5	0.0	-5.00	November	15-54	27.8	+2.63
December	1-4	25.0	+1.50	December	11-48	22.9	-0.81
January	0-4	0.0	-4.00	January	9-38	23.7	-12.39
February	1-6	16.7	-1.50	February	2-21	9.5	-12.75
March	1-4	25.0	-1.80	March	8-37	21.6	-1.29
April	2-7	28.6	-1.13	April	8-36	22.2	-5.87

Chases	W-R	Per cent	£1 Level Stake	Totals	W-R	Per cent	£1 Level Stake
May	4-10	40.0	+11.38	May	9-21	42.9	+15.69
June	3-8	37.5	+3.73	June	5-17	29.4	+1.98
July	2-8	25.0	-2.10	July	3-11	27.3	-3.10
August	2-10	20.0	-3.00	August	2-10	20.0	-3.00
September	1-6	16.7	-4.56	September	1-6	16.7	-4.56
October	6-26	23.1	-2.71	October	15-58	25.9	+3.85
November	10-43	23.3	-1.74	November	25-102	24.5	-4.11
December	8-43	18.6	-18.23	December	20-95	21.1	-17.54
January	7-32	21.9	-16.38	January	16-74	21.6	-32.77
February	2-20	10.0	-15.40	February	5-47	10.6	-29.65
March	7-34	20.6	-18.48	March	16-75	21.3	-21.57
April	11-39	28.2	+40.66	April	21-82	25.6	+33.66

DISTANCE

Hurdles	W-R	Per cent	£1 Level Stake	Chases	W-R	Per cent	£1 Level Stake
2m-2m3f	32-127	25.2	+15.57	2m-2m3f	22-76	28.9	-10.31
2m4f-2m7f	20-96	20.8	-20.82	2m4f-2m7f	26-104	25.0	-10.56
3m+	16-57	28.1	-13.20	3m+	15-99	15.2	-5.96

TYPE OF RACE

Non-Handicaps	W-R	Per cent	£1 Level Stake	Handicaps	W-R	Per cent	£1 Level Stake
Nov Hrdls	22-92	23.9	-23.11	Nov Hrdls	3-7	42.9	+10.25
Hrdls	17-69	24.6	-12.51	Hrdls	25-110	22.7	+7.20
Chases	7-44	15.9	-17.80	Chases	18-118	15.3	+6.75
Sell/Claim	1-2	50.0	-0.27	Sell/Claim	0-0	0.0	0.00

RACE CLASS / FIRST TIME OUT

Race Class	W-R	Per cent	£1 Level Stake	First Time Out	W-R	Per cent	£1 Level Stake
Class 1	33-180	18.3	-15.81	Bumpers	5-28	17.9	-10.04
Class 2	23-100	23.0	+6.10	Hurdles	30-86	34.9	+17.12
Class 3	26-130	20.0	-44.40	Chases	17-68	25.0	-9.62
Class 4	44-135	32.6	+11.59				
Class 5	8-26	30.8	-6.22	Totals	52-182	28.6	-2.54
Class 6	4-27	14.8	-12.38				

National hopes Alfie Sherrin and Sunnyhillboy lead promising squad

ONE of my earliest racing recollections is from 1979 and the picture of Jonjo O'Neill cradling the head of the stricken Alverton, the Gold Cup winner killed in a fall in the Grand National – it moved me then and it still does. Tragically, history repeated itself last season when Synchronised won the Gold Cup for the trainer and, four weeks later, broke his leg when running free after falling at Becher's first time around at Aintree. It was a terrible end to what had been a fine season for O'Neill with just three winners shy of a century and with more than £1.1 million in prize-money.

Synchronised was one of three winners for O'Neill at the Cheltenham Festival, along with Alfie Sherrin and Sunnyhillboy.

Alfie Sherrin has been a talking horse several times during his career. Originally owned by Harry Findlay and trained by Paul Nicholls, he was bought by O'Neill at the owner's dispersal sale in August 2010 for £110,000 on behalf of JP McManus. While with Nicholls, Alfie Sherrin won three of his five starts – a bumper, a novice hurdle and a handicap hurdle – and was described by his trainer as talented but immature.

O'Neill sent him straight over fences and, on his good days, Alfie Sherrin has shown

decent form but has been hard to keep sound.

Last season started badly with a fall in Leopardstown's valuable Paddy Power Chase but after that things started to improve, and he showed promise on his next two starts, hinting he was no back number. At Cheltenham Alfie Sherrin won the JLT Speciality Handicap Chase over an extended three miles when fitted with first-time cheekpieces. After that he ran a creditable third in the Irish National and it looks as though the horse's career is back on track.

"He took a while to find himself, but he did it on the right day and at the right place. All being well he'll be aimed at all the better long-distance chases and he could end up in the Grand National. He's had his share of problems and it's a matter of keeping him right but he's a sound jumper and if he took to Aintree he would be interesting."

Sunnyhillboy won the Kim Muir at the festival, storming up the hill in fine style to win going away. He then went to Aintree for the National and ran an absolute blinder, looking all over the winner before starting to fade in the final 100 yards. He was beaten a nose by Neptune Collonges and was later found to have struck into his off-fore tendon. The injury was serious and thought at the time to be career-threatening.

"The plan is to have another crack at the National as long as we can keep him sound."

Get Me Out Of Here was consistent last season, winning at Fairyhouse in May as well as finishing second in the Relkeel, the Betfair Hurdle and the Coral Cup.

"He's a great horse, especially considering

he has a lot of problems. When he's right he's very good and he's been a bit unlucky in some of his races, such as at Newbury when he would have maybe won if he hadn't been hampered badly just as he was starting his run. We schooled him over fences a couple of years ago but probably because of his problems he wasn't good at it, so he'll stay over hurdles and run in similar races to last season."

It's A Gimme *(above, right)* is interesting. He won his bumper the season before last and won over hurdles at Newbury and Southwell. At Aintree he was going well but, after a blunder two from home went out like a light, suggesting he didn't get the two-and-a-half-mile trip.

"He was a bit disappointing last year and is another who's had a few problems. However, if they come all right then he could just turn out to be okay this season. I'm not sure what his best trip is – I always thought he'd get further than two miles, but when I tried him over further he didn't seem to stay. He'll stay handicap hurdling and I'll start him out again at two miles."

Johns Spirit won his bumper at the start of last season and then went over hurdles. He won twice and was placed on four other occasions.

"He'll be going chasing. Things sometimes haven't quite worked out for him: when he was right the races maybe weren't ideal, and when he got in the right race maybe he was a touch below his best. He won at Market Rasen in April as he was entitled to, and in that kind of race he can look really good, but in tougher fights it sometimes just doesn't happen for him. We're still learning with him but we'll try him over fences.

"**Valley View** is back. He's a lovely big horse but he's had his problems. He'll be going chasing at two and a half or three miles, and he's useful if we can keep him right."

It's not easy to win three bumpers but **Shutthefrontdoor** achieved that. He

started at Ffos Las on bottomless ground last November, followed up at Ascot, staying on really well, and then rounded things off at Newbury in what was undoubtedly a hot event, again looking as though the further he went the better he got.

"He's a lovely, big, fine chasing type and he did really well last season. I'm looking forward to him going chasing next season but he'll have a year over hurdles first as he needs to learn what the game is about. I'll be disappointed if he doesn't win over hurdles. Whatever he does I think he'll be even better over fences.

"**Listen And Learn** isn't the biggest and we don't think he's a superstar but he's done nothing wrong so far. He's a nice, honest horse who goes well, and I think he should win his share of races."

Lookout Mountain is firmly in the 'could be anything' category. The dogs had been barking ahead of his debut as he went off at odds of 1-2, but he won as an odds-on

shot should, landing a heavy-ground Ffos Las bumper by six lengths.

"He did it well. We like him and he goes nicely at home – he's also big enough to go on and jump fences at some stage, but we'll start over hurdles and see how we get on.

"**Abnaki** is a great little horse who loves soft ground. Not the biggest, I think we'll start off again in three-mile handicap hurdles but if that doesn't work out then we'll consider fences.

"We bought **Dursey Sound** at Doncaster – he was second in a bumper at Galway for Charlie Swan. We've schooled him over hurdles and, while he isn't the most natural of jumpers, he'll be ready to run fairly soon as it looks as though he likes good ground.

"**Holywell** won his maiden at Chepstow, and I would imagine he'll be going chasing. I think he'll stay, so three miles shouldn't be a problem for him."

Among the new arrivals, **Beckhani** was bought at the Cheltenham Sales in April.

JONJO O'NEILL
CHELTENHAM, GLOUCS

	No. of Hrs	Races Run	1st	2nd	3rd	Unpl	Per cent	£1 Level Stake
NH Flat	32	45	9	7	7	22	20.0	-5.42
Hurdles	113	378	55	43	26	254	14.6	-67.18
Chases	60	226	33	31	20	142	14.6	-34.43
Totals	157	649	97	81	53	418	14.9	-107.03
10-11	189	757	97	70	76	514	12.8	-154.16
09-10	185	729	105	77	64	483	14.4	-190.67

BY MONTH

NH Flat	W-R	Per cent	£1 Level Stake	Hurdles	W-R	Per cent	£1 Level Stake
May	0-3	0.0	-3.00	May	2-14	14.3	+8.00
June	1-3	33.3	+2.00	June	3-18	16.7	-1.63
July	0-3	0.0	-3.00	July	4-16	25.0	+1.23
August	1-3	33.3	-0.38	August	3-17	17.6	+1.38
September	2-3	66.7	+6.00	September	2-17	11.8	-6.50
October	0-5	0.0	-5.00	October	9-39	23.1	+3.40
November	2-6	33.3	+0.13	November	8-60	13.3	-23.97
December	1-3	33.3	+2.50	December	8-52	15.4	-19.25
January	0-3	0.0	-3.00	January	5-38	13.2	-13.88
February	1-5	20.0	-0.67	February	7-40	17.5	+0.13
March	0-2	0.0	-2.00	March	2-36	5.6	-10.00
April	1-6	16.7	+1.00	April	2-31	6.5	-6.09

Chases	W-R	Per cent	£1 Level Stake	Totals	W-R	Per cent	£1 Level Stake
May	3-17	17.6	-5.50	May	5-34	14.7	-0.50
June	6-15	40.0	+1.75	June	10-36	27.8	+2.12
July	1-15	6.7	-8.00	July	5-34	14.7	-9.77
August	4-16	25.0	+2.00	August	8-36	22.2	+3.00
September	2-9	22.2	+0.25	September	6-29	20.7	-0.25
October	1-26	3.8	-22.50	October	10-70	14.3	-24.10
November	5-39	12.8	+19.00	November	15-105	14.3	-4.84
December	4-31	12.9	-5.50	December	13-86	15.1	-22.25
January	1-18	5.6	-15.75	January	6-59	10.2	-32.63
February	0-9	0.0	-9.00	February	8-54	14.8	-9.54
March	4-14	28.6	+19.88	March	6-52	11.5	+7.88
April	2-17	11.8	-11.05	April	5-54	9.3	-16.14

DISTANCE

Hurdles	W-R	Per cent	£1 Level Stake	Chases	W-R	Per cent	£1 Level Stake
2m-2m3f	16-170	9.4	-68.33	2m-2m3f	3-37	8.1	-18.75
2m4f-2m7f	27-138	19.6	-7.84	2m4f-2m7f	13-94	13.8	-20.38
3m+	12-70	17.1	+9.00	3m+	17-95	17.9	+4.70

TYPE OF RACE

Non-Handicaps	W-R	Per cent	£1 Level Stake	Handicaps	W-R	Per cent	£1 Level Stake
Nov Hrdls	10-105	9.5	-40.34	Nov Hrdls	5-30	16.7	+12.00
Hrdls	6-51	11.8	-14.90	Hrdls	34-189	18.0	-20.94
Nov Chs	4-12	33.3	+2.50	Nov Chs	1-27	3.7	-24.00
Chases	2-12	16.7	-0.80	Chases	26-175	14.9	-12.13
Sell/Claim	0-3	0.0	-3.00	Sell/Claim	0-0	0.0	0.00

RACE CLASS

	W-R	Per cent	£1 Level Stake
Class 1	6-37	16.2	+10.33
Class 2	2-28	7.1	-13.00
Class 3	11-110	10.0	+9.75
Class 4	56-374	15.0	-113.15
Class 5	14-60	23.3	+8.10
Class 6	8-40	20.0	-8.05

FIRST TIME OUT

	W-R	Per cent	£1 Level Stake
Bumpers	5-32	15.6	-7.25
Hurdles	11-83	13.3	-40.56
Chases	11-42	26.2	+25.45
Totals	27-157	17.2	-22.36

He was placed in two bumpers for Charlie Brooks. "He's a grand, big, chasing type, and we'll probably go straight over hurdles with him.

"**Mr Watson** was third in the Racing Post Champion Point-to-Point bumper at Fairyhouse in April. He's a lovely chasing prospect – I'm hoping he's as good as he looks. I'd say we'd go straight over hurdles with him."

There are, as usual, a number of recruits from the point-to-point arena, with names like **Catching On**, **Classical Twist**, **Dreamsoftheatre**, **Minella Fifty**, **Presence Felt** and **Theatre Evening** all catching the eye.

"They're all lovely big chasing types but until they run you never know what you've got. That said, we're delighted with them all at this stage – this is the time of year when all the dreams are still alive. They look well going up the gallop, they're healthy and well, and you have to be hopeful."

As always Jackdaws Castle houses a strong team, and O'Neill has good prospects of achieving a century of winners for the eighth time. [CB]

otepool mobile

bet **tote**pool on the go...

your favourite
totepool
bets on your
mobile!

Available on the
App Store

to get started text **TOTE**
to **89660**

O'NEILL AND THE STATS

Last season was a good one for O'Neill. He might have been just short of the century barrier with 97 winners but that was an increase, albeit slight, on his previous total of 94, while the £1.1 million prize-money amassed last term was a significant increase on the £860,000 in 2010-11. The festival was a resounding success for O'Neill as the valuable handicaps landed by Alfie Sherrin and Sunnyhillboy supplemented the Gold Cup victory of the ill-fated Synchronised, proving once again that he knows how to peak his string for showpiece meetings, *writes Kevin Morley*.

Following O'Neill's runners at the Cheltenham Festival often reaps dividends and that is one of the more reliable betting methods punters can benefit from. However, backing the trainer blind throughout the season will almost certainly incur a loss as it has done for the last 11 seasons and it doesn't really help to break the figures down into hurdlers, chasers and bumper runners as he has recorded significant deficits in each area.

Given the large backing of JP McManus, it's hardly a shock to see Tony McCoy leading the winners list at Jackdaws Castle but, as you would expect, the bookies see the team coming a mile away and price them up accordingly. Even backing those ridden by back-up pilot Richie McLernon returns a substantial loss, so you have to look a little deeper regarding riding arrangements if you want to find a moneyspinner.

Maurice Linehan must be one of the most talented 7lb claimers in the weighing room and his rides for O'Neill recorded a steady +9.13 profit with an 18 per cent strike-rate. The conditional has started the 2012-13 campaign well for the yard and should continue to pay his way.

Noel Fehily is often entrusted on the yard's chasers and is worth following in that area. Since 2008-09, he has ridden ten winners from 54 rides over fences for O'Neill (19 per cent / +13.56pt).

Beware if choosing to follow O'Neill's horses blind for any length of time as he is prone to cold spells more than any of the other leading jumps yards. The winners did flow for the large part of last season but they gradually dried up after the festival. He sent out just two winners from 42 runners in the last few weeks of the 2011-12 campaign during April (5 per cent / -17.09pt).

As with most trainers, O'Neill has his favourite tracks and it's something that punters can benefit from. His runners at Fontwell, Ludlow, Towcester and Worcester are regular sources of profit, although his most impressive figures last term came at Ffos Las with ten winners from 33 runners (30 per cent / 37.88pt). His record at the Welsh venue read similarly in 2009-10 (ten from 32 / 31 per cent / +5.54pt).

King George the early target for Pipe's exciting flagbearer Grands Crus

LAST season was an excellent one for David Pipe and his team, with 101 winners at a strike-rate of 16 per cent and almost £1 million in prize-money.

The star of the show was **Grands Crus**, a 167-rated hurdler who made the switch to fences with aplomb. His debut at Cheltenham in November was spectacular. He jumped well and showed an impressive turn of foot to settle matters going to the last. After that it was a Grade 2 at Newbury where he was, if anything, even better, jumping cleanly over the three-mile trip. In the Feltham at Kempton he was better still, and on the back of that was made a hot favourite for the RSA Chase at the Cheltenham Festival.

On the big day he was sent off 6-5 favourite but found little when asked to make his challenge, proving one of the most expensive flops of the meeting. He looked as though he didn't stay that day, but that's hard to believe, so was it just a bad day at the office?

"He was beaten a long way out and wasn't 100 per cent after the race, and I'm certain that wasn't his true running. However, that's in the past, and the main thing is that he's back in, looks well, and we're raring to go this season. He could start off in the Paddy Power, but it's more likely it will be the Betfair Chase with the King George as the first big target. After that the hope is that he'll make up into a Gold Cup contender."

Dynaste followed in the footsteps of Grands Crus when taking the Fixed Brush Handicap Hurdle at Haydock in November. In the Long Walk at Ascot he met Big Buck's for the first time but came unstuck in the closing stages after trying to make all. He got a lot closer to the great one in the Cleeve Hurdle, getting Big Buck's off the bridle but, as so many have done before, he came off second best. In the World Hurdle he wore a tongue-tie for the first time but failed to give his true running and finished a well-beaten eighth.

"He didn't run up to his best at the festival but he was very good at Haydock and in the Cleeve. There were a few possible reasons why he was below par in the World Hurdle, and one of them could be that he didn't like the tongue-tie. He's still lightly raced and at six is a young horse. The plan is to send him novice chasing and he should be a really exciting prospect. We might give him a run over hurdles first."

Notus De La Tour won his first two outings over fences and ran well both times he was sent to Leopardstown, but his season ended on a sour note when he took a crashing fall in the Byrne Group Plate at the festival.

"He's given his owners a lot of fun – we've sent him to Ireland and France as well as running him here, and I think we'll probably do the same this season. He took a while to get over Cheltenham as he got a nasty kick from the horse who was behind him when he fell, but he's fine now – in fact, looking better than ever in my opinion. He'll be running in the better two and two-and-a-half-mile handicap chases."

Salut Flo run just twice last season, coming back at Cheltenham in December after 20 months off and then when winning the Byrne Group Plate in impressive style.

"It's great when a plan comes together. His owner was very patient, allowing me to keep him for the big day and not run him for three months. Unfortunately Salut Flo has had to have an operation for colic and I hope we'll get him back later in the season – it's possible he could go straight to Cheltenham.

"Things fell into place for **Ashkazar** *(below)* at Cheltenham in April, with a small field, rain all day that turned the ground soft, and a wonderful ride from Timmy Murphy. That was his first run back over fences since October 2009 – he was beaten at Cheltenham on that occasion, but when you look back he had Weird Al and Knockara Beau in front of him that day so the form was very strong. He isn't the easiest to train and his chase mark was more than a stone below his hurdles rating, so we thought the Cheltenham race was a good opportunity for him to get his head in front. I would imagine we'll mix and match over fences and hurdles this season.

"**Our Father** won a handicap hurdle at Ascot in December and we fancied him for the Pertemps Final at the festival, but I don't think he was suited by the hustle and bustle of a big field. He then disappointed at Aintree but the track and ground were probably too quick for him – it was more a question of him needing further experience. So, we're on a fact-finding mission with him when he comes back. He went up 19lb for his Ascot win but we might run him initially over hurdles before going over fences – he was bought as a chaser and that's what we'll do.

"**Balgarry** was coming back from an injury last season, and it was all a bit of a rush. He won easily at Newbury, which he needed to do to get into the handicap at Cheltenham for the Coral Cup but it was then very close to the festival and, looking back, he'd probably have been better off in the County Hurdle rather than racing over 2m5f. However, Newbury showed he's decent and very fluent at his hurdles, so we'll stick with them for now. He's on a mark of 144 so life will be tougher, but he's lightly raced so hopefully there's more to come from him.

"**The Tracey Shuffle** hasn't quite lived up to our expectations. He ran well when winning at Ayr and when third at Punchestown, but we were disappointed with him at Haydock on his final start. He isn't the easiest to keep sound, but he has a fair bit of ability and he'll be going novice chasing.

"**Close House** had very little experience going into the festival but he ran a cracker to finish fourth in the Neptune Investment Management Novices' Hurdle. They caught him a bit flat-footed at the top of the hill, but he was staying on strongly after the last. Before that he'd won at Towcester, again staying on really well. He's one to look forward to, and he could be exciting over hurdles or fences."

Master Overseer rounded off his season with a win in the Midlands Grand National at Uttoxeter in March. He stayed on really well over a marathon trip, showing a great attitude and battling up the straight.

"It was great to get him back because we had high hopes for him at the start of the season – we thought he was our Welsh National horse. He'd started out well with a handicap hurdle win but then disappointed us twice at Chepstow – he has always liked soft ground but didn't seem to like it there.

"He's probably the slowest in the yard but he keeps galloping and when he's on top form he's a good handicapper. Despite not performing at Chepstow last season, I think we have to try again, so he'll be aimed at the Welsh National – it looks like the right sort of race for him.

"**Weekend Millionair** won well at Ffos Las and then ran really well on atrocious ground at Punchestown when he was second in a two-and-a-half-mile handicap hurdle. He has been a raw individual who never carries a lot of condition, but he summered really well and strengthened up. He's a novice over hurdles until the end of October, so hopefully we can find him a race before we need to decide whether to go handicap hurdling or send him over fences.

"**Kazlian** is a good-looking horse who travels well in his races, sometimes a bit too well. He looked like he might win the Fred Winter Juvenile Handicap at the festival but the hill just caught him out. Things then didn't go right for him at Aintree, but he still finished seventh, not beaten very far.

"As you know, life can be tough for second-

*Master Overseer:
Midlands National winner
will be aimed at the Welsh
National this season*

season four-year-old hurdlers, but we'll start him off in two-mile handicaps and see how we go. He doesn't have to make the running but he does like to be prominent in his races."

Zaynar, formerly trained by Nicky Henderson, and then by Nick Williams, has joined Pipe's team. Good enough at his best to finish third in a Champion Hurdle, he showed some decent form over fences, but he blotted his copybook with a temperamental display at Kempton in February where he put on the brakes and tried to refuse at the first. After that he moved to Pipe and had just the one run, finishing down the field in the Jewson Handicap at the festival.

"We didn't have him for long, and it was a race against the clock to get him to Cheltenham – with the benefit of hindsight he probably shouldn't have run. The form

book probably tells you more about him than I can at this stage, but he has some top-class form and from what I've seen he still has plenty of ability. He could mix it with very good company over hurdles or fences."

Successful owner Malcolm Denmark has moved a number of horses to Pipe, and on paper the best of them looks to be **Knight Pass**, winner of two bumpers and a novice hurdle and a handicap.

"He was third favourite for the Champion Bumper a couple of seasons ago and probably hasn't quite lived up to expectations. He's a lovely, big horse and I imagine chasing will be his game. He ran twice at last season's festival and that probably didn't suit him but he's had a nice summer off and I'm pleased with what I've seen of him so far."

Problema Tic joined Pipe towards the

end of last season from Nicky Henderson's team, having been bought privately after not making his reserve at the sales. He ran just the once for his new connections, winning an Ayr handicap chase off 137. For his previous trainer he had won two of his three novice chases, showing marked improvement when stepped up to three miles.

"He's lightly raced and was impressive at Ayr. He's gradually creeping up the handicap but has some very good form – he seems to be an out-and-out stayer."

Investissement was trained in France by Andre Fabre, for whom he won over ten furlongs, and was placed in Group 3 company. He then had two runs over hurdles for Evan Williams before going to John Gosden. He won over a mile and three-quarters at Goodwood off a mark of 95 and finished third in the Ebor off 99. If he takes to hurdles second time around he will be a very interesting recruit.

"He's clearly a very good horse and if we can get him to translate his Flat form to hurdles then he'll be exciting. He's had a few injury problems and John Gosden thought the swimming pool down here would help him – if we can keep him in one piece he has a lot of potential.

"**Palace Jester** was bought cheaply [£14,000] at Doncaster Sales but he has some good form even if he a bit in and out. He's still a novice chaser and if we can get his jumping together then that's what we'll do – if not it will be handicap hurdles.

"There are a couple of interesting ex-French new arrivals at Pipe's yard. **Garynella** has some good hurdles form and will be novice chasing. **Katkeau** won a handicap hurdle at Auteuil last time out – at this stage I think we'll keep him to hurdles for the time being."

Pipe has an exceptionally strong team of horses this season and I would expect him to have another good year, and more than likely a personal best. [CB]

DAVID PIPE
NICHOLASHAYNE, DEVON

	No. of Hrs	Races Run	1st	2nd	3rd	Unpl	Per cent	£1 Level Stake
NH Flat	24	39	5	7	7	20	12.8	-25.23
Hurdles	117	419	67	47	44	261	16.0	-109.29
Chases	59	173	29	20	19	105	16.8	-13.76
Totals	156	631	101	74	70	386	16.0	-148.28
10-11	134	511	70	63	47	331	13.7	-82.39
09-10	142	567	103	54	40	370	18.2	+77.42

BY MONTH

NH Flat	W-R	Per cent	£1 Level Stake	Hurdles	W-R	Per cent	£1 Level Stake
May	2-3	66.7	+1.57	May	1-18	5.6	-15.75
June	0-3	0.0	-3.00	June	2-16	12.5	-10.13
July	0-4	0.0	-4.00	July	1-15	6.7	-12.38
August	0-1	0.0	-1.00	August	5-17	29.4	+1.55
September	0-1	0.0	-1.00	September	2-19	10.5	-12.50
October	0-1	0.0	-1.00	October	7-43	16.3	-25.68
November	1-5	20.0	-2.00	November	7-51	13.7	-8.46
December	2-8	25.0	-1.80	December	8-60	13.3	-25.65
January	0-6	0.0	-6.00	January	9-44	20.5	+2.55
February	0-4	0.0	-4.00	February	7-34	20.6	-0.32
March	0-2	0.0	-2.00	March	11-60	18.3	+3.90
April	0-1	0.0	-1.00	April	7-42	16.7	-6.42

Chases	W-R	Per cent	£1 Level Stake	Totals	W-R	Per cent	£1 Level Stake
May	2-9	22.2	-0.25	May	5-30	16.7	-14.43
June	2-6	33.3	+1.23	June	4-25	16.0	-11.90
July	1-8	12.5	+0.50	July	2-27	7.4	-15.88
August	1-12	8.3	-10.50	August	6-30	20.0	-9.95
September	0-7	0.0	-7.00	September	2-27	7.4	-20.50
October	2-8	25.0	-1.50	October	9-52	17.3	-28.18
November	7-27	25.9	+10.23	November	15-83	18.1	-0.23
December	3-27	11.1	-16.47	December	13-95	13.7	-43.92
January	1-18	5.6	-7.00	January	10-68	14.7	-10.45
February	3-12	25.0	+5.50	February	10-50	20.0	+1.18
March	3-25	12.0	-4.00	March	14-87	16.1	-2.10
April	4-14	28.6	+15.50	April	11-57	19.3	+8.08

DISTANCE

Hurdles	W-R	Per cent	£1 Level Stake	Chases	W-R	Per cent	£1 Level Stake
2m-2m3f	29-195	14.9	-79.97	2m-2m3f	2-30	6.7	-16.00
2m4f-2m7f	29-154	18.8	-0.11	2m4f-2m7f	17-67	25.4	+15.75
3m+	9-70	12.9	-29.21	3m+	10-76	13.2	-13.51

TYPE OF RACE

Non-Handicaps	W-R	Per cent	£1 Level Stake	Handicaps	W-R	Per cent	£1 Level Stake
Nov Hrdls	19-84	22.6	-15.12	Nov Hrdls	4-26	15.4	-7.25
Hrdls	10-51	19.6	+4.85	Hrdls	30-244	12.3	-91.07
Chases	8-22	36.4	-2.82	Nov Chs	2-10	20.0	-1.27
Chases	0-9	0.0	-9.00	Chases	19-132	14.4	-0.67
Sell/Claim	4-14	28.6	-0.70	Sell/Claim	0-0	0.0	0.00

RACE CLASS / FIRST TIME OUT

Race Class	W-R	Per cent	£1 Level Stake	First Time Out	W-R	Per cent	£1 Level Stake
Class 1	8-92	8.7	-35.51	Bumpers	4-24	16.7	-14.23
Class 2	9-90	10.0	-36.17	Hurdles	14-92	15.2	-11.28
Class 3	14-102	13.7	+14.54	Chases	8-40	20.0	-4.25
Class 4	47-230	20.4	-51.09				
Class 5	18-83	21.7	-19.82	Totals	26-156	16.7	-29.76
Class 6	5-34	14.7	-20.23				

PIPE AND THE STATS

Last season was a good one on the numbers front for Pipe as his tally of 101 just about broke the century barrier. It is difficult to predict whether he will repeat that in 2012-13, though, as his seasonal tally for the four prevous seasons reads 65, 102, 76 and 100. The inconsistency could perhaps be explained by his reliance on handicappers. They accounted for more than half of his winners in each of the last four seasons and it can sometimes take a horse a whole term to drop down to a winnable mark following a successful spell, *writes Kevin Morley*.

Pipe does adopt a scattergun approach to handicaps, though, so a level-stakes loss is almost certain and while he has plenty of decent horses to scoop some valuable pots in that area, he lacks some quality for the top graded races. Only Grands Crus threatened to make the breakthrough in novice chases last term and while he managed to win the Feltham at Kempton over Christmas, he was ultimately disappointing at Cheltenham in the RSA.

His level-stakes loss stood at -149.28pt last season, which gives an indication that finding profitable methods to follow the Pipe stable in some way is more difficult than other trainers. Pipe has recorded a loss of a whopping -429.72pt with his hurdlers over the last five seasons and although the chasers fare much better in that respect, they still record a loss of -27.31pt. Bumper runners offer more hope with a profit of +19.55pt (19%) although his runners underperformed in that area last term with a 14% strike-rate (-26.23pt).

Given the sheer volume of runners Pipe has, it's hardly surprising to learn that backing all of stable jockey Tom Scudamore's rides leaves you massively in the red but Tony McCoy, so successful for Pipe's father Martin, is a booking for the yard. With 16 winners from 57 mounts since the beginning of the 2008-09 campaign (28 per cent /+18.77pt), it's an angle punters can use to their advantage.

However, it's always worth noting Pipe's use of conditional riders and he has given plenty of opportunities to claiming jockeys, sometimes on big occasions. The likes of Johnny Farrelly, Danny Cook, Hadden Frost and Conor O'Farrell have all ridden winners for the Nicholashayne handler at the Cheltenham Festival while O'Farrell was profitable to follow for the yard two seasons ago in 2010-11.

That wasn't the case last season, though, and now O'Farrell has lost his claim, punters may lose the edge in siding with the trainer-jockey combination religiously. Perhaps the void will be filled by Tom Bellamy who won on five of his 19 rides for Pipe last term (26 per cent /+3.99pt). With his 7lb claim still intact, punters may benefit from backing his mounts this term.

The best way to find a profitable angle with the Pipe stable is to look at his record at certain tracks. He boasts steady if not spectacular strike-rates at Ascot (16 per cent /+6.88pt) and Newbury (13 per cent /+48.62pt) but those that oblige often do so at generous prices. His runners at Chepstow and Uttoxeter also provide a steady stream of winners with healthy profits.

Big names who should wrap up plenty of the biggest races this season

After interviewing the leading British trainers **Colin Boag** picks his most promising ten to follow

Cinders And Ashes Donald McCain

Read McCain's comments about the horse, including what Jason Maguire said on dismounting after his Supreme Novices' win. He has to be one to follow this season.

Comeonginger Paul Nicholls

Yet to run under rules but was successful in the point-to-point arena and this brother to Cheltenham Festival winner Brindisi Breeze can make a big name for himself in novice hurdle company.

Dynaste David Pipe

High class over hurdles and is his trainer's chaster to follow, which is a good enough tip in itself. Could well have what it takes to become an RSA Chase contender

Fingal Bay Philip Hobbs

Although Hobbs has the RSA Chase in mind for Fingal Bay, it might just be that he is best at a bit short of that trip. However it pans out, though, there is no denying he has the look of an exciting novice chaser.

Grands Crus David Pipe

It could be best to forgive this exciting performer for his below-par effort in the RSA Chase as he clearly wasn't right. On the basis of his previous runs he is a very high class chaser who looks Gold Cup material.

Grumeti Alan King

King trained Katchit to win the Triumph Hurdle and he went on to win the Champion Hurdle the next year. So, when King says Grumeti is the best juvenile hurdler he has ever trained we should take note.

Sanctuaire Paul Nicholls

Nicholls is very bullish about Sanctuaire and sounds as though he's relishing the prospect of a clash with Sprinter Sacre. If all goes well, their meeting in the Queen Mother Champion Chase would be very special.

Simonsig Nicky Henderson

Did a double over hurdles at the Cheltenham and Aintree festivals and now goes novice chasing. Could develop into a principal contender for the Arkle.

Sprinter Sacre Nicky Henderson

Impossible to leave off any list of. Already very good, he could just be a special one.

Zarkandar Paul Nicholls

Not 100 per cent right last season, but thought to be a different horse this time. Will head down the Champion Hurdle route and should win races along the way.

Mullins holds all the aces with Gold Cup looking up for grabs

Johnny Ward looks at the jumps scene in Ireland and assesses the various divisions

THE cyclical nature of matters in life, from sporting trends to fashion, should always be on our minds as we attempt to analyse the present with a view to the future.

Given the good health of point-to-point racing in Ireland, the fact Ireland has been rather starved of Gold Cup success in recent years has engendered much debate. The collapse of the economy has been a factor – for example, both the owner of 2005 Cheltenham hero Kicking King and 2006 third Forget The Past have had their fortunes wiped out by the property crash. So it is to be expected that some of the most promising pointers will, as has been the case in the past, end up in Britain.

Our Champion Chase dominance looks as dead as our World Hurdle hopes until Big Buck's retires, while Hurricane Fly's eclipse last season suggest he is likely on the wane. With nothing close to an outstanding novice hurdler in Ireland last term, we have only a sporting chance of regaining that most thrilling feature of the first day. However, in Sir Des Champs, Ireland has a realistic chance of bagging one of the four championship races in 2013.

It will be mainly on the shoulders of his trainer Willie Mullins that Irish hopes rest in 2012-13. The genius son of a genius father, based in the little town of Muine Beag, has

another formidable team to go to war with as the season develops.

Indeed, his stranglehold on racing in Ireland seems to be gaining ever more of a grip. Mullins' total prize-money accumulated in Ireland alone last season was over €2.3m, comfortably more than three times what nearest rival Noel Meade achieved.

Yet the Gold Cup has eluded Mullins and it is entirely appropriate that he is the man on the cusp of delivering an Irish winner in the race this season.

SENIOR CHASERS

Has the Gold Cup ever looked so open? Synchronised is sadly gone, Kauto Star is finished with a view to the race and Long Run produced so many underwhelming performances last season as to make one wonder what he has left. Surely a new order is nigh.

Remarkably, three of the first five in the betting for the race are trained in Ireland and, in Sir Des Champs, Willie Mullins has a horse that really appeals as a Gold Cup winner. Although his cv as a novice is hardly spectacular – winning the Jewson and a Grade 1 at Punchestown that was there for the taking – everything about the horse points to him developing into a formidable Gold Cup contender this season.

He has won all seven races since coming to Ireland and is two from two at Cheltenham. He jumps with a little swagger and real efficiency, seemingly saving a bit for a finishing burst.

And yet, it was Flemenstar whose heroics as a novice garnered the bulk of the plaudits in Ireland last term. Justifiably so, too. After his first outing he routed every rival with powerful displays of awesome jumping at a cruising speed that left good horses heartless and hopeless.

The big question for Flemenstar is whether he can make the step up to the staying division. He could easily improve over three miles, but another three-quarters of a mile and the hill at Cheltenham is another matter altogether.

Another horse who has huge promise and who might have escaped widespread British attention as he has yet to run out of Ireland is Last Instalment. He was an outstanding novice chaser for us last year and there was something of the Denman about the son of Anshan, who is unbeaten over fences and looked within a sniff of stardom when hammering First Lieutenant at Leopardstown in December.

There is a niggling concern that he might not be able to deliver on that immense potential – any time a horse gets a tendon injury there has to deep concern – but his injury might not be the most severe and his trainer Philip Fenton deserves a bit of luck.

That other Gigginstown ace, First Lieutenant, ran a blinder behind Bobs Worth in the RSA Chase and will be trained for the Gold Cup.

As for the Queen Mother Champion Chase hopefuls, it hardly needs reiteration that Sprinter Sacre will run away with this race and the two-mile division if he stays sound, but what of the Irish pretenders?

Sizing Europe's limitations were seemingly exposed at Cheltenham last year. He ought to remain a big player in this division once he does not take on the Henderson freak but, with Big Zeb all but finished and Flemenstar set to step up in trip, Ireland will have a relatively weak team this season.

What of the Grand National? Seabass performed with immense credit in finishing third to Neptune Collonges despite perhaps not quite staying the trip. No doubt the nine-year-old will be trained for a repeat bid, albeit off a little higher mark, while On His Own is one to keep in mind too. Sent off 14-1 at Aintree in April, the eight-year-old traded at under 4-1 in-running in the race until falling on the second circuit at Bechers. He could be the one to beat next year.

SENIOR HURDLERS

Hurricane Fly is still Champion Hurdle favourite but a predictably uneasy one. The adage comes to mind: fool me once shame on you; fool me twice, shame on me. Willie Mullins could not explain his defeat in the Champion Hurdle last season and, while he got his Grade 1 reward at Punchestown, a workmanlike win over Zaidpour, who

'Last Instalment was an outstanding novice chaser last season and there was something of the Denman about him. He is unbeaten over fences and looked within a sniff of stardom when hammering First Lieutentant'

has twice since been beaten, was hardly something to celebrate.

What Mullins said just after the race at Punchestown was noteworthy. "We were worried about him being very keen and he probably settled too well at Cheltenham and here, so we might now ride him like a normal horse next year."

Hurricane Fly owes nothing to anybody and this remarkable son of Montjeu is still only eight years old so it is, of course, entirely possible he will thrive this season. The feeling is, nonetheless, that he is far from unbeatable.

Beyond 'The Fly', there is not a single Irish horse in the top ten in the betting for the Champion Hurdle. Our best sophomore hurdlers are Trifolium, Alderwood and Hisaabaat. It will be also interesting to see how Galway Hurdle winner Rebel Fitz develops this term.

In the staying hurdle picture, Big Buck's still rules over all, but the Colm Murphy-trained Voler La Vedette is a classy mare who could justifiably be deemed the best of the rest. She flirted with odds-on approaching the final flight in the World Hurdle last March and probably struggled on the ground at Punchestown when second to the legendary Quevega.

Both these mares are set to have lucrative campaigns again, while Zaidpour should earn his owner plenty of prize-money and is versatile regarding trips, although he does need deep ground ideally.

NOVICES

Yet again, Willie Mullins has the key in his hand – at least with the young chasers.

However, Gordon Elliott's Don Cossack is perhaps our most exciting novice hurdler, having achieved a Racing Post Rating of 146 when winning at Fairyhouse in April, his third successive win in bumpers.

Don Cossack, a son of Sholokov, is rather unproven on decent ground. The Dermot Weld-trained pair, Waaheb and Rock Critic, are both exciting, while Minsk could yet be a smart second-season novice for Dessie Hughes.

Our rookie steeplechasers are generally an exciting bunch. The whole of Ireland seemed to back Boston Bob to win last year's Albert Bartlett at the festival and, although he was beaten, he was not shamed and Willie Mullins expects fences to bring out some improvement.

Champagne Fever, last year's Champion Bumper winner, is due to bypass hurdling in advance of a novice chase career and this scopey sort should be exciting in two-mile chases.

Back In Focus, who represents the same connections as Boston Bob, routed his rivals on his chasing debut at Listowel and looks a natural already.

Owner Graham Wylie and Mullins could have a cracking campaign, as Felix Yonger – second to Simonsig at Cheltenham last year – also has the credentials to go a long way as a chaser.

Sir Des Champs leads the way for team who can bag plethora of races

Johnny Ward with a squad he expects to do well over the coming months and score plenty of points

Flemenstar Peter Casey

There will surely be few Ten to Follow lists that omit this one. Unbeaten after a blowout on his chase debut, Flemenstar is a punters' dream: he lies up with the pace, jumps like a natural and finds plenty for pressure. He also is reasonably ground versatile.

Casey says he hopes Flemenstar is a Gold Cup horse. Stamina is still a big question mark, but the seven-year-old should have plenty of other options in Ireland, even before trying three miles and beyond.

Sir Des Champs Willie Mullins

That Sir Des Champs is clear favourite for the Cheltenham Gold Cup says much about the limited regard in which the 2012 Cheltenham protagonists are held. Synchronised is gone, Kauto Star is nearing the end and Long Run has questions to answer.

Sir Des Champs is seven from seven over jumps since moving to Mullins and looks more of a Gold Cup horse at this stage than Flemenstar. Stamina seems assured, he jumps with aplomb and achieved his highest Racing Post rating at Cheltenham (when winning the Jewson). The ground was good then but winter conditions will be fine too. Expect him to mop up plenty of races in Ireland over the winter.

Don Cossack Gordon Elliott

This five-year-old earned an RPR of 146 for winning a Fairyhouse bumper by 17 lengths in April, a figure that suggests he is the best bumper horse in Ireland.

His worst performance came on his debut on decent ground, so time will reveal how he copes with good conditions. However, we can assume that, given typical winter terrain, he should make some novice hurdler. He ought to be versatile distance-wise.

Hurricane Fly Willie Mullins

It seems unlikely Hurricane Fly will be at the peak of his powers again as last season's Champion Hurdle disappointment and subsequent Punchestown effort were not that of the horse we knew, or thought we knew. But his trainer will recognise last year's Irish novices were an ordinary crop and, with Hurricane Fly still much the best of the senior hurdlers over two to two and a half miles, he can be expected to add one or two more Grade 1s to his tally.

Boston Bob Willie Mullins

Boston Bob was sent off 6-5 favourite for the Albert Bartlett at the Cheltenham Festival last season, and his defeat to Brindisi Breeze came as a shock to the pockets of many Irish punters. Nevertheless, he remains a cracking prospect for novice chasing this season and, assuming he takes to fences, Mullins' toughest job will be choosing which races to miss.

Boston Bob (right) looks sure to take high rank over fences this season

Voler La Vedette Colm Murphy

Ireland probably has its best staying hurdler for several years in Voler La Vedette. She gave Big Buck's something of a fright last March in the World Hurdle and, although she was unable to beat Quevega on deep ground at Punchestown afterwards, she nevertheless looks destined to dominate the staying hurdling scene in Ireland this season.

Champagne Fever Willie Mullins

Expect Champagne Fever to go straight over fences with the potential to prove a powerful force in the novice ranks. He has a high cruising speed and the scope to be a smashing chaser. He has proven equally impressive on good and heavy ground, which increases his options.

On His Own Willie Mullins

A faller when going well in the Grand National last season, this Presenting eight-year-old had hacked up in the Thyestes Chase previously. His trainer is likely to attack that race again and he looks primed to win at Graded level or land another big handicap.

Rubi Light Robert Hennessy

This horse's prospects may hinge on whether he can avoid Sir Des Champs and Flemenstar. Nevertheless, he is a proven top-class performer on easy ground over two and a half miles, which means he can be targetted at the Grade 1 John Durkan, two Grade 2 chases at Gowran and plenty more.

Minsk Dessie Hughes

He was favourite for the Triumph Hurdle for much of last season having been a smart performer on the Flat for John Oxx. He shaped with promise when finishing second on his only hurdling start, and two-mile novice hurdles look likely to dominate his agenda, although he should get further.

'He's seven from seven over jumps since arriving in Ireland – expect him to mop up plenty of races over the winter'

Promising Alpancho can leave first runs behind and prove useful recruit

Brian Morgan with ten horses who have stayed away from the public eye and could prove worth following

Alpancho Anthony Honeyball

The debut of this six-year-old, in a Sandown bumper in February, was promising. A physically imposing presence in a small field. he was pretty much unfancied at 12-1 and was waited with on the widest route by Aidan Coleman. The pace was non-existent until the straight and he emerged with credit in a vain attempt to match Sky Watch for speed in a quarter-mile sprint that would not have played to his strengths.

On his only other appearance, in a Chepstow bumper two months later, assistant trainer Rachael Green held him up before mounting a challenge from three out – again he was left a little lacking in pace and faded into fifth.

For a horse who stands 17hh, these were creditable first efforts. By Alflora, he can be expected to get much better as he grows into his frame and matures. Over jumps he's likely to come into his own over further than the minimum trip and he'll probably handle most ground conditions.

Civil Disobedience Richard Woollacott

Woollacott has risen from a prolific point-to-point jockey and trainer into another fine leading West Country member of the jumps fraternity. One of his lesser known charges is this eight-year-old gelding with winning point form who has yet to make the frame in five efforts under rules.

On his debut at Warwick last December he was bang there until running out of gas in the closing stages and then, on his second run under rules, he again raced prominently in a two-and-a-half-mile maiden hurdle at Bangor until tapped for toe when the pace quickened, but he kept on doggedly up the straight for fourth.

Upped in class at Newbury he could never go the pace over a furlong shorter but then, in his first try at novice chasing, he was impressive at Warwick. Sent off the 16-1 outsider of five he jumped beautifully, apart from one slowish leap, and the further they went the better he looked. Nick Scholfield eased him past hot favourite Lively Baron rounding the turn and the race was his until a fall two out.

He ran no race on his only other start, but a summer break is sure to have done him good and I expect him to come back stronger, lose his maiden tag and claim some decent prizes.

Fine Parchment Charlie Mann

One of our more mature quiet achievers, he's not won since March 2011 when landing a Newbury handicap chase over two and a half miles. He ran a cracker in the same race last March, finishing fourth after getting outsprinted in a dash for the line.

It's possible he needs longer trips at the age of nine, unless there's a fortunate combination of a stiff track and soft ground. Usually a very safe conveyance, his only blemish in jumping terms has been an unseating over the National fences, which can be easily forgiven. With a fair handicap mark and the right conditions I can envisage him winning at least a couple of handicap chases this season.

Font Lawney Hill

I was really pleased to see this great character back on the track during the summer, running on the Flat at Goodwood and then in handicap chases at Stratford and Uttoxeter.

In a somewhat chequered career, his record of five wins includes the commendable hat-trick of a victory on the Flat, over hurdles and in a chase, so versatility has never been a weakness.

Following Font is not for the faint-hearted, but he's a real fun sort to have in our virtual stable, and he's sure to be noticed for one reason or another in all of his races. On the pretty safe assumption that his top-class trainer has him in the right mental and physical shape, I reckon he's one to support this term off handy hurdle and chase marks.

Giorgio Quercus Nicky Henderson

In 2009 this ex-French gelding landed the John Smith's Scottish Triumph Hurdle Trial at Musselburgh on his trainer's debut at the track, and since then has gone on to be just as effective over fences.

His six wins from 16 starts in Britain have been at Haydock, Hereford, Kempton (slow, all-weather), Leicester, Musselburgh and Sandown, which tends to suggest a preference for flatter tracks. In fact, if one removes his runs at Cheltenham and Chepstow, his record is six wins and two seconds from just 11 races.

Last season's four appearances brought a win and a second in graduation chases and a clear round over the National fences in the Topham Chase.

He acts well on goodish ground but even better when it's soft or heavy, and now we know he stays two and a half miles there are more options.

Meganisi Rebecca Curtis

After an error-strewn maiden hurdle debut at Cheltenham last October, this five-year-old had a seven-month layoff before reappearing in a two-mile novice event on heavy ground at Wincanton. He was sent off at 7-1 but made a mockery of those odds – prominent throughout and tackling the obstacles fluently, he took it up just after the home turn for Tony McCoy and won in a canter by 11 lengths.

Just nine days later he switched codes and was raised significantly in class to contest a Listed race at Newbury. Again apparently unfancied at 16-1 in a six-horse race, he overcame a sluggish break under a positive ride from Neil Callan and finished second.

He could make up into a decent hurdler this term, where a combination of a high cruising speed, stamina and pace should translate into winning ways – and he looks to have enough scope to go chasing in time, too.

Nafaath Neil King

Successful three times for Kevin Prendergast in Ireland this six-year-old recorded one win and two places from eight runs over jumps for Howard Johnson. He's yet to leave the ground for his current handler, but showed his wellbeing with a staying-on third at a big price from a poor draw in the Ascot Stakes Handicap in June.

There seems little doubt he's improving with age and, given that he's yet to try any stamina test over obstacles, in jumping terms he could be anything. With a high cruising speed and the ability to act on decent to very testing ground, I'm convinced that 'anything' will become something very interesting.

Victors Serenade Anthony Honeyball

This Old Vic gelding has had only 12 runs in three season, but with only four of them out of the frame, each appearance has been worth waiting for.

The most notable run of that opening 2009-10 campaign was a fast-finishing third at 66-1 in a Taunton novice hurdle over two miles and a furlong. It was a big clue that further was needed to bring the best out of him and he has since won four races, three of them over three miles. His first success came from a mark of 104 in a handicap at Exeter, and his most recent success was off 128, for which he earned a Racing Post rating of 150.

He's now on a mark of 140 and it must surely be onwards and upwards this season, and he's my long-range fancy for the Welsh National.

Vintage Vixon Tim Vaughan

This Moscow Society mare's five runs have all been in point-to-points in Ireland. Bought by an existing owner of Vaughan's, she could enjoy plenty of success in the burgeoning field of mares' only races.

After a fairly anonymous debut her record

She acts on soft and heavy ground for sure, has generally been a good jumper, and at only five has bags of room for improvement. She's in excellent hands and I can see her making into a nice prospect for this season and several more to come

in her other four maiden points reads 2321: impressive on paper but, as any Irish point devotee will tell you, it could mean something or nothing.

When winning at Lismore on her final start in March she was well clear when making a right hash of the last yet still went on to record a 20-length success.

She acts on soft and heavy ground for sure, has generally been a good jumper, and at only five has bags of room for improvement. She's in excellent hands and can make up into a nice prospect for this season and several more to come.

Wyck Hill David Bridgwater

This eight-year-old Pierre gelding has relatively few racing miles on the clock. After three runs in bumpers in the 2009-10 season, he was sent novice hurdling for the next campaign and managed a return of two thirds and two fourth-placed finishes from five appearances. But it's his four outings over fences between October and December in 2011 that gain him a spot in this list.

In the first of these, plunged into novice handicap company over an inadequate two miles and three furlongs at Chepstow, he was sent into an early lead by Tom Scudamore and refused to let anything past him for very long, fending off challengers and staying on in the gamest fashion to win by a couple of lengths.

A fortnight later at Market Rasen, upped in class, by 9lbs in weight and by almost half a mile in distance, he was again at the head of affairs and it was between him and Mister Hyde until he was left clear two out by the latter's fall.

Wyck Hill's third Chase, at Newbury, told us little as he put in a short one at the third and took a heavy fall, while his season ended back at the same course shortly before Christmas, when he put in a foot-perfect round until the last two and was the only one to give Penny Max a race, albeit well beaten off into second.

He's got everything I look for in a chaser to follow: he jumps well, has a great engine, gives it his all, and is in love with the game.

otepool.com

bet £5
get £10 free

when you open an account at totepool.com
- home of racing, sports, casino, games & bingo!

 @totepool   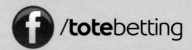 /totebetting

Don't strike off Long Run – he looks a serious player to reclaim Gold Cup crown

 Paul Kealy with six hurdlers and chasers who can make it to this season's big meetings

CHASERS

Sprinter Sacre Nicky Henderson

If there's one racing certainty this jumps season it's that not all of the previous season's star novices, whether over hurdles or fences, will live up to their potential.

We will have high hopes for any number of top prospects from last year, but a look at what happened to the class of Cheltenham 2011 reveals a sorry tale. Between them, the winners of the 2011 Arkle, Jewson and RSA Chases managed just a solitary win in a three-runner chase at odds of 1-3 last term.

Having said all that, it would be a major surprise if Sprinter Sacre was to join the list of one-season wonders. Henderson had always said we would see the best of this six-year-old once he was sent over fences, and so dominant was he in last season's two-mile novice division that Racing Post handicapper Steve Mason already rates him the best two-mile chaser in Britain or Ireland.

A perfect five from five last term, his wins came by an aggregate of 66 lengths and included a Grade 2 against open company and sublime victories in the Arkle and the Maghull at Aintree. All roads will lead towards the Queen Mother Champion Chase, with Sandown's Tingle Creek in December the stated starting point.

Long Run Nicky Henderson

Henderson has by common consent the most powerful stable in Britain this term yet the only Gold Cup winner he has ever trained is in danger of being overlooked. That could prove folly as no matter how disappointing he was last season, he has still reached a level that, pre Kauto Star and Denman, so few horses ever manage. Indeed, on the best of last season's performances, he still has upwards of 10lb in hand of any likely rival at Cheltenham in March.

He may have won a second King George had he not clouted the last at Kempton in December and, while his effort when third in the Gold Cup was laboured, that was clearly not his best form.

Yet to finish out of the first three, he is still surely by far the most likely to be crowned champion stayer for a second time and, still being only a seven-year-old, there is no real reason so suspect he's in decline.

Simonsig Nicky Henderson

Sorry to bore you with another Seven Barrows inmate, but how could this exciting grey be left out? Indeed, the real dilemma was whether to put him in with the hurdlers or the chasers as, while Henderson has five of the top 11 in the Champion Hurdle betting, he's actually the shortest. By all accounts, however, this six-year-old is set to embark on a career over fences. He could not have been more impressive in his novice hurdle campaign, suffering his only defeat at the hands of Fingal Bay at Sandown in December

For Non Stop: could be good enough for a crack at the Ryanair Chase at the festival in March

before stepping up on that form to saunter home in the Neptune at Cheltenham and then follow up by 15 lengths at Aintree.

Those runs were at around two and a half miles, but Simonsig is anything but short of pace and the plan is to keep him to the minimum trip in his first season, which is no doubt why one firm already has him as short as 5-2 for the Arkle. He wasn't the most fluent over hurdles, but this type of horse often gives more respect to fences and there can't be many as exciting as him this term.

For Non Stop Nick Williams

Williams's seven-year-old possibly didn't get the credit he deserved for a fine first season over fences. He would almost certainly have won first time up had he not fallen at Cheltenham in October and, after running fine races against Al Ferof and Cue Card (second both times), he got off the mark in a Grade 1 at Newbury before running a respectable third to Sir Des Champs in the Jewson. Those runs suggest he might just fall short of top class, but he has run only 15 times, has improved with every season and, importantly, seems perfectly well at home in strongly-run contests.

He would have finished second in the 2011 Coral Cup had he not fallen at the last and if he doesn't quite make Ryanair standard, he could well be the sort to run a big race in one of the festival handicaps.

Smad Place Alan King

This five-year-old could not quite hack it in one of the hottest Triumph Hurdles ever run two seasons ago, but he became much more of a man last term when upped in trip, defying a big weight to land a two-and-a-half-mile handicap hurdle at Ascot in January before going on to run third to Big Buck's in the World Hurdle. He would almost certainly have been second to that great stayer next time at Aintree but for unseating at the ninth, and this season he should be seen to better effect over fences.

By the same sire as Nacarat (Smadoun), he

shapes as though he'll get three miles better than his ageing fellow grey and is one to keep an eye on in staying novice chases.

On His Own Willie Mullins

You've got to have one stab at the Grand National in a list like this and On His Own is more than just a token effort. Willie Mullins's eight-year-old was short on experience when running in the race last year but took to it like a duck to water until falling at second Becher's when going as well as anything.

As long as that run hasn't left his mark, there is no reason for him not to be targeted at the race again this season and Ruby Walsh will have to be really impressed by something else to jump ship in April.

Few horses win big handicaps chases as easily as he won January's Thyestes and there is no reason why there isn't more to come.

HURDLERS
Darlan Nicky Henderson

Sometimes you can be wrong about a horse and my suspicion that Darlan was little more than a bridle merchant after seeing him win a soft novice hurdle by a nose at odds-on in December could not have proved more inaccurate.

I still wasn't convinced he had found much even though he was cantering when falling two out in the Betfair Hurdle at Newbury but his next two runs made me change my mind.

The first came in the Supreme Novices' at Cheltenham when, perhaps remembering his heavy fall, he never looked that happy from an early stage. He was also held up in a race with surprisingly little pace and was trapped out wide, but he still gave his all to finish second to Cinders And Ashes and I'd have no qualms about backing him to reverse the form. He again displayed battling qualities to win at Aintree and gives Henderson a very strong hand for the Champion Hurdle.

Grandouet Nicky Henderson

Another horse in danger of being forgotten,

if only because he missed last season's Champion Hurdle due to swelling in a hind leg, which turned into an internal infection. The road to recovery was apparently slow over the summer, but Henderson believes he has him back on the right track and, arguably, no hurdler had been more impressive in the first half of last season.

Grandouet was cantering over Celestial Halo when falling two out at Wincanton on his first run out of juvenile company, then went on to and effortless success in a four-year-olds' conditions event at Haydock before winning the International Hurdle at Cheltenham. Many, including this writer, had doubted Grandouet's ability see it out up the Cheltenham hill, but he ran out a smooth winner from Overturn, and although he was getting 4lb, that form suggests he'd have been right on the heels of Rock On Ruby in the Champion Hurdle in March. If he has fully recovered (and given it was an infection and not tendon or bone damage there must be a good chance he has) he can only be stronger as a six-year-old this year.

Moscow Mannon Brian Hamilton

It's too early to say how the 2012 Champion Bumper is going to work out, but with winner Champagne Fever following up at Punchestown and the sixth winning at Aintree the signs are good. Moscow Mannon went into March's contest boasting some of the best form credentials but the fastish ground may have been against him and he also raced keenly in the early stages. He still stayed on powerfully up the hill for fourth. He will certainly go over fences at some stage, but staying hurdles are likely to prove his forte this season and it will be no surprise if he returns to Cheltenham as a leading contender for the Albert Bartlett, if not the Neptune.

Royal Guardsman Colin Tizzard

An impressive winner on his bumper debut in April 2011, Royal Guardsman flopped badly on his return in October, but proved that running all wrong when bouncing back with a fluent seven-length success in a decent bumper at Ascot in February. Indeed, so impressive was he for Cue Card's trainer Colin Tizzard that he was sent off second favourite to emulate his stablemate by winning the Champion Bumper. He finished only tenth there but lost his place when hitting trouble at the top of the hill and was then asked to make his ground too quickly.

He showed plenty of courage to work his way into fourth halfway up the straight, though, and that attitude will serve him well over hurdles. He boasts enough natural ability to be a contender for one of the top novices at the season's end.

Well Sharp Jonjo O'Neill

A fairly useful performer when owned by Andrew Tinkler and trained by Michael Dods on the Flat, he showed his best form when third to Brown Panther on rain-softened ground at Royal Ascot in June 2011.

Picked up for 250,000gns by JP McManus and sent to O'Neill, he had two outings during the summer jumps season, winning at Wetherby in May and Market Rasen in August, both times without breaking sweat. Clearly useful, he apparently took time to get used to hurdling, so it's no bad thing he's got some experience under his belt already.

The handicapper will struggle to hit him too hard for what he has done so far and he could prove interesting for something like the Betfair Hurdle, which the same connections won with the novice Get Me Out Of Here in 2010 and may well have done again with Darlan last term had he not fallen two out. After that, he should be up for the Supreme.

Zarkandar Paul Nicholls

There comes a time when all great champions are dethroned and that time may be upon Big Buck's, who had to work harder than ever to land his fourth World Hurdle at Cheltenham in March. It's hard to win any major championship event once you pass the age of nine (neither Kauto Star nor Denman could manage in the Gold Cup) and only one horse aged older than nine has ever won the World Hurdle when aged in double figures.

Big Buck's hits ten in January and the main danger to his crown could reside in the same stable, provided trainer Paul Nicholls sees the light and switches his 2011 Triumph Hurdle winner away from the two-milers.

Yes, he did have the pace to win the Betfair Hurdle *(below)*, but he appeared particularly well handicapped given how well the Triumph form had worked out and he looked badly short of the required pace when only fifth in the big one in March. Upped to two and a half miles at Aintree next time, he fell before we could tell what he was capable of, but I have no doubt he would have stayed nor that he will stay even further.

Henderson's Grandouet has what it takes to lift Champion Hurdle crown

 Racing & Football Outlook's **Nicholas Watts** looks at likely big-race contenders

IF any reminder were needed, the recent losses of Spirit Son, Invictus and Batonnier prove what a hard game jumps racing is. Bearing that in mind, it may not seem a great place to start by talking up the chances of Nicky Henderson's **Grandouet** but, injury permitting, he could well win the Champion Hurdle.

He might have done so last season but for an injury that occurred before his warm-up race in the Kingwell Hurdle. He was running all over Celestial Halo at Wincanton only to fall two out, and then won two in a row, including the International Hurdle. That Cheltenham victory was an important one as it quashed any doubts about his ability to get up the hill and, as long as he is fully recovered from injury, there's no reason why he won't return even better.

Strictly speaking, Last Instalment should be just about favourite for the Gold Cup following his seven-length demolition of First Lieutenant in a Grade 1 at Leopardstown last Christmas.

That success saw a superb display of jumping and gives him the beating of Bobs Worth on RSA Chase form. The dilemma, however, is that he succumbed to injury after winning another Grade 1 in February and, although he is due to come back this season, soft ground seems a prerequisite for him.

More solid, therefore, is Henderson's **Bobs Worth**. His Cheltenham record is amazing. He's won all his four outings at the track, including two festival successes, and he devours the hill. Don't back him for the King George – he was well beaten in the Feltham and in the Reynoldstown going right-handed – but he has to be top of the list for Cheltenham.

The two-mile division looks likely to be cornered by Sprinter Sacre and Sanctuaire, and it looks like a simple choice between the two as to who wins the Champion Chase.

Sanctuaire is exciting and put in the best round of jumping at speed round Sandown for some considerable time. He was faultless. However, it will be harder for him this season to maintain those trailblazing tactics, and it may only serve to give Sprinter Sacre a nice lead and one he can settle off.

It is quite a rarity to witness such a one-sided Arkle as we did in 2012, but Sprinter Sacre was awesome, making Cue Card and Menorah (a Grade 1 winner on his next start) look decidedly average. If he enjoys another 100 per cent campaign he'll start to be revered like **Big Buck's**, who also looks sure to be a hefty points scorer again with little in the way of credible rivals.

In his three races preceding his fourth World Hurdle win, his starting prices were 1-8, 30-100 and 1-4, highlighting the fact that opposition to him is in thin on the ground. It is likely to be a similar story this season, and there's no reason why his powers should start to wane now he's rising ten.

Another from the Paul Nicholls camp to have on side is **Silviniaco Conti**, who

Arvika Ligeonniere looks a likely sort to make it to the festival

could well be the successor to Kauto Star in the King George. He was beaten by Grands Crus in the Feltham, but finished his season much better by slamming Champion Court at Aintree. He often comes to hand quite early in the season and, having proved his effectiveness at Kempton already, he must be accorded plenty of respect.

In the novice chase division, Willie Mullins' **Arvika Ligeonniere** makes plenty of appeal as an Arkle/Jewson/RSA prospect. It's hard to quite pin down his best trip yet, but he looked fantastic on his chase debut at Punchestown over two and a half miles in May which gives him options back at two miles or up to three.

In contrast, **Captain Conan** is likely to stay at around two miles over fences and this imposing type, who won the Tolworth so well

last season, could give Henderson another Arkle winner next March.

The Grand National is a long way off, but already Rebecca Curtis's **Teaforthree** should be top of the list. His jumping as a novice was extremely fluent, and it's hard to remember him making any mistakes when winning the four-miler at Cheltenham in March. He is a thorough stayer, and is likely to go for the Welsh National first off. With winning form already at Chepstow, it's not impossible he could win both.

Two other chasers capable of better again this season are Victor Dartnall's **Roudoudou Ville**, a slightly unlucky loser at Cheltenham last December, and David Pipe's **Notus De La Tour**. Both could have good handicaps in them and look set for profitable campaigns.

Obvious, but Big Buck's and Sprinter Sacre are a must for any lists

Ten to Follow comment writer **Dylan Hill** with ten who can score heavily

Big Buck's Paul Nicholls

It's conceivable that the first cracks in Big Buck's might come this season as he will be ten by the time of the World Hurdle, but there are so few serious contenders in the staying hurdle division that anyone not including the four-time champion in their list would potentially be putting themselves out of the running, especially as he takes more races to get fit these days and might possibly be seen more often.

Cue Card Colin Tizzard

Forget about Sprinter Sacre – as many trainers will wish they could this season – and Cue Card would have won this year's Arkle Trophy by 22 lengths from subsequent Grade 1 winner Menorah. It was a superb effort to keep Sprinter Sacre in his sights for so long as Cue Card did, realising the immense potential he had shown when running away with the 2010 Champion Bumper. His connections might not need to worry about Sprinter Sacre this season, though, as a step up in trip should suit Cue Card well.

Darlan Nicky Henderson

This one might well develop into a leading contender for the Champion Hurdle as he looks ideally equipped for the trials, which are likely to revert to their usual slowly-run formula this season with Overturn probably going chasing. Darlan is full of speed, as he showed with a win at Aintree last time, yet he stayed on well into second in the Supreme Novices' Hurdle after losing his place.

Grands Crus David Pipe

Pipe's super jumper would have close in last year's King George given the way he won the Feltham earlier in the afternoon, and he should have a leading chance this time with another year on his back. Things didn't go right at Cheltenham, where he possibly didn't stay the trip in the RSA, although he scoped badly afterwards anyway. If connections opt for shorter trips after Kempton, he has the speed to win the Ryanair, notching more crucial points.

Shutthefrontdoor Jonjo O'Neill

The winner of a Listed bumper at Newbury last season, this JP McManus-owned five-year-old is a terrific novice hurdle prospect. He's a particularly interesting dark horse for this competition as McManus has a habit of running his best novices in the Betfair Hurdle and that is where Shutthefrontdoor could end up if things go according to plan. Get Me Out Of Here won the race as a novice for McManus in 2010 and his Darlan was going well when falling last season.

Sir Des Champs Willie Mullins

Many punters' idea of next year's Gold Cup

winner, Sir Des Champs *(right)* has reserved his best for Cheltenham in each of the last two seasons, winning the Martin Pipe Hurdle in 2011 before he was hugely impressive in the Jewson Chase last season. He's also the type to rack up wins before March given he is yet to be beaten. His first run over three miles at Punchestown taught us little, but he has always looked likely to appreciate the trip.

Sizing Europe Henry De Bromhead

There may not be many willing to put a horse rising 11 in their team but, while it's pointless expecting Sizing Europe to regain his Champion Chase crown should the likes of Sprinter Sacre and Sanctuaire stay fit, he may easily pick up plenty of soft points beforehand. Last season's two-mile novice chasers in Ireland were a modest bunch and there are plenty of decent prizes around that trip in which Sizing Europe could make hay.

Sprinter Sacre Nicky Henderson

Even more so than Big Buck's, this one surely cannot be left out of any lists. Sprinter Sacre was magnificent last season and it can hardly be argued that he wasn't taking on the best, even in novice company, because Cue Card has long looked top-class and Al Ferof, third in the Victor Chandler, was pushed into mistakes by his relentless galloping. A banker for the Champion Chase.

Time For Rupert Paul Webber

A major letdown last season, Time For Rupert proved his form for most of the campaign had been all wrong when he bounced back with a fine fifth in the Cheltenham Gold Cup. The handicapper hasn't reacted harshly as his chase mark remains well below his hurdling peak, and it's hard not to see him scaling at least those heights over fences given his superb jumping. He will be a leading candidate for the Hennessy Gold Cup at Newbury, for which 25 bonus points are on offer.

Zarkandar Paul Nicholls

The 2011 Triumph Hurdle worked out very well last season and there may be more to come from the winner Zarkandar. Little went right last season as he missed most of the campaign, was under the weather before his fifth in the Champion Hurdle and then fell in the Aintree Hurdle. He still won the Betfair Hurdle when not fully fit and should be much better over two and a half miles, and he would also be capable of doing better in the Champion Hurdle off a strong gallop.

Competition might be a little different but keeping it simple is still the key

Editor **David Dew** with some ideas on how to tackle the new-look Ten to Follow

THE first thing to do before entering this year's jumps Ten to Follow is take a good look at pages 103-104 in this guide. There have been several changes to the way the competition is run and these pages contain everything you need to know on that count.

Finding the winners of the bonus races is going to be as crucial as ever. Just like last year there are 15 of these contests, and each has an additional 25 points up for grabs. Take note that the International Hurdle at Cheltenham and Aintree Hurdle have been introduced this time, replacing the former Racing Post Chase and Betfair Hurdle.

You will be well served by finding horses with the potential to run in several bonus races. Grandouet, for example, is likely to go for the International and the Champion Hurdle, while an improving staying chaser could go for the Hennessy and, if successful, go on to the King George and Gold Cup. There is no bonus window in the competition this time, so getting your choices right is more important than ever.

Who's your star?

Last year's top entry amassed 703 points, 135 coming courtesy of Big Buck's. With a campaign identical to last year's already mapped out for Paul Nicholls' ace staying hurdler, he will surely be at the top of most lists. However, be wary of adding him as your 'Star Horse'.

This new innovation rewards double points according to starting price and while the recording-breaking Big Buck's has topped the 100-point barrier for the last few years, he has been sent off at odds-on for his last 14 starts and looks sure to do so again each time this season. The same is likely apply to the likes of Sprinter Sacre and Hurricane Fly. While they will earn supporters bundles of points, it is best to look elsewhere for your star.

In doing so, you will need one from the list of 400 who is likely to run regularly. The likes of Darlan might fit the bill. He ran six times last season, winning four times. He is likely to take in the various Champion Hurdle trials en route to the big race at Cheltenham in March but, given there should be decent competition in such contests, is unlikely to start particularly short in the betting.

Another worthy of consideration is Champion Court. He won just two of his seven races as a novice chaser last year and earned only 16 Ten to Follow points. However, he ran regularly and was placed on every other completed start, filling minor places behind the likes of Sir Des Champs, Silviniaco Conto, Join Together and Grands Crus. Having had only five runs before the start of last term, he is clearly open to further progess and looks sure to give his supporters plenty of fun.

Trained away from the glare of the media spotlight by Martin Keighley, his odds are likely to be more generous than if he was with one of the big guns, which will help

when it comes to those bonus points awarded for starting price.

Is it worth waiting a little longer?

The Paddy Power Gold Cup offers the first chance for bonus points as usual, but it is not obligatory to get your entry in before the Open meeting at Cheltenham. Instead, the doors stay open for an extra couple of weeks with a November 30 deadline.

So, should you get your entry in nice and early, or wait a little longer? It is interesting to note that last year's Paddy Power winner did not feature on the lists of any of the top ten winning entries. Rewind 12 months and the same comment applies to Little Josh. Go back a year earlier and it was the same with Tranquil Sea. So, although you might think that passing up the chance to nab an early 25 points is not a good strategy, recent history suggests it would do no harm. And, if you wait an extra couple of weeks to place your entry, you are likely to be more clued up on running plans for horses you are considering – and you will also have a good idea of how the Hennessy Gold Cup is shaping up, and that's the second bonus race.

It's cheaper to enter this time

It took 676 points to scrape into the top ten in last year's Ten to Follow. That's just 27 points less than the number needed to finish top, which goes to show that every point counts. As well as the option to enter later this time, the entry fee has been halved to just £5. This is good news for players with a long list of horses they are keen on – permutations will become more affordable, enhancing your chance to bag that guaranteed quarter of a million pounds.

Some names to consider

Sir Des Champs heads the antepost Gold Cup market and looks a must. He notched a Racing Post rating of 168 in winning the Jewson at last year's festival. To put that performance into perspective, the average RPR of the previous five winners of that contest was a little more than 154, meaning Willie Mullins's crack performer is a stone in front of a typical Jewson winner. That figure of 168 would have seen Sir Des Champs finish fourth in last year's Gold Cup and it would have been enough for fifth in race in 2011. Given that, as a six-year-old, he is open to any amount of improvement, he can be expected to be right up there in this year's Gold Cup. And he will be incredibly difficult to beat throughout the winter in valuable graded contests in Ireland.

Hurricane Fly is a far from original suggestion, but time and time again this competition has rewarded plenty of points for being unoriginal. The former Champion Hurdle winner earned 150 points in 2010-11 and, despite being eclipsed at Cheltenham and generally a little below his best last season, he notched 50 points and featured on the every list in the top ten. He is the antepost favourite to regain his crown in March and should bag plenty of points along the way.

Former festival winners can often be a little overlooked. In the same way as Hurricane Fly is thought by some to be on the wane, 2011 Gold Cup winner **Long Run** is probably not an obvious candidate for inclusion. He earned only 27 points from his sole win last season but, with a similar campaign in the pipeline this time, it is surely likely he will better that tally.

Nicky Henderson's seven-year-old twice finished behind Kauto Star and had it not been for the dual Gold Cup winner, Long Run would have bagged Haydock's Betfair Chase and the King George and plenty more points. Kauto's future is still in the balance but, even if he continues, you would have to fancy Long Run to have his beating this season.

Finding a horse with the potential to run up a sequence is a way to earn valuable points. **Simonsig** did just that last season when winning four of his five starts over hurdles, including the Neptune Novices' Hurdle at the festival. He could do the same when switched to fences this term, but with the potential to earn bonus points in the Arkle, for which he is currently antepost favourite.

Arkle runner-up Cue Card looks well treated with big handicap looking formality

Steve Mason picks out ten who have impressed on Racing Post ratings

Close House David Pipe

Decent bumper performer who picked up an ordinary Towcester novice hurdle before finishing a commendable fourth in the Neptune at the festival. Raised just over a stone to mark of 133 for that effort, but it could have been worse and it will be surprising if he is not placed to advantage by his shrewd connections.

Cotton Mill John Ferguson

He beat the 150-rated Ambion Wood when landing a Grade 2 at Warwick in January and was in the process of giving the brilliant Simonsig a race when veering left and unseating Denis O'Regan at the second-last in the Neptune. Subsequently failed to see out the three-mile trip in Grade 1 company at Aintree, but should be able to pick up a decent handicap off his current mark of 145.

Cue Card Colin Tizzard

Top notch in bumpers and as a novice hurdler but has developed into an even better chaser. No match for the imperious Sprinter Sacre in the Arkle, but finished miles clear of the rest and an official mark of 157 would appear to seriously underestimate the worth of that run. Can surely pick up a very decent handicap if connections opt to go that way.

Darlan Nicky Henderson

Smart bumper horse who enjoyed an excellent first season over hurdles, culminating in an impressive success in a Grade 2 at Aintree. That was arguably the best two-mile performance from a novice hurdler last season and there should be plenty more to come.

Dildar Paul Nicholls

Failed to translate his smart French Flat form to hurdles last season but reportedly took a long time to get over a gelding operation and much better can be expected in his second season. His form of the level marks him down as a potential 150+ hurdler.

Grands Crus David Pipe

Failed to give his running behind Bobs Worth in the RSA Chase at the festival but had previously posted one of the best staying performances from a novice in recent seasons when slamming subsequent Aintree winner Silviniaco Conti and Bobs Worth in the Grade 1 Feltham at Kempton. He should develop into a contender for top honours this season but a mark of 157 gives him the option of running in a big handicap.

Ile De Re Donald McCain

Decent on the Flat in 2011 for Ian Williams but stepped up a level to land the Chester Cup-Northumberland Plate double on his only starts for his current yard to date. Won

Cotton Mill: should be capable of winning a good handicap hurdle

a couple of ordinary novice hurdles for his previous stable, but his current official mark of 123 is around two stone shy of what could reasonably be expected of a Flat horse with a mark of 105.

Oscar Nominee Nicky Henderson

Dual novice hurdle winner who showed signs of inexperience en route to a strong-finishing third in the ultra-competitive Martin Pipe handicap hurdle at the Cheltenham Festival. Not one of his stable's stars but handicapped to do some damage off a mark of 139.

Ted Spread Paul Nicholls

Another whose hurdle form to date falls

some way below what could be expected given the 100+ figures he posted on the level. His trainer reports he has benefited from a recent breathing operation and, given his current hurdle mark of 134, he should be well capable of picking up at least one valuable two-mile handicap.

Time For Rupert Paul Webber

Connections opted not to run him off 159 in last year's Hennessy, but no harm done as he can run off 157 this term. It could be significant that his only win last season came at Newbury where he handed a comfortable beating to subsequent Gold Cup second The Giant Bolster.

Stick with Zarkandar – he has potential to reach the top over hurdles

Dave Edwards (Topspeed) with the pick of those who left a lasting impression from a speed perspective

Allthekingshorses Philip Hobbs

A successful pointer, he beat a decent pair on his hurdling debut at Exeter in November but then had breathing problems when a disappointing favourite at Newcastle a fortnight later.

Below his best on ground too soft and trip too far at Huntingdon, he showed his true colours at Doncaster in February when scoring in a time almost four seconds faster than par. Seemingly treading water with a circuit to go, he came into his own on the second lap and stayed on dourly to land the spoils. Good ground brings out the best in him and he could exploit a reasonable handicap mark.

Baby Shine Lucy Wadham

Although her small team is based in Newmarket, Wadham has won some decent prizes over jumps and this mare could boost her tally further. A dual bumper winner, she landed a mares' only hurdle in good style on her debut over jumps at Leicester in January and did not enjoy the run of the race and also sustained a nick when inched out at Southwell the following month. Pitched in at the deep end at Aintree in April, she was a fine third behind Simonsig but failed to fire at Punchestown in April and is capable of much better.

Oscar Nominee Nicky Henderson

This five-year-old cost £100,000 at Doncaster Bloodstock Sales in May 2010 and his first two starts in bumpers a year later were ordinary at best. He was a different proposition in a maiden hurdle at Southwell in January, however, coasting home for a wide-margin success after jumping fluently. Last of three behind Cinders And Ashes at Haydock he jumped indifferently on the testing ground but under the circumstances was far from disgraced. He showed his true colours at the Cheltenham Festival in March, running a blinder to finish third, beaten a couple of necks behind Attaglance in the Martin Pipe handicap hurdle. He will have learned plenty from that and is likely to prove effective at around three miles on decent ground.

Roudoudou Ville Victor Dartnall

He won a couple of bumpers in France but made an inauspicious start to his career in Britain. However, he has made giant strides since his breathing was sorted out. A measure of his progress can be gauged from the fact that between March and December last year his official rating leapt from 114 to 145 – and he can still prove competitive from that mark.

At his best on good or quick ground, he scored with authority at Wincanton and Chepstow then found one too good at Perth, He resumed winning ways at Sandown and at Cheltenham in December he chased home Quantitativeeasing and Medermit. Sidelined since, he can make up for lost time when underfoot conditions are favourable.

Tap Night Lucinda Russell

Successful on dirt in the States he was purchased at Keenland sales by current connections in November 2010 and has not looked back since sent hurdling. Placed in his first three outings, all at Perth, he then enjoyed a deserved wide-margin Carlisle success and then landed the odds at Newcastle. He competed his hat-trick in the Grade 2 Premier Hurdle at Kelso and signed off at Aintree in April when not disgraced behind Lovcen in the Sefton Novices Hurdle. He appeared to find the extended three miles beyond him at Liverpool but seems effective on both good and soft ground and a decent prize at around two and a half miles could come his way.

Teaforthree Rebecca Curtis

Winner of the four-miler at the Cheltenham Festival last season, this doughty stayer has the Welsh National as his first target this time.

Some long-distance chases turn into one-lap sprints which surely defeats the object, but he has proved a searching gallop throughout holds no fears and has already won over three miles twice at Chepstow. Effective on decent ground, he has also won on both soft and heavy which is another positive with the Welsh marathon in mind. In the main he is a sound jumper and appears best on a left-handed track.

Ubaltique Donald McCain

Emphatically won his only start in France on heavy ground at Pau in January and on his first start in Britain was given a tough assignment in a hot Kelso contest the following month. Never a factor he beat only one home but enjoyed a confidence-booster at Perth in April, clearly relishing the soft ground. Asked to quicken he strode purposefully clear with the promise of better to come as he matures. An official mark of 130 may prove a conservative guide to his talents.

Vendor Alan King

This four-year-old had mixed fortunes in half a dozen outings in France when let down by his jumping but was clearly expected when landing the odds at Newbury at the turn of the year on his first run for new connections.

Favourite for the Fred Winter at Cheltenham, he found the searching pace and big field a different ball game but nonetheless finished a creditable third and more importantly will have learned valuable lessons. He should have much more to offer.

Wyse Hill Teabags Jim Goldie

He cost only 500guineas as a yearling and has had problems but is an above-average performer on his day.

Successful in an Ayr bumper in March 2010, he subsequently landed novice hurdles at Musselburgh and Kelso and on his handicap bow finished a close third behind Russian War in a hot Aintree contest. On his reappearance last November he divided Any Given Day and Attaglance and was then made favourite for a similar race at Aintree. However, he was tailed off and pulled up and later scoped dirty. He unseated on his chasing debut at the end of September but still has a very workable mark over hurdles.

Zarkandar Paul Nicholls

He won the Triumph Hurdle in 2011, scoring in a faster time than more seasoned handicappers in the County Hurdle. Despite an interrupted preparation he followed up in the Anniversary Hurdle at Aintree.

Various setbacks delayed his reappearance until the Betfair Hurdle in February last season, but despite the layoff he proved too strong for the opposition. His success was all the more remarkable as he coughed a couple of days later, although that hindered his build-up to the Champion Hurdle in which he finished fifth. He took a crashing fall at Aintree before the race began in earnest but, granted an injury-free campaign, he could still be a major player this season.

RACING POST RATINGS TOP 600 CHASERS

KEY: *Horse name, Best RPR figure, Finishing position when earning figure, (details of race where figure was earned)*

A New Story (IRE) 145 2 (3m 7f, Chel, GF, Mar 13)
Abbeybraney (IRE) 137 3 (2m 6f 110y, Kels, Gd, Mar 3)
According To Pete 153 1 (3m, Hayd, Hvy, Jan 21)
Ace High 138 1 (3m, Chep, Gd, Oct 22)
Ackertac (IRE) 140 5 (2m 4f 110y, Chel, Gd, Mar 13)
Action Master 136 2 (2m 4f, List, Sft, Sep 12)
Ad Idem 156 2 (3m, Nava, Hvy, Nov 27)
Adams Island (IRE) 137 4 (3m, Gowr, Hvy, Jan 26)
Aerial (FR) 159 2 (2m 5f, Chel, GS, Apr 18)
Aigle D'or 143 6 (3m, Leop, Yld, Dec 27)
Aiteen Thirtythree (IRE) 154 2 (2m 4f 110y, Kemp, Gd, Oct 31)
Al Ferof (FR) 163 3 (2m 1f, Asco, GS, Jan 21)
Albertas Run (IRE) 169 2 (2m 5f, Chel, Gd, Mar 15)
Alderley Rover (IRE) 139 1 (2m, Live, Gd, May 6)
Alfa Beat (IRE) 162 1 (3m, List, Hvy, Sep 14)
Alfie Sherrin 142 3 (3m 5f, Fair, GS, Apr 9)
Alfie Spinner (IRE) 145 3 (3m, Asco, GS, Feb 18)
Allee Garde (FR) 148 3 (3m, Leop, Gd, Dec 28)
Alpha Ridge (IRE) 139 2 (2m 6f, Galw, Hvy, Oct 23)
Always Right (IRE) 152 1 (2m 6f 110y, Kels, Sft, Dec 4)
Always Waining (IRE) 149 1 (2m 5f 110y, Live, Gd, Apr 13)
Amaury De Lusignan (IRE) 140 1 (2m 1f, Plum, GS, Feb 27)
Another Jewel (IRE) 135 1 (4m 1f, Punc, Fm, May 5)
Anquetta (IRE) 140 4 (2m 110y, Chel, Gd, Mar 16)
Any Currency (IRE) 136 3 (3m 5f 110y, Sand, GS, Dec 3)
Apt Approach (IRE) 153 1 (2m 4f, Thur, Sft, Jan 19)
Arabella Boy (IRE) 138 2 (3m, Naas, Sft, Mar 11)
Araldur (FR) 149 2 (2m 4f 110y, Weth, Gd, Oct 28)
Aran Concerto (IRE) 146 6 (2m 4f, Punc, Gd, May 4)
Archie Boy (IRE) 146 2 (2m 4f, Dowr, GF, May 2)
Armaramak (IRE) 140 1 (2m 4f 120y, Kill, Sft, Aug 25)
As De Fer (FR) 151 1 (3m, Ffos, Sft, Nov 28)
Ashkazar (FR) 148 1 (3m 1f 110y, Chel, Sft, Apr 19)
Askanna (IRE) 136 1 (2m 4f, Fair, Sft, Apr 10)
Astracad (FR) 150 2 (2m, Live, GS, Apr 12)
Aura About You (IRE) 138 5 (2m 4f, Fair, Gd, Apr 25)
Auroras Encore (IRE) 156 2 (4m 110y, Ayr, Gd, Apr 21)
Australia Day (IRE) 149 1 (2m, Kemp, Gd, Oct 16)
Back Of The Pack (IRE) 141 1 (2m 4f, Cork, Gd, May 27)
Bahrain Storm (IRE) 138 1 (2m 1f, Kill, Gd, Jul 11)
Baile Anrai (IRE) 143 1 (3m 1f, Mark, Sft, Apr 15)
Ballabriggs (IRE) 158 6 (4m 4f, Live, Gd, Apr 14)
Ballycarney (IRE) 137 4 (3m, Asco, Gd, Nov 18)
Ballyfitz 137 2 (3m 3f 110y, Chel, GS, Nov 12)
Ballyfoy (IRE) 134 1 (3m 4f 110y, Chel, GS, Apr 18)
Ballyholland (IRE) 144 1 (2m 6f, Galw, Gd, Aug 27)
Balthazar King (IRE) 145 1 (3m 7f, Chel, GF, Mar 13)
Balzaccio (FR) 138 1 (2m 4f 110y, Hunt, Gd, Oct 30)
Banjaxed Girl 135 2 (2m 4f, Fair, Sft, Apr 10)
Barbers Shop 135 1 (3m 110y, Fake, GS, Feb 17)
Barizan (IRE) 140 1 (2m 110y, Newt, GF, Aug 1)
Battle Group 147 2 (3m 1f, Live, Gd, Apr 14)
Be There In Five (IRE) 135 7 (3m 1f 110y, Chel, Gd, Mar 15)
Beamazed 137 1 (3m 2f, Carl, Hvy, Feb 20)
Bear's Affair (IRE) 134 2 (2m 4f 110y, Weth, GS, Dec 3)
Beau Michael 134 4 (2m 6f, Wexf, Sft, Oct 30)
Beautiful Sound (IRE) 141 2 (3m 1f, Punc, Yld, May 7)
Becauseicouldntsee (IRE) 148 2 (3m 1f 110y, Chel, Gd, Mar 15)
Bellvano (GER) 153 (2m 1f, Fair, Sft, Apr 10)
Benbane Head (USA) 144 1 (2m 5f, Utto, GF, Sep 18)
Benny Be Good 161 2 (3m, Donc, GS, Dec 10)
Berties Dream (IRE) 140 1 (3m, Thur, Hvy, Jan 7)

Beshabar (IRE) 151 5 (3m 2f 110y, Newb, Gd, Nov 26)
Best Lover (FR) 137 1 (2m, Weth, GS, Nov 23)
Bideford Legend (IRE) 153 2 (3m, Lime, Sft, Oct 9)
Big Zeb (IRE) 175 1 (2m, Punc, Yld, May 3)
Billie Magern 144 5 (3m 110y, Chel, Gd, Mar 13)
Bishopsfurze (IRE) 143 5 (2m 4f, Fair, Gd, Apr 8)
Black Apalachi (IRE) 147 2 (3m 1f, Fair, Sft, Feb 25)
Black Jack Blues (IRE) 144 1 (2m, Ffos, GF, Jun 16)
Blackstairmountain (IRE) 148 2 (2m, Punc, Hvy, Apr 27)
Blazing Bailey 142 8 (3m 2f 110y, Newb, Gd, Nov 26)
Blazing Beacon (IRE) 140 1 (2m 4f, Nava, Gd, Sep 24)
Blazing Tempo (IRE) 159 1 (2m 1f, Fair, Sft, Jan 22)
Blenheim Brook (IRE) 137 1 (3m 1f, Ayr, Sft, Feb 6)
Bless The Wings (IRE) 142 1 (2m 5f, Chel, GS, Jan 28)
Bob Lingo (IRE) 146 1 (2m 1f, Fair, Sft, Apr 10)
Bobs Worth (IRE) 166 1 (3m 110y, Chel, Gd, Mar 14)
Bog Warrior (IRE) 162 1 (2m, Naas, Hvy, Feb 11)
Bold Addition (FR) 138 2 (2m 6f, Hayd, Gd, Nov 18)
Bold Sir Brian (IRE) 152 1 (2m 4f, Muss, GS, Feb 11)
Bostons Angel (IRE) 153 3 (3m 110y, Sand, GS, Dec 2)
Bradley 141 2 (3m 1f 110y, Chel, Sft, Apr 19)
Brooklyn Brownie (IRE) 134 5 (3m, Pert, Gd, Apr 27)
Bruslini (FR) 135 1 (3m 1f 110y, Here, Gd, Mar 27)
Buck Mulligan 138 2 (2m 4f, Chel, GF, Oct 15)
Burton Port (IRE) 171 2 (3m, Newb, GS, Feb 17)
Byerley Bear (IRE) 134 2 (2m 2f, Gowr, Sft, Oct 1)
Cadogan (FR) 141 1 (3m, Nava, Sft, Mar 18)
Caduceus (IRE) 138 1 (2m 6f 100y, Fair, Sft, Apr 9)
Calgary Bay (IRE) 161 1 (3m, Donc, GS, Jan 28)
Call The Police (IRE) 153 3 (3m 110y, Chel, Gd, Mar 14)
Campbonnais (FR) 134 1 (3m 100y, Rosc, Yld, Jun 12)
Cannington Brook (IRE) 150 1 (2m 4f, Hayd, Hvy, Feb 18)
Cape Tribulation 141 5 (2m 5f, Chel, GS, Jan 1)
Cappa Bleu (IRE) 152 3 (3m, Asco, GS, Feb 18)
Captain Cee Bee (IRE) 166 3 (2m, Punc, Yld, May 3)
Captain Chris (IRE) 166 1 (2m, Punc, Gd, May 5)
Carloswayback (IRE) 135 1 (2m 4f, Punc, Hvy, Jan 14)
Carpincho (FR) 138 1 (2m 6f, Font, Sft, Jan 12)
Carrickboy (IRE) 146 1 (2m 3f, Here, Sft, Mar 5)
Carrigmartin (IRE) 144 1 (2m, Punc, Gd, May 18)
Carruthers 153 1 (3m 2f 110y, Newb, Gd, Nov 26)
Cedre Bleu (FR) 137 1 (2m 1f, Newb, GS, Jan 18)
Chamirey (FR) 135 1 (3m 6f, Sedg, Sft, Apr 3)
Champion Court (IRE) 161 2 (2m 4f, Chel, Gd, Mar 15)
Chance Du Roy (FR) 155 2 (3m 2f 110y, Live, Gd, Apr 13)
Chapoturgeon (FR) 147 2 (3m 2f 110y, Chel, Gd, Mar 16)
Charingworth (IRE) 136 (2m 4f, Ayr, Sft, Feb 14)
Chariot Charger (IRE) 140 1 (3m, Utto, GS, Nov 12)
Charminster (IRE) 139 4 (2m 5f, Chel, GS, Jan 28)
Chester Lad 138 1 (2m 110y, Newc, Sft, Jan 26)
Chicago Grey (IRE) 154 (3m 110y, Chel, GF, Oct 15)
China Rock (IRE) 149 5 (3m, Leop, GS, Feb 12)
Clash Duff (IRE) 141 1 (3m 6f 110y, Devo, Gd, Mar 6)
Colbert Station (IRE) 137 3 (2m 5f, Leop, Gd, Mar 4)
Columbus Secret (IRE) 141 1 (3m, Pert, Gd, Apr 28)
Come To The Party (IRE) 134 1 (2m 5f 50y, Tram, Sft, Dec 31)
Comehomequietly (IRE) 134 1 (3m, Ffos, Gd, Oct 9)
Connak (IRE) 136 1 (3m, Devo, GS, Nov 9)
Consigliere (FR) 152 1 (2m 5f, Winc, Sft, Jan 7)
Cool Mission (IRE) 134 2 (3m 6f, Catt, GS, Jan 12)
Coolcashin (IRE) 152 2 (2m 4f, Gowr, Sft, Oct 1)
Cooldine (IRE) 141 2 (2m 6f, Thur, Hvy, Nov 3)
Cootehill (IRE) 138 2 (2m 4f, Ludl, Gd, Apr 5)
Corkage (IRE) 138 1 (2m 4f 110y, Sout, GS, Jan 18)
Cornas (NZ) 158 3 (2m, Sand, GS, Dec 3)

Coscorrig (IRE) 142 2 (2m, Punc, Gd, May 5)
Court Red Handed (IRE) 135 2 (3m, Hunt, Sft, Jan 27)
Court Victory (IRE) 135 3 (3m 110y, Warw, GS, Jan 14)
Crack Away Jack 148 5 (2m, Chel, Gd, Nov 11)
Crash (IRE) 136 2 (3m, Naas, Hvy, Jan 21)
Crescent Island (IRE) 148 2 (2m 4f, Newb, Gd, Nov 26)
Cristal Bonus (FR) 157 2 (2m 4f, Live, GS, Apr 12)
Cross Appeal (IRE) 138 1 (3m, Leop, Yld, Dec 27)
Cruising Katie (IRE) 140 2 (2m 4f, Fair, Gd, Apr 25)
Cucumber Run (IRE) 139 1 (2m 4f 110y, Weth, Sft, Jan 23)
Cue Card 167 2 (2m, Chel, Gd, Mar 13)
Current Event (FR) 141 1 (2m 1f, Plum, Sft, Apr 9)
Daffern Seal (IRE) 139 6 (4m, Chel, Gd, Mar 14)
Dan Breen (IRE) 152 2 (2m 4f, Newb, Gd, Mar 3)
Dancing Tornado (IRE) 151 5 (3m, List, Hvy, Sep 14)
Darceys Dancer (IRE) 136 5 (2m 1f, Asco, Gd, Nov 19)
Darna 144 1 (2m 5f 110y, Asco, Gd, Apr 1)
Dave's Dream (IRE) 138 7 (2m, Sand, GS, Jan 7)
Days Hotel (IRE) 147 1 (2m, Punc, Sft, Nov 20)
De Boitron (FR) 142 2 (2m 4f, Ayr, Gd, Apr 20)
De Valira (IRE) 143 1 (2m 4f, Cork, Yld, Oct 16)
Deep Purple 159 1 (3m 5f 110y, Sand, GS, Dec 3)
Diamond Harry 165 4 (3m, Hayd, GS, Nov 19)
Dinarius 137 1 (2m 3f 110y, Chep, GS, Apr 14)
Divers (FR) 150 3 (2m 4f 110y, Chel, GS, Nov 12)
Divine Intavention (IRE) 134 1 (3m, Ludl, Gd, Mar 1)
Doctor David 145 2 (2m, Hayd, Gd, Nov 18)
Doeslessthanme (IRE) 152 1 (2m, Ayr, Gd, Apr 21)
Domtaline (FR) 135 1 (2m 4f, Ludl, Gd, Apr 5)
Donnas Palm (IRE) 145 1 (2m 1f, Nava, Sft, Feb 19)
Door Boy (IRE) 138 2 (2m 4f, Hayd, GS, Mar 21)
Dover's Hill 146 1 (3m 110y, Sand, Gd, Mar 10)
Down In Neworleans (IRE) 145 1 (2m 1f, Galw, Gd, Aug 27)
Dr Whizz (IRE) 137 1 (2m, Punc, Gd, May 5)
Duke Of Lucca (IRE) 146 1 (3m 1f 110y, Chel, GS, Apr 18)
Dundrum (IRE) 135 3 (2m 3f, List, Gd, Jun 6)
Dunowen Point (IRE) 135 2 (2m 4f 110y, Bang, Gd, Sep 29)
Eagle's Pass (IRE) 136 1 (2m 1f, Galw, Gd, Aug 28)
Earth Dream (IRE) 137 1 (3m 110y, Fake, GS, Apr 9)
Echo Bob (IRE) 135 2 (2m 1f, Kill, Gd, Jul 11)
Edgardo Sol (FR) 160 1 (2m, Live, GS, Apr 12)
Edge Of Town (IRE) 135 1 (2m 7f, Hexh, Hvy, Dec 7)
Educated Evans (IRE) 140 2 (2m 110y, Chep, Sft, Feb 25)
Eleazar (GER) 134 2 (3m 110y, Fake, GS, Feb 17)
Emmaslegend 138 1 (3m 1f, Folk, Gd, Dec 13)
Eradicate (IRE) 149 2 (2m, Sand, GS, Nov 5)
Escort'men (FR) 138 2 (2m 4f, Font, Gd, Oct 19)
Estates Recovery (IRE) 140 1 (3m 2f 110y, Newt, GF, Jul 4)
Exmoor Ranger (IRE) 149 1 (3m, Asco, Gd, Oct 29)
Faasel (IRE) 145 1 (3m, Donc, Gd, Feb 22)
Fabalu (IRE) 134 2 (3m, Asco, Gd, Apr 1)
Fair Along (GER) 149 (3m 6f, Punc, Yld, May 6)
Falcon Island 141 2 (2m, Sand, Gd, Feb 24)
False Economy (IRE) 146 3 (2m 4f, Fair, Gd, Apr 8)
Far Away So Close (IRE) 136 (2m 3f 120y, Lime, Sft, Oct 9)
Far More Serious (IRE) 137 3 (3m 110y, Bang, GS, Nov 9)
Fiendish Flame (IRE) 153 1 (2m 4f, Muss, Gd, Jan 1)
Fine Parchment (IRE) 140 2 (2m 4f, Live, Gd, Oct 22)
Finger Onthe Pulse (IRE) 150 1 (2m 4f, List, Hvy, Sep 16)
Finian's Rainbow (IRE) 175 1 (2m 4f, Live, Gd, Apr 13)
First Lieutenant (IRE) 164 2 (3m 110y, Chel, Gd, Mar 14)
Fistral Beach (IRE) 151 3 (2m 5f 110y, Live, Gd, Apr 13)
Fists Of Fury (IRE) 142 2 (2m 5f, Leop, Yld, Jan 28)
Fix The Rib (IRE) 136 3 (2m 4f 110y, Kemp, Gd, Jan 14)
Flaming Gorge (IRE) 135 2 (2m 5f, Winc, Sft, Feb 18)
Flemenstar (IRE) 164 1 (2m 4f, Fair, Gd, Apr 8)
Foildubh (IRE) 149 2 (2m 1f, Fair, Sft, Apr 10)
Follow The Plan (IRE) 168 1 (3m 1f, Live, GS, Apr 12)

For A Finish 134 3 (2m 4f, List, Hvy, Sep 11)
For Bill (IRE) 145 2 (2m 4f, List, Hvy, Sep 16)
For Non Stop (IRE) 154 3 (2m 4f, Chel, Gd, Mar 15)
Forpadydeplasterer (IRE) 160 3 (2m 1f, Leop, Yld, Dec 27)
Fortification (USA) 140 1 (3m 5f, Warw, Gd, Feb 24)
Four Commanders (IRE) 149 3 (4m, Chel, Gd, Mar 14)
Frascati Park (IRE) 146 1 (3m 110y, Warw, GS, Jan 14)
Fredo (IRE) 136 2 (3m 5f, Warw, GS, Jan 14)
Free World (FR) 144 1 (2m 1f, Ball, Yld, Aug 21)
French Opera 162 2 (2m 1f, Newb, GS, Feb 17)
Frisco Depot 149 (3m 1f, Punc, Hvy, Apr 24)
Frontier Spirit (IRE) 137 2 (2m 3f 110y, Ffos, Hvy, Dec 26)
Fruity O'Rooney 151 2 (3m 110y, Chel, Gd, Mar 13)
Gala Dancer (IRE) 140 1 (3m, Clon, Gd, Sep 25)
Galaxy Rock (IRE) 153 1 (3m 3f 110y, Chel, GS, Nov 12)
Gansey (IRE) 140 3 (2m 4f, Hayd, Gd, Apr 7)
Garde Champetre (FR) 146 2 (3m 7f, Chel, Fm, Nov 11)
Garleton (IRE) 145 1 (3m, Newc, Gd, Mar 29)
Gates Of Rome (IRE) 137 1 (2m 3f, Naas, Hvy, Feb 11)
Gauvain (GER) 166 1 (2m 4f 110y, Hunt, GS, Dec 8)
Ghizao (GER) 155 6 (2m 5f, Chel, Gd, Dec 10)
Gift Of Dgab (IRE) 145 2 (2m 1f, Leop, Hvy, Jan 29)
Giles Cross (IRE) 149 1 (3m 4f, Hayd, Hvy, Feb 18)
Giorgio Quercus (FR) 156 1 (2m 5f, Hayd, Hvy, Jan 21)
Glenwood Knight (IRE) 134 5 (3m 2f, Carl, Sft, Nov 27)
Going Wrong 138 1 (2m 110y, Sedg, Sft, Jan 5)
Golan Way 151 1 (3m 110y, Sand, GS, Dec 2)
Golden Chieftain (IRE) 143 1 (3m, Utto, GS, Nov 24)
Golden Silver (FR) 153 1 (2m 100y, Cork, Hvy, Dec 11)
Gone To Lunch (IRE) 134 3 (3m 3f 110y, Winc, GF, Apr 5)
Got Attitude (IRE) 134 4 (2m 2f, Gowr, Sft, Sep 30)
Gracchus (USA) 136 2 (2m, Warw, GS, Jan 14)
Grands Crus (FR) 168 1 (3m, Kemp, GS, Dec 26)
Great Endeavour (IRE) 164 1 (2m 4f 110y, Chel, GS, Nov 12)
Groody Hill (IRE) 141 3 (3m, Punc, Hvy, Apr 24)
Gullible Gordon (IRE) 142 4 (3m 3f 110y, Winc, Gd, Oct 23)
Gwanako (FR) 142 1 (2m 4f 110y, Sand, Gd, Mar 9)
Habbie Simpson 137 2 (3m 3f, Donc, GS, Dec 29)
Halley (FR) 139 2 (2m 5f, Hayd, Hvy, Jan 21)
Hampshire Express (IRE) 135 2 (2m 6f, Tram, GF, Aug 14)
Harry The Viking 149 2 (4m, Chel, Gd, Mar 14)
Havingotascoobydo (IRE) 141 2 (2m, Chel, Gd, Nov 11)
Head Of The Posse (IRE) 147 3 (3m 1f, Punc, Yld, May 3)
Hector's Choice (FR) 154 1 (2m 5f, Chel, GS, Apr 18)
Hello Bud (IRE) 134 5 (3m 5f, Warw, GS, Jan 14)
Helpston 147 2 (3m 1f, Weth, Sft, Dec 26)
Hey Big Spender (IRE) 164 1 (3m 5f, Warw, GS, Jan 14)
Hidden Cyclone (IRE) 140 2 (3m 5f, Leop, Yld, Jan 28)
Hidden Keel 145 4 (2m 4f 110y, Hunt, GS, Dec 8)
Hold Fast (IRE) 149 1 (2m, Sand, GS, Jan 7)
Hold On Julio (IRE) 150 1 (3m 110y, Sand, GS, Jan 7)
Hollo Ladies (IRE) 135 2 (2m 4f, Sedg, GF, Apr 26)
Holmwood Legend 140 5 (2m 5f, Winc, Sft, Feb 18)
Hoo La Baloo (FR) 137 3 (2m 5f 110y, Newt, GS, Aug 21)
How's Business 135 2 (2m 6f 110y, Newb, Gd, Mar 24)
Humbie (IRE) 134 1 (3m 110y, Carl, Gd, Oct 7)
Hunt Ball (IRE) 165 3 (3m 1f, Live, GS, Apr 12)
I Have Dreamed (IRE) 140 1 (2m 4f 110y, Kemp, Gd, Apr 17)
I Hear A Symphony (IRE) 138 1 (2m, Dowr, Sft, Nov 4)
I'm So Lucky 150 3 (2m 1f, Newb, GS, Feb 17)
I'msingingtheblues (IRE) 159 2 (2m 5f 110y, Asco, GS, Jan 21)
Idarah (USA) 140 1 (2m 1f, Fair, Gd, Apr 26)
Ikorodu Road 143 1 (3m 2f 110y, Newb, Gd, Mar 24)
In Compliance (IRE) 136 5 (4m 4f, Live, Gd, Apr 14)
Inside Dealer (IRE) 134 (3m, Kemp, Gd, Dec 27)
Intac (IRE) 135 1 (3m 3f, Here, Gd, Aug 31)
Invictus (IRE) 155 1 (3m, Asco, GS, Feb 18)
Invisible Man (FR) 137 2 (2m 5f 110y, Stra, Gd, May 28)

Jack Absolute (IRE) 135 1 (2m 2f, Gowr, Sft, Feb 18)
Jack The Bus (IRE) 139 5 (3m, Gowr, Hvy, Jan 26)
Jadanli (IRE) 134 3 (3m, Gowr, Hvy, Jan 26)
Jim Will Fix It (IRE) 142 2 (2m 1f, Nava, Hvy, Dec 10)
Join Together (IRE) 156 1 (3m 1f 110y, Chel, Gd, Dec 10)
Joncol (IRE) 162 2 (2m 4f, Punc, Hvy, Dec 11)
Junior 161 2 (3m 2f, Donc, Gd, Mar 3)
Kakagh (IRE) 134 3 (2m 4f, Clon, Sft, Nov 10)
Kalahari King (FR) 139 5 (2m 1f, Kels, Gd, Nov 5)
Karasenir (IRE) 136 1 (2m 5f, Utto, GF, Oct 2)
Kauto Star (FR) 182 1 (3m, Kemp, GS, Dec 26)
Kauto Stone (FR) 166 2 (2m, Sand, GS, Dec 3)
Keki Buku (FR) 134 4 (2m, Chel, Gd, Nov 11)
Kid Cassidy (IRE) 150 1 (2m 110y, Donc, GS, Jan 28)
Kilcrea Kim (IRE) 135 (2m 5f, Winc, GS, Nov 5)
Killyglen (IRE) 147 1 (3m 2f, Dowr, Sft, Mar 17)
King Edmund 146 1 (2m 1f, Asco, Sft, Dec 17)
King Fontaine (IRE) 135 3 (4m 110y, Ayr, Gd, Apr 21)
King High (IRE) 142 1 (2m, Cork, Sft, Oct 16)
King's Legacy (IRE) 139 1 (2m 4f 110y, Worc, Gd, Jun 5)
Kings Grey (IRE) 135 3 (2m 110y, Donc, GS, Jan 28)
Knight Legend (IRE) 134 1 (2m 4f, Mark, Gd, Aug 20)
Knighton Combe 135 1 (3m, Asco, Gd, Apr 1)
Knockara Beau (IRE) 156 6 (3m 2f 110y, Chel, Gd, Mar 16)
Knockfierna (IRE) 143 1 (2m 6f, Lime, Hvy, Mar 18)
Kudu Country (IRE) 141 1 (2m, Sout, Gd, Feb 29)
Kumbeshwar 151 3 (2m 110y, Chel, Gd, Mar 16)
Lackamon 141 2 (3m 1f, Ayr, Gd, Apr 21)
Lambro (IRE) 146 3 (2m 5f, Leop, GS, Feb 12)
Lancetto (FR) 144 1 (2m 110y, Newt, Gd, Sep 20)
Last Instalment (IRE) 154 1 (3m, Leop, Gd, Dec 28)
Lastoftheleaders (IRE) 146 1 (2m 1f, Hvy, Dec 3)
Le Beau Bai (FR) 145 1 (3m 5f 110y, Chep, Hvy, Dec 27)
Leanne (IRE) 139 1 (2m 5f, Leop, Gd, Mar 4)
Lenabane (IRE) 146 3 (3m, List, Hvy, Sep 14)
Lidar (FR) 146 1 (2m, Hayd, Gd, Apr 7)
Lie Forrit (IRE) 140 2 (2m 6f 110y, Kels, Sft, Dec 29)
Lightening Rod 141 2 (2m 110y, Donc, Gd, Dec 9)
Lion Na Bearnai (IRE) 153 1 (3m 5f, Fair, GS, Apr 9)
Little Josh (IRE) 140 6 (3m 1f 110y, Chel, GS, Jan 28)
Lively Baron (IRE) 136 3 (3m, Donc, GS, Dec 10)
Logans Run (IRE) 140 1 (2m 4f 110y, Hexh, Gd, May 24)
Long Run (FR) 181 1 (3m, Newb, GS, Feb 17)
Loose Preformer (IRE) 142 1 (2m 7f 110y, Leic, GF, Dec 28)
Loosen My Load (IRE) 152 2 (2m 4f, Fair, Gd, Apr 24)
Lord Jay Jay (IRE) 134 1 (2m 1f 110y, Stra, GF, Aug 18)
Lucky William (IRE) 149 1 (2m, Punc, Hvy, Apr 27)
Lucky Wish 142 2 (2m 4f, Punc, Gd, May 4)
Mad Max (IRE) 135 3 (2m 5f, Hayd, Hvy, Jan 21)
Mad Moose (IRE) 140 1 (2m 5f, Chel, Sft, Apr 19)
Made In Taipan (IRE) 142 6 (2m 1f, Fair, Gd, Apr 26)
Magnanimity (IRE) 148 4 (3m 1f, Fair, Sft, Feb 5)
Major Malarkey (IRE) 139 2 (4m 1f 110y, Utto, GS, Mar 17)
Mamlook (IRE) 137 6 (2m 5f 110y, Newt, GS, Aug 21)
Manger Hanagment (IRE) 141 1 (2m 5f 110y, Here, Gd, Aug 31)
Maringo Bay (IRE) 134 3 (2m 4f, Plum, Sft, Dec 5)
Marodima (FR) 142 1 (2m 4f, Font, Sft, Jan 12)
Massini's Maguire (IRE) 158 1 (3m, Asco, GS, Feb 18)
Master Minded (FR) 175 1 (2m 3f, Asco, Gd, Nov 19)
Master Of The Hall (IRE) 158 1 (2m 6f 110y, Kels, Gd, Mar 3)
Master Overseer (IRE) 138 1 (4m 1f 110y, Utto, GS, Mar 17)
Matuhi 142 3 (2m 5f, Chel, GS, Jan 1)
Max Bygraves 138 1 (2m 4f 110y, Hunt, GF, Oct 2)
Meanus Dandy (IRE) 142 2 (3m 1f 110y, Winc, GS, Nov 5)
Medermit (FR) 170 3 (2m 5f, Chel, Gd, Mar 15)
Medical Card (IRE) 136 1 (3m, Naas, Hvy, Jan 21)
Menorah (IRE) 164 1 (2m 4f, Live, GS, Apr 12)
Merigo (FR) 149 1 (4m 110y, Ayr, Gd, Apr 21)

Mic's Delight (IRE) 134 2 (3m, Devo, Sft, Jan 1)
Micheal Flips (IRE) 151 1 (2m 3f, Taun, GS, Jan 19)
Michel Le Bon (FR) 137 (3m 2f 110y, Newb, Gd, Nov 26)
Midnight Appeal 139 1 (3m 110y, Sand, Gd, Feb 17)
Midnight Chase 168 1 (3m 1f 110y, Chel, GS, Jan 28)
Midnight Haze 140 1 (3m 1f 110y, Ludl, GS, Dec 8)
Mikael D'Haguenet (FR) 144 4 (2m 4f, Fair, Gd, Apr 24)
Minella Class (IRE) 143 2 (2m 1f 110y, Bang, GS, Nov 26)
Mister Hyde (IRE) 134 2 (2m 4f, Utto, Sft, Dec 16)
Mister Marker (IRE) 142 1 (3m 1f, Ayr, Sft, Feb 6)
Mohayer (IRE) 140 1 (3m 1f 110y, Ffos, Hvy, Dec 21)
Mon Mome (FR) 148 2 (3m 2f 110y, Chel, GS, Jan 1)
Mon Parrain (FR) 160 3 (3m 1f 110y, Chel, Gd, Dec 9)
Monastrell 134 1 (2m, Naas, Hvy, Oct 29)
Monkerty Tunkerty 134 1 (3m 110y, Warw, GS, Jan 26)
Montan (FR) 145 4 (2m 5f, Leop, Yld, Jan 28)
Moon Indigo 138 3 (2m 6f 110y, Kels, Sft, Dec 29)
Mossey Joe (IRE) 158 1 (3m, Cork, Gd, May 27)
Mossley (IRE) 143 2 (3m 1f 110y, Chel, Gd, Dec 10)
Mostly Bob (IRE) 137 1 (3m 2f 110y, Chel, GS, Jan 1)
Mount Oscar (IRE) 146 3 (2m 5f, Winc, Sft, Feb 18)
Mr Cracker (IRE) 149 3 (2m 4f, Fair, Gd, Apr 24)
Mr Moonshine (IRE) 154 1 (2m 6f, Hayd, Gd, Nov 18)
Mr Moss (IRE) 135 1 (2m 7f, Stra, Gd, Apr 22)
Muirhead (IRE) 157 1 (3m, Lime, Sft, Oct 9)
Mush Mir (IRE) 138 1 (2m 6f, Font, Gd, Apr 3)
My Moment (IRE) 134 1 (3m 110y, Fake, Gd, Oct 21)
Nacarat (FR) 168 1 (3m, Kemp, Gd, Feb 25)
Nadiya De La Vega (FR) 144 1 (2m, Hayd, Gd, Nov 18)
Nakajima Nate (IRE) 135 2 (2m, Rosc, Sft, Sep 26)
Nearest The Pin (IRE) 138 2 (2m 3f, Leop, Yld, Dec 29)
Neptune Collonges (FR) 169 1 (4m 4f, Live, Gd, Apr 14)
Neptune Equester 140 1 (3m 4f, Hayd, GS, Nov 19)
Nez Rouge (FR) 135 1 (2m 6f 110y, Mark, GS, Jul 16)
Niceonefrankie 138 1 (2m 1f, Newb, Gd, Mar 2)
Niche Market (IRE) 152 2 (3m 2f 110y, Newb, Gd, Mar 3)
Nicto De Beauchene (FR) 140 2 (3m 110y, Bang, GS, Nov 9)
Nine Stories (IRE) 135 1 (2m, Pert, Gd, Apr 27)
Ninetieth Minute (IRE) 139 1 (3m 6f 100y, Fair, Sft, Feb 25)
No Loose Change (IRE) 137 1 (3m, Newb, Gd, Mar 23)
Noble Alan (GER) 146 (2m 6f 110y, Mark, Gd, Sep 24)
Noble Prince (GER) 165 2 (2m 1f, Fair, Sft, Jan 22)
Noble Request (FR) 139 (2m 1f 110y, Stra, Gd, Jul 10)
Noland 153 5 (3m, Leop, Gd, Dec 28)
Nomecheki (FR) 136 3 (2m 110y, Taun, GS, Jan 31)
Norther Bay (FR) 135 2 (2m 1f, Galw, Gd, Jul 31)
Notus De La Tour (FR) 152 3 (2m 3f 110y, Devo, GS, Dec 2)
Oceana Gold 140 1 (2m, Winc, Gd, Apr 2)
Odonimee (IRE) 135 1 (2m 1f, Worf, Sft, Mar 17)
Ogee 137 2 (3m 110y, Fake, GS, Feb 17)
Oh Crick (FR) 151 1 (2m 110y, Chep, Sft, Feb 25)
Oiseau De Nuit (FR) 156 4 (2m 110y, Chel, Gd, Dec 10)
On Borrowed Wings (IRE) 141 3 (3m 2f 110y, Newb, Gd, Mar 24)
On His Own (IRE) 153 1 (3m, Gowr, Hvy, Jan 26)
On The Fringe (IRE) 140 2 (3m 1f, Fair, Sft, Apr 10)
Ordinary Man (IRE) 135 3 (3m, Lime, Gd, Apr 1)
Organisedconfusion (IRE) 150 1 (3m 5f, Fair, Gd, Apr 25)
Osana (FR) 151 2 (2m 1f, Fair, Gd, Apr 26)
Oscar Delta (IRE) 136 3 (3m 2f 110y, Chel, Gd, Mar 16)
Oscar Gogo (IRE) 137 1 (3m 2f 110y, Ffos, Hvy, Dec 26)
Osirixamix (IRE) 149 (2m 100y, Cork, Hvy, Dec 11)
Ostland (GER) 147 1 (3m, Hunt, GF, Oct 11)
Our Mick 153 3 (3m 110y, Chel, Gd, Mar 13)
Our Victoria (IRE) 140 4 (4m, Chel, Gd, Mar 14)
Out Now (IRE) 144 2 (3m 5f, Fair, GS, Apr 9)
Outlaw Pete (IRE) 140 1 (3m, Punc, Fm, May 3)
Ouzbeck (FR) 143 2 (3m 2f 110y, Newb, Gd, Mar 24)
Owen Glendower (IRE) 144 (2m 4f, Hayd, Gd, Apr 7)

Pacha Du Polder (FR) 147 1 (2m 4f, Ayr, Gd, Apr 21)
Paddy Pub (IRE) 134 4 (3m 5f, Fair, GS, Apr 9)
Paddy The Oscar (IRE) 134 1 (3m, Thur, Hvy, Mar 1)
Paint The Clouds 139 1 (2m 7f, Worc, Gd, May 8)
Painter Man (FR) 136 1 (2m 5f, Winc, Sft, Feb 18)
Pasco (SWI) 140 4 (3m, Newb, Sft, Dec 14)
Passato (GER) 143 2 (2m 1f, Newb, Gd, Nov 25)
Pearlysteps 147 (3m, Hayd, Hvy, Dec 17)
Peddlers Cross (IRE) 159 1 (2m 1f 110y, Bang, GS, Nov 26)
Penny Max (IRE) 141 1 (3m, Devo, Sft, Jan 1)
Pentiffic (NZ) 138 (3m 2f, Donc, Gd, Mar 3)
Pepite Rose (FR) 150 1 (2m 6f 110y, Newb, Gd, Mar 24)
Perfect Smile (IRE) 134 3 (2m 1f, Nava, Gd, Mar 31)
Pickamus (FR) 144 1 (2m 7f, Stra, Gd, Mar 31)
Pilgrims Lane (IRE) 135 1 (2m 5f 110y, Fake, GF, May 22)
Piraya (FR) 139 3 (2m 3f, Asco, Gd, Nov 18)
Planet Of Sound 161 2 (3m 2f 110y, Newb, Gd, Nov 26)
Pomme Tiepy (FR) 138 3 (3m 6f, Punc, Yld, May 6)
Ponmeoath (IRE) 137 8 (3m, List, Hvy, Sep 14)
Popcorn (FR) 139 1 (2m 2f, Thur, Hvy, Nov 17)
Poquelin (FR) 172 2 (2m 5f, Chel, GS, Jan 28)
Portrait King (IRE) 148 1 (4m 1f, Newc, Gd, Feb 25)
Postmaster 140 1 (3m 110y, Bang, Gd, Aug 19)
Premier Sagas (FR) 142 2 (2m 4f 110y, Bang, Gd, Mar 24)
Pret A Thou (FR) 143 2 (2m, Weth, Sft, Dec 27)
Prince De Beauchene (FR) 155 1 (3m 1f, Fair, Sft, Feb 25)
Prince Of Pirates (IRE) 143 1 (2m 7f 110y, Leic, Gd, Feb 16)
Problema Tic (FR) 148 1 (3m 1f, Ayr, Gd, Apr 21)
Promising Anshan (IRE) 140 (3m, Kemp, Gd, Dec 27)
Psycho (IRE) 156 4 (2m 1f, Fair, Sft, Jan 22)
Pure Faith (IRE) 150 2 (2m 4f, Live, Gd, Oct 22)
Qhilimar (FR) 140 3 (3m 110y, Sand, GS, Jan 7)
Qianshan Leader (IRE) 138 1 (3m, Donc, GS, Dec 10)
Quantitativeeasing (IRE) 157 1 (2m 5f, Chel, Gd, Dec 10)
Quarryvale (IRE) 141 1 (2m 6f, Thur, Hvy, Feb 9)
Quel Esprit (FR) 160 1 (3m, Leop, GS, Feb 12)
Quentin Collonges (FR) 140 2 (3m, Kemp, Gd, Mar 17)
Quicuyo (GER) 145 1 (2m 110y, Donc, GS, Jan 28)
Quincy Des Pictons (FR) 136 1 (2m 3f 110y, Chep, Hvy, Dec 27)
Quiscover Fontaine (FR) 150 4 (3m 5f, Fair, Gd, Apr 25)
Quito De La Roque (FR) 167 1 (3m, Dowr, Sft, Nov 5)
Quito Du Tresor (FR) 138 1 (2m 3f, Asco, Gd, Nov 18)
Qulinton (FR) 150 1 (2m 6f 110y, Mark, GS, Jul 16)
Railway Dillon (IRE) 145 1 (3m, Pert, Sft, Apr 26)
Raptor (FR) 137 1 (2m 4f, Punc, Sft, Nov 19)
Rare Bob (IRE) 147 3 (3m, Naas, Sft, Mar 11)
Rathlin 154 1 (2m 4f, Naas, Sft, Feb 26)
Razor Royale (IRE) 149 2 (3m, Asco, Gd, Oct 29)
Realt Dubh (IRE) 169 2 (2m, Punc, Hvy, Apr 24)
Realt Mor (IRE) 141 (2m 4f 110y, Weth, GS, Dec 3)
Rebel Du Maquis (FR) 154 1 (2m 5f 110y, Stra, Gd, May 28)
Relax (FR) 137 2 (2m 4f 110y, Bang, Gd, Apr 21)
Renard (FR) 148 1 (2m 110y, Taun, GS, Jan 31)
Requin (FR) 137 (3m, Asco, Sft, Dec 17)
Restezen D'Armor (FR) 135 1 (2m 4f 110y, Worc, Gd, Oct 19)
Restless Harry 146 2 (3m, Chep, Hvy, Dec 3)
Reve De Sivola (FR) 145 4 (3m 1f, Punc, Yld, May 3)
Riguez Dancer 136 1 (2m 3f, Asco, Gd, Apr 1)
Rileyev (FR) 138 3 (2m 4f, Newb, Gd, Mar 3)
Rival D'Estruval (FR) 135 2 (2m 4f, Ayr, Gd, Apr 21)
Rivaliste (FR) 139 3 (2m 1f 110y, Stra, GF, May 15)
Riverside Theatre 172 1 (2m 5f 110y, Asco, GS, Feb 18)
Roalco De Farges (FR) 143 1 (2m 6f 110y, Newb, Gd, Nov 26)
Roberto Goldback (IRE) 159 (3m 1f, Punc, Gd, May 4)
Rockyaboya (IRE) 135 1 (2m 1f, Lime, Sft, Nov 14)
Roi Du Mee (FR) 156 1 (2m 7f, Punc, Sft, Oct 13)
Roudoudou Ville (FR) 154 3 (2m 5f, Chel, Gd, Dec 10)
Rougham 140 2 (2m 1f 110y, Devo, Hvy, Dec 15)

Rubi Light (FR) 169 1 (2m 4f, Gowr, Sft, Feb 18)
Sa Suffit (FR) 150 3 (2m 6f 110y, Kels, Sft, Dec 4)
Saddlers Storm (IRE) 138 2 (3m 2f, Dowr, Sft, Mar 17)
Safari Journey (USA) 146 3 (2m 2f, Font, Gd, Sep 30)
Saint Are (FR) 148 1 (3m 1f, Live, Gd, Apr 14)
Salesin 141 1 (2m 3f, Wexf, Gd, Jul 1)
Salsify (IRE) 148 1 (3m 2f 110y, Chel, Gd, Mar 16)
Saludos (IRE) 148 3 (2m, Punc, Gd, May 5)
Salut Flo (FR) 151 1 (2m 5f, Chel, Gd, Mar 15)
Sanctuaire (FR) 159 1 (2m, Sand, Gd, Mar 10)
Santa's Son (IRE) 140 2 (3m 1f, Live, Gd, Oct 22)
Sarando 142 1 (3m 110y, Carl, GS, Nov 7)
Sarteano (FR) 141 4 (3m 1f, Punc, Yld, May 7)
Schelm (GER) 144 2 (2m 1f, Ball, Yld, Aug 21)
Schindler's Gold (IRE) 138 1 (2m 4f 110y, Worc, Gd, Jun 15)
Scotsirish (IRE) 162 1 (2m 4f, Punc, Gd, May 4)
Seabass (IRE) 158 3 (4m 4f, Live, Gd, Apr 14)
Sebadee (IRE) 135 1 (2m 6f, Tram, GF, Aug 14)
Shakalakaboomboom (IRE) 153 2 (3m, Donc, GS, Jan 28)
Shakervilz (FR) 140 7 (3m 5f, Fair, Gd, Apr 25)
Shinrock Paddy (IRE) 136 2 (2m 3f, Naas, Hvy, Feb 11)
Shop Dj (IRE) 136 2 (2m 1f, Cork, Hvy, Dec 11)
Shot From The Hip (GER) 137 2 (2m 4f, Naas, Sft, Feb 26)
Silk Drum (IRE) 141 2 (2m 110y, Donc, Gd, Mar 3)
Silviniaco Conti (FR) 166 1 (3m 1f, Live, Gd, Apr 13)
Sir Des Champs (FR) 168 1 (2m 4f, Chel, Gd, Mar 15)
Sir Ian (IRE) 147 2 (2m 4f 110y, Worc, Gd, May 8)
Sizing Australia (IRE) 142 4 (3m 7f, Chel, GF, Mar 13)
Sizing Europe (IRE) 174 2 (2m, Chel, Gd, Mar 14)
Skip Two (IRE) 135 5 (2m 6f, Lime, Gd, Jul 3)
Skippers Brig (IRE) 148 2 (2m 6f 110y, Kels, Sft, Dec 4)
Slieveardagh (IRE) 147 2 (2m, Naas, Hvy, Feb 11)
Slippers Percy (IRE) 136 3 (3m 1f, Fair, Gd, Apr 25)
Smoking Aces (IRE) 136 1 (3m 5f, Fair, Hvy, Dec 4)
Solix (FR) 156 2 (2m 5f, Chel, GS, Jan 1)
Soll 140 2 (3m, Punc, Hvy, Dec 31)
Some Target (IRE) 142 4 (3m, Nava, Hvy, Nov 27)
Somersby (IRE) 169 1 (2m 1f, Asco, GS, Jan 21)
Son Amix (FR) 142 1 (3m, Punc, Hvy, Dec 31)
Song Sung Blue (IRE) 136 1 (2m, Sand, Gd, Feb 24)
Sonny Mullen (IRE) 141 1 (3m, Pert, Gd, Jun 5)
Sonofvic (IRE) 154 2 (3m, Newb, Gd, Nov 24)
Sprinter Sacre (FR) 176 1 (2m, Chel, Gd, Mar 13)
St Devote (FR) 136 1 (2m, Rosc, Sft, Sep 26)
Stagecoach Pearl 156 2 (2m 110y, Donc, GS, Jan 28)
Start Me Up (IRE) 138 3 (3m, Nava, Sft, Feb 19)
Stewarts House (IRE) 146 1 (2m 5f 110y, Live, Hvy, Dec 3)
Strongbows Legend 137 3 (3m 5f, Warw, GS, Jan 14)
Sunnyhillboy (IRE) 154 2 (4m 4f, Live, Gd, Apr 14)
Sweeps Hill (NZ) 142 1 (2m 1f, Galw, Hvy, Oct 22)
Swincombe Rock 142 2 (3m, Chep, Gd, Oct 8)
Swing Bill (FR) 149 1 (3m 110y, Chel, Gd, Nov 11)
Sybarite (FR) 136 2 (2m 5f, Chel, Gd, Dec 9)
Synchronised (IRE) 175 1 (3m 2f 110y, Chel, Gd, Mar 16)
Take The Breeze (FR) 142 4 (2m 3f 110y, Chep, Hvy, Dec 27)
Takeroc (FR) 152 1 (2m, Live, Gd, Oct 23)
Taking Stock (IRE) 139 3 (3m 1f, Punc, Yld, May 7)
Tamarinbleu (FR) 153 1 (2m 5f, Hayd, Hvy, Dec 30)
Tanks For That (IRE) 159 2 (2m 110y, Chel, Gd, Mar 16)
Tara Royal 141 1 (2m, Muss, GS, Feb 11)
Tartak (FR) 152 5 (2m 5f, Chel, Gd, Mar 15)
Tataniano (FR) 167 1 (2m 110y, Chep, Gd, Oct 22)
Tatenen (FR) 150 1 (2m 5f 110y, Asco, GS, Jan 21)
Tchico Polos (FR) 159 3 (2m 1f, Kels, Gd, Nov 5)
Teaforthree (IRE) 153 1 (3m, Chep, Sft, Feb 25)
Templer (FR) 139 3 (3m 2f 110y, Newt, Gd, Sep 20)
Tharawaat (IRE) 148 1 (2m 6f, Galw, Hvy, Oct 23)
That'll Do 137 5 (2m 5f 110y, Newt, GS, Aug 21)

That'lldoboy (FR) 138 (2m 4f 110y, Kemp, GS, Dec 26)
That's Rhythm (FR) 140 3 (3m 1f, Hexh, GF, Apr 30)
The Cockney Mackem (IRE) 136 2 (2m 5f, Chel, Gd, Mar 15)
The Fonze (IRE) 142 3 (2m 5f 50y, Tram, Hvy, Jan 1)
The Giant Bolster 172 2 (3m 2f 110y, Chel, Gd, Mar 16)
The Hollinwell 142 2 (3m, Newc, GS, Nov 26)
The Jigsaw Man (IRE) 142 2 (2m 1f 110y, Stra, Gd, Jul 10)
The Knoxs (IRE) 146 1 (2m 4f, Ayr, Gd, Apr 20)
The Last Derby (FR) 141 2 (3m, Cork, Gd, May 27)
The Midnight Club (IRE) 140 4 (2m 5f 50y, Tram, Hvy, Jan 1)
The Minack (IRE) 161 1 (3m, Asco, Sft, Dec 17)
The Nightingale (FR) 160 3 (3m, Dowr, Sft, Nov 5)
The Package 145 4 (3m 110y, Chel, Gd, Mar 13)
The Panama Kid (IRE) 145 3 (2m 6f 110y, Kels, Sft, Dec 4)
The Sawyer (BEL) 137 5 (3m, Asco, Sft, Dec 17)
The Sneezer (IRE) 135 1 (2m 2f, Gowr, Sft, Mar 10)
Tidal Bay (IRE) 162 2 (3m 1f 110y, Chel, GS, Jan 28)
Tiger O'Toole (IRE) 136 3 (2m 4f, Hayd, GS, Mar 21)
Time For Rupert (IRE) 164 5 (3m 2f 110y, Chel, Gd, Mar 16)
Time For Spring (IRE) 135 2 (2m 7f 110y, Taun, GS, Jan 9)
Tinakellylad (IRE) 135 2 (2m 4f, Cork, Hvy, Jan 2)
Torphichen 150 2 (2m 4f, Hayd, Gd, Apr 7)
Toubab (FR) 150 2 (2m, Live, Gd, Apr 14)
Traffic Article (IRE) 142 1 (3m 110y, Chel, GF, Oct 14)
Trafford Lad 138 2 (2m 4f, Clon, Hvy, Feb 2)
Tranquil Sea (IRE) 163 1 (2m 4f, Clon, Sft, Nov 10)
Treacle (IRE) 151 3 (3m, Leop, GS, Feb 12)
Triangular (USA) 145 1 (2m 6f 110y, Newb, Gd, Mar 23)
Triolo D'Alene (FR) 137 1 (2m 3f, Asco, GS, Jan 21)
Trooper Clarence 137 1 (2m 1f 110y, Devo, Fm, Oct 18)
Truckers Delight (IRE) 144 1 (2m 1f, Galw, Gd, Jul 31)
Tullamore Dew (IRE) 147 2 (3m, Asco, GS, Feb 18)
Ultimate 144 1 (2m 110y, Donc, Gd, Mar 3)

Un Hinged (IRE) 136 1 (2m 1f, Fair, Gd, Apr 25)
Uncle Junior (IRE) 146 8 (3m 7f, Chel, GF, Mar 13)
Uncle Tom Cobley (IRE) 139 2 (2m 1f, Fair, Gd, Apr 25)
Universal Soldier (IRE) 146 1 (3m 110y, Towc, GS, Jan 22)
Up The Beat 147 2 (3m 4f, Punc, Hvy, Feb 5)
Vic Venturi (IRE) 143 2 (3m 1f, Punc, Gd, May 4)
Victors Serenade (IRE) 150 1 (3m, Ffos, Sft, Mar 17)
Viking Blond (FR) 145 4 (3m 110y, Chel, GS, Nov 12)
Vino Griego (FR) 143 2 (3m, Asco, Sft, Dec 17)
Wake Board (FR) 135 1 (2m, Worc, Gd, Sep 23)
Walkon (FR) 156 1 (2m 3f 110y, Devo, GS, Dec 2)
Wayward Prince 146 4 (3m 1f, Weth, Sft, Dec 26)
Weird Al (IRE) 170 3 (3m, Hayd, GS, Nov 19)
West End Rocker (IRE) 155 1 (3m 2f, Live, Hvy, Dec 3)
West With The Wind 155 1 (2m, Ffos, GF, Aug 25)
Western Charmer (IRE) 152 2 (3m 5f, Fair, Gd, Apr 25)
Westmeath 135 1 (2m 2f, Gowr, Sft, Oct 1)
What A Friend 167 3 (3m, Newb, GS, Feb 17)
White Star Line (IRE) 142 2 (2m 4f 110y, Chel, Gd, Mar 13)
Whodoyouthink (IRE) 142 2 (2m 2f, Thur, Hvy, Jan 7)
Wise Old Owl (IRE) 154 2 (2m 6f, Galw, Gd, Jul 27)
Wishfull Thinking 168 2 (2m 4f, Live, Gd, Apr 13)
Wogan 135 4 (2m 7f, Worc, GF, May 18)
Woody Waller 135 2 (2m, Muss, GS, Feb 11)
Woolcombe Folly (IRE) 163 3 (2m 110y, Chep, Gd, Oct 22)
Wymott (IRE) 143 6 (3m 2f 110y, Newb, Gd, Nov 26)
Yes Tom (IRE) 140 1 (2m 4f, Ayr, GS, Jan 17)
Your Busy (IRE) 136 2 (3m, Lime, Gd, Apr 1)
Zaarito (IRE) 151 2 (2m, Naas, Sft, Feb 26)
Zarrafakt (IRE) 155 1 (3m 1f 110y, Winc, GS, Jan 21)
Zaynar (FR) 156 1 (2m 3f, Asco, Sft, Dec 16)
Zitenka (IRE) 136 2 (2m 4f 110y, Pert, Sft, Apr 26)

RACING POST RATINGS TOP 600 HURDLERS

KEY: Horse name, Best RPR figure, Finishing position when earning figure, (details of race where figure was earned)

A Media Luz (FR) 135 3 (2m, Asco, Gd, Oct 29)
Abergavenny 136 3 (2m 110y, Chel, GS, Nov 13)
Abou Ben (IRE) 141 1 (2m, Fair, Hvy, Feb 4)
Across The Bay (IRE) 142 3 (3m 110y, Live, GS, Apr 12)
Act Of Kalanisi (IRE) 138 3 (2m 5f, Kemp, Gd, Jan 14)
Action Master 132 1 (2m, Punc, Gd, May 25)
Ad Idem 138 2 (2m 4f, Naas, Hvy, Oct 29)
Adams Island (IRE) 139 3 (3m, Leop, Sft, Dec 29)
Afsoun (FR) 135 1 (2m, Newc, GS, Dec 17)
Agent Archie (USA) 133 (2m 110y, Chel, Gd, Mar 13)
Aikideau (FR) 132 3 (2m 4f, Sand, GS, Mar 10)
Aikman (IRE) 139 1 (2m 6f 110y, Kels, GS, Oct 2)
Ainama (IRE) 148 4 (2m 4f, Punc, Gd, May 7)
Alaivan (IRE) 151 5 (2m, Fair, Gd, Apr 26)
Aland Islands (IRE) 140 1 (2m 3f 110y, Donc, Gd, Mar 3)
Alarazi (IRE) 138 3 (2m, Asco, Sft, Dec 17)
Alasi 136 4 (2m 4f, Chel, Gd, Mar 13)
Alderwood (IRE) 148 1 (2m, Punc, Hvy, Apr 24)
All The Aces (IRE) 134 1 (2m 110y, Newb, Sft, Dec 31)
Alla Svelta (IRE) 136 1 (3m 3f, Newt, GF, Aug 9)
Allee Garde (FR) 132 4 (3m, Punc, Gd, May 4)
Allthekingshorses (IRE) 133 1 (3m 110y, Donc, Gd, Feb 22)
Allure Of Illusion (IRE) 140 2 (2m, Fair, GS, Apr 9)
Ambion Wood (IRE) 153 1 (3m 110y, Pert, Sft, Apr 25)
American Spin 137 2 (3m 110y, Live, GS, Apr 12)
American Trilogy (IRE) 139 2 (2m 5f 110y, Ayr, Gd, Apr 21)
Anshan Dreams 133 2 (2m, Cork, Sft, Apr 23)

Any Given Day (IRE) 159 1 (2m 4f, Hayd, GS, Nov 19)
Arab League (IRE) 136 1 (2m 3f 110y, Taun, Fm, Mar 28)
Archie Meade (IRE) 137 1 (3m, Fair, Gd, Apr 8)
Arnaud (IRE) 134 5 (2m 110y, Chel, Gd, Mar 14)
Art Professor (IRE) 135 5 (2m 4f 110y, Chel, Gd, Mar 16)
Arthurian Legend 137 3 (2m 110y, Chep, Sft, Feb 25)
Asaid 132 (2m 1f, Chel, Gd, Mar 16)
Askanna (IRE) 143 1 (3m, Punc, Gd, May 4)
Askthemaster (IRE) 134 1 (2m 2f, Leop, Sft, Dec 26)
Attaglance 152 1 (2m 4f, Live, Gd, Apr 13)
Baby Mix (FR) 139 1 (2m, Kemp, Gd, Feb 25)
Baby Whizz (IRE) 135 1 (2m, Nava, Hvy, Jan 15)
Bagber 137 3 (2m 4f, Punc, Gd, May 5)
Baile Anrai (IRE) 132 2 (2m 4f, Chep, Gd, Oct 22)
Balder Succes (FR) 138 1 (2m, Asco, GS, Feb 18)
Balgarry (FR) 143 1 (2m 110y, Newb, GS, Mar 3)
Bally Legend 139 4 (2m 1f, Taun, GS, Jan 19)
Ballynacree (IRE) 135 1 (2m, Fair, GS, Apr 10)
Ballyrock (IRE) 144 2 (2m 5f, Newb, Sft, Dec 31)
Ballysteen (IRE) 137 3 (2m, Punc, Hvy, Dec 11)
Barbatos (FR) 141 1 (2m 4f 110y, Chel, GS, Jan 1)
Barizan (IRE) 135 6 (2m, Hayd, Gd, May 7)
Barker (IRE) 151 2 (2m 4f, Punc, Gd, May 7)
Barnhill Brownie (IRE) 134 2 (3m 3f, Stra, Gd, May 27)
Barwell Bridge 137 3 (3m 1f, Warw, GS, Jan 14)
Batonnier (FR) 142 1 (2m 4f 110y, Chel, GS, Jan 28)
Battle Group 138 (2m 1f, Chel, GS, Jan 28)
Bear's Affair (IRE) 140 1 (2m 5f, Kemp, Gd, Mar 17)
Beau Michael 138 3 (2m 4f, Tipp, Sft, Oct 2)
Beckett Rock (IRE) 136 3 (3m, Thur, GF, Apr 3)

Bellflower Boy (IRE) 136 1 (3m 1f, Warw, GS, Jan 26)
Benash (IRE) 151 2 (2m, Punc, Hvy, Apr 24)
Benefficient (IRE) 147 1 (2m 2f, Leop, GS, Feb 12)
Benefit Of Porter (IRE) 135 2 (2m 4f, Wexf, GF, Apr 20)
Benheir (IRE) 133 1 (3m, Bang, Gd, Apr 21)
Benny Be Good 149 2 (3m, Hayd, GS, Nov 19)
Berties Dream (IRE) 137 6 (2m 4f, Nava, Sft, Nov 13)
Best Served Cold 139 2 (3m, Cork, Hvy, Dec 11)
Bideford Legend (IRE) 138 2 (3m, List, Gd, Jun 6)
Big Buck's (FR) 173 1 (3m, Chel, Gd, Mar 15)
Big Easy (GER) 137 3 (2m 4f 110y, Chel, GS, Apr 18)
Big Occasion (IRE) 134 1 (2m 4f, Carl, Sft, Feb 20)
Binocular (FR) 170 1 (2m, Winc, Sft, Feb 18)
Bishopsfurze (IRE) 132 7 (3m, Punc, Gd, May 4)
Black Thunder (FR) 139 1 (2m 110y, Chep, Sft, Apr 9)
Blackstairmountain (IRE) 159 2 (2m 4f, Fair, Gd, Apr 25)
Blackwell Synergy (FR) 135 1 (3m, Clon, Sft, Oct 27)
Blazing Beacon (IRE) 140 1 (2m 3f, Naas, Gd, Aug 1)
Blenheim Brook (IRE) 140 1 (3m 110y, Pert, Gd, Apr 27)
Bob Lingo (IRE) 132 4 (2m 7f, Nava, Hvy, Dec 10)
Bocciani (GER) 136 2 (2m 3f 110y, Donc, GS, Jan 28)
Boland's Corner (GER) 133 4 (2m 4f, Fair, Hvy, Dec 3)
Bold Addition (FR) 138 2 (2m 5f, Chel, GF, Oct 14)
Bold Chief (IRE) 133 2 (2m 4f 110y, Chel, GS, Apr 18)
Boston Bob (IRE) 156 1 (2m 4f, Leop, Hvy, Jan 29)
Bourne 136 9 (2m 4f 110y, Chel, Gd, Mar 16)
Brampour (IRE) 161 3 (2m 1f, Chel, Gd, Dec 10)
Bridgets Pet (IRE) 144 2 (2m 4f, Fair, Gd, Apr 8)
Bright New Dawn (IRE) 133 7 (2m, Naas, Sft, Feb 26)
Brindisi Breeze (IRE) 154 1 (3m, Hayd, Hvy, Feb 18)
Broadbackbob (IRE) 148 2 (2m 4f 110y, Chel, GS, Jan 28)
Bullock Harbour (IRE) 135 2 (2m 4f, List, Hvy, Sep 14)
Burn And Turn (IRE) 133 2 (2m 4f, Fair, Gd, Apr 8)
Burrenbridge Lodge (IRE) 132 1 (2m, Fair, Hvy, Feb 25)
Cairdin (IRE) 136 4 (3m, Fair, Gd, Apr 8)
Cantlow (IRE) 147 3 (3m, Chel, Gd, Mar 15)
Caolaneoin (IRE) 140 4 (2m 4f, Thur, Hvy, Mar 1)
Cape Dutch (IRE) 134 1 (2m 4f, Muss, GS, Feb 11)
Cape Tribulation (IRE) 158 1 (3m 110y, Live, GS, Apr 12)
Capellanus (IRE) 137 2 (2m, Punc, Sft, Nov 20)
Captain Cee Bee (IRE) 152 8 (2m, Galw, Gd, Jul 28)
Captain Conan (FR) 150 2 (2m 110y, Live, Gd, Apr 13)
Captain Sunshine 135 1 (2m 4f 110y, Chel, GS, Apr 18)
Carlingford Lough (IRE) 132 1 (2m, Galw, Gd, Jul 25)
Carlito Brigante (IRE) 157 3 (3m, Punc, Gd, May 5)
Carrigmartin (IRE) 136 1 (3m 3f, Cork, Gd, Apr 8)
Casa Jove (IRE) 140 1 (2m, Tram, Sft, Dec 31)
Cash And Go (IRE) 143 1 (2m, Leop, Yld, Dec 27)
Cass Bligh (IRE) 145 4 (2m 3f, Naas, Sft, Mar 11)
Castle Wings (IRE) 143 2 (3m, Naas, Sft, Feb 26)
Catch Me (GER) 151 2 (3m, Chel, Gd, Mar 15)
Catcherinscratcher (IRE) 132 1 (3m, Tipp, Gd, Jul 17)
Celestial Halo (IRE) 164 1 (2m 110y, Newb, Sft, Dec 31)
Celtic Folklore (IRE) 132 2 (2m, Punc, Gd, May 6)
Ceol Rua (IRE) 135 (2m, Punc, Hvy, Apr 24)
Changing Times (IRE) 133 1 (2m 4f, Fair, Hvy, Feb 4)
Charm School 133 1 (2m 110y, Newb, GS, Mar 2)
Chicago Grey (IRE) 136 3 (3m, Gowr, Hvy, Jan 26)
Ciceron (IRE) 136 1 (2m 110y, Sand, Sft, Jan 7)
Cinders And Ashes (IRE) 151 1 (2m 110y, Chel, Gd, Mar 13)
Citizenship 135 1 (2m, Leop, Yld, Jan 28)
Clerk's Choice (IRE) 149 3 (2m, Ayr, Gd, Apr 21)
Close House 139 4 (2m 5f, Chel, Gd, Mar 14)
Cloudy Spirit 135 2 (3m 110y, Kemp, Gd, Nov 21)
Cloudy Too (IRE) 134 1 (3m, Newc, Gd, Mar 17)
Cockney Trucker (IRE) 143 5 (2m 5f, Chel, Gd, Mar 14)
Colour Squadron (IRE) 148 2 (2m 4f, Punc, Hvy, Apr 27)
Conquisto 135 2 (2m 110y, Live, Gd, Apr 14)

Cootamundra (IRE) 140 6 (2m 3f, Naas, Sft, Mar 11)
Corbally Ghost (IRE) 133 1 (3m, Cork, Hvy, Dec 11)
Corkage (IRE) 138 1 (3m 110y, Donc, Gd, Mar 3)
Cotillion 132 2 (2m 4f, Muss, GS, Feb 11)
Cotton Mill 153 (2m 5f, Chel, Gd, Mar 14)
Cottrelsbooley (IRE) 135 3 (2m 4f, Naas, Hvy, Oct 29)
Countrywide Flame 147 2 (2m 110y, Live, GS, Apr 12)
Court In Session (IRE) 132 1 (2m, Asco, Gd, Oct 29)
Cousin Vinny (IRE) 148 1 (2m, Punc, Hvy, Feb 22)
Crack Away Jack 147 2 (3m 110y, Live, GS, Apr 12)
Cross Kennon (IRE) 151 2 (3m, Hayd, Hvy, Feb 18)
Cucumber Run (IRE) 139 1 (2m 5f 110y, Ayr, Gd, Apr 21)
Dare Me (IRE) 134 3 (2m 1f, Taun, GS, Feb 21)
Dare To Doubt 147 1 (2m, Punc, Sft, Nov 20)
Dariak (FR) 136 1 (2m 4f, Punc, Sft, Nov 19)
Daring Article (IRE) 135 2 (3m, Cork, Yld, Mar 22)
Dark Glacier (IRE) 133 1 (2m 6f, Newc, Gd, Feb 25)
Darlan 156 1 (2m 110y, Live, Gd, Apr 13)
Darwins Fox (FR) 140 3 (2m, Gowr, Sft, Feb 18)
Datokepe (IRE) 139 2 (3m, Clon, Sft, Oct 27)
Dawn Commander (GER) 133 2 (3m, Bang, Gd, Feb 29)
Dazzling Susie (IRE) 133 1 (2m, Punc, Gd, May 25)
De Valira (IRE) 143 2 (2m 2f, Cork, Gd, Aug 1)
Decoy (FR) 133 1 (2m 5f, Chel, Gd, Nov 11)
Dedigout (IRE) 152 1 (2m 4f, Punc, Hvy, Apr 27)
Dee Ee Williams (IRE) 142 5 (2m 110y, Live, Gd, Apr 14)
Deireadh Re (IRE) 139 5 (3m 110y, Live, GS, Apr 12)
Desert Cry (IRE) 143 2 (2m, Hayd, Hvy, Jan 21)
Deutschland (USA) 140 4 (2m 4f, Fair, Gd, Apr 25)
Devils Bit (IRE) 133 1 (2m, Gowr, Gd, Jun 19)
Dirar (IRE) 147 3 (2m, Galw, Gd, Jul 28)
Distant Memories (IRE) 136 8 (2m 110y, Chel, Gd, Mar 13)
Doctor Deejay (IRE) 135 (2m 4f, Punc, Gd, May 7)
Dodging Bullets 141 4 (2m 1f, Chel, Gd, Mar 16)
Dolphin Bay (IRE) 138 3 (2m, Fair, Gd, Apr 26)
Domtaline (FR) 138 1 (2m 110y, Chep, Gd, Oct 8)
Donnas Palm (IRE) 154 3 (2m, Tipp, Sft, Oct 2)
Dorset Square (IRE) 138 7 (2m 4f, Punc, Gd, May 7)
Double Double (FR) 132 1 (2m, Gowr, Sft, Mar 10)
Double Ross (IRE) 134 2 (2m, Hayd, Hvy, Jan 21)
Double Seven (IRE) 144 1 (2m 4f, Tipp, Sft, Oct 2)
Dream Esteem 142 4 (2m 110y, Live, Gd, Apr 14)
Dream Function (IRE) 136 1 (2m 3f, Devo, Sft, Nov 9)
Dreamy Gent (IRE) 139 6 (2m, Gowr, GF, Jun 19)
Dressedtothenines (IRE) 132 2 (2m, Naas, Sft, Feb 26)
Drill Sergeant 139 4 (2m 4f 110y, Chel, GS, Jan 1)
Dualla Lord (IRE) 132 2 (2m 3f 110y, Taun, GS, Jan 19)
Duc De Regniere (FR) 135 3 (2m 4f, Font, GS, Feb 26)
Dul Ar An Ol (IRE) 132 1 (2m, Leop, GS, Feb 12)
Dunraven Storm (IRE) 138 4 (2m 3f 110y, Asco, GS, Feb 18)
Dylan Ross (IRE) 145 2 (2m, Naas, Hvy, Jan 21)
Dynaste (FR) 162 2 (3m, Chel, GS, Jan 28)
Edeymi (IRE) 139 2 (2m 110y, Chel, Gd, Mar 14)
Edgardo Sol (FR) 144 2 (2m 1f, Chel, Gd, Mar 16)
Eightybarackstreet (IRE) 139 1 (2m, Fair, Gd, Apr 8)
Empire Levant (USA) 141 2 (2m 110y, Newb, GS, Nov 26)
Empire Theatre (IRE) 133 2 (3m, Thur, GF, Apr 3)
Eradicate (IRE) 155 1 (2m, Hayd, Gd, May 7)
Eyesontheprize (IRE) 138 1 (2m, Thur, Hvy, Nov 3)
Fair Along (GER) 149 2 (3m 1f, Weth, Gd, Oct 29)
False Economy (IRE) 140 1 (2m, Lime, Gd, Apr 1)
Faltering Fullback 136 2 (2m 4f, List, Hvy, Sep 23)
Far Away So Close (IRE) 137 3 (2m, Punc, Yld, May 3)
Featherbed Lane (IRE) 154 2 (2m 5f, Kemp, Gd, Jan 14)
Felix Yonger (IRE) 153 2 (2m 5f, Chel, Gd, Mar 14)
Fiendish Flame (IRE) 147 1 (2m 4f 110y, Leic, Gd, Dec 1)
Fill The Power (IRE) 134 1 (2m 6f, Newc, GS, Nov 26)
Final Approach 150 1 (2m, Cork, Hvy, Jan 2)

Fingal Bay (IRE) 156 1 (2m 4f, Sand, GS, Dec 2)
First Fandango 141 4 (2m 110y, Newb, GS, Nov 26)
First In The Queue (IRE) 134 2 (2m 1f, Chel, Gd, Dec 9)
First Lieutenant (IRE) 146 3 (2m 4f, Punc, Gd, May 6)
Five Dream (FR) 152 2 (3m 1f, Asco, Sft, Dec 17)
Flemenstar (IRE) 135 4 (2m 4f, Fair, Gd, Apr 26)
Flycorn (IRE) 135 4 (2m 4f, Live, Gd, Apr 14)
Folsom Blue (IRE) 154 1 (2m 6f, Clon, Hvy, Feb 2)
For Non Stop (IRE) 135 2 (2m 3f 110y, Asco, Gd, Nov 19)
Forgotten Gold (IRE) 134 3 (2m 4f 110y, Chel, GS, Jan 1)
Formidableopponent (IRE) 134 4 (2m, Leop, Yld, Dec 27)
Fosters Cross (IRE) 151 3 (2m 1f, Kill, Yld, May 15)
Four Chimneys (IRE) 139 2 (2m 4f, Fair, Hvy, Feb 25)
Fox Appeal (IRE) 137 1 (3m 110y, Taun, GS, Jan 19)
Frisco Depot 136 4 (2m 4f, Punc, Gd, May 6)
Fully Funded (USA) 146 2 (2m 6f, Punc, Sft, Nov 20)
Gagewell Flyer (IRE) 137 5 (2m 4f, Punc, Gd, May 6)
Gala Dancer (IRE) 139 1 (3m, Galw, Yld, Jul 27)
Galant Ferns (IRE) 139 1 (2m 6f, Fair, Hvy, Jan 1)
Galaxy Rock (IRE) 133 3 (3m, Bang, Gd, Mar 24)
Galileo's Choice (IRE) 151 2 (2m, Fair, Hvy, Dec 4)
General Miller 146 2 (2m 110y, Pert, Gd, Aug 20)
Geneva Geyser (GER) 132 2 (2m 4f 110y, Utto, GF, Sep 7)
Get Me Out Of Here (IRE) 159 2 (2m 5f, Chel, Gd, Mar 14)
Gibb River (IRE) 145 3 (2m 110y, Live, Gd, Apr 14)
Gimli's Rock (IRE) 143 (2m, Leop, GS, Feb 12)
Global Power (IRE) 136 2 (2m 4f, Chep, Gd, Oct 22)
Golan Way 138 3 (3m, Chel, Sft, Apr 19)
Golanbrook (IRE) 133 1 (2m 4f, Wexf, GF, Apr 20)
Golden Call (IRE) 143 1 (3m, Bang, Gd, Mar 24)
Golden Sunbird (IRE) 141 2 (2m 4f, Fair, Gd, Apr 24)
Good Fella (IRE) 132 1 (2m 4f, Nava, Sft, Mar 3)
Gormanstown Cuckoo 135 1 (3m 110y, Live, Gd, Oct 22)
Got Attitude (IRE) 134 3 (2m 6f, Thur, Gd, Oct 20)
Grand Vision (IRE) 151 3 (3m, Chel, Gd, Mar 16)
Grandads Horse 138 1 (2m 4f, Hayd, Gd, Apr 7)
Grandouet (FR) 166 1 (2m 1f, Chel, Gd, Dec 10)
Grey Gold (IRE) 133 4 (2m 1f, Taun, GS, Jan 31)
Grey Soldier (IRE) 142 8 (2m 1f, Kill, Yld, May 15)
Grumeti 148 1 (2m 110y, Live, GS, Apr 12)
Gullinbursti (IRE) 143 2 (3m 110y, Newb, GS, Feb 17)
Hans Crescent (FR) 133 1 (2m 4f, Fair, Hvy, Feb 25)
Hard To Swallow (IRE) 137 4 (2m 4f 110y, Chel, GS, Jan 28)
Harry Topper 139 2 (3m, Hayd, Hvy, Feb 18)
Havingotascoobydo (IRE) 137 2 (2m 110y, Sand, Sft, Jan 7)
Hawkes Point 138 2 (2m 6f, Sand, GS, Mar 9)
He'llberemembered (IRE) 145 2 (2m 3f, Cork, Gd, Apr 8)
He's A Delight (IRE) 132 1 (2m 6f 110y, Down, Yld, Oct 15)
Head Of The Posse (IRE) 142 2 (2m, Fair, Hvy, Dec 3)
Hearthstead Dream 132 2 (2m 4f 110y, Pert, Gd, Apr 28)
Heather Royal 134 2 (2m 5f, Newb, Gd, Mar 24)
Hidden Universe (IRE) 140 2 (2m, Punc, Yld, May 3)
Higgy's Ragazzo (FR) 137 2 (2m, Kemp, GS, Dec 27)
Highland Lodge (IRE) 137 1 (2m 4f, Hayd, Hvy, Dec 17)
Highway Code (USA) 133 1 (2m 1f, Devo, Hvy, Dec 15)
Hildisvini (IRE) 134 1 (2m 6f, Sand, GS, Mar 9)
His Excellency (IRE) 136 8 (2m 1f, Chel, Gd, Mar 16)
Hisaabaat (IRE) 142 2 (2m 1f, Chel, Gd, Mar 16)
Hollow Tree 140 3 (2m 1f, Chel, GS, Jan 28)
Houblon Des Obeaux (FR) 145 4 (3m, Chel, Gd, Mar 15)
Hunterview 138 3 (2m, Hayd, Gd, May 7)
Hunting Tower 139 3 (2m 4f, Bell, GF, Jul 2)
Hurricane Fly (IRE) 173 1 (2m, Leop, Hvy, Jan 29)
Idarah (USA) 136 3 (2m 1f, Kill, Gd, Jul 14)
Ifyouletmefinish (IRE) 136 1 (2m 1f, Taun, GS, Feb 21)
Il Fenomeno (ITY) 141 3 (2m 2f, Leop, GS, Feb 12)
Immediate Response (IRE) 143 1 (2m, Lime, Hvy, Mar 19)
Ingleby Spirit 137 1 (2m, Muss, Gd, Jan 25)

Inspector Clouseau (IRE) 141 5 (2m, Fair, Hvy, Dec 3)
Ipsos Du Berlais (FR) 147 1 (2m 4f, Punc, Hvy, Jan 14)
Irish Soul (IRE) 135 1 (3m, Clon, Sft, Nov 10)
It's A Gimme (IRE) 141 1 (2m 110y, Newb, GS, Nov 25)
Jack Cool (IRE) 151 1 (2m, Fair, Gd, Apr 26)
Jacksonslady (IRE) 133 3 (2m, Fair, GS, Apr 9)
Jenari (IRE) 148 1 (2m 4f, Fair, Gd, Apr 8)
Jetson (IRE) 148 2 (3m, Fair, Gd, Apr 8)
Jim Will Fix It (IRE) 138 1 (2m 4f, Ball, Gd, May 31)
Jimbill (IRE) 134 (2m 110y, Chel, Gd, Mar 13)
Joe Smooth 133 (2m, Punc, Gd, May 6)
Johnny Mcgeeney (IRE) 138 1 (2m, Punc, Yld, May 3)
Johns Spirit (IRE) 133 1 (2m 1f, Mark, Sft, Apr 15)
Joker Choker (IRE) 137 4 (2m 5f, Chel, GS, Nov 13)
Jumbo Rio (IRE) 143 4 (2m, Tipp, Gd, Jul 17)
Jump City (FR) 133 1 (2m 3f, Newt, Gd, Apr 12)
Just For Joe (IRE) 135 2 (2m 4f, Galw, Hvy, Oct 22)
Kaffie 132 2 (2m 4f, Sand, Sft, Jan 7)
Kalann (IRE) 143 2 (2m, Gowr, Sft, Feb 18)
Kandari (FR) 132 2 (2m 3f, Mark, GS, Feb 19)
Kangaroo Court (IRE) 136 4 (3m, Worc, Gd, Jun 22)
Karabak (FR) 145 1 (2m 4f, Nava, Sft, Nov 13)
Kasbadali (FR) 133 1 (3m, Asco, Gd, Apr 1)
Katchmore (IRE) 134 1 (2m 1f, Devo, Gd, Mar 20)
Kayf Aramis 137 2 (3m, Chel, GS, Jan 1)
Kazlian (FR) 134 4 (2m 110y, Chel, Gd, Mar 14)
Kells Belle (IRE) 144 1 (2m 5f 110y, Chel, Sft, Apr 19)
Kentford Grey Lady 133 1 (3m 110y, Kemp, GS, Dec 27)
Kerb Appeal (IRE) 148 1 (3m, Punc, Gd, May 5)
Keys (IRE) 137 2 (2m 1f, Live, Sft, Dec 3)
Kid Cassidy (IRE) 145 1 (2m, Punc, Gd, May 6)
Killyglen (IRE) 132 3 (3m, Gowr, Sft, Sep 30)
Kilmacowen (IRE) 139 1 (3m 1f, Warw, Gd, Mar 11)
King Ali (IRE) 134 3 (2m 5f 190y, Galw, Hvy, Oct 23)
King In Waiting (IRE) 135 2 (2m 1f, Mark, Gd, Sep 24)
King Of The Night (GER) 159 1 (2m 5f, Kemp, Gd, Oct 31)
King Of The Refs (IRE) 134 2 (2m 4f, Fair, Sft, Feb 15)
Knight Pass (IRE) 135 1 (2m 5f, Kemp, GS, Dec 26)
Knock A Hand (IRE) 144 1 (3m 110y, Newb, GS, Feb 17)
Knockara Beau (IRE) 139 2 (2m 2f, Kels, GS, Feb 15)
Knockfierna (IRE) 143 1 (2m 4f, Fair, Gd, Apr 24)
Kumbeshwar 137 2 (2m, Punc, Gd, May 7)
Kylenoe Fairy (IRE) 134 2 (2m 1f, Mark, GS, Jul 16)
Laganbank (IRE) 140 5 (2m 4f, Fair, Gd, Apr 8)
Lambro (IRE) 143 1 (2m 4f, Fair, Gd, Apr 26)
Lancetto (FR) 135 3 (2m 4f, Ffos, GF, Aug 25)
Last Instalment (IRE) 137 3 (2m 4f, Fair, Gd, Apr 26)
Liberate 141 1 (3m, Hayd, Gd, May 7)
Lifestyle 144 1 (2m 110y, Live, Gd, Apr 14)
Lightning Strike (GER) 134 3 (3m 2f, Hunt, Sft, Jan 27)
Like Minded 136 3 (2m 5f, Kemp, GS, Dec 26)
Little Green (IRE) 135 2 (2m, Cork, Hvy, Jan 2)
Local Hero (GER) 142 2 (2m, Ayr, Gd, Apr 21)
Loch Ard (IRE) 140 1 (2m, Punc, Hvy, Apr 25)
London Bridge 135 2 (2m, Galw, Gd, Jul 26)
Lord Windermere (IRE) 139 1 (2m, Naas, Sft, Mar 11)
Lough Ferrib (IRE) 132 5 (2m 4f, Punc, Gd, May 7)
Loveen (GER) 154 1 (3m 110y, Live, Gd, Apr 13)
Lucky Spring (IRE) 143 1 (2m, Dowr, Sft, Nov 5)
Luska Lad (IRE) 154 2 (2m, Tipp, Sft, Oct 2)
Lyreen Legend (IRE) 148 3 (2m 4f, Punc, Hvy, Apr 27)
Mackeys Forge (IRE) 141 2 (2m 4f, Fair, Gd, Apr 26)
Mad Moose (IRE) 143 1 (2m 6f, Newt, GS, Aug 20)
Madame Mado (FR) 137 1 (2m, Cork, Hvy, Dec 11)
Magnifique Etoile 135 3 (2m 110y, Sand, Sft, Jan 7)
Make A Track (IRE) 142 4 (2m 4f 110y, Chel, Gd, Mar 16)
Make Your Mark (IRE) 137 3 (2m 4f, Leop, Hvy, Jan 29)
Makethe Mostofnow (IRE) 140 1 (3m, Ffos, Sft, Mar 17)

Maller Tree 142 4 (2m 4f, Fair, Gd, Apr 8)
Malt Master (IRE) 136 2 (2m, Punc, Hvy, Apr 27)
Manger Hanagment (IRE) 135 1 (2m 5f 110y, Sedg, Gd, Sep 27)
Marasonnien (FR) 144 1 (3m, Punc, Hvy, Apr 25)
Marlay Park (IRE) 147 1 (2m 6f, Fair, Gd, Apr 25)
Marodima (FR) 142 1 (2m, Towc, GS, Mar 15)
Marsh Warbler 149 3 (2m, Hayd, Hvy, Jan 21)
Mart Lane (IRE) 135 2 (2m 4f, Nava, Hvy, Dec 10)
Meister Eckhart (IRE) 144 5 (3m, Chel, Gd, Mar 16)
Memories Of Milan (IRE) 132 (2m 6f, Kill, Sft, Aug 25)
Menorah (IRE) 157 4 (2m 1f, Chel, Gd, Dec 10)
Micheal Flips (IRE) 137 6 (3m, Hayd, Gd, May 7)
Michel Le Bon (FR) 140 1 (3m, Chel, Sft, Apr 19)
Mickelson (IRE) 132 1 (2m, Fair, Hvy, Jan 11)
Midnight Game 146 1 (2m, Naas, Hvy, Jan 21)
Mikael D'Haguenet (FR) 159 1 (2m 3f, Naas, Hvy, Jan 21)
Minella Humour (IRE) 133 3 (3m, Wexf, Sft, Oct 31)
Mister Carter (IRE) 134 3 (2m, Lime, Hvy, Dec 26)
Module (FR) 140 1 (2m 1f, Chel, GS, Jan 28)
Molotof (FR) 141 1 (2m, Hayd, GS, Nov 18)
Monksland (IRE) 148 3 (2m 5f, Chel, Gd, Mar 14)
Mono Man (IRE) 141 3 (2m 110y, Newb, GS, Nov 25)
Montan (FR) 144 2 (2m, Fair, Hvy, Dec 3)
Montbazon (FR) 148 4 (2m 110y, Chel, Gd, Mar 13)
Moon Dice (IRE) 149 4 (2m 110y, Chel, GS, Nov 13)
Mossey Joe (IRE) 146 2 (3m, Punc, Gd, May 4)
Mount Benbulben (IRE) 148 2 (2m 4f, Nava, Hvy, Dec 18)
Mount Helicon 132 5 (2m 4f, Galw, Gd, Aug 28)
Mourad (IRE) 163 2 (3m, Punc, Gd, May 5)
Much Acclaimed (IRE) 135 1 (2m, List, Sft, Sep 13)
Mush Mir (IRE) 135 1 (2m 4f 110y, Sout, Gd, Nov 7)
My Murphy (IRE) 142 1 (2m 7f, Nava, Sft, Mar 18)
Nagpur (FR) 135 1 (2m 5f, Plum, GS, Apr 27)
Native Gallery (IRE) 137 3 (2m 4f 110y, Chel, GS, Apr 18)
Nearby 139 (2m 110y, Chel, GS, Nov 9)
Nearest The Pin (IRE) 134 2 (2m, Punc, Yld, May 3)
Nelson's Bridge (IRE) 132 1 (2m 3f 110y, Taun, GS, Jan 19)
New Phase (IRE) 141 1 (2m, Cork, Hvy, Nov 23)
Noble Alan (GER) 134 4 (2m 110y, Pert, Gd, Aug 20)
Noras Fancy (IRE) 135 1 (2m, Lime, Hvy, Mar 18)
Novarov (GER) 135 2 (3m, Punc, Hvy, Apr 26)
Now This Is It (IRE) 142 2 (2m 5f 190y, Galw, Gd, Jul 30)
Ohio Gold (IRE) 132 1 (2m 5f, Plum, Sft, Dec 19)
Oilily (IRE) 147 1 (2m 4f, Cork, Yld, Mar 22)
Olofi (FR) 138 5 (2m 110y, Newb, GS, Feb 17)
Oneeightofamile (IRE) 150 1 (2m 2f, Cork, Gd, Aug 1)
Ongenstown Lad (IRE) 142 1 (3m 1f 110y, Chel, GF, Oct 15)
Open Hearted 139 1 (2m 4f, Fake, GS, Feb 17)
Organisedconfusion (IRE) 132 3 (3m, Fair, Sft, Nov 16)
Original Option (IRE) 142 1 (2m 4f, List, Hvy, Sep 14)
Orsippus (USA) 135 4 (2m 2f, Kels, GS, Feb 15)
Oscar Dan Dan (IRE) 154 3 (2m 4f, Fair, Gd, Apr 25)
Oscar Hill (IRE) 135 1 (2m 2f 50y, Down, Sft, Mar 7)
Oscar Nominee (IRE) 143 3 (2m 4f 110y, Chel, Gd, Mar 16)
Oscar Prairie (IRE) 136 3 (2m 5f, Kemp, Gd, Mar 17)
Oscar Whisky (IRE) 167 1 (2m 4f 110y, Chel, GS, Jan 1)
Oscara Dara (IRE) 138 1 (2m, Punc, Hvy, Apr 27)
Oscargo (IRE) 141 1 (3m, Chel, Gd, Mar 16)
Oscars Well (IRE) 164 6 (2m 110y, Chel, Gd, Mar 13)
Osirixamix (IRE) 141 1 (2m, Fair, Hvy, Jan 1)
Our Father (IRE) 147 1 (2m 6f, Asco, Sft, Dec 16)
Our Girl Salley (IRE) 143 3 (2m, Fair, Hvy, Dec 3)
Our Joe Mac (IRE) 132 2 (2m, Hayd, GS, Nov 18)
Overturn (IRE) 167 2 (2m 110y, Chel, Gd, Mar 13)
Owega Star (IRE) 136 4 (2m 4f, Naas, Hvy, Mar 18)
Owen Glendower (IRE) 133 4 (2m 3f, Newt, GF, May 16)
Owennacurra Milan (IRE) 134 3 (2m 4f, Gowr, Hvy, Mar 24)
Paintball (IRE) 137 1 (2m 110y, Sand, GS, Mar 10)

Palace Jester 138 1 (3m, Chep, Hvy, Dec 27)
Palawi (IRE) 140 1 (2m, Newc, Gd, Feb 25)
Pateese (FR) 140 1 (2m 110y, Sand, Sft, Nov 5)
Pearl Swan (FR) 143 (2m 1f, Chel, Gd, Mar 16)
Peckhamecho (IRE) 139 1 (2m 1f, Bang, GS, Nov 26)
Pepe Simo (IRE) 137 1 (2m, Kemp, Gd, Oct 16)
Persian Gayle (IRE) 135 3 (2m 4f, Leop, Hvy, Jan 29)
Petit Robin (FR) 147 3 (2m 110y, Newb, GS, Mar 23)
Pettifour (IRE) 147 3 (3m 110y, Newb, GS, Nov 26)
Pickapocketortwo (IRE) 141 1 (2m 6f 110y, Thur, Hvy, Nov 17)
Pineau De Re (FR) 148 4 (3m, Punc, Hvy, Feb 5)
Pires 133 2 (2m, Leop, Gd, Dec 28)
Pittoni (IRE) 154 3 (2m, Punc, Sft, Nov 20)
Plan A (IRE) 141 4 (2m 1f, Chel, Gd, Mar 16)
Platinum (IRE) 135 1 (2m, Ludl, Gd, Nov 21)
Please Talk (IRE) 140 2 (3m, Lime, Hvy, Dec 28)
Plenty Pocket (FR) 134 3 (2m, Hayd, GS, Nov 18)
Poole Master 144 1 (2m 5f, Newb, GS, Mar 2)
Poungach (FR) 154 2 (2m 4f 110y, Chel, GS, Jan 1)
Powerstation (FR) 154 3 (3m, Clon, Sft, Nov 10)
Pozyc (FR) 136 7 (2m, Leop, GS, Feb 12)
Premier Grand Cru (FR) 135 1 (2m 4f, Live, Gd, May 6)
Prima Vista 148 2 (2m 4f, Punc, Gd, May 6)
Primroseandblue (IRE) 134 1 (2m 100y, Clon, Sft, Mar 8)
Prince Of Fire (GER) 134 5 (2m 1f, Kill, Yld, May 15)
Prince Rudi (IRE) 137 5 (2m 6f, Fair, Gd, Apr 25)
Princely Player (IRE) 136 2 (2m 110y, Chep, Sft, Apr 9)
Princeton Plains (IRE) 142 1 (2m, List, Sft, Sep 15)
Priors Gold 133 4 (2m, Nava, Sft, Nov 13)
Prospect Wells (FR) 146 5 (2m 110y, Chel, Gd, Mar 13)
Quevega (FR) 159 1 (3m, Punc, Hvy, Apr 26)
Quiscover Fontaine (FR) 135 1 (2m, Leop, Gd, Dec 28)
Rajdhani Express 134 8 (2m, Asco, Sft, Dec 17)
Ranjaan (FR) 137 1 (2m 1f, Taun, GS, Jan 19)
Rathlin 142 2 (2m, Fair, Gd, Apr 25)
Rattan (USA) 137 2 (2m 6f, Kill, Sft, Aug 25)
Raya Star (IRE) 149 1 (2m, Ayr, Gd, Apr 21)
Real Milan (IRE) 134 4 (3m, Hayd, Hvy, Feb 18)
Rebel Fitz (FR) 149 2 (2m 4f, Nava, Hvy, Nov 27)
Red Merlin (IRE) 137 4 (2m, Ayr, Gd, Apr 21)
Redera (IRE) 142 1 (2m, Rosc, Sft, Jun 13)
Reindeer Dippin 142 1 (3m, Hayd, Hvy, Jan 21)
Reizovic (IRE) 133 4 (2m 4f, Nava, Hvy, Dec 10)
Restless Harry 156 1 (3m, Hayd, Hvy, Feb 18)
Rev It Up (IRE) 135 1 (3m, Chep, Hvy, Dec 27)
Rick (FR) 142 3 (2m 5f, Nava, Sft, Feb 19)
Rigidity 135 2 (2m, Asco, Sft, Dec 17)
Rigour Back Bob (IRE) 144 2 (2m 6f, Thur, Gd, Oct 20)
Ringaroses 136 4 (3m 110y, Live, GS, Apr 12)
Rivage D'Or (FR) 150 2 (3m, Punc, Gd, May 5)
Rival D'Estruval (FR) 135 2 (2m 6f, Newc, Gd, Feb 25)
Robinson Collonges (FR) 137 3 (2m 4f, Chep, Gd, Oct 22)
Rock On Ruby (IRE) 171 1 (2m 110y, Chel, Gd, Mar 13)
Rocky Creek (IRE) 142 1 (3m 110y, Donc, GS, Jan 28)
Royal Charm (FR) 134 7 (2m 3f 110y, Asco, GS, Jan 21)
Royal Reveille (IRE) 142 1 (2m 5f, Lime, Sft, Oct 9)
Rumble Of Thunder (IRE) 136 1 (2m 1f, Live, GS, Oct 22)
Run With The Wind (IRE) 133 2 (2m, Punc, Sft, Oct 13)
Russian War (IRE) 142 5 (3m, Chel, GF, Oct 14)
Sa Suffit (FR) 137 2 (3m, Hayd, Hvy, Feb 18)
Sadler's Risk (IRE) 137 6 (2m 1f, Chel, Gd, Mar 16)
Safari Sunup (IRE) 134 1 (2m 4f, Rosc, Yld, Jul 5)
Sailors Warn (IRE) 149 3 (2m 1f, Chel, Gd, Mar 16)
Saint Gervais (IRE) 139 1 (2m, Cork, Sft, Apr 23)
Salesin 141 1 (2m 3f, Cork, Gd, Apr 24)
Sam Bass (IRE) 133 1 (2m, Fair, Hvy, Dec 4)
Same Difference (IRE) 140 1 (2m 4f, Ffos, GS, Apr 23)
Sanctuaire (FR) 151 8 (2m 110y, Chel, GS, Nov 13)

Saphir River (FR) 135 4 (2m 4f, Live, Gd, Apr 13)
Savello (IRE) 140 1 (2m, Fair, Sft, Nov 16)
Scotsbrook Cloud 134 2 (3m 3f, Font, Gd, Sep 30)
Sea Of Thunder (IRE) 141 (3m, Chel, Gd, Dec 10)
Sebadee (IRE) 137 1 (2m 6f, Kill, Gd, Jul 13)
See U Bob (IRE) 134 2 (2m 4f, Punc, Sft, Nov 19)
Sergent Guib's (FR) 152 3 (3m, Punc, Hvy, Feb 5)
Shadow Catcher 138 2 (2m, Leop, GS, Feb 12)
Shadow Eile (IRE) 133 1 (2m 4f, Fair, Gd, Apr 8)
Shakervilz (FR) 145 3 (3m, Leop, Gd, Dec 28)
Shamiran (IRE) 136 1 (2m 4f, Punc, Hvy, Apr 25)
Shoegazer (IRE) 139 1 (2m 4f, Chep, Sft, Apr 9)
Shop Dj (IRE) 141 1 (2m 2f, Punc, Gd, May 7)
Shoreacres (IRE) 140 2 (2m 3f 110y, Asco, GS, Jan 21)
Shot From The Hip (GER) 150 1 (2m, Punc, Yld, May 3)
Si C'etait Vrai (FR) 136 5 (2m 4f, Punc, Gd, May 5)
Sicilian Secret (IRE) 133 1 (2m 4f, Ball, Yld, Jul 19)
Silk Hall (UAE) 140 1 (2m 4f, Galw, Gd, Aug 28)
Silverhand (IRE) 141 6 (2m, Galw, Gd, Jul 28)
Simenon (IRE) 140 3 (2m, Punc, Hvy, Apr 24)
Simonsig 162 1 (2m 4f, Live, Gd, Apr 14)
Sire De Grugy (FR) 149 3 (2m 110y, Sand, GS, Mar 10)
Sivola De Sivola (FR) 135 4 (2m 1f, Chel, GS, Jan 28)
Sizing Symphony (IRE) 144 1 (2m 5f, Chel, GF, Oct 14)
Slieveardagh (IRE) 137 (2m 1f, Kill, Yld, May 15)
Smad Place (FR) 164 3 (3m, Chel, Gd, Mar 15)
Snap Tie (IRE) 158 1 (2m, Punc, Hvy, Apr 24)
So Young (FR) 155 1 (2m, Nava, Hvy, Jan 15)
Some Present (IRE) 139 4 (2m, Punc, Sft, Nov 20)
Some Target (IRE) 142 2 (3m, Clon, Sft, Nov 10)
Son Amix (FR) 143 9 (2m, Galw, Gd, Jul 28)
Son Of Flicka 142 1 (2m 5f, Chel, Gd, Mar 14)
Sonofvic (IRE) 141 (3m, Chel, Gd, Mar 15)
Sous Les Cieux (FR) 153 1 (2m, Fair, Hvy, Dec 4)
Sparky May 144 4 (3m 110y, Newb, GS, Nov 26)
Spirit Of Adjisa (IRE) 148 1 (2m 4f, Punc, Gd, May 6)
Spirit River (FR) 146 (2m 5f, Chel, Gd, Mar 14)
Spring Heeled (IRE) 135 1 (2m 4f, Lime, Gd, Apr 1)
Springfield Way (IRE) 133 1 (2m 2f 50y, Down, Hvy, Dec 21)
St Devote (FR) 139 3 (2m 4f, Punc, Gd, May 7)
Star In Flight 133 1 (2m 3f, Catt, Gd, Feb 28)
Star Neuville (FR) 138 2 (2m 6f, Thur, Sft, Jan 19)
Star Of Angels 141 1 (2m 4f, Winc, Sft, Jan 7)
Starluck (IRE) 144 (2m 1f, Chel, Gd, Mar 16)
Start Me Up (IRE) 133 4 (3m, Fair, Gd, Apr 24)
Staying Article (IRE) 155 3 (2m, Leop, Yld, Jan 28)
Steps To Freedom (IRE) 141 5 (2m, Fair, GS, Apr 9)
Stonemaster (IRE) 145 (2m, Leop, Gd, Mar 4)
Street Entertainer (IRE) 137 3 (2m 1f, Mark, GS, Jul 16)
Sunnyhillboy (IRE) 138 7 (3m, Hayd, GS, Nov 19)
Super Duty (IRE) 142 2 (2m 4f, Live, Gd, Apr 14)
Sweet My Lord (FR) 152 4 (2m, Leop, Yld, Jan 28)
Swincombe Flame 135 3 (2m 3f 110y, Asco, GS, Feb 18)
Sword Of Destiny (IRE) 146 1 (3m, Cork, Sft, Nov 6)
Synchronised (IRE) 152 3 (3m, Hayd, GS, Nov 19)
Take The Breeze (FR) 138 6 (3m 110y, Live, Gd, Oct 23)
Talkonthestreet (IRE) 134 3 (3m 110y, Pert, Sft, Apr 25)
Tamarinbleu (FR) 138 3 (3m, Hayd, Hvy, Feb 18)
Tango De Juilley (FR) 133 4 (2m 1f, Chel, GS, Jan 28)
Tap Night (USA) 140 1 (2m 2f, Kels, Gd, Mar 3)
Tavern Times (IRE) 151 1 (2m, Tipp, Sft, Oct 2)
Tawaagg 139 4 (2m, List, Sft, Sep 15)
Ted Spread 136 1 (2m 1f, Taun, GS, Jan 31)
Tenor Nivernais (FR) 144 1 (2m 4f, Carl, Sft, Feb 20)
Terminal (FR) 134 3 (2m, Fair, Sft, Feb 5)
Tetlami (IRE) 142 1 (2m, Kemp, GS, Dec 26)
Texas Jack (IRE) 143 1 (2m 4f, Clon, Sft, Nov 10)
That'll Do 136 1 (2m 6f, Winc, GF, Apr 5)

The Bishop Looney (IRE) 136 1 (2m 4f, Punc, Hvy, Feb 22)
The Bull Hayes (IRE) 148 3 (2m, List, Sft, Sep 15)
The Druids Nephew (IRE) 137 6 (3m, Chel, Gd, Mar 16)
The Giant Bolster 140 4 (2m 4f, Chep, Gd, Oct 22)
The Jigsaw Man (IRE) 146 6 (2m, Punc, Yld, May 3)
The Knoxs (IRE) 152 1 (2m 7f 110y, Devo, Sft, Nov 9)
The Real Article (IRE) 158 1 (2m, Tipp, Sft, Oct 2)
The Tracey Shuffle (IRE) 140 3 (2m 4f, Punc, Hvy, Apr 26)
The Way We Were (IRE) 140 2 (2m, Fair, GS, Apr 10)
Thehillofuisneach (IRE) 138 1 (3m 1f, Warw, GS, Jan 14)
Themilanhorse (IRE) 133 1 (2m 4f, Winc, GF, Mar 25)
Third Intention (IRE) 151 1 (2m 4f, Font, GS, Feb 26)
Thousand Stars (IRE) 165 2 (2m 4f, Live, Gd, Apr 14)
Tidal Bay (IRE) 160 3 (3m, Chel, GS, Jan 1)
Tillahow (IRE) 134 6 (3m, Punc, Hvy, Feb 5)
Timesawastin (IRE) 137 1 (2m 4f, Hayd, Gd, Mar 21)
Tofino Bay (IRE) 150 1 (2m 4f, Punc, Hvy, Apr 26)
Tom Horn (IRE) 134 3 (2m 7f, Nava, Sft, Mar 18)
Toner D'Oudairies (FR) 145 2 (2m 4f 110y, Chel, Gd, Mar 16)
Topolski (IRE) 140 2 (2m 4f, Font, GS, Feb 26)
Tornado Bob (IRE) 139 3 (2m 5f 110y, Ayr, Gd, Apr 21)
Tornedo Shay (IRE) 143 1 (2m 4f, Punc, Gd, May 5)
Torphichen 141 2 (2m 110y, Newb, Sft, Dec 31)
Total Excitement (IRE) 139 4 (2m 1f, Kill, Yld, May 15)
Touch Back (IRE) 136 6 (2m, Fair, GS, Apr 10)
Tour D'Argent (FR) 137 2 (2m 4f, Live, Gd, Apr 13)
Trifolium (FR) 147 2 (2m, Punc, Hvy, Apr 24)
Truckers Delight (IRE) 144 1 (2m 4f, Punc, Gd, May 7)
Trustan Times (IRE) 135 3 (3m 110y, Live, GS, Apr 12)
Tullamore Dew (IRE) 137 5 (2m 4f, Chep, Gd, Oct 22)
Turban (FR) 146 2 (2m 4f, Punc, Hvy, Apr 26)
Turner Brown (IRE) 133 3 (2m 4f, Fair, Hvy, Feb 25)
Twinlight (FR) 137 3 (2m, Punc, Gd, May 7)
Ubi Ace 145 2 (2m, Muss, GS, Feb 11)
Unaccompanied (IRE) 153 1 (2m, Leop, Sft, Dec 29)
Uncle Junior (IRE) 136 4 (2m 4f, Slig, Gd, Aug 4)
Une Artiste (FR) 133 1 (2m 1f, Chel, Sft, Apr 19)
Up For The Match (IRE) 133 1 (2m 3f, Naas, Sft, Mar 11)
Urbain De Sivola (FR) 134 1 (2m 1f, Taun, GS, Feb 21)
Ut De Sivola (FR) 140 1 (2m, Punc, Hvy, Jan 14)
Vast Consumption (IRE) 143 1 (2m, Fair, GS, Apr 10)
Veiled 139 3 (2m 5f, Chel, Gd, Mar 14)
Vendor (FR) 133 3 (2m 110y, Chel, Gd, Mar 14)
Vesper Bell (IRE) 141 2 (3m, Punc, Hvy, Apr 25)
Via Galilei (IRE) 145 5 (2m 1f, Chel, Gd, Mar 16)
Viaduct Joey (IRE) 133 4 (3m, Clon, Sft, Nov 10)
Vics Canvas (IRE) 136 (3m, Punc, Gd, May 5)
Violin Davis (FR) 137 1 (2m 6f, Winc, GS, Nov 5)
Viva Colonia (IRE) 139 1 (2m 1f 110y, Cart, Sft, Aug 27)
Volador (IRE) 137 1 (2m 4f 110y, Utto, GS, Mar 17)
Voler La Vedette (IRE) 163 2 (3m, Chel, Gd, Mar 15)
Vulcanite (IRE) 139 5 (2m 110y, Live, Gd, Apr 13)
Water Garden (FR) 133 2 (3m, Chel, GS, Apr 18)
Weekend Millionair (IRE) 137 2 (2m 4f, Punc, Hvy, Apr 25)
Well Regarded (IRE) 133 4 (2m 5f, Kemp, Gd, Jan 14)
Western Leader (IRE) 144 2 (2m 4f, Punc, Hvy, Jan 14)
Westmeath 135 8 (2m 4f, Punc, Gd, May 7)
Whatever Jacksays (IRE) 134 1 (3m, Punc, Hvy, Apr 26)
Whatuthink (IRE) 150 4 (3m, Punc, Hvy, Apr 26)
Whodoyouthink (IRE) 136 1 (2m 4f, Wexf, Sft, Mar 17)
Whoops A Daisy 136 1 (3m 110y, Kemp, Gd, Nov 21)
Wilde Wit Pleasure (IRE) 133 2 (2m 4f, Wexf, Sft, Mar 17)
Wingtips (FR) 137 5 (2m 1f, Chel, Gd, Mar 16)
Won In The Dark (IRE) 154 6 (3m, Punc, Gd, May 5)
Wyse Hill Teabags 140 2 (2m 4f, Hayd, GS, Nov 19)
Zaidpour (FR) 166 2 (2m, Punc, Hvy, Apr 27)
Zarkandar (IRE) 164 5 (2m 110y, Chel, Gd, Mar 13)

TOPSPEED LEADING CHASERS (RATED 130 AND OVER)

KEY: Horse Name, Best RPR figure, Finishing position when earning figure, (details of race where figure was earned)

Abergavenny 133 3 (2m 110y, Chel, GS, Nov 13)
Across The Bay (IRE) 137 4 (3m, Hayd, GS, Nov 19)
Allure Of Illusion (IRE) 136 6 (2m 110y, Chel, Gd, Mar 13)
American Spin 132 2 (3m 110y, Live, GS, Apr 12)
Any Given Day (IRE) 155 1 (2m 4f, Hayd, GS, Nov 19)
Arnaud (IRE) 132 5 (2m 110y, Chel, Gd, Mar 14)
Attaglance 138 1 (2m 3f, Mark, GS, Feb 19)
Barbatos (FR) 132 1 (2m 4f 110y, Chel, GS, Jan 1)
Batonnier (FR) 132 1 (2m 4f 110y, Chel, GS, Jan 28)
Bear's Affair (IRE) 140 1 (2m 5f, Kemp, Gd, Mar 17)
Benny Be Good 144 2 (3m, Hayd, GS, Nov 19)
Big Buck's (FR) 161 1 (3m, Chel, Gd, Mar 15)
Binocular (FR) 160 4 (2m 110y, Chel, Gd, Mar 13)
Boston Bob (IRE) 132 2 (3m, Chel, Gd, Mar 16)
Brampour (IRE) 155 1 (2m 110y, Chel, GS, Nov 13)
Brindisi Breeze (IRE) 142 1 (3m, Hayd, Hvy, Feb 18)
Broadbackbob (IRE) 136 2 (2m 4f 110y, Chel, GS, Jan 28)
Cantlow (IRE) 143 3 (3m, Chel, Gd, Mar 15)
Cape Tribulation 153 1 (3m 110y, Live, GS, Apr 12)
Captain Cee Bee (IRE) 134 8 (2m, Galw, Gd, Jul 28)
Catch Me (GER) 145 2 (3m, Chel, Gd, Mar 15)
Celestial Halo (IRE) 147 1 (2m, Hayd, Hvy, Jan 21)
Ciceron (IRE) 136 1 (2m 110y, Sand, Sft, Jan 7)
Cinders And Ashes 149 1 (2m 110y, Chel, Gd, Mar 13)
Clerk's Choice (IRE) 136 3 (2m, Ayr, Gd, Apr 21)
Close House 135 4 (2m 5f, Chel, Gd, Mar 14)
Cockney Trucker (IRE) 137 5 (2m 5f, Chel, Gd, Mar 14)
Conquisto 134 2 (2m 110y, Live, Gd, Apr 14)
Countrywide Flame 134 2 (2m 110y, Live, GS, Apr 12)
Cross Kennon (IRE) 140 2 (3m, Hayd, Hvy, Feb 18)
Darlan 147 2 (2m 110y, Chel, Gd, Mar 13)
Dee Ee Williams (IRE) 140 5 (2m 110y, Live, Gd, Apr 14)
Deireadh Re (IRE) 133 5 (3m 110y, Live, GS, Apr 12)
Desert Cry (IRE) 137 1 (2m, Hayd, Gd, Nov 18)
Distant Memories (IRE) 133 8 (2m 110y, Chel, Gd, Mar 13)
Donnas Palm (IRE) 136 3 (2m, Tipp, Sft, Oct 2)
Dontpaytheferryman (USA) 131 3 (2m, Muss, GS, Feb 11)
Dream Esteem 141 4 (2m 110y, Live, Gd, Apr 14)
Dynaste (FR) 148 1 (3m, Hayd, GS, Nov 19)
Edeymi (IRE) 138 2 (2m 110y, Chel, Gd, Mar 14)
Edgardo Sol (FR) 137 1 (2m 110y, Chel, GS, Nov 12)
Empire Levant (USA) 137 2 (2m 110y, Newb, GS, Nov 26)
Enfant De Lune (FR) 134 2 (2m 4f, Ayr, Gd, Apr 21)
Featherbed Lane (IRE) 143 1 (2m 4f, Live, Sft, Dec 3)
Felix Yonger (IRE) 149 2 (2m 5f, Chel, Gd, Mar 14)
First Fandango 134 4 (2m 110y, Newb, GS, Nov 26)
Five Dream (FR) 148 2 (3m 1f, Asco, Sft, Dec 17)
Fosters Cross (IRE) 139 3 (2m 1f, Kill, Yld, May 15)
Galaxy Rock (IRE) 131 3 (3m, Bang, Gd, Mar 24)
Galileo's Choice (IRE) 135 7 (2m 110y, Chel, Gd, Mar 13)
General Miller 139 2 (2m 110y, Pert, Gd, Aug 20)
Get Me Out Of Here (IRE) 152 2 (2m 5f, Chel, Gd, Mar 14)
Gibb River (IRE) 144 3 (2m 110y, Live, Gd, Apr 14)
Golden Call (IRE) 137 1 (3m, Bang, Gd, Mar 24)
Grand Vision (IRE) 132 1 (3m, Hayd, Hvy, Feb 18)
Grandads Horse 137 1 (2m 4f, Hayd, Gd, Apr 7)
Grandouet (FR) 158 1 (2m 1f, Chel, Gd, Dec 10)
Grumeti 135 1 (2m 110y, Live, GS, Apr 12)
Harry Topper 132 2 (3m, Hayd, Hvy, Feb 18)
Havingotascoobydo (IRE) 138 2 (2m 110y, Sand, Sft, Jan 7)
Hidden Universe (IRE) 134 2 (2m, Punc, Yld, May 3)
Houblon Des Obeaux (FR) 143 4 (3m, Chel, Gd, Mar 15)
Hurricane Fly (IRE) 161 3 (2m 110y, Chel, Gd, Mar 13)
Ingleby Spirit 135 4 (2m, Muss, GS, Feb 11)
Jack Cool (IRE) 132 (2m 110y, Chel, GS, Nov 13)
Kazlian (FR) 131 4 (2m 110y, Chel, Gd, Mar 14)

Kerb Appeal (IRE) 135 1 (3m, Punc, Gd, May 5)
Kid Cassidy (IRE) 135 1 (2m, Punc, Gd, May 6)
King Of The Night (GER) 145 1 (2m 5f, Kemp, Gd, Oct 31)
Kylenoe Fairy (IRE) 136 2 (2m 1f, Mark, GS, Jul 16)
Lifestyle 143 1 (2m 110y, Live, Gd, Apr 14)
Luska Lad (IRE) 136 2 (2m, Tipp, Sft, Oct 2)
Marsh Warbler 139 3 (2m, Hayd, Hvy, Jan 21)
Menorah (IRE) 147 4 (2m 1f, Chel, Gd, Dec 10)
Molotof (FR) 134 1 (2m, Asco, Sft, Dec 16)
Monksland (IRE) 139 3 (2m 5f, Chel, Gd, Mar 14)
Montbazon (FR) 145 4 (2m 110y, Chel, Gd, Mar 13)
Moon Dice (IRE) 146 4 (2m 110y, Chel, GS, Nov 13)
Nearby 131 (2m 110y, Chel, GS, Nov 13)
Now This Is It (IRE) 133 3 (2m 110y, Pert, Gd, Aug 20)
Olofi (FR) 133 2 (2m 110y, Chel, GS, Nov 13)
Oscar Nominee (IRE) 131 3 (2m 4f 110y, Chel, Gd, Mar 16)
Oscar Prairie (IRE) 138 3 (2m 5f, Kemp, Gd, Mar 17)
Oscar Whisky (IRE) 147 5 (3m, Chel, Gd, Mar 15)
Oscars Well (IRE) 157 6 (2m 110y, Chel, Gd, Mar 13)
Overturn (IRE) 163 2 (2m 110y, Chel, Gd, Mar 13)
Pantxoa (FR) 133 2 (2m 5f, Kemp, Gd, Mar 17)
Pateese (FR) 134 1 (2m 110y, Sand, Sft, Nov 5)
Peckhamecho (IRE) 132 2 (2m, Asco, Sft, Dec 16)
Pittoni (IRE) 135 3 (2m, Punc, Sft, Nov 20)
Poungach (FR) 141 1 (2m 6f, Sand, GS, Dec 3)
Premier Grand Cru (FR) 134 1 (2m 4f, Live, Gd, May 6)
Prospect Wells (FR) 144 5 (2m 110y, Chel, Gd, Mar 13)
Raya Star (IRE) 135 1 (2m, Ayr, Gd, Apr 21)
Reindeer Dippin 136 1 (3m, Hayd, Hvy, Jan 21)
Restless Harry 147 3 (3m 1f, Asco, Sft, Dec 17)
Rick (FR) 134 6 (3m, Chel, Gd, Mar 15)
Ringaroses 132 4 (3m 110y, Live, GS, Apr 12)
Rivage D'Or (FR) 137 2 (3m, Punc, Gd, May 5)
Rock On Ruby (IRE) 167 1 (2m 110y, Chel, Gd, Mar 13)
Russian War (IRE) 135 9 (3m, Chel, Gd, Mar 15)
Sa Suffit (FR) 135 2 (3m, Hayd, Hvy, Feb 18)
Sanctuaire (FR) 147 8 (2m 110y, Chel, GS, Nov 13)
Shot From The Hip (GER) 144 1 (2m, Punc, Yld, May 3)
Silverhand (IRE) 134 4 (2m 5f, Chel, Gd, Mar 14)
Simonsig 155 1 (2m 5f, Chel, Gd, Mar 14)
Sire De Grugy (FR) 142 8 (2m 110y, Live, Gd, Apr 14)
Smad Place (FR) 152 3 (3m, Chel, Gd, Mar 15)
Son Of Flicka 135 1 (2m 5f, Chel, Gd, Mar 14)
Sous Les Cieux (FR) 136 1 (2m, Fair, Hvy, Dec 4)
Staying Article (IRE) 142 3 (2m, Leop, Yld, Jan 28)
Stonemaster (IRE) 131 6 (2m 5f, Chel, Gd, Mar 14)
Street Entertainer (IRE) 137 3 (2m 1f, Mark, GS, Jul 16)
Sunnyhillboy (IRE) 137 3 (3m, Hayd, GS, Nov 19)
Sweet My Lord (FR) 139 4 (2m, Leop, Yld, Jan 28)
Synchronised (IRE) 147 3 (3m, Hayd, GS, Nov 19)
Tamarinbleu (FR) 133 3 (3m, Hayd, Hvy, Feb 18)
Tetlami (IRE) 132 9 (2m 110y, Chel, Gd, Mar 14)
The Real Article (IRE) 140 1 (2m, Tipp, Sft, Oct 2)
Third Intention (IRE) 139 7 (2m 110y, Chel, GS, Nov 13)
Thousand Stars (FR) 149 4 (3m, Chel, Gd, Mar 15)
Toner D'oudairies (FR) 133 2 (2m 4f 110y, Chel, Gd, Mar 16)
Trifolium (FR) 146 3 (2m 110y, Chel, Gd, Mar 13)
Ubi Ace 146 2 (2m, Muss, GS, Feb 11)
Unaccompanied (IRE) 141 1 (2m, Leop, Sft, Dec 29)
Une Artiste (FR) 132 1 (2m 110y, Chel, Gd, Mar 14)
Veiled 132 3 (2m 5f, Chel, Gd, Mar 14)
Vendor (FR) 132 1 (2m 110y, Chel, Gd, Mar 14)
Via Galilei (IRE) 138 6 (2m 110y, Chel, GS, Nov 13)
Viva Colonia (IRE) 136 5 (2m 110y, Chel, GS, Nov 13)
Voler La Vedette (IRE) 152 2 (2m 110y, Chel, Gd, Mar 15)
Wyse Hill Teabags 135 2 (2m 4f, Hayd, GS, Nov 19)
Zaidpour (FR) 152 8 (2m 110y, Chel, Gd, Mar 13)
Zarkandar (IRE) 159 5 (2m 110y, Chel, Gd, Mar 13)

TOPSPEED LEADING HURDLERS (RATED 130 AND OVER)

*KEY: Horse name, Best RPR figure, Finishing position when
earning figure, (details of race where figure was earned)*

Abergavenny 133 3 (2m 110y, Chel, GS, Nov 13)
Across The Bay (IRE) 137 4 (3m, Hayd, GS, Nov 19)
Allure Of Illusion (IRE) 136 6 (2m 110y, Chel, Gd, Mar 13)
American Spin 132 2 (3m 110y, Live, GS, Apr 12)
Any Given Day (IRE) 155 1 (2m 4f, Hayd, GS, Nov 19)
Arnaud (IRE) 132 5 (2m 110y, Chel, Gd, Mar 14)
Attaglance 138 1 (2m 3f, Mark, GS, Feb 19)
Barbatos (FR) 132 1 (2m 4f 110y, Chel, GS, Jan 1)
Batonnier (FR) 132 1 (2m 4f 110y, Chel, GS, Jan 28)
Bear's Affair (IRE) 140 1 (2m 5f, Kemp, Gd, Mar 17)
Benny Be Good 144 2 (3m, Hayd, GS, Nov 19)
Big Buck's (FR) 161 1 (3m, Chel, Gd, Mar 15)
Binocular (FR) 160 4 (2m 110y, Chel, Gd, Mar 13)
Boston Bob (IRE) 132 2 (3m, Chel, Gd, Mar 16)
Brampour (IRE) 155 1 (2m 110y, Chel, GS, Nov 13)
Brindisi Breeze (IRE) 142 1 (3m, Hayd, Hvy, Feb 18)
Broadbackbob (IRE) 136 2 (2m 4f 110y, Chel, GS, Jan 28)
Cantlow (IRE) 143 3 (3m, Chel, Gd, Mar 15)
Cape Tribulation 153 1 (3m 110y, Live, GS, Apr 12)
Captain Cee Bee (IRE) 134 8 (2m, Galw, Gd, Jul 28)
Catch Me (GER) 145 2 (3m, Chel, Gd, Mar 15)
Celestial Halo (IRE) 147 1 (2m, Hayd, Hvy, Jan 21)
Ciceron (IRE) 136 1 (2m 110y, Sand, Sft, Jan 7)
Cinders And Ashes 149 1 (2m 110y, Chel, Gd, Mar 13)
Clerk's Choice (IRE) 136 3 (2m, Ayr, Gd, Apr 21)
Close House 135 4 (2m 5f, Chel, Gd, Mar 14)
Cockney Trucker (IRE) 137 5 (2m 5f, Chel, Gd, Mar 14)
Conquisto 134 2 (2m 110y, Live, Gd, Apr 14)
Countrywide Flame 134 2 (2m 110y, Live, GS, Apr 12)
Cross Kennon (IRE) 140 2 (3m, Hayd, Hvy, Feb 18)
Darlan 147 2 (2m 110y, Chel, Gd, Mar 13)
Dee Ee Williams (IRE) 140 5 (2m 110y, Live, Gd, Apr 14)
Deireadh Re (IRE) 133 5 (3m 110y, Live, GS, Apr 12)
Desert Cry (IRE) 137 1 (2m, Hayd, Gd, Nov 18)
Distant Memories (IRE) 133 8 (2m 110y, Chel, Gd, Mar 13)
Donnas Palm (IRE) 136 3 (2m, Tipp, Sft, Oct 2)
Dontpaytheferryman (USA) 131 3 (2m, Muss, GS, Feb 11)
Dream Esteem 141 4 (2m 110y, Live, Gd, Apr 14)
Dynaste (FR) 148 1 (3m, Hayd, GS, Nov 19)
Edeymi (IRE) 138 2 (2m 110y, Chel, Gd, Mar 14)
Edgardo Sol (FR) 137 1 (2m 110y, Chel, GS, Nov 12)
Empire Levant (USA) 137 2 (2m 110y, Newb, GS, Nov 26)
Enfant De Lune (FR) 134 2 (2m 4f, Ayr, Gd, Apr 21)
Featherbed Lane (IRE) 143 1 (?m 4f, Live, Sft, Dec 3)
Felix Yonger (IRE) 149 2 (2m 5f, Chel, Gd, Mar 14)
First Fandango 134 4 (2m 110y, Newb, GS, Nov 26)
Five Dream (FR) 148 2 (3m 1f, Asco, Sft, Dec 17)
Fosters Cross (IRE) 139 3 (2m 1f, Kill, Yld, May 15)
Galaxy Rock (IRE) 131 3 (3m, Bang, Gd, Mar 24)
Galileo's Choice (IRE) 135 7 (2m 110y, Chel, Gd, Mar 13)
General Miller 139 2 (2m 110y, Pert, Gd, Aug 20)
Get Me Out Of Here (IRE) 152 2 (2m 5f, Chel, Gd, Mar 14)
Gibb River (IRE) 144 3 (2m 110y, Live, Gd, Apr 14)
Golden Call (IRE) 137 1 (3m, Bang, Gd, Mar 24)
Grand Vision (IRE) 132 1 (3m, Hayd, Hvy, Feb 18)
Grandads Horse 137 1 (2m 4f, Hayd, Gd, Apr 7)
Grandouet (FR) 158 1 (2m 1f, Chel, Gd, Dec 10)
Grumeti 135 1 (2m 110y, Live, GS, Apr 12)
Harry Topper 132 2 (3m, Hayd, Hvy, Feb 18)
Havingotascoobydo (IRE) 138 2 (2m 110y, Sand, Sft, Jan 7)
Hidden Universe (IRE) 136 1 (2m, Punc, Yld, May 3)
Houblon Des Obeaux (FR) 143 4 (3m, Chel, Gd, Mar 15)
Hurricane Fly (IRE) 161 3 (2m 110y, Chel, Gd, Mar 13)
Ingleby Spirit 135 4 (2m, Muss, GS, Feb 11)
Jack Cool (IRE) 132 (2m 110y, Chel, GS, Nov 13)
Kazlian (FR) 131 4 (2m 110y, Chel, Gd, Mar 14)

Kerb Appeal (IRE) 135 1 (3m, Punc, Gd, May 5)
Kid Cassidy (IRE) 135 1 (2m, Punc, Gd, May 6)
King Of The Night (GER) 145 1 (2m 5f, Kemp, Gd, Oct 31)
Kylenoe Fairy (IRE) 136 2 (2m 1f, Mark, GS, Jul 16)
Lifestyle 143 1 (2m 110y, Live, Gd, Apr 14)
Luska Lad (IRE) 136 2 (2m, Tipp, Sft, Oct 2)
Marsh Warbler 139 3 (2m, Hayd, Hvy, Jan 21)
Menorah (IRE) 147 4 (2m 1f, Chel, Gd, Dec 10)
Molotof (FR) 134 1 (2m, Asco, Sft, Dec 16)
Monksland (IRE) 139 3 (2m 5f, Chel, Gd, Mar 14)
Montbazon (FR) 145 4 (2m 110y, Chel, Gd, Mar 13)
Moon Dice (IRE) 146 4 (2m 110y, Chel, GS, Nov 13)
Nearby 131 (2m 110y, Chel, GS, Nov 13)
Now This Is It (IRE) 133 3 (2m 110y, Pert, Gd, Aug 20)
Olofi (FR) 133 2 (2m 110y, Chel, GS, Nov 13)
Oscar Nominee (IRE) 131 3 (2m 4f 110y, Chel, Gd, Mar 16)
Oscar Prairie (IRE) 138 3 (2m 5f, Kemp, Gd, Mar 17)
Oscar Whisky (IRE) 147 5 (3m, Chel, Gd, Mar 15)
Oscars Well (IRE) 157 6 (2m 110y, Chel, Gd, Mar 13)
Overturn (IRE) 163 2 (2m 110y, Chel, Gd, Mar 13)
Pantxoa (FR) 133 2 (2m 5f, Kemp, Gd, Mar 17)
Pateese (FR) 134 1 (2m 110y, Sand, Sft, Nov 5)
Peckhamecho (IRE) 132 2 (2m, Asco, Sft, Dec 16)
Pittoni (IRE) 135 3 (2m, Punc, Sft, Nov 20)
Poungach (FR) 141 1 (2m 6f, Sand, GS, Dec 3)
Premier Grand Cru (FR) 134 1 (2m 4f, Live, Gd, May 6)
Prospect Wells (FR) 144 5 (2m 110y, Chel, Gd, Mar 13)
Raya Star (IRE) 135 1 (2m, Ayr, Gd, Apr 21)
Reindeer Dippin 136 1 (3m, Hayd, Hvy, Jan 21)
Restless Harry 147 3 (3m 1f, Asco, Sft, Dec 17)
Rick (FR) 134 6 (3m, Chel, Gd, Mar 15)
Ringaroses 132 4 (3m 110y, Live, GS, Apr 12)
Rivage D'or (FR) 137 2 (3m, Punc, Gd, May 5)
Rock On Ruby (IRE) 167 1 (2m 110y, Chel, Gd, Mar 13)
Russian War (IRE) 135 9 (3m, Chel, Gd, Mar 15)
Sa Suffit (FR) 135 2 (3m, Hayd, Hvy, Feb 18)
Sanctuaire (FR) 147 8 (2m 110y, Chel, GS, Nov 13)
Shot From The Hip (GER) 144 1 (2m, Punc, Yld, May 3)
Silverhand (IRE) 134 4 (2m 5f, Chel, Gd, Mar 14)
Simonsig 155 1 (2m 5f, Chel, Gd, Mar 14)
Sire De Grugy (FR) 142 8 (2m 110y, Live, Gd, Apr 14)
Smad Place (FR) 152 3 (3m, Chel, Gd, Mar 15)
Son Of Flicka 135 1 (2m 5f, Chel, Gd, Mar 14)
Sous Les Cieux (FR) 136 1 (2m, Fair, Hvy, Dec 4)
Staying Article (IRE) 142 3 (2m, Leop, Yld, Jan 28)
Stonemaster (IRE) 131 6 (2m 5f, Chel, Gd, Mar 14)
Street Entertainer (IRE) 137 3 (2m 1f, Mark, GS, Jul 16)
Sunnyhillboy (IRE) 134 7 (3m, Hayd, GS, Nov 19)
Sweet My Lord (FR) 139 4 (2m, Leop, Yld, Jan 28)
Synchronised (IRE) 147 3 (3m, Hayd, GS, Nov 19)
Tamarinbleu (FR) 135 3 (3m, Hayd, Hvy, Feb 18)
Tetlami (IRE) 132 9 (2m 110y, Chel, Gd, Mar 13)
The Real Article (IRE) 140 1 (2m, Tipp, Sft, Oct 2)
Third Intention (IRE) 137 (2m 110y, Chel, GS, Nov 13)
Thousand Stars (FR) 149 4 (3m, Chel, Gd, Mar 15)
Toner D'oudairies (FR) 133 2 (2m 4f 110y, Chel, Gd, Mar 16)
Trifolium (FR) 146 3 (2m 110y, Chel, Gd, Mar 13)
Ubi Ace 146 2 (2m, Muss, GS, Feb 11)
Unaccompanied (IRE) 141 1 (2m, Leop, Sft, Dec 29)
Une Artiste (FR) 134 1 (2m 110y, Chel, Gd, Mar 14)
Veiled 132 3 (2m 5f, Chel, Gd, Mar 14)
Vendor (FR) 132 3 (2m 110y, Chel, Gd, Mar 14)
Via Galilei (IRE) 138 6 (2m 110y, Chel, GS, Nov 13)
Viva Colonia (IRE) 136 5 (2m 110y, Chel, GS, Nov 13)
Voler La Vedette (IRE) 152 2 (3m, Chel, Gd, Mar 15)
Wyse Hill Teabags 135 2 (2m 4f, Hayd, GS, Nov 19)
Zaidpour (FR) 152 8 (2m 110y, Chel, Gd, Mar 13)
Zarkandar (IRE) 159 5 (2m 110y, Chel, Gd, Mar 13)

HOW TO ENTER

You can enter the competition by two methods:

1. Online at racingpost.com/ttf from mid-October until midnight on November 30, 2012.

2. In any Betfred betting shop using one of the Ten to Follow betting slips provided in the shop. Any player entering in a Betfred betting shop will be able to view their online standings from December 8, 2012.

Simply select ten horses from the list of 400 horses starting on page 105 to compete in the 2012-2013 Jumps Ten to Follow competition which runs from Friday, November 16, 2012 to Saturday, April 6 2013. The competition remains open until midnight on November 30, 2012. However, to stand the best chance of winning the life-changing prizes on offer in the season-long competition try to get your entries in before the first race on Friday, November 16, 2012.

PRIZE STRUCTURE

Overall prize

Entries to the competition will cost £5 each. There will be a guaranteed minimum dividend payout of £250,000 to the overall winner. All stake monies, will be aggregated and paid out in dividends after a 30 per cent deduction to cover administration costs. The remaining 70 per cent of all stakes will be divided as follows to the overall winners:

First	70 per cent
Second	10 per cent
Third	5 per cent
Fourth	4.5 per cent
Fifth	3 per cent
Sixth	2.5 per cent
Seventh	2 per cent
Eighth	1.5 per cent
Ninth	1 per cent
Tenth	0.5 per cent

In the event of a tie for any places, the dividend(s) for the places concerned will be shared.

POINT-SCORING

Selections winning jump races (under the rules of racing in Great Britain or Ireland) during the period of the competition will be awarded points as follows:

In a race worth £30,000 or more to the winner **25**

In a race worth £25,000 up to £29,999 to the winner **20**

In a race worth £15,000 up to £24,999 to the winner **15**

In a race worth £10,000 up to £14,999 to the winner **12**

In a race worth les than £10,000 to the winner **10**

Prize-money will be taken as the published racecard penalty value to the winner. For races in Ireland, prize money published in Euro will be converted to Sterling at the official conversion rate of €1.25 to £1 as of September 22, 2012. In the event of a dead-heat, points will be divided by the number of horses dead-heating with fractions rounded down. No points for a walkover. The official result on the day will be used for the calculation of points with any subsequent disqualifications disregarded.

BONUS RACES

An additional 25 points will be awarded to the winner and 12 points to the runner-up in each of the following races:

Paddy Power Gold Cup, Cheltenham, November 17, 2012

Hennessy Gold Cup, Newbury, December 1, 2012

International Hurdle, Cheltenham, December 15, 2012

King George VI Chase, Kempton, December 26, 2012

Irish Champion Hurdle, Leopardstown, January 27, 2013

Irish Hennessy Gold Cup, Leopardstown, February 10, 2013

Champion Hurdle, Cheltenham, March 12, 2013

Racing Post Arkle Challenge Trophy, Cheltenham, March 12, 2013

Queen Mother Champion Chase, Cheltenham, March 13, 2013

RSA Chase, Cheltenham, March 13, 2013

World Hurdle, Cheltenham, March 14, 2013

Ryanair Chase, Cheltenham, March 14, 2013

Cheltenham Gold Cup, Cheltenham, March 15, 2013

Aintree Hurdle, Aintree, April 6, 2013

Grand National, Aintree, April 6, 2013

Any of the above races which take place outside the dates of the competition will not be included in the competition.

TEN TO FOLLOW
JUMPS RACING 2012/13

BONUS POINTS

Bonus points will be awarded according to the official Tote win and Tote place dividend odds, including a £1 unit stake, as follows:

Win dividend – straight conversion from £s to points. For example for a £9.40 win dividend the horse is awarded 9.40 points, £15.30 is awarded 15.30 points etc.

Horses who finished placed receive no race points (unless second in one of the bonus races listed), but will receive the place dividend declared by the Tote. This will be on the same criteria as above – i.e. £7.20 equates to 7.2 points.

The maximum points conversion will be capped at 50 for any one horse in any race. If no Tote Win dividend is declared, the starting price will determine any bonus points. Should neither a Tote win dividend nor a starting price be returned, bonus points will not apply.

STAR HORSES

Players nominate one horse to be their 'Star Horse' in each entry. This horse scores double points on the bonus points system, detailed above, for a win or place in any race. For example a horse wins and returns the following dividend:

Win £6.20. As the horse is the 'Star Horse' the return will be doubled for a total combined return of 12.4 points.

The maximum points conversion will be capped at 50 for any one horse in any race.

MINI-LEAGUES

Ten to Follow players will be able to enter separate public and private TTF mini-leagues. You can only enter one stable per mini-league. Entry to mini-leagues and the ability to create a mini-league ends at midnight on Friday, November 30, 2012.

TERMS AND CONDITIONS

1. You must be aged 18 or over to enter and may be required to provide proof of age before receiving payment of any winnings.

2. Entries are accepted subject to independent age verification checks and by placing an entry you authorise Totepool to undertake any such age verification as may be required to confirm that you are aged 18 or over. If age cannot be verified the entry will be void.

3. The Tote Ten to Follow competition is operated by Totepool whose Head Office is: Westgate House, Chapel Lane, Wigan, WN3 4HS.

4. Selections cannot be changed or cancelled after an entry has been placed.

5. Members of staff (or their immediate families) of Totepool, Betfred, Grand Parade, Gaming Media Solutions, Centurycomm or any other commercial partner are not eligible to enter.

6. The names of winning/leading stables will be published on the game site. Any disagreement with the published list must be made in writing and received within five days of the publication date at: Tote Ten to Follow, PO Box 116, Wigan WN3 4WW OR by email at: tentofollow@betfred.com Claims received after the five-day period or telephone enquiries will not be considered.

7. Totepool reserves the right to refuse to accept or disqualify any entries which, in its sole opinion, do not comply with any of the information stated herein. In all cases the decision of Totepool is final.

8. Totepool reserves the right to change any stable or mini-league names which are inappropriate or offensive. In all cases the decision of Totepool is final.

9. Once accepted, entries are non-refundable.

10. All online winners will be paid out by cheque no later than 5pm on Friday, April 12, 2013.

11. Any customer who has entered via a BetFred shop must contact customer services quoting their unique bet ID to arrange for a cheque to be dispatched. By phone: 0800 666 160. By Post, Ten to Follow Jumps winner, PO Box 116, Wigan, WN3 4WW. By email: tentofollow@betfred.com

12. To enter the competition online you must sign up for a totepool.com account. If you have previously been restricted to play online at totepool.com then you will not be eligible to play the Ten to Follow Competition.

13. Retail entrants to the competition will be able to view their online standings from December 8, 2012.

14. If you place an entry from outside of the UK it is your responsibility to ensure that you comply with any laws applicable to betting in the country in which you are located when the bet is placed. Any entries taken in error from such territories will be made void.

15. It is your responsibility to ensure your credit or debit card issuer allowed to be used for gambling purposes.

16. Mini-leagues: there are no official prizes associated with public or private mini-leagues. Should a third party offer a prize in return for winning a mini-league then Totepool accepts no responsibility for fulfilment of the prize on offer.

17. Totepool/Betfred betting rules apply to any point not covered above.

18. In all cases the Tote's decision is final.

Reading the Ten to Follow profiles Each of the 400 profiles listed on the following pages contains the number to put on your entry form; age, colour, sex, sire, dam and dam's sire; trainer; career form figures to September 15, 2012; owner; current Racing Post rating; details of career wins; summary of achievements and, where known, possible running plans

1000 Ackertac (Ire)
7 ch g Anshan - Clonsingle Native (Be My Native)
Nigel Twiston-Davies   Mark Aspey & Steve Catton

PLACINGS: 22/115B0260/P23325P-   **RPR 140+c**

Starts	1st	2nd	3rd	4th	Win & Pl
20	3	5	2	-	£21,815
	10/10	Uttx	2m6¹/₂f Cls4 Nov Hdl good		£2,212
	9/10	Uttx	2m4¹/₂f Cls4 Nov Hdl good		£2,212
	11/09	Ludl	2m Cls5 Mdn NHF 4-6yo soft		£2,602

Without a win since novice hurdles in late 2010 but showed progressive form over fences last season and ran well to finish fifth to Hunt Ball in novice handicap chase at Cheltenham Festival; should have opportunities in novice and handicap races.

1001 Ad Idem
8 b g Kayf Tara - Major Hoolihan (Soldier Rose)
Pauline Gavin (Ir)   Mrs A F Mee

PLACINGS: 342126/F2122/P22800-   **RPR 156+c**

Starts	1st	2nd	3rd	4th	Win & Pl
18	2	8	1	1	£68,270
	1/11	Navn	2m6f Ch soft		£9,517
	2/10	Thur	2m6f Mdn Hdl soft		£4,580

Promising novice chaser two seasons ago and began last campaign in good form, just losing to Groody Hill in good handicap chase at Navan; not beaten far at Leopardstown next time but then went off the boil; capable of landing a big prize if back to form.

1002 Aerial (Fr)
6 b g Turgeon - Fille Formidable (Trempolino)
Paul Nicholls   Tony Hayward & Barry Fulton

PLACINGS: 3223/315F4712/41412-   **RPR 159c**

Starts	1st	2nd	3rd	4th	Win & Pl
20	4	4	4	3	£157,297
149	3/12	Newb	2m4f Cls1 Gd3 132-158 Ch Hcap good	£22,780
	12/11	Asct	2m5¹/₂f Cls2 Ch soft		£15,698
126	2/11	Winc	2m5f Cls3 108-126 Ch Hcap gd-sft	£6,505
	6/10	Autl	2m2¹/₂f Ch 4yo v soft		£21,239

Steadily worked his way up the handicap last season with a string of solid performances at around 2m4f, gaining biggest win by a short head in Grade 3 at Newbury; young enough to make further progress, though set to start this season on 11lb higher mark.

1003 Al Ferof (Fr) (above)
7 gr g Dom Alco - Maralta (Altayan)
Paul Nicholls   J Hales

PLACINGS: F13112/F3111/11343-   **RPR 163c**

Starts	1st	2nd	3rd	4th	Win & Pl
14	7	1	4	1	£160,174
	12/11	Sand	2m Cls1 Nov Gd1 Ch gd-sft		£20,787
	11/11	Chel	2m Cls1 Nov Gd2 Ch gd sft		£13,668
	3/11	Chel	2m Cls1 Nov Gd1 Hdl good		£57,010
	2/11	Newb	2m¹/₂f Cls3 Nov Hdl gd-sft		£5,204
	1/11	Tntn	2m3¹/₂f Cls4 Nov Hdl 4-7yo gd-sft		£3,426
	2/10	Newb	2m¹/₂f Cls1 Gd2 NHF 4-6yo gd-sft		£10,832
	12/09	Fair	2m NHF 4yo heavy		£6,038

Supreme Novices' Hurdle winner in 2011 who

made excellent start to chasing career last season before disappointing at Cheltenham and Aintree; produced best efforts over 2m but seems likely to want further and even looked outpaced over 2m4f on final start.

1004 Albertas Run (Ire)

11 b g Accordion - Holly Grove Lass (Le Moss)

Jonjo O'Neill   Trevor Hemmings

PLACINGS: 3/P136211/4FP12/123-   RPR **169**c

Starts	1st	2nd	3rd	4th	Win & Pl
35	15	5	5	3	£908,584
168	10/11 Aint	2m4f Cls1 Gd2 158-178 Ch Hcap good			£28,475
	3/11 Chel	2m5f Cls1 Gd1 Ch good			£154,896
	4/10 Aint	2m4f Cls1 Gd1 Ch good			£99,768
	3/10 Chel	2m5f Cls1 Gd1 Ch good			£142,525
	11/09 Asct	2m3f Cls1 Gd2 Ch good			£31,356
	3/08 Chel	3m¹/₂f Cls1 Gd1 Ch gd-sft			£96,934
	2/08 Asct	3m Cls1 Nov Gd2 Ch good			£22,536
	11/07 Chel	3m¹/₂f Cls2 Nov Ch good			£12,700
	10/07 Towc	2m¹/₂f Cls4 Ch good			£3,578
128	4/07 Aint	3m¹/₂f Cls1 List 128-150 Hdl Hcap good			£28,510
115	3/07 Sand	2m4f Cls1 Nov Gd3 106-132 Hdl 4-7yo Hcap heavy			£34,212
107	1/07 Hntg	2m5¹/₂f Cls4 97-115 Hdl Hcap soft			£3,253
	10/06 Uttx	2m Cls4 Nov Hdl 4-6yo soft			£3,904
	1/06 Hayd	2m Cls6 NHF 4-6yo soft			£1,713
	11/05 Hayd	2m Cls6 NHF 4-6yo gd-sft			£1,932

Outstanding performer at around 2m4f in recent seasons, winning successive renewals of Ryanair Chase before being denied the hat-trick by half a length last season; had missed much of campaign with leg injury and below-par at Aintree on final start.

1005 Alderwood (Ire)

8 b g Alderbrook - Clamit Falls (Homo Sapien)

Thomas Mullins (Ir)   John P McManus

PLACINGS: 420036/41610120111-   RPR **148**h

Starts	1st	2nd	3rd	4th	Win & Pl
17	6	2	1	2	£135,429
	4/12 Punc	2m Nov Gd1 Hdl sft-hvy			£41,333
	4/12 Fair	2m Nov Gd2 Hdl gd-sft			£21,667
139	3/12 Chel	2m1f Cls1 Gd3 132-150 Hdl Hcap good			£39,865
123	8/11 Klny	2m6f 103-125 Hdl Hcap yld-sft			£12,888
116	7/11 Klny	2m1f 98-123 Hdl Hcap good			£8,625
	5/11 Klny	2m6f Mdn Hdl good			£4,759

Late developer who returned from a winter break to win three big races last spring, including the County Hurdle at Cheltenham; went on to Grade 1 glory at Punchestown when beating Trifolium, proving effectiveness in all conditions; set for novice chasing.

1006 Alfie Sherrin

9 b g Kayf Tara - Mandys Native (Be My Native)

Jonjo O'Neill   John P McManus

PLACINGS: /11/310/413P/PF7513-   RPR **142**c

Starts	1st	2nd	3rd	4th	Win & Pl
15	5	-	3	1	£84,493
129	3/12 Chel	3m¹/₂f Cls1 Gd3 129-155 Ch Hcap good			£42,713
	1/11 Weth	2m4¹/₂f Cls3 Nov Ch gd-sft			£3,332
132	2/10 Newb	3m¹/₂f Cls2 116-140 Hdl Hcap gd-sft			£10,019
	2/09 Font	2m6¹/₂f Cls4 Nov Hdl good			£2,927
	11/08 Chep	2m¹/₂f Cls6 NHF 4-6yo gd-sft			£1,370

Had badly lost his way until bouncing back to form last spring, winning 3m handicap chase at Cheltenham Festival and arguably running equally well when third in Irish National (may not have quite stayed 3m5f); could land more top handicaps.

1007 Alfie Spinner (Ire)

7 b g Afflora - Little Red Spider (Bustino)

Nick Williams   Alan Beard & Brian Beard

PLACINGS: /371145/4220/241235-   RPR **145**c

Starts	1st	2nd	3rd	4th	Win & Pl
19	3	5	2	4	£44,272
	12/11 Chep	3m Cls4 Ch heavy			£2,859
115	1/10 Newb	2m3f Cls2 115-133 Hdl Hcap soft			£10,408
	12/09 Extr	2m1f Cls4 Nov Hdl 4-6yo heavy			£3,903

Showed steady improvement over fences last season, finishing third in Reynoldstown Chase on penultimate start before good fifth in National Hunt Chase (best of those not ridden prominently); could win good races if progressing again.

1008 Allee Garde (Fr)

7 b g Kapgarde - Allee Du Port (Port Etienne)

Willie Mullins (Ir)   Doran Bros (London) Limited

PLACINGS: 20/223191/4133FP-   RPR **148**c

Starts	1st	2nd	3rd	4th	Win & Pl
14	3	3	3	1	£29,541
	12/11 Clon	2m4f Ch heavy			£4,759
	4/11 Gowr	3m Hdl good			£7,733
	2/11 DRoy	2m4f Mdn Hdl yld-sft			£3,103

Won well on his chasing debut over inadequate 2m4f last season before fair third in Grade 1 behind Last Instalment; well fancied for National Hunt Chase when stepped up to 4m but fell early and then pulled up in Irish National; should do well in staying handicaps.

1009 Allure Of Illusion (Ire)
6 ch g Captain Rio - Sixhills (Sabrehill)

Willie Mullins (Ir)   Mrs S Ricci

PLACINGS: 13/2162-   RPR **140**+h

Starts	1st	2nd	3rd	4th	Win & Pl
6	2	2	1	-	£20,874

2/12	Punc	2m4f Mdn Hdl 5-6yo heavy	£3,542
8/10	Klny	2m1f NHF 4yo yield	£4,580

Missed the first half of last season but soon proved a surprise package in the top novice hurdles, finishing sixth at 40-1 in the Supreme and chasing home Alderwood at Fairyhouse; seems to improve after just four runs over hurdles.

1010 Ambion Wood (Ire)
6 b g Oscar - Dorans Grove (Gildoran)

Victor Dartnall   O C R Wynne & Mrs S J Wynne

PLACINGS: 21/3212511-   RPR **153**+h

Starts	1st	2nd	3rd	4th	Win & Pl
9	4	3	1	-	£48,060

4/12	Prth	3m¹/₂f Cls2 Nov Hdl soft	£7,798
132 3/12	Sand	2m4f Cls1 Nov Gd3 120-132 Hdl 4-7yo Hcap gd-sft	£28,475
12/11	Chep	2m4f Cls4 Mdn Hdl heavy	£2,372
3/11	Uttx	2m Cls6 NHF 4-6yo gd-sft	£1,821

Highly progressive in novice hurdles last season and finished campaign with a wide-margin win at Perth; had previously defied top-weight in Grade 3 handicap hurdle at Sandown after running Cotton Mill to half a length at Warwick; set to go novice chasing.

1011 American Spin
8 ch g Groom Dancer - Sea Vixen (Machiavellian)

Luke Dace   G Collacott & Mrs Louise Dace

PLACINGS: 22123P2-1   RPR **143**+h

Starts	1st	2nd	3rd	4th	Win & Pl
8	2	4	1	-	£31,979

137 5/12	Hayd	3m Cls2 124-150 Hdl Hcap soft	£15,640
10/11	Font	3m3f Cls4 Nov Hdl soft	£2,274

Thorough stayer who stepped up on fair form in novice hurdles when granted a more strongly-run race in big-field handicaps, finishing second at Aintree at end of last season before winning at Haydock; should do even better on soft ground; good novice chase prospect.

1012 Any Given Day (Ire)
7 gr g Clodovil - Five Of Wands (Caerleon)

Donald McCain   T G Leslie

PLACINGS: 11232570/2142247/14-   RPR **159**h

Starts	1st	2nd	3rd	4th	Win & Pl
18	5	5	1	3	£85,521

155 11/11	Hayd	2m4f Cls2 129-155 Hdl Hcap gd-sft	£22,743
137 10/10	Chep	2m4f Cls1 List 122-148 Hdl Hcap soft	£17,103
7/09	MRas	2m1¹/₂f Cls4 Nov Hdl good	£4,554
6/09	Uttx	2m Cls4 Nov Hdl gd-fm	£3,253
5/09	Kels	2m2f Cls4 Nov Hdl good	£3,253

Developed into a smart hurdler from 2m to 3m two seasons ago, producing best efforts when second in valuable contests at Cheltenham, and won well over that trip at Haydock last season; injured after finishing fourth next time but reportedly fit again this summer.

1013 Apt Approach (Ire)
9 ch g Bob Back - Imminent Approach (Lord Americo)

Willie Mullins (Ir)   Greenstar Syndicate

PLACINGS: /1/2212/52/FU111386-   RPR **153**c

Starts	1st	2nd	3rd	4th	Win & Pl
18	6	4	1	-	£82,059

1/12	Thur	2m4f Gd2 Ch soft	£24,375
1/12	Tram	2m5f List Ch heavy	£16,250
11/11	Thur	3m Ch heavy	£6,841
12/09	Clon	2m1f Ch heavy	£5,702
3/09	Fair	2m Mdn Hdl heavy	£5,367
2/08	Gowr	2m1f NHF 5yo soft	£5,589

Sharply progressive in first half of last season, completing a hat-trick in Grade 2 race at Thurles (first or second all four starts at that course); failed to figure in three more competitive races and may find it hard to win unless found easier opportunities.

1014 Araldur (Fr)
8 ch g Spadoun - Aimessa (Tropular)

Alan King   David Sewell

PLACINGS: 6131114/522211/206P-   RPR **149**+c

Starts	1st	2nd	3rd	4th	Win & Pl
19	6	4	1	1	£56,245

3/11	Towc	2m Cls4 Nov Hdl good	£2,277
3/11	Kemp	2m5f Cls4 Nov Hdl good	£2,602
12/08	Sand	2m Cls1 Nov Gd2 Ch gd-sft	£22,804
11/08	Wwck	2m Cls3 Nov Ch 4yo soft	£8,996
112 11/08	Chep	2m1¹/₂f Cls4 105-113 Ch Hcap gd-sft	£3,903
7/08	Vitt	2m2f Ch 4-5yo good	£4,941

Won a Grade 2 novice chase in November 2008 but missed most of next two seasons through injury; returned to fences last season after showing fair form in novice hurdles but suffered jumping problems; on a good mark but unclear how much ability remains.

1015 Arvika Ligeonniere (Fr)
7 b g Arvico - Daraka (Akarad)

Willie Mullins (Ir)   Mrs S Ricci

PLACINGS: 2/41241/1   RPR **150**+c

Starts	1st	2nd	3rd	4th	Win & Pl
7	3	2	-	2	£46,376

5/12	Punc	2m4f Ch yield	£6,900
4/10	Punc	2m Nov Hdl good	£14,381
1/10	Fair	2m4f Mdn Hdl 4-6yo heavy	£6,727

Returned from more than two years out through injury to win well on chasing debut in May before being put away; had been a very smart novice hurdler in 2010, not quite staying 3m when fourth in Grade 1 at Cheltenham, and could go far over fences.

1016 As De Fer (Fr)

6 b g Passing Sale - Miss Hollywood (True Brave)

Anthony Honeyball · Midd Shire Racing

PLACINGS: 432P/1239113/1P0- · **RPR 151+c**

Starts	1st	2nd	3rd	4th	Win & Pl
14	4	2	3	1	£41,415

135	11/11	Ffos	3m Cls3 115-135 Ch Hcap soft.....................£5,507
122	2/11	Extr	2m3¹/₂f Cls3 111-130 Ch Hcap heavy...................£4,554
110	1/11	Ffos	2m5f Cls4 Nov 89-113 Ch Hcap gd-sft..............£3,253
	7/10	Claf	2m1f Hdl 4yo gd-sft....................£7,221

Looked a useful staying handicapper in the making when romping home at Ffos Las on his return last season for his third win in four starts in British chases; failed to stay 3m5f on heavy ground in Welsh National before disappointing over hurdles.

1017 Ashkazar (Fr)

8 b g Sadler's Wells - Asharna (Darshaan)

David Pipe · D A Johnson

PLACINGS: 69068711/48510/P701- · **RPR 148+c**

Starts	1st	2nd	3rd	4th	Win & Pl
27	9	1	-	3	£160,949

137	4/12	Chel	3m1¹/₂f Cls2 120-144 Ch Hcap soft..........£10,441
152	1/11	Chel	3m Cls2 129-152 Hdl Hcap gd-sft..........£9,393
	4/10	Sand	2m Cls1 List Hdl good..........£11,603
135	4/10	Chel	2m1f Cls4 110-135 Hdl Hcap good..........£8,454
	10/09	Strf	2m4f Cls4 Ch good..........£4,764
	2/09	Winc	2m Cls1 Gd2 Hdl soft..........£45,608
135	3/08	Sand	2m1¹/₂f Cls1 List 117-141 Hdl Hcap good..........£34,212
	2/08	Sand	2m¹/₂f Cls3 Nov Hdl 4yo soft..........£6,506
	12/07	Winc	2m Cls4 Nov Hdl 3yo gd-sft..........£3,083

Disappointing over hurdles last season (had been high-class at his best) but took advantage of much lower chase mark with smooth win in slowly-run race at Cheltenham; still potentially well handicapped over fences.

1018 Astracad (Fr)

6 br g Cadoudal - Astre Eria (Garde Royale)

Nigel Twiston-Davies · H R Mould

PLACINGS: 50/11318660/1321721- · **RPR 150c**

Starts	1st	2nd	3rd	4th	Win & Pl
19	6	3	2	-	£65,827

	4/12	Prth	2m Cls3 Nov Ch soft..........£5,991
138	12/11	Chel	2m¹/₂f Cls2 127-152 Ch Hcap good..........£15,640
	9/11	Prth	2m4¹/₂f Cls4 Nov Ch gd-sft..........£4,549
128	10/10	Chel	2m¹/₂f Cls3 111-131 Hdl Hcap good..........£6,262
110	5/10	Aint	2m4f Cls3 104-124 Hdl Hcap good..........£5,204
103	4/10	Hrfd	2m4f Cls4 90-106 Hdl Hcap good..........£2,992

Ran well against good novice chasers before making successful step up into handicap company to win by a head at Cheltenham; below best when 11-2 for Grand Annual Chase but easily beat all bar Edgardo Sol at Aintree; should still be improving.

1019 Attaglance (above, left)

6 b g Passing Glance - Our Ethel (Be My Chief)

Malcolm Jefferson · H Young, G Eifert & R Snyder

PLACINGS: 53/4741612/8135P111- · **RPR 152h**

Starts	1st	2nd	3rd	4th	Win & Pl
19	6	1	3	2	£71,716

144	4/12	Aint	2m4f Cls1 List 130-144 Hdl Hcap good..........£22,780
139	3/12	Chel	2m4¹/₂f Cls2 132-145 Cond Hdl Hcap good..........£28,152
130	2/12	MRas	2m3f Cls3 105-130 Hdl Hcap gd-sft..........£4,549
121	10/11	Carl	2m1f Cls3 104-123 Hdl Hcap gd-sft..........£4,549
	3/11	Hexm	2m1¹/₂f Cls4 Nov Hdl gd-sft..........£2,055
	11/10	MRas	2m3f Cls4 Nov Hdl gd-sft..........£2,740

Landed Cheltenham/Aintree double last season, getting up close home on both occasions having been pushed along to keep up; seems sure to stay 3m on that evidence; hit with 11lb rise for latest win but had been set for novice chases anyway.

1020 Auroras Encore (Ire)

10 b g Second Empire - Sama Veda (Rainbow Quest)

Sue Smith   Mrs Alicia Skene & W S Skene

PLACINGS: R4052F/1P50/06312-U0   RPR **156**c

Starts	1st	2nd	3rd	4th	Win & Pl
38	7	7	1	1	£173,014

134	4/12	Hayd	2m4f Cls2 124-144 Ch Hcap good	£32,490
139	5/10	Uttx	3m Cls1 List 132-150 Ch Hcap soft	£28,505
129	4/09	Ayr	3m1f Cls2 Nov 106-130 Ch Hcap good	£12,685
	3/09	Carl	2m Cls3 Nov Ch good	£6,337
	12/08	Sedg	2m4f Cls4 Ch soft	£4,436
129	4/08	Aint	2m4f Cls1 List 120-143 Hdl Hcap good	£34,206
	12/07	Sedg	2m5¹/₂f Cls4 Nov Hdl gd-sft	£2,928

Returned from long injury absence last January and soon bounced back to best form when easily winning at Haydock; proved stamina for extreme distances when just run out of Scottish National by Merigo subsequently; should remain a force in top handicaps.

1021 Baby Mix (Fr)

4 gr g Al Namix - Douchka (Fijar Tango)

Tom George   Gdm Partnership

PLACINGS: 5/1619-   RPR **139**+h

Starts	1st	2nd	3rd	4th	Win & Pl
5	2	-	-	-	£24,551

	2/12	Kemp	2m Cls1 Gd2 Hdl 4yo good	£12,073
	12/11	Chel	2m1f Cls2 Hdl 3yo good	£10,010

Won at 14-1 on his British debut after arriving from France last season and built on that promise when winning Grade 2 juvenile hurdle at Kempton; raced too keenly when fading into ninth in the Triumph Hurdle; capable of better and could make a fine chaser.

1022 Baile Anrai (Ire)

8 b g Norwich - Rose Ana (Roselier)

Ian Williams   Massive

PLACINGS: 61/44U212/2F11F01-   RPR **143**+c

Starts	1st	2nd	3rd	4th	Win & Pl
13	4	3	-	2	£23,427

	4/12	MRas	3m1f Cls3 Nov Ch soft	£7,148
	1/12	Leic	2m7¹/₂f Cls4 Nov Ch good	£5,198
	12/11	Towc	2m6f Cls5 Ch gd-sft	£1,949
	3/11	Folk	2m6¹/₂f Cls5 Mdn Hdl good	£1,918

Won three small-field novice chases last season and was running well falling three out when still in contention in the Reynoldstown Chase at Ascot; flopped in 3m handicap chase at Cheltenham Festival but still a potentially smart staying handicapper.

1023 Baily Green (Ire)

6 b g King's Theatre - Dream On Boys (Anshan)

Mouse Morris (Ir)   R A Scott

PLACINGS: 393F41/63435677-1111   RPR **142**+c

Starts	1st	2nd	3rd	4th	Win & Pl
18	5	-	4	2	£46,817

121	9/12	Klny	2m1f 108-134 Hdl Hcap yld-sft	£15,438
	7/12	Limk	2m3¹/₂f Nov Ch good	£10,063
	6/12	Rosc	2m Cls4 Nov Ch gd-sft	£7,188
	5/12	Rosc	2m Ch good	£4,600
	3/11	Cork	2m Mdn Hdl 3yo yield	£5,948

Not up to Grade 1 level when highly tried in novice chases last season but benefited from that experience to run up a hat-trick this summer in slightly lesser company; remains a novice and may now be able to hold his own in stronger races; prefers good ground.

1024 Balder Succes (Fr)

4 b g Goldneyev - Frija Eria (Kadalko)

Alan King   Masterson Holdings Limited

PLACINGS: 1111FU-   RPR **138+**h

Starts	1st	2nd	3rd	4th	Win & Pl
6	4	-	-	-	£41,067
	2/12	Asct	2m Cls2 Nov Hdl gd-sft		£10,010
	1/12	Asct	2m Cls3 Hdl 4yo gd-sft		£5,630
	1/12	Plum	2m Cls4 Nov Hdl heavy		£2,669
	10/11	Autl	2m2f Hdl 3yo v soft		£22,759

Notched hat-trick in impressive fashion last season, most notably when romping home at Ascot against older novices; expected to handle quicker ground but crashed out early when fancied at Cheltenham and Punchestown; could be well handicapped.

1025 Balgarry (Fr)

5 ch g Ballingarry - Marie De Motreff (Kendor)

David Pipe   Brocade Racing

PLACINGS: 2/1/17-   RPR **143+**h

Starts	1st	2nd	3rd	4th	Win & Pl
4	2	1	-	-	£32,167
129	3/12	Newb	2m¹/₂f Cls3 115-131 Hdl Hcap gd-sft		£6,256
	8/10	Claf	2m2f Hdl 3yo v soft		£16,142

Had winning form in France in 2010 but then off the track for 18 months before winning British debut at Newbury in March; fair seventh in Coral Cup when turned out again quickly, possibly not staying 2m5f; up again in handicap but full of potential.

1026 Ballabriggs (Ire)

11 b g Presenting - Papoose (Little Bighorn)

Donald McCain   Trevor Hemmings

PLACINGS: F212/0/3111/1121/46-   RPR **158**c

Starts	1st	2nd	3rd	4th	Win & Pl
24	7	7	1	1	£621,908
150	4/11	Aint	4m4f Cls1 Gd3 138-160 Ch Hcap good		£535,135
	1/11	Ayr	2m4f Cls4 Nov Hdl good		£2,602
	1/11	Winc	2m6f Cls4 Nov Hdl soft		£2,277
140	3/10	Chel	3m1¹/₂f Cls2 127-140 Am Ch Hcap good		£33,011
130	2/10	Ayr	3m1t Cls2 114-134 Ch Hcap good		£11,272
119	1/10	Catt	3m1¹/₂f Cls3 93-119 Ch Hcap soft		£5,855
	3/08	Bang	3m¹/₂f Cls4 Ch soft		£3,666

Brilliantly laid out to win 2011 Grand National and made a bold defence of his crown last season, finishing sixth off 10lb higher mark; likely to head to Aintree again but trainer has promised to run more often before then and has prolific record over fences.

1027 Ballyrock (Ire)

6 b g Milan - Ardent Love (Ardross)

Tim Vaughan   Pearn's Pharmacies Ltd

PLACINGS: 82/216/12P-   RPR **144**h

Starts	1st	2nd	3rd	4th	Win & Pl
4	1	1	-	-	£8,295
	12/11	Hrfd	2m4f Cls5 Mdn Hdl soft		£1,884

Second in last season's Challow Hurdle on second

run over hurdles (flattered to finish close to Fingal Bay but beat rest easily); flopped on quicker ground at Aintree, though he has won a point-to-point on good to firm; should make mark over fences.

1028 Balthazar King (Ire)

8 b g King's Theatre - Afdala (Hernando)

Philip Hobbs   The Brushmakers

PLACINGS: F06/1142511P/15P001-   RPR **145**c

Starts	1st	2nd	3rd	4th	Win & Pl
33	9	6	1	4	£89,703
139	3/12	Chel	3m7f Cls2 130-156 Ch Hcap gd-fm		£25,024
136	10/11	Chel	3m1¹/₂f Cls2 124-150 Ch Hcap gd-fm		£15,698
	4/11	Chel	3m1¹/₂f Cls2 Nov Ch good		£9,480
	3/11	Hrfd	3m1¹/₂f Cls4 Nov Ch gd-sft		£3,253
	10/10	Chep	3m Cls3 Nov Ch gd-sft		£5,204
	9/10	Worc	2m7f Cls4 Ch good		£3,253
	10/09	Kemp	2m5f Cls4 Nov Hdl gd-fm		£3,253
	10/09	Ffos	2m4f Cls4 Mdn Hdl good		£3,253
	11/08	Plum	2m2f Cls6 Mdn NHF 4-6yo gd-sft		£1,713

Lost his way early last season after comeback win but relished switch to cross-country racing when winning at Cheltenham and successfully recovered from subsequent heart trouble; could flourish in that sphere and may have more to offer in top staying handicaps.

1029 Barbatos (Fr)

6 gr g Martaline - Peace Bay (Alamo Bay)

Ian Williams   Power Panels Electrical Systems Ltd

PLACINGS: 35552/1231-   RPR **141+**h

Starts	1st	2nd	3rd	4th	Win & Pl
9	3	2	2	-	£25,884
	1/12	Chel	2m4¹/₂f Cls3 Nov Hdl gd-sft		£6,256
	10/11	Aint	2m4f Cls4 Nov Hdl 4-6yo good		£3,899

Placed behind Spirit Son in a Listed hurdle in France in 2010 but slow to come to hand in Britain until blossoming midway through last season, winning good novice hurdle at Cheltenham from Grade 2 winner Batonnier; recovered from injury and may well progress again.

1030 Battle Group

7 b g Beat Hollow - Cantanta (Top Ville)

David Pipe   Jolly Boys Outing

PLACINGS: 344141/3092U20542-22   RPR **147**c

Starts	1st	2nd	3rd	4th	Win & Pl
31	6	7	2	6	£84,217
137	4/11	Aint	3m1¹/₂f Cls1 Gd3 130-148 Hdl Hcap good		£28,505
	2/11	Newc	2m6f Cls3 Nov Hdl heavy		£4,476
120	8/10	MRas	2m3f Cls3 105-128 Hdl Hcap good		£5,204
107	6/10	NAbb	2m1f Cls4 98-115 Hdl Hcap good		£3,383
	5/10	Strf	2m1¹/₂f Cls4 Nov Hdl good		£4,228
	7/09	Prth	2m1¹/₂f Cls5 NHF 4-6yo good		£2,055

Looked most unwilling when initially sent over fences last season but revitalised by first-time blinkers when fourth behind Hunt Ball at Cheltenham and only just beaten by Saint Are at Aintree; has enough ability to win good races if putting his mind to it.

1031 Becauseicouldntsee (Ire)

9 ch g Beneficial - Ath Dara (Duky)

Noel Glynn (Ir)   N F Glynn

PLACINGS: 15F42212/42F/63F22F-   **RPR 148c**

Starts	1st	2nd	3rd	4th	Win & Pl
17	2	6	1	2	£81,023
2/10	Fair	2m6½f Ch soft			£10,381
7/09	Klny	2m1f NHF 5-7yo gd-yld			£5,032

Yet to land the big race he has long threatened having chased home Sunnyhillboy in last season's Kim Muir at Cheltenham (also second in National Hunt Chase and Paddy Power Chase in 2010); fell early when fancied for last two runnings of the Grand National.

1032 Benefficient (Ire)

6 ch g Beneficial - Supreme Breda (Supreme Leader)

Tony Martin (Ir)   A Shiels & Niall Reilly

PLACINGS: 313/0U1P107-   **RPR 147h**

Starts	1st	2nd	3rd	4th	Win & Pl
8	2	-	1	-	£49,764
2/12	Leop	2m2f Nov Gd1 Hdl gd-sft			£43,333
12/11	Navn	2m4f Mdn Hdl heavy			£5,948

Surprise 50-1 winner of Grade 1 novice hurdle at Leopardstown in February when dictating a modest gallop and failed to follow it up at Cheltenham and Punchestown; still maturing and could do better over fences (already won a point-to-point) at around 3m.

1033 Benny Be Good

9 b g Benny The Dip - Hembane (Kenmare)

Keith Reveley   John Wade

PLACINGS: /6123U41/114224635P-   **RPR 161+c**

Starts	1st	2nd	3rd	4th	Win & Pl
24	7	4	4	3	£90,971
143	9/11	MRas	2m6½f Cls1 List 123-147 Ch Hcap good	£28,475
135	4/11	Sedg	2m4f Cls2 114-135 Ch Hcap gd-fm	£10,056
	4/11	Sedg	2m5f Cls4 Nov Ch gd-fm	£2,992
	11/10	Sedg	2m4f Cls4 Nov Ch gd-sft	£3,169
120	3/10	Hayd	2m4½f Cls2 112-133 Hdl Hcap soft	£9,758
	2/10	Sedg	2m4f Cls4 Nov Hdl heavy	£2,992
	11/09	Sedg	2m1f Cls6 NHF 4-6yo good	£1,301

Hit hard by handicapper for 20-1 win in Listed handicap chase at Market Rasen early last season and subsequently mixed hurdles and fences with moderate results; chase mark has fallen rapidly as a result and may prosper again on favoured quick ground.

1034 Berties Dream (Ire) (above)

9 b g Golden Tornado - Orla's Pride (Brush Aside)

Henry De Bromhead (Ir)   Half A Keg Syndicate

PLACINGS: F341/44566/P462151P-   **RPR 140+c**

Starts	1st	2nd	3rd	4th	Win & Pl
29	6	3	2	4	£115,168
	4/12	Thur	3m Hdl gd-fm	£6,900
	1/12	Thur	3m Ch heavy	£4,600
	3/10	Chel	3m Cls1 Nov Gd1 Hdl good	£57,010
	8/09	Gway	2m4f Hdl heavy	£13,273
	8/09	Slig	2m4f Nov Hdl soft	£7,715
90	7/09	Slig	2m4f 83-107 Hdl Hcap sft-hvy	£7,715

Has had limitations exposed since surprise win

in Albert Bartlett Hurdle at Cheltenham in 2010 but got back to winning ways last season with game front-running performances; equally effective over hurdles and fences and acts on extremes of going.

1035 Big Buck's (Fr)

9 b/br g Cadoudal - Buck'S (Le Glorieux)

Paul Nicholls   The Stewart Family

PLACINGS: 111/1111/1111/11111-   RPR **173**+h

Starts	1st	2nd	3rd	4th	Win & Pl
37	22	4	3	2	£1,275,332

4/12	Aint	3m¹/₂f Cls1 Gd1 Hdl gd-sft........................£56,736
3/12	Chel	3m Cls1 Gd1 Hdl good........................£148,070
1/12	Chel	3m Cls1 Gd2 Hdl gd-sft........................£28,475
12/11	Asct	3m1f Cls1 Gd1 Hdl soft........................£42,203
11/11	Newb	3m¹/₂f Cls1 Gd2 Hdl gd-sft........................£17,165
4/11	Aint	3m¹/₂f Cls1 Gd1 Hdl gd-sft........................£57,010
3/11	Chel	3m Cls1 Gd1 Hdl good........................£148,226
12/10	Newb	3m¹/₂f Cls1 Gd1 Hdl gd-sft........................£22,638
11/10	Newb	3m¹/₂f Cls1 Gd2 Hdl gd-sft........................£28,505
4/10	Aint	3m¹/₂f Cls1 Gd1 Hdl good........................£57,010
3/10	Chel	3m Cls1 Gd1 Hdl good........................£148,226
12/09	Newb	3m¹/₂f Cls1 Gd1 Hdl heavy........................£39,465
11/09	Newb	3m¹/₂f Cls1 Gd1 Hdl gd-sft........................£28,639
4/09	Aint	3m¹/₂f Cls1 Gd2 Hdl good........................£57,010
3/09	Chel	3m Cls1 Gd1 Hdl gd-sft........................£148,226
1/09	Chel	3m Cls1 Gd2 Hdl heavy........................£34,206
151	1/09	Chel	2m Cls2 126-152 Hdl Hcap gd-sft........................£15,655
4/08	Aint	3m1f Cls1 Nov Gd2 Ch good........................£45,608
1/08	Newb	2m1f Cls3 Nov Ch soft........................£6,506
12/07	Newb	2m1f Cls3 Ch soft........................£6,417
5/07	Autl	2m3¹/₂f Gd2 Hdl 4yo v soft........................£53,209
3/07	Autl	2m2f Hdl 4yo Hcap heavy........................£27,365

Outstanding staying hurdler who set new jumps record when landing 17th successive victory in winning at Aintree in April; had been as dominant as ever in staying hurdles all season, including when landing fourth World Hurdle crown at Cheltenham; reaching an age where he may be more vulnerable to improving youngsters, but is the one they all have to beat in his division and sure to be at the top of many Ten to Follow lists as usual.

1036 Big Zeb (Ire)

11 b g Oscar - Our Siveen (Deep Run)

Colm Murphy (Ir)   Patrick Joseph Redmond

PLACINGS: 1/21411/1122/111233-   RPR **167**+c

Starts	1st	2nd	3rd	4th	Win & Pl
31	13	10	3	1	£805,359

12/11	Leop	2m1f Gd1 Ch gd-yld........................£56,034
11/11	Navn	2m Gd2 Ch yld-sft........................£21,013
5/11	Punc	2m Gd1 Ch gd-yld........................£74,828
12/10	Leop	2m1f Gd1 Ch heavy........................£57,522
11/10	Navn	2m Gd2 Ch soft........................£24,159
3/10	Chel	2m Cls1 Gd1 Ch good........................£182,432
1/10	Punc	2m Gd2 Ch heavy........................£23,044
11/09	Navn	2m Gd2 Ch sft-hvy........................£28,442
4/09	Fair	2m Hdl good........................£15,801
12/08	Leop	2m1f Gd1 Ch yld-sft........................£47,794
4/08	Punc	2m Nov Gd1 Ch good........................£50,147
1/08	Fair	2m5¹/₂f Ch sft-hvy........................£7,875
3/07	Fair	2m Mdn Hdl sft-hvy........................£5,603

Won the Champion Chase in 2010 before finishing second to Sizing Europe the following year and beating that horse at Punchestown; not quite the same force last season but still landed soft Grade 1 at Leopardstown before twice finishing third against top two-milers.

1037 Billie Magern

8 b g Alderbrook - Outfield (Monksfield)

Nigel Twiston-Davies   Exors Of The Late Roger Nicholls

PLACINGS: /F111135028/15PP35F-   RPR **144**c

Starts	1st	2nd	3rd	4th	Win & Pl
34	9	4	4	-	£79,440

133	10/11	Chel	2m4f Cls2 125-143 Ch Hcap gd-fm........................£15,640
9/10	MRas	2m6¹/₂f Cls2 Nov Ch good........................£9,758
7/10	Prth	2m4¹/₂f Cls3 Nov Ch gd-fm........................£5,529
7/10	Prth	3m Cls4 Nov Ch good........................£4,753
6/10	Strf	2m7f Cls4 Nov Ch good........................£4,554
9/09	Prth	3m¹/₂f Cls4 Nov Hdl gd-fm........................£2,797
8/09	Strf	2m6¹/₂f Cls3 Nov Hdl gd-fm........................£6,337
7/09	Strf	2m6¹/₂f Cls4 Nov Hdl good........................£4,554
7/09	Worc	2m4f Cls4 Nov Hdl good........................£3,253

Has run vast majority of his recent races at Cheltenham (pulled up only two starts elsewhere last season); won good handicap chase last October and continued to run well in top races, including when fifth in Paddy Power Gold Cup and at Cheltenham Festival.

1038 Binocular (Fr)

8 b g Enrique - Bleu Ciel Et Blanc (Pistolet Bleu)

Nicky Henderson   John P McManus

PLACINGS: 113/5311/3114/32114-   RPR **170**+h

Starts	1st	2nd	3rd	4th	Win & Pl
20	11	2	4	2	£739,529

2/12	Winc	2m Cls1 Gd2 Hdl soft........................£34,170
12/11	Kemp	2m Cls1 Gd1 Hdl gd-sft........................£37,018
2/11	Sand	2m¹/₂f Cls1 List Hdl good........................£9,122
1/11	Kemp	2m Cls1 Gd1 Hdl gd-sft........................£42,758
3/10	Chel	2m Cls1 Gd1 Hdl gd-sft........................£210,937
2/10	Sand	2m¹/₂f Cls1 List Hdl soft........................£14,253
12/08	Asct	2m Cls1 Gd2 Hdl gd-sft........................£114,020
11/08	Hayd	2m¹/₂f Cls2 Hdl 4yo good........................£31,310
4/08	Aint	2m¹/₂f Cls1 Nov Gd1 Hdl 4yo good........................£74,113
2/08	Sand	2m Cls1 Nov Gd2 Hdl 4yo good........................£14,255
1/08	Asct	2m Cls3 Nov Hdl 4yo soft........................£6,576

Won what proved to be a moderate Champion Hurdle in 2010 and bounced back to similar level of form last season, doing best when touching off Rock On Ruby in Christmas Hurdle before fair fourth at Cheltenham; may well pick up one or two major 2m hurdles again.

1039 Bishopsfurze (Ire)

7 b g Broadway Flyer - Supreme Dipper (Supreme Leader)

Willie Mullins (Ir)   Mrs C M Hurley

PLACINGS: 171/15114/71F15-8   RPR **143**c

Starts	1st	2nd	3rd	4th	Win & Pl
14	7	-	-	1	£54,476

2/12	Clon	2m Ch soft........................£6,613
11/11	Thur	2m2f Ch heavy........................£7,138
2/11	Clon	2m6f Nov List Hdl sft-hvy........................£14,849
1/11	Thur	2m6f Nov Hdl soft........................£8,328
12/10	Cork	2m Mdn Hdl 4-5yo soft........................£4,673
4/10	Punc	2m NHF 4-7yo good........................£7,327
2/10	Fair	2m NHF 4-7yo heavy........................£4,580

Has a big reputation (sent off favourite on ten of first 12 starts) but finished no better than fourth in five starts at graded level; showed modest form in novice chases, gaining both wins by narrow margins, but could be better than handicap mark.

1040 Blackstairmountain (Ire)

7 b g Imperial Ballet - Sixhills (Sabrehill)

Willie Mullins (Ir)　　　　　　　　　Mrs S Ricci

PLACINGS: /11021/527/2611552-3　　　RPR **148**+c

Starts	1st	2nd	3rd	4th	Win & Pl
20	6	5	1	-	£170,761
12/11	Leop	2m1f Nov Gd1 Ch yld-sft			£47,629
12/11	Clon	2m1f Ch heavy			£4,759
4/10	Punc	2m Nov Gd1 Hdl good			£46,637
1/10	Punc	2m Mdn Hdl 5yo heavy			£6,421
6/09	Tipp	2m NHF 4yo good			£7,044
2/09	Thur	2m NHF 4yo sft-hvy			£5,032

Among the leading 2m novice chasers in Ireland last season, winning Grade 1 at Leopardstown over Christmas and chasing home Lucky William at Punchestown on final start, though thrashed by Sprinter Sacre at Cheltenham; looks on a fair handicap mark.

1041 Bless The Wings (Ire)

7 b g Winged Love - Silva Venture (Mandalus)

Alan King　　　　　　　　　　　　Mrs Lesley Field

PLACINGS: 644/2462/1210-5　　　　RPR **142**+c

Starts	1st	2nd	3rd	4th	Win & Pl
12	2	3		3	£23,839
130	1/12	Chel	2m5f Cls2 Nov 114-140 Ch Hcap gd-sft		£15,640
119	11/11	Extr	2m3¹/₂f Cls4 Nov 99-120 Ch Hcap gd-sft		£3,574

Fairly moderate over hurdles but always expected to do better over fences and ran exclusively in novice handicap chases last season to exploit low mark, gaining best win at Cheltenham; disappointed back there in March when possibly finding ground too quick.

1042 Bob Lingo (Ire)

10 b g Bob's Return - Pharlingo (Phardante)

Thomas Mullins (Ir)　　　　　　　John P McManus

PLACINGS: 27/PP0049870213-0511　　RPR **149**c

Starts	1st	2nd	3rd	4th	Win & Pl
32	6	4	4	3	£193,521
119	8/12	Klny	2m6f 109-137 Hdl Hcap soft		£12,458
139	8/12	Gway	2m6f 132-160 Ch Hcap soft		£100,333
130	4/12	Fair	2m1f 127-148 Ch Hcap soft		£40,625
	1/11	Fair	2m5¹/₂f Ch sft-hvy		£7,435
	10/08	Punc	2m Mdn Hdl sft-hvy		£5,081
	4/08	Punc	2m2f NHF 5-7yo good		£8,129

Disappointing for much of last season but started to come good when winning at Fairyhouse and maintained progress with fine win in Galway Plate; hit hard by handicapper but clearly talented.

1043 Bobs Worth (Ire)

7 b g Bob Back - Fashionista (King's Theatre)

Nicky Henderson　　　　The Not Afraid Partnership

PLACINGS: 21/1111/1321-　　　　　RPR **166**+c

Starts	1st	2nd	3rd	4th	Win & Pl
10	7	2	1	-	£179,485
3/12	Chel	3m¹/₂f Cls1 Gd1 Ch good			£74,035
11/11	Newb	2m4f Cls1 Nov Gd2 Ch good			£13,668
3/11	Chel	3m Cls1 Nov Gd1 Hdl good			£57,010
1/11	Chel	2m4¹/₂f Cls1 Nov Gd2 Hdl gd-sft			£14,253
1/11	Chel	2m4¹/₂f Cls3 Nov Hdl gd-sft			£6,262
11/10	Kemp	2m Cls4 Nov Hdl 4-6yo good			£2,602
4/10	Kemp	2m Cls6 NHF 4-6yo good			£1,370

Has won at Cheltenham Festival for last two seasons, maintaining unbeaten record over hurdles in 2011 and returning to claim RSA Chase last season; less convincing over fences before that but better going left-handed and may have benefited from wind operation.

1044 Bog Warrior (Ire)

8 b g Strategic Choice - Kilmac Princess (King's Ride)

Tony Martin (Ir)　　　　　Gigginstown House Stud

PLACINGS: 1F1/11F13-　　　　　　RPR **162**+c

Starts	1st	2nd	3rd	4th	Win & Pl
8	5		1	-	£74,097
2/12	Naas	2m Nov Ch sft-hvy			£9,488
12/11	Fair	2m Nov Gd1 Ch sft-hvy			£42,026
11/11	Navn	2m Ch yld-sft			£9,517
3/11	Cork	2m4f Mdn Hdl yield			£5,948
1/11	Fair	2m NHF 5-7yo sft-hvy			£5,056

Made a huge impression in first two starts over fences last season, beating Flemenstar before landing Drinmore Chase by 31 lengths; fell next time out and bitterly disappointing on final start; remains a fine prospect but may be reliant on soft ground.

1045 Bold Sir Brian (Ire)

6 b g Brian Boru - Black Queen (Bob Back)

Lucinda Russell　　　　　　　　　　A R Trotter

PLACINGS: 12/417/221114-　　　　RPR **152**+c

Starts	1st	2nd	3rd	4th	Win & Pl
11	5	3		2	£36,862
2/12	Muss	2m4f Cls3 Nov Ch gd-sft			£7,988
12/11	Kels	2m6¹/₂f Cls4 Nov Ch soft			£4,549
12/11	Hexm	2m¹/₂f Cls5 Ch heavy			£1,949
3/11	Kels	2m2f Cls1 Gd2 Hdl gd-sft			£17,103
12/09	Ayr	1m6f Cls5 NHF 3yo soft			£1,953

Very impressive when running up a hat-trick in novice chases last season before disappointing

fourth on handicap debut at Haydock, finishing very tired over 2m4f; has won over further but only in very slowly-run affair so expected to stick to shorter trips.

1046 Boston Bob (Ire)

7 b g Bob Back - Bavaway (Le Bavard)

Willie Mullins (Ir)   Graham Wylie

PLACINGS: 1/31/1112-   RPR **156+**h

Starts	1st	2nd	3rd	4th	Win & Pl
6	4	1	1	-	£92,200
	1/12	Leop	2m4f Nov Gd2 Hdl heavy................................£21,396
	12/11	Navn	2m4f Nov Gd1 Hdl sft-hvy...............................£39,224
	11/11	Navn	2m4f Mdn Hdl yld-sft.......................................£8,328
	3/11	Hexm	2m¹/₂f Cls5 Mdn NHF 4-6yo gd-sft.................£1,370

Showed high-class form in winning three novice hurdles last season, all in testing conditions; sent off 6-5 when stepped up to 3m at Cheltenham Festival but didn't travel smoothly on good ground, though saw out trip well to finish second; exciting chasing prospect.

1047 Bostons Angel (Ire)

8 b g Winged Love - Lady Boston (Mansonnien)

Jessica Harrington (Ir)   E A P Scouller

PLACINGS: /71311P/214111/U36P-   RPR **153**c

Starts	1st	2nd	3rd	4th	Win & Pl
20	8	2	3	1	£210,340
	3/11	Chel	3m¹/₂f Cls1 Gd3 Ch good................................£74,113
	2/11	Leop	2m5f Nov Gd1 Ch heavy................................£44,828
	12/10	Leop	3m Nov Gd1 Ch heavy...................................£43,142
	11/10	DRoy	2m4f Ch yld-sft...£7,633
	1/10	Donc	2m3¹/₂f Cls3 Nov Hdl 4-7yo gd-sft................£5,855
	1/10	Cork	2m2f Hdl soft..£9,173
	11/09	Navn	2m Mdn Hdl heavy.......................................£10,399
	3/09	DRoy	2m NHF 5-7yo yld-sft......................................£5,032

Leading novice chaser two seasons ago when completing a hat-trick of Grade 1 wins with gutsy success in RSA Chase; seemed to lose confidence last season after early jumping problems; plenty to prove but has fallen to good handicap mark if bouncing back to form.

1048 Bradley

8 ch g Karinga Bay - Good Taste (Handsome Sailor)

Fergal O'Brien   J C Collett

PLACINGS: 1/4F3111/12/521812-1   RPR **141**c

Starts	1st	2nd	3rd	4th	Win & Pl
9	4	3	-	1	£29,171
125	5/12	Chel	3m2¹/₂f Cls4 Am Hunt Ch soft..............................£4,679
	4/12	Hayd	3m4f Cls3 111-125 Ch Hcap good......................£7,148
	2/12	Sand	3m¹/₂f Cls3 Am Ch good...................................£5,428
	5/10	Chel	3m1¹/₂f Cls4 Am Hunt Ch good.........................£4,372

Showed fair form in hunter chases last season but did much better under professional handling when winning a handicap chase at Haydock and finishing second at Cheltenham; likely to stick to long-distance handicaps and should do well.

1049 Brampour (Ire)

5 b g Daylami - Brusca (Grindstone)

Paul Nicholls   Banks, Blackshaw & Gannon

PLACINGS: 3199/113077-   RPR **161**h

Starts	1st	2nd	3rd	4th	Win & Pl
10	3	-	2	-	£102,898
149	11/11	Chel	2m¹/₂f Cls1 Gd3 125-150 Hdl Hcap gd-sft...........£56,950
139	10/11	Asct	2m Cls1 List 128-150 Hdl Hcap good.................£28,135
	2/11	Tntn	2m1f Cls4 Mdn Hdl good £3,426

Struck up a terrific relationship with 7lb claimer Harry Derham last season, winning valuable handicap hurdles at Ascot and Cheltenham following successful breathing operation; had limitations exposed later, though still ran well in seventh in Champion Hurdle.

1050 Bridgets Pet (Ire)

5 ch g Arakan - Classy Act (Lycius)

Anthony Mullins (Ir)   Barry Connell

PLACINGS: U42113P132P-   RPR **144**h

Starts	1st	2nd	3rd	4th	Win & Pl
11	3	2	2	1	£29,130
	2/12	Naas	2m3f Mdn Hdl sft-hvy.....................................£5,750
	10/11	Gway	2m NHF 4-7yo heavy.......................................£6,543
	9/11	Dpat	2m2f NHF 4-7yo gd-yld...................................£4,164

Dual bumper winner early last season and swiftly made up into a useful novice hurdler, twice finishing fast to get placed in Grade 2 races over 2m4f; seems sure to improve over 3m despite being pulled up on only run at that trip on bad ground at Punchestown.

1051 Broadbackbob (Ire)

7 b g Broadway Flyer - Back Home (Bob Back)

Nicky Henderson   Anthony Speelman

PLACINGS: U32/64216/112-   RPR **148+**h

Starts	1st	2nd	3rd	4th	Win & Pl
7	3	1	-	1	£16,967
	12/11	Newb	2m3f Cls4 Nov Hdl 4-6yo soft............................£2,599
	11/11	Asct	2m Cls3 Hdl good...£6,882
	1/11	Catt	2m Cls6 Am NHF 4-6yo gd-sft...........................£1,370

66-1 sixth in Aintree bumper in 2011 when trained in Ireland and made bright start for new trainer when winning pair of novice hurdles last season; jumping frailties exposed when second at Cheltenham last time but remains a bright chasing prospect.

1052 Buckers Bridge (Ire)

6 b g Pelder - La Fiere Dame (Lafontaine)

Henry De Bromhead (Ir)   Ann & Alan Potts Partnership

PLACINGS: 111-   RPR **138+**b

Starts	1st	2nd	3rd	4th	Win & Pl
2	2	-	-	-	£10,925
	4/12	Punc	2m NHF 4-7yo good..£6,325
	3/12	Gowr	2m2f NHF 4-7yo soft......................................£4,600

Won his sole point-to-point last November and put stamina to good use when running away with his second bumper at Punchestown in heavy ground in April; trainer expects him to handle a quicker surface and could make a smart staying novice hurdler.

1053 Burton Port (Ire)

8 b g Bob Back - Depute (Be My Native)

Nicky Henderson   Trevor Hemmings

PLACINGS: 13342/1211121/2/242-   RPR **171+c**

Starts	1st	2nd	3rd	4th	Win & Pl
17	7	6	2	2	£262,636

4/10	Aint	3m1f Cls1 Nov Gd2 Ch good	£45,608
2/10	Asct	3m Cls1 Nov Gd2 Ch gd-sft	£16,899
2/10	Sthl	3m¹/₂f Cls3 Nov Ch soft	£7,806
12/09	Ling	3m Cls1 Nov Gd2 Ch heavy	£18,813
11/09	Bang	2m4¹/₂f Cls4 Ch soft	£4,228
1/09	Hrfd	2m1f Cls4 Nov Hdl soft	£2,927
12/08	Hrfd	2m1f Cls6 NHF 4-6yo soft	£1,691

Former RSA Chase and Hennessy Gold Cup runner-up who returned as good as ever from 15-month injury absence last season, finishing fourth in Gold Cup and second in Betfred Bowl; seems to just come up short at top level but should continue to threaten in good races.

1054 Calgary Bay (Ire)

9 b g Taipan - Dante's Thatch (Phardante)

Mick Channon   Mrs T P Radford

PLACINGS: /P0164/56242F/85110-   RPR **161c**

Starts	1st	2nd	3rd	4th	Win & Pl
29	5	9		3	£180,931

151	1/12	Donc	3m Cls1 List 126-151 Ch Hcap gd-sft	£42,713
145	1/12	Chel	2m5f Cls1 Gd3 141-167 Ch Hcap gd-sft	£22,780
142	12/09	Donc	3m Cls2 120-144 Ch Hcap good	£19,515
	1/09	Chel	2m5f Cls1 Nov Gd2 Ch gd-sft	£19,954
	12/07	Chel	2m1f Cls2 Nov Hdl 4-6yo good	£9,395

Belatedly started to fulfil promise of novice days (once a leading fancy for 2009 Arkle Trophy) when winning valuable handicaps at Cheltenham and Doncaster before finishing down the field in Grand National; sure to find things tougher off much higher mark.

1055 Call The Police (Ire)

9 b g Accordion - Evangelica (Dahar)

Willie Mullins (Ir)   Dd Racing Syndicate

PLACINGS: P/114/210/P1234-F   RPR **153+c**

Starts	1st	2nd	3rd	4th	Win & Pl
12	4	2	1	2	£71,773

11/11	Gowr	2m4f Cls6 Ch soft	£9,517
2/11	Punc	2m4f Hdl heavy	£8,625
11/09	Limk	2m Mdn Hdl heavy	£3,102
5/09	Clon	2m NHF 5-7yo heavy	£5,032

Did well when pitched into Grade 1 company after just one win over fences last season, chasing home Last Instalment at Leopardstown before fine third in RSA Chase; would have won good handicap chase at Punchestown but for final-fence fall; should improve.

1056 Cannington Brook (Ire)

8 b g Winged Love - Rosie Brook (Be My Native)

Colin Tizzard   Mrs Sara Biggins & Mrs Celia Djivanovic

PLACINGS: 1/2P213/3622/315185-   RPR **150+c**

Starts	1st	2nd	3rd	4th	Win & Pl
15	3	4	3	-	£52,466

135	2/12	Hayd	2m4f Cls3 Nov 115-135 Ch Hcap heavy	£8,123
128	12/11	Hayd	3m Cls2 119-145 Ch Hcap heavy	£19,494
	2/10	Ludl	3m Cls4 Mdn Hdl soft	£3,253

Twice won on heavy ground at Haydock last season but slightly disappointing when distant fifth in Welsh National in between and struggled after 15lb rise; copes with good ground (third in Grade 1 novice hurdle at Aintree in 2010) but needs stiff stamina test.

1057 Cantlow (Ire)

7 b g Kayf Tara - Winnowing (Strong Gale)

Paul Webber   R V Shaw

PLACINGS: 2412/40203-5   RPR **147h**

Starts	1st	2nd	3rd	4th	Win & Pl
9	1	2	1	2	£36,457

2/11	Ludl	3m Cls5 Mdn Hdl gd-sft	£2,277

Finished second in Grade 1 novice hurdle at Aintree in 2011 and belatedly built on that last season when close third in Pertemps Final at Cheltenham (winner followed up at Aintree); bred to be a better chaser.

1058 Caolaneoin (Ire)

6 b g King's Theatre - Queen Plaisir (Grand Plaisir)

Seamus Fahey (Ir)   Michael J Mulligan

PLACINGS: 21/021344-5   RPR **140h**

Starts	1st	2nd	3rd	4th	Win & Pl
9	2	2	1	2	£19,114

1/12	Fair	2m Mdn Hdl soft	£5,750
2/11	Leop	2m NHF 4-7yo heavy	£4,759

Won maiden hurdle at Fairyhouse last season before showing fair form in a couple of Grade 2 races and a handicap hurdle; only fifth on chasing debut at Killarney but hung badly on good ground (had flopped on only other start on similar surface).

1059 Cape Tribulation

8 b g Hernando - Gay Fantastic (Ela-Mana-Mou)

Malcolm Jefferson   J David Abell

PLACINGS: /2440/1P22/5P50411-0   RPR **158h**

Starts	1st	2nd	3rd	4th	Win & Pl
23	6	2	4	3	£133,230

150	4/12	Aint	3m¹/₂f Cls1 Gd3 130-150 Hdl Hcap gd-sft	£25,628
142	3/12	Chel	3m Cls1 List 137-157 Hdl Hcap good	£39,865
	10/10	Hexm	3m1f Cls3 Nov Ch soft	£6,337
	1/09	Donc	3m¹/₂f Cls1 Nov Gd2 Hdl soft	£17,850
	11/08	Uttx	2m4¹/₂f Cls4 Nov Hdl gd-sft	£3,903
	3/08	Uttx	2m Cls4 NHF 4-6yo gd-sft	£2,342
	3/08	MRas	2m1¹/₂f Cls6 NHF 4-6yo good	£1,370

Had become slightly disappointing over fences last

season but was revitalised by switch to hurdles and won staying handicaps at Cheltenham and Aintree in terrific fashion; remains on a terrific mark for chasing if managing to transfer improvement.

1060 Cappa Bleu (Ire)

10 b g Pistolet Bleu - Cappagale (Strong Gale)

Evan Williams   Mr & Mrs William Rucker

PLACINGS: F21/1111/3F2P/1334-   **RPR 152+c**

Starts	1st	2nd	3rd	4th	Win & Pl
9	2	1	3	1	£111,056
140	11/11	Hayd	3m Cls2 126-141 Ch Hcap gd-sft		£18,768
	3/09	Chel	3m2¹/₂f Cls2 Hunt Ch gd-sft		£24,008

Struggled to fulfil potential of 2009 Cheltenham Foxhunter win but benefited from return to point-to-point when back under rules last season; ran consistently well in top staying handicaps, including when fourth in Grand National; needs an extreme stamina test.

1061 Captain Chris (Ire)

8 b g King's Theatre - Function Dream (Strong Gale)

Philip Hobbs   Mrs Diana L Whateley

PLACINGS: 4111/222211/1U3P4-   **RPR 165c**

Starts	1st	2nd	3rd	4th	Win & Pl
15	6	4	1	2	£204,863
160	05/11	Pun	2m Nov Gd1 Ch Gd		£48,103
153	03/11	Chel	2m Nov Gd1 Ch Gd		£74,113
153	02/11	Kemp	2m4¹/₂f Nov Gd2 Ch gd-sft		£13,340
146	04/10	Chel	2m1f Cls2 Hdl Gd		£8,453
	3/10	Kemp	2m Cls4 Hdl Gd		£2,602
	3/10	Kemp	2m Cls4 Hdl Gd		£3,252

Patchy chasing record but talented on his day, as when winning Arkle Trophy in 2011 and finishing good fourth in Ryanair Chase last season; tends to jump to his right; likely type for King George (third after interrupted preparation last season).

1062 Captain Conan (Fr)

5 b g Kingsalsa - Lavandou (Sadler's Wells)

Nicky Henderson   Triermore Stud

PLACINGS: 3411622-   **RPR 150h**

Starts	1st	2nd	3rd	4th	Win & Pl
7	2	2	1	1	£60,425
1/12	Sand	2m¹/₂f Cls1 Gd1 Hdl soft			£17,286
6/11	Autl	2m2f Hdl 4yo v soft			£19,862

Strapping chasing type who was flattered to land the Tolworth Hurdle on his British debut with main rivals below best but showed more ability when putting two poor efforts behind him to chase home Darlan at Aintree; seems sure to go far over fences.

1063 Carlingford Lough (Ire)

6 b g King's Theatre - Baden (Furry Glen)

John Kiely (Ir)   John P McManus

PLACINGS: 711-6113   **RPR 148+h**

Starts	1st	2nd	3rd	4th	Win & Pl
7	4		1	-	£48,357
129	8/12	Gway	2m6f 114-142 Hdl Hcap sft-hvy		£21,667
119	7/12	Bell	2m4f 116-135 Hdl Hcap soft		£12,729
109	7/11	Gway	2m 95-116 Hdl Hcap good		£8,625
	7/11	Rosc	2m Mdn Hdl 4-5yo good		£4,461

Off the track for nearly a year after winning pair of hurdles last summer but soon made up for lost time with two wins in handicap company; balloted out of Galway Hurdle when favourite before winning lesser event at same meeting; seems very promising.

1064 Carlito Brigante (Ire)

6 b g Haafhd - Desert Magic (Green Desert)

Gordon Elliott (Ir) Gigginstown House Stud

PLACINGS: 011142/10214/35P-13 **RPR 138+c**

Starts		1st	2nd	3rd	4th	Win & Pl
16		6	2	2	2	£168,612
	5/12	Klny	2m6f Nov Ch good			£6,900
142	3/11	Chel	2m5f Cls1 Gd3 128-154 Hdl Hcap good			£39,907
	11/10	Hayd	2m Cls2 Hdl 4yo gd-sft			£25,048
	2/10	Muss	2m Cls2 Nov Hdl 4yo gd-sft			£18,786
	12/09	Leop	2m Gd2 Hdl 3yo yield			£31,602
	11/09	Muss	2m Cls4 Nov Hdl 3yo gd-sft			£3,253

Won the Coral Cup in 2011 having finished fourth in the Triumph Hurdle the previous year; failed to make a mark over hurdles last season (seemingly too high in handicap) but looked rejuvenated when winning on chasing debut in May; could do well over fences.

1065 Carrickboy (Ire)

8 b g Silver Patriarch - Alaskan Princess (Prince Rupert)

Venetia Williams Trevor Hemmings

PLACINGS: S11704/2U83/P1216PP- **RPR 146+c**

Starts		1st	2nd	3rd	4th	Win & Pl
19		4	3	2	1	£35,717
128	3/12	Hrfd	2m3f Cls3 108-134 Ch Hcap soft			£3,899
	1/12	Catt	2m3f Cls4 Ch gd-sft			£3,899
120	2/09	MRas	2m1½f Cls2 117-135 Hdl Hcap soft			£15,655
	2/09	Tntn	2m1f Cls4 Mdn Hdl heavy			£4,033

Took six runs to get off the mark over fences at Catterick before soon winning again at Hereford; good sixth behind Hunt Ball at Cheltenham Festival and back to same mark after being pulled up twice; can win good races if resuming upward curve.

1066 Carruthers (above, left)

9 b g Kayf Tara - Plaid Maid (Executive Perk)

Mark Bradstock The Oaksey Partnership

PLACINGS: 14/51242/6649/31P09- **RPR 153+c**

Starts		1st	2nd	3rd	4th	Win & Pl
24		7	5	1	3	£271,157
146	11/11	Newb	3m2½f Cls1 Gd3 142-168 Ch Hcap good			£85,425
	12/09	Newb	3m Cls2 Ch heavy			£19,515
	2/09	Asct	3m Cls1 Nov Gd2 Ch heavy			£23,240
	1/09	Fknm	3m½f Cls4 Ch good			£5,204
	2/08	Bang	3m Cls3 Nov Hdl soft			£6,181
	1/08	Wwck	2m5f Cls1 Nov Gd2 Hdl heavy			£22,808
	11/07	Chep	2m4f Cls4 Nov Hdl gd-sft			£2,407

Hugely popular front-running chaser who finally landed a major victory when landing an admittedly weak renewal of the Hennessy Gold Cup last season; badly out of sorts on all three subsequent starts but dropping back to a winnable mark once again.

1067 Cash And Go (Ire)

5 b g Sulamani - Calcida (Konigsstuhl)

Nicky Henderson David Monaghan

PLACINGS: 14/31115- **RPR 143h**

Starts		1st	2nd	3rd	4th	Win & Pl
7		4	-	1	1	£62,646
	12/11	Leop	2m Nov Gd1 Hdl gd-yld			£44,828
	11/11	Gowr	2m Nov Hdl 4yo soft			£7,733
	10/11	Wxfd	2m Mdn Hdl 4yo soft			£4,461
	2/11	Thur	2m NHF 4yo heavy			£4,164

Had excuses for sole defeat over hurdles last season when fifth behind Benefficient at Leopardstown (slightly lame and scoped badly); winning form not strong by Grade 1 standards but remains an exciting prospect and could be even better over fences.

1068 Catch Me (Ger)

10 b g Law Society - Calcida (Konigsstuhl)

Edward O'Grady (Ir)   John P McManus

PLACINGS: 43/3035F333/63752P-3   **RPR 151+h**

Starts	1st	2nd	3rd	4th	Win & Pl
35	9	2	9	2	£281,985

10/09	Cork	2m4f Nov Ch good	£14,537
2/09	Navn	2m5f Gd2 Hdl heavy	£36,342
12/08	Leop	3m Gd2 Hdl yield	£23,934
11/08	Fair	2m4f Gd1 Hdl soft	£43,015
11/08	Navn	2m4f Gd2 Hdl soft	£23,934
2/08	Gowr	2m Gd2 Hdl soft	£47,868
12/07	Fair	2m2f Hdl yld-sft	£11,876
11/06	Naas	2m Hdl 4yo yld-sft	£6,672
10/06	Naas	2m Mdn Hdl 4yo soft	£4,766

Former Grade 1 winner over hurdles who bounced back to form with a tremendous second in Pertemps Final at Cheltenham last season; disappointing in Irish National next time but could still be laid out for another tilt at a major spring handicap.

1069 Cause Of Causes (USA)

4 b g Dynaformer - Angel In My Heart (Rainbow Quest)

Gordon Elliott (Ir)   Timeform Betfair Racing Club Ltd

PLACINGS: F22-17126   **RPR 139+h**

Starts	1st	2nd	3rd	4th	Win & Pl
8	2	3	-	-	£54,352

7/12	Dpat	2m2f Hdl good	£5,750
5/12	Kbgn	2m3f Mdn Hdl 4yo good	£4,313

Ran a huge race for a horse of limited experience when beaten a head in the Galway Hurdle this summer; had only begun his hurdling career in February and remains eligible for novice hurdles having not won until May; should continue to win races.

1070 Celestial Halo (Ire)

8 b g Galileo - Pay The Bank (High Top)

Paul Nicholls   The Stewart Family

PLACINGS: 244F/F333218/131129-   **RPR 164h**

Starts	1st	2nd	3rd	4th	Win & Pl
26	8	7	4	2	£486,349

1/12	Hayd	2m Cls1 Gd2 Hdl heavy	£28,475
160	12/11	Newb	2m¹/₂f Cls2 134-160 Hdl Hcap soft	£31,280
160	11/11	Winc	2m Cls1 Gd2 140-160 Hdl Hcap gd-sft	£28,810
2/11	Font	2m4f Cls1 Gd2 Hdl soft	£18,528
165	11/09	Winc	2m Cls1 Gd2 145-165 Hdl Hcap gd-sft	£34,206
1/09	Sand	2m¹/₂f Cls1 List Hdl soft	£17,103
3/08	Chel	2m1f Cls1 Gd1 Hdl 4yo gd-sft	£68,424
12/07	Newb	2m¹/₂f Cls3 Nov Hdl 3yo soft	£6,506

Former Champion Hurdle runner-up who benefited from return to 2m last season when winning three times; producing best effort when defying big weight in competitive handicap hurdle

at Newbury, though may need more help from assessor to win again; out until new year.

1071 Champagne Fever (Ire)

5 gr g Stowaway - Forever Bubbles (Roselier)

Willie Mullins (Ir)   Mrs S Ricci

PLACINGS: 12111-   **RPR 142+b**

Starts	1st	2nd	3rd	4th	Win & Pl
4	4	-	-	-	£78,961

4/12	Punc	2m Gd1 NHF 4-7yo good	£40,625
3/12	Chel	2m¹/₂f Cls1 Gd1 NHF 4-6yo good	£31,323
1/12	Fair	2m NHF 4-7yo soft	£4,600

Top-class bumper performer last season, winning at Cheltenham and grinding out victory at Punchestown to prove effectiveness in all conditions; won a point-to-point last April and could go straight into novice chases; seems sure to stay well beyond 2m.

1072 Champion Court (Ire)

7 b g Court Cave - Mooneys Hill (Supreme Leader)

Martin Keighley   M Boothright

PLACINGS: 12194/U123122-   **RPR 161c**

Starts	1st	2nd	3rd	4th	Win & Pl
12	4	4	1	1	£85,221

1/12	Chel	2m5f Cls1 Nov Gd2 Ch gd-sft	£14,238
10/11	Aint	2m4f Cls3 Nov Ch good	£6,330
11/10	Chel	2m5f Cls1 Nov Gd2 Hdl gd-sft	£14,253
5/10	Kbgn	2m NHF 5yo yield	£4,274

Went from strength to strength in novice chases last season, landing best win in Grade 2 at Cheltenham before chasing home Sir Des Champs in Jewson Chase with high-class field well strung out behind; didn't seem quite as effective when twice stepped up to 3m.

1073 Chance Du Roy (Fr)

8 ch g Morespeed - La Chance Au Roy (Rex Magna)

Philip Hobbs   Miss I D Du Pre

PLACINGS: /94411/7313P/125412-   **RPR 155c**

Starts	1st	2nd	3rd	4th	Win & Pl
24	7	2	3	4	£95,068

143	3/12	Hayd	2m4f Cls2 119-145 Ch Hcap gd-sft	£12,996
137	11/11	Newb	2m4f Cls2 126-145 Ch Hcap good	£15,640
130	1/11	Chep	2m3¹/₂f Cls2 121-147 Ch Hcap soft	£10,408
121	4/10	Ludl	2m4f Cls3 102-120 Ch Hcap soft	£7,514
116	3/10	Chep	2m3¹/₂f Cls3 100-120 Ch Hcap good	£6,505
115	3/08	Extr	2m1f Cls4 105-115 Hdl Hcap soft	£4,229
12/07	Newb	2m¹/₂f Cls4 Nov Hdl 3yo gd-sft	£3,904

Steadily progressive throughout last two campaigns and went out on a high last season when winning at Haydock and only just outstayed in Topham Chase at Aintree; seems sure to head to Aintree again and could pick up further decent prizes.

1074 Cheltenian (Fr)

6 b g Astarabad - Salamaite (Mansonnien)

Philip Hobbs   R S Brookhouse

PLACINGS: 211/

Starts	1st	2nd	3rd	4th	Win & Pl
3	2	1	-	-	£34,271
	3/11	Chel	2m¹/₂f Cls1 Gd1 NHF 4-6yo good		£31,356
	2/11	Kemp	2m Cls5 Mdn NHF 4-6yo gd-sft		£1,713

Missed last season through injury having won the Champion Bumper at Cheltenham in 2011; that race generally worked out badly despite success of Cinders And Ashes (fifth) so something to prove, though clearly has potential to do well in novice hurdles.

1075 Chicago Grey (Ire)

9 gr g Luso - Carrigeen Acer (Lord Americo)

Gordon Elliott (Ir)   John Earls

PLACINGS: /313211F2518/U3732B-   RPR **154**+c

Starts	1st	2nd	3rd	4th	Win & Pl
31	7	5	8	-	£140,178
	3/11	Chel	4m Cls2 Nov Am Ch good		£45,015
	10/10	Chel	3m¹/₂f Cls2 Nov Ch good		£9,393
	9/10	Navn	2m4f Ch yield		£12,080
	7/10	Leop	2m6f Ch gd-fm		£9,770
	12/09	Thur	2m List Hdl sft-hvy		£18,013
	11/09	Thur	2m Hdl heavy		£7,044
	4/09	Prth	2m4¹/₂f Cls4 Mdn Hdl good		£3,578

Won National Hunt Chase at Cheltenham two seasons ago but hasn't added to that victory since then; generally disappointing last season, though seemed to be coming to a peak in time for Grand National at Aintree only to be brought down in early stages.

1076 China Rock (Ire)

9 ch g Presenting - Kigali (Torus)

Mouse Morris (Ir)   Michael O'Flynn

PLACINGS: 3145442/1134P/45841-   RPR **168**+c

Starts	1st	2nd	3rd	4th	Win & Pl
25	6	2	2	8	£199,278
	4/12	Punc	3m1f Gd1 Ch heavy		£70,000
	10/10	Chel	2m7f Gd3 Ch good		£18,119
	10/10	Gowr	2m4f Gd2 Ch yld-sft		£23,009
	10/09	Gway	2m6f Ch soft		£12,076
	1/09	Cork	2m2f Hdl yield		£10,734
	9/08	List	2m4f Mdn Hdl 5yo soft		£7,367

Finally realised abundant talent when landing Grade 1 at Punchestown at end of last season;

has travelled strongly for a long way in last two runnings of Cheltenham Gold Cup (finished distressed first time); could be a force in top races.

1077 Cinders And Ashes

5 b g Beat Hollow - Moon Search (Rainbow Quest)

Donald McCain   Dermot Hanafin & Phil Cunningham

PLACINGS: 1250/21111-   RPR **151**+h

Starts	1st	2nd	3rd	4th	Win & Pl
9	5	2	-	-	£84,872
	3/12	Chel	2m¹/₂f Cls1 Nov Gd1 Hdl good		£56,950
	1/12	Hayd	2m Cls1 Nov Gd2 Hdl heavy		£12,073
	12/11	Hayd	2m Cls4 Nov Hdl 4-6yo heavy		£3,249
	12/11	Aint	2m1f Cls4 Mdn Hdl soft		£4,549
	12/10	Sthl	1m6f Cls5 NHF 3yo std slw		£1,713
	10/10	Font	1m6f Cls6 NHF 3yo gd-sft		£1,370

Unlucky not to be unbeaten over hurdles last season, losing narrowly at Ascot before landing four successive wins; barely tested for first three wins but did superbly to edge out Darlan in Supreme Novices' Hurdle; likely to improve again.

1078 Citizenship

6 b g Beat Hollow - Three More (Sanglamore)

Jessica Harrington (Ir)   Fresh By Nature Syndicate

PLACINGS: 00/7132106-F   RPR **135**+h

Starts	1st	2nd	3rd	4th	Win & Pl
10	2	1	1	-	£63,116
	1/12	Leop	2m 111-139 Hdl Hcap yield		£50,000
	11/11	Punc	2m Nov 90-102 Hdl Hcap soft		£5,948

Progressed well in 2m handicap hurdles last season and showed a stunning turn of foot to win the valuable Boylesports Hurdle at Leopardstown; had no luck in running when beaten favourite in County Hurdle and unsuited by heavy ground at Punchestown.

1079 Clerk's Choice (Ire)

6 b g Bachelor Duke - Credit Crunch (Caerleon)

Oliver Sherwood   M C Banks

PLACINGS: 31/1114462/7403-0   RPR **149**h

Starts	1st	2nd	3rd	4th	Win & Pl
14	4	1	2	3	£68,094
	10/10	Chel	2m¹/₂f Cls2 Hdl 4yo good		£31,310
	5/10	Strf	2m¹/₂f Cls4 Nov Hdl good		£4,228
	5/10	Hntg	2m¹/₂f Cls4 Nov Hdl gd-sft		£2,602
	4/10	Kemp	2m Cls4 Nov Hdl good		£3,253

Has largely struggled since 31lb rise for runaway Cheltenham win in October 2010, not helped by close-up sixth in that season's Champion Hurdle; slowly slipped down handicap last season and back

to a fair mark judged on third in Scottish Champion Hurdle.

1080 Clonbanan Lad (Ire)

6 b g Rudimentary - Flute Orchestra (Deep Run)

Michael John O'Connor (Ir)   Edward M Walsh

PLACINGS: 32/U11107-   **RPR 135**b

Starts	1st	2nd	3rd	4th	Win & Pl
4	2	-	-	-	£10,806
	2/12	Naas	2m3f NHF 4-7yo sft-hvy		£5,750
	12/11	Limk	2m NHF 4-5yo heavy		£5,056

High-class bumper performer last season, producing a devastating victory at Naas; disappointed at Cheltenham having been widely expected to struggle on quicker ground and easily forgiven flop at Punchestown in virtually unraceable conditions.

1081 Close House

5 b g Generous - Not Now Nellie (Saddlers' Hall)

David Pipe   R S Brookhouse

PLACINGS: 212/314-   **RPR 139**h

Starts	1st	2nd	3rd	4th	Win & Pl
6	2	2	1	1	£20,952
	12/11	Towc	2m Cls5 Mdn Hdl gd-sft		£1,689
	1/11	Ayr	1m6f Cls6 NHF 4yo good		£1,370

Showed plenty of promise at a much lower level before running a cracker when stepped up significantly in class for the Neptune Hurdle at Cheltenham, staying on well in fourth; likely to stay 3m on that evidence despite not winning beyond 2m.

1082 Colour Squadron (Ire)

6 b g Old Vic - That's The Goose (Be My Native)

Philip Hobbs   John P McManus

PLACINGS: 1212F0F2-   **RPR 148**h

Starts	1st	2nd	3rd	4th	Win & Pl
8	2	3	-	-	£24,897
	12/11	Newb	2m¹/₂f Cls4 Mdn Hdl soft		£2,599
	10/11	Chep	2m¹/₂f Cls5 NHF 4-6yo soft		£1,779

Massively underachieved in novice hurdles last season, hanging left to throw away the Tolworth Hurdle and falling twice when in contention (albeit when unlikely to beat Simonsig at Aintree); good second at Punchestown on final start; looks well handicapped.

1083 Cornas (NZ) (above)

10 b g Prized - Duvessa (Sound Reason)

Nick Williams   The Gascoigne Brookes Partnership III

PLACINGS: 1545/1641793/2238F8-   **RPR 158**c

Starts	1st	2nd	3rd	4th	Win & Pl
33	5	5	3	4	£161,155
148	1/11	Sand	2m Cls2 132-158 Ch Hcap soft		£12,524
	10/10	Limk	2m1f Gd3 Ch good		£18,119
	12/09	Extr	2m1¹/₂f Cls2 Ch soft		£18,786
	1/09	Ludl	2m Cls4 Ch soft		£5,010
	4/08	Winc	2m Cls4 Nov Hdl good		£3,083

Desperately unlucky to have won only four times over fences despite string of good efforts during last four seasons; placed in Haldon Gold Cup and Tingle Creek Chase last season but only eighth in Grand Annual Chase and may need more help from handicapper.

1084 Cotton Mill

5 b g Tiger Hill - Mill Line (Mill Reef)

John Ferguson   Bloomfields

PLACINGS: 111U3-   RPR 153+h

Starts	1st	2nd	3rd	4th	Win & Pl
5	3	-	1	-	£29,136
	1/12	Wwck	2m5f Cls1 Nov Gd2 Hdl gd-sft		£14,238
	12/11	Fknm	2m4f Cls4 Nov Hdl good		£2,599
	11/11	Hrfd	2m4f Cls5 Mdn Hdl good		£1,689

Showed lots of largely unfulfilled talent last season, attempting to run out at the second-last when set to give Simonsig a race at Cheltenham (has shown a good attitude otherwise) and then finding 3m beyond him at Aintree; capable of winning good races.

1085 Countrywide Flame

4 b g Haafhd - Third Party (Terimon)

John Quinn   Estio Pinnacle Racing

PLACINGS: 11212312-   RPR 147+h

Starts	1st	2nd	3rd	4th	Win & Pl
8	4	3	1	-	£103,668
	3/12	Chel	2m1f Cls1 Gd1 Hdl 4yo good		£56,950
	11/11	Sedg	2m1f Cls4 Hdl 3yo gd-sft		£2,534
	8/11	Ctml	2m1¹/₂f Cls4 Hdl 3yo soft		£2,599
	7/11	MRas	2m1f Cls3 Hdl 3yo gd-sft		£5,198

Took an unusual route to Triumph Hurdle glory having raced 12 times during 2011 (last five over hurdles); suffered three defeats before Cheltenham but seemed to relish good gallop and big field before another fine effort in second to Grumeti at Aintree.

1086 Court In Motion (Ire)

7 br g Fruits Of Love - Peace Time Girl (Buckskin)

Emma Lavelle   N Mustoe

PLACINGS: 3F2/12123F/

Starts	1st	2nd	3rd	4th	Win & Pl
9	2	3	2	-	£42,881
	1/11	Wwck	2m5f Cls4 Nov Gd2 Hdl heavy		£14,253
	11/10	Extr	2m5¹/₂f Cls3 Nov Hdl soft		£4,228

Among leading staying novice hurdlers two seasons ago when twice placed at top level and hacking up in Grade 2 at Warwick by 21 lengths; missed last season through injury when set to go novice chasing and should do well in that sphere; acts on any going.

1087 Crack Away Jack

8 ch g Gold Away - Jolly Harbour (Rudimentary)

Tom George   Gdm Partnership

PLACINGS: 11/1254/124/8P/50P2-   RPR 148+c

Starts	1st	2nd	3rd	4th	Win & Pl
17	4	3	1	2	£165,653
	11/09	Sand	2m Cls3 Ch good		£6,505
149	10/08	Chep	2m¹/₂f Cls2 129-149 Hdl 4yo Hcap good		£31,310
133	3/08	Chel	2m¹/₂f Cls1 Nov List 122-135 Hdl 4yo Hcap gd-sft		£42,765
	2/08	Sand	2m1¹/₂f Cls3 Nov Hdl 4yo good		£4,554

Good enough to finish fourth in 2009 Champion

Hurdle at his peak but had been bitterly disappointing since long injury lay-off until finishing second to Big Buck's at Aintree on first run for new yard; very well handicapped on old form if that sparks a revival.

1088 Cristal Bonus (Fr)

6 b g Della Francesca - Cristal Springs (Loup Solitaire)

Paul Nicholls   R J H Geffen

PLACINGS: 14/8211/16257/11P2-   RPR 157c

Starts	1st	2nd	3rd	4th	Win & Pl
15	6	3	-	1	£230,489
	2/12	Kemp	2m4¹/₂f Cls1 Nov Gd2 Ch good		£13,561
	1/12	Chep	2m3¹/₂f Cls4 Ch heavy		£2,599
	9/10	Autl	2m2f List Hdl 4yo v soft		£36,106
	11/09	Engh	2m1¹/₂f Gd3 Hdl 3yo heavy		£56,796
	10/09	Engh	2m1¹/₂f Hdl 3yo heavy		£22,369
	3/09	Pari	1m7f Hdl 3yo gd-sft		£7,456

Former high-class hurdler in France (Grade 1 runner-up); did well in novice chases last season, twice winning modest contests by wide margins before good second to Menorah at Aintree; pulled up at Cheltenham in between (third below-par effort at that track).

1089 Cue Card

6 b g King's Theatre - Wicked Crack (King's Ride)

Colin Tizzard   Mrs Jean R Bishop

PLACINGS: 11/11242/1U212-   RPR 167c

Starts	1st	2nd	3rd	4th	Win & Pl
12	6	4	-	1	£151,012
	12/11	Newb	2m2¹/₂f Cls3 Nov Ch soft		£7,323
	10/11	Chep	2m3¹/₂f Cls3 Nov Ch good		£7,148
	11/10	Chel	2m1¹/₂f Cls1 Nov Gd2 Hdl good		£14,253
	10/10	Aint	2m4f Cls3 Nov Hdl 4-6yo gd-sft		£4,554
	3/10	Chel	2m1¹/₂f Cls1 Gd1 NHF 4-6yo good		£34,206
	1/10	Font	1m6f Cls6 NHF 4-6yo soft		£1,431

Carried big reputation since winning Champion Bumper at Cheltenham in 2010; lived up to that promise as a novice chaser last season despite being no match for Sprinter Sacre in the Arkle, finishing a clear second; could be top-class over 2m4f or beyond.

1090 Darlan

5 br g Milan - Darbela (Doyoun)

Nicky Henderson   John P McManus

PLACINGS: 1/111F21-   RPR 156+h

Starts	1st	2nd	3rd	4th	Win & Pl
7	5	1	-	-	£66,261
	4/12	Aint	2m¹/₂f Cls1 Nov Gd2 Hdl good		£28,475
	1/12	Tntn	2m1f Cls3 Nov Hdl gd-sft		£5,848
	12/11	Chel	2m1f Cls3 Nov Hdl 4-6yo good		£6,256
	11/11	Kemp	2m Cls4 Nov Hdl 4-6yo good		£2,599
	4/11	Hayd	2m Cls5 NHF 4-6yo good		£1,713

Arguably last season's best 2m novice hurdler having stepped on form of his Supreme Novices' Hurdle second to win well at Aintree; had also been going well when falling two out in Betfair Hurdle at Newbury; strong traveller who may have a lot more to come.

1091 Darna

6 b g Alflora - Dutch Dyane (Midyan)

Kim Bailey   Mrs Julie Martin And David R Martin

PLACINGS: 23/611/01P11-   RPR **144+c**

Starts	1st	2nd	3rd	4th	Win & Pl
10	5	1	1	-	£25,992

4/12	Asct	2m5^1/$_2$f Cls3 Nov Ch good		£6,882
3/12	Extr	2m3^1/$_2$f Cls3 Nov Ch good		£6,498
11/11	Ling	2m Cls5 Ch good		£2,053
1/11	Ayr	2m Cls4 Nov Hdl good		£2,602
1/11	Ayr	2m Cls5 Mdn Hdl soft		£1,952

Beaten only twice over jumps and suffered sole chasing defeat when going wrong early at Ludlow; returned from subsequent break to win well at Exeter and Ascot, stepping steadily up in trip; unproven in bigger fields but has a fine engine.

1092 Days Hotel (Ire)

7 b g Oscar - Call Catherine (Strong Gale)

Henry De Brodhead (Ir)   James Treacy

PLACINGS: 29/47414/11-   RPR **147+c**

Starts	1st	2nd	3rd	4th	Win & Pl
7	3	-	-	2	£34,622

11/11	Punc	2m Nov Gd2 Ch soft		£22,414
10/11	Punc	2m Ch heavy		£7,138
3/11	Clon	2m1^1/$_2$f Mdn Hdl soft		£4,461

Useful point-to-pointer (second to Boston Bob in 2010) who left hurdling form behind when winning both novice chases early last season, most notably Grade 2 at Punchestown in November; due to return from injury and could be very smart; best on soft ground.

1093 De Boitron (Fr)

8 b g Sassanian - Pondiki (Sicyos)

Ferdy Murphy   Mrs J Morgan & Mrs Lindsey J Shaw

PLACINGS: 333113/0243/7783602-   RPR **142c**

Starts	1st	2nd	3rd	4th	Win & Pl
36	6	4	7	3	£90,299

126	4/10	Chel	2m^1/$_2$f Cls3 117-135 Cond Ch Hcap good		£6,262
120	3/10	Donc	2m^1/$_2$f Cls2 118-142 Ch Hcap good		£16,263
109	4/09	Strf	2m4f Cls3 106-125 Ch Hcap good		£7,828
96	1/09	Catt	2m3f Cls3 94-116 Ch Hcap soft		£6,440
	3/08	Autl	2m1^1/$_2$f Ch 4yo v soft		£7,412
	12/07	Pau	2m1^1/$_2$f Hdl 3yo gd-sft		£5,189

Knocking on the door in a string of top 2m handicap chases during last two seasons, including when fourth and sixth in the Grand Annual at Cheltenham; benefited from stepping up to 2m4f when good second at Ayr on final start last season.

1094 Dedigout (Ire)

6 b g Bob Back - Dainty Daisy (Buckskin)

Tony Martin (Ir)   Gigginstown House Stud

PLACINGS: 2/211311-   RPR **152+h**

Starts	1st	2nd	3rd	4th	Win & Pl
6	4	1	1	-	£73,905

	4/12	Punc	2m4f Nov Gd1 Hdl heavy		£41,333
132	4/12	Fair	2m6f 106-134 Hdl Hcap gd-sft		£12,458
	12/11	Navn	2m4f Nov Hdl sft-hvy		£7,733
	11/11	Punc	2m4f Mdn Hdl soft		£8,328

Beaten only once over hurdles last season when no match for Monksland over 2m4f; benefited from step up in trip to win handicap hurdle at Fairyhouse before outstaying decent field in Grade 1 at Punchestown; should relish 3m over fences.

1095 Definity (Ire)

9 br g Definite Article - Ebony Jane (Roselier)

Paul Nicholls — C G Roach

PLACINGS: 1112/4125/

Starts	1st	2nd	3rd	4th	Win & Pl
7	3	2	-	1	£22,175

	1/11	Font	2m4f Cls4 Ch gd-sft	£3,253
	2/09	Newb	3m¹/₂f Cls3 Nov Hdl good	£5,204
	11/08	Winc	2m6f Cls4 Nov Hdl gd-sft	£4,554

Has missed two of the last three seasons through injury but showed lots of potential in novice chases when last seen, finishing fifth when 3-1 favourite for novice handicap chase at Cheltenham Festival in 2011; possible candidate for major handicaps at around 2m5f.

1096 Divers (Fr)

8 gr g Highest Honor - Divination (Groom Dancer)

Ferdy Murphy — Let's Live Racing

PLACINGS: 83V02/031511/P3U047- **RPR 150c**

Starts	1st	2nd	3rd	4th	Win & Pl
32	4	7	4	1	£88,930

132	3/11	Chel	2m4¹/₂f Cls1 Nov List 132-140 Ch Hcap good	£28,505
	2/11	Muss	2m4f Cls3 Nov Ch soft	£7,806
	10/10	Carl	2m Cls3 Nov Ch good	£5,855
	12/08	Muss	2m4f Cls5 Mdn Hdl good	£2,602

Won novice handicap chase at Cheltenham Festival in 2011 and ran well over that course and distance last season when third in Paddy Power Gold Cup and fourth in Byrne Group Plate (main threat to winner both times before fading); could land decent prize.

1097 Dodging Bullets

4 b g Dubawi - Nova Cyngi (Kris S)

Paul Nicholls — Martin Broughton & Friends

PLACINGS: 246- **RPR 141h**

Starts	1st	2nd	3rd	4th	Win & Pl
3	-	1	-	1	£11,247

Did brilliantly to make big mark in top juvenile hurdles last season given he didn't run until February, finishing fourth in Triumph Hurdle despite pulling hard; badly hampered at Aintree next time; retains novice status and should relish big-field handicaps.

1098 Doeslessthanme (Ire) (above, left)

8 ch g Definite Article - Damemill (Danehill)

Paul Nicholls — Andrea & Graham Wylie

PLACINGS: F1/23620/1/1F222111- **RPR 152+c**

Starts	1st	2nd	3rd	4th	Win & Pl
21	10	5	2	-	£67,696

144	4/12	Ayr	2m Cls2 122-145 Ch Hcap good	£16,245
137	4/12	NAbb	2m¹/₂f Cls2 125-145 Ch Hcap gd-fm	£12,660
	3/12	Hrfd	2m Cls3 Nov Ch soft	£3,899
	10/11	Font	2m4f Cls4 Nov Ch gd-sft	£3,054
127	11/10	Kels	2m¹/₂f Cls3 104-130 Hdl Hcap soft	£4,554
	4/09	Kels	2m2f Cls4 Nov Hdl good	£2,927
	12/08	Muss	2m Cls4 Nov Hdl good	£3,253
	10/08	Kels	2m¹/₂f Cls5 Mdn Hdl gd-sft	£2,602
	3/08	Donc	2m¹/₂f Cls5 Am NHF 4-6yo good	£2,056
	2/08	Muss	2m Cls5 NHF 4-6yo gd-sft	£1,627

Had a busy campaign as a novice chaser last season but showed rapid progress in the spring, completing a hat-trick with an impressive win in a handicap chase at Ayr; needs to improve again off

higher mark but effective from 2m to 2m4f and acts on any going.

1099 Don Cossack (Ger)

5 br g Sholokhov - Depeche Toi (Konigsstuhl)

Gordon Elliott (Ir)   Gigginstown House Stud

PLACINGS: 5111-					RPR **146+b**
Starts	1st	2nd	3rd	4th	Win & Pl
4	3	-	-	-	£27,944

4/12	Fair	2m NHF 4-7yo soft		£7,479
12/11	Navn	2m Gd2 NHF 4-7yo sft-hvy		£15,409
10/11	Naas	2m3f NHF 4-7yo heavy		£5,056

Completed a hat-trick in bumpers in terrific fashion at Fairyhouse having made up lots of ground to land previous start at Navan; looks a terrific prospect for staying novice hurdles, though he was beaten on his only start on ground quicker than soft.

1100 Donnas Palm (Ire)

8 gr g Great Palm - Donna's Tarquin (Husyan)

Noel Meade (Ir)   Grand Alliance Racing Club

PLACINGS: 1122/1392/532136412-					RPR **154h**
Starts	1st	2nd	3rd	4th	Win & Pl
26	9	7	3	1	£203,979

2/12	Navn	2m1f Nov Gd2 Ch soft		£20,313
10/11	Wxfd	2m3f Ch soft		£5,651
10/10	Tipp	2m Gd2 Hdl yield		£31,637
12/09	Navn	2m4f Gd2 Hdl sft-hvy		£26,546
11/09	Fair	2m2f Hdl heavy		£13,589
10/09	Punc	2m List Hdl gd-yld		£17,697
12/08	Navn	2m Hdl 4yo heavy		£8,129
10/08	Naas	2m Mdn Hdl 4yo sft-hvy		£6,097
9/08	Navn	2m NHF 4-7yo gd-yld		£5,081

Smart Grade 2 winner over hurdles; failed to reach that level when sent novice chasing last season despite winning in that grade in moderate contest at Navan and no match for Slieveardagh next time but has dropped down handicap in both codes.

1101 Down In Neworleans (Ire)

7 b g Saddlers' Hall - Miss Muppet (Supreme Leader)

Mags Mullins (Ir)   P J Magnier

PLACINGS: 0/5153336163/111-					
Starts	1st	2nd	3rd	4th	Win & Pl
14	5	-	4	-	£39,994

8/11	Gway	2m1f Nov Ch good		£12,328
7/11	Gway	2m1f Nov Ch good		£12,888
5/11	Rosc	2m Ch gd-yld		£4,759
2/11	Clon	2m1/2f Mdn Hdl 5-6yo sft-hvy		£3,103
6/10	Clon	2m NHF 4-7yo good		£4,274

Won only once in seven runs over hurdles and proved much better when sent chasing last summer, completing a hat-trick in usual front-running style at Galway; missed rest of season through injury but due to return; superb jumper who remains a very exciting prospect.

1102 Dream Esteem (above)

7 b m Mark Of Esteem - City Of Angels (Woodman)

David Pipe   R S Brookhouse

PLACINGS: 120/3272/3114-4					RPR **144h**
Starts	1st	2nd	3rd	4th	Win & Pl
12	3	3	2	2	£29,338

135	3/12	Newb	2m1/2f Cls2 119-145 Hdl Hcap gd-sft		£10,397
126	2/12	Chep	2m1/2f Cls3 116-134 Hdl Hcap soft		£5,848
	1/10	Ffos	2m Cls4 Mdn Hdl gd-sft		£2,927

Front-running hurdler who was much improved last season, winning handicaps at Chepstow and

Newbury and remaining competitive off much higher mark when close fourth at Aintree (led at the last); could do better if more amenable to restraint.

1103 Drive Time (USA)

7 b g King Cugat - Arbusha (Danzig)

Willie Mullins (Ir)   Graham Wylie & Andrea Wylie

PLACINGS: 1P1F/1-F   RPR **147+h**

Starts	1st	2nd	3rd	4th	Win & Pl
6	3	-	-	-	£47,616
125	4/12	Punc	2m4f 117-142 Hdl Hcap heavy		£41,333
	3/11	Donc	2m3¹/₂f Cls3 Nov Hdl good		£4,228
	1/11	Donc	2m3¹/₂f Cls4 Nov Hdl good		£2,055

Absent for just over a year after falling in Grade 2 novice hurdle at Aintree for Howard Johnson in 2011; won first start for new trainer in April and followed up on the Flat before falling early when 4-1 favourite for Galway Hurdle; remains interesting for big handicap hurdles.

1104 Duke Of Lucca (Ire)

7 b g Milan - Derravaragh Native (Be My Native)

Philip Hobbs   Mrs Lesley Field

PLACINGS: 0123/04450/221P2511-   RPR **146+c**

Starts	1st	2nd	3rd	4th	Win & Pl
20	6	5	1	2	£66,850
	4/12	Chel	3m1¹/₂f Cls2 Nov Ch gd-sft		£10,256
	3/12	Bang	3m1¹/₂f Cls4 Nov Ch good		£4,328
	12/11	Winc	2m5f Cls4 Ch gd-sft		£3,249
	3/10	Tntn	2m3¹/₂f Cls3 Nov Hdl gd-sft		£5,692
	12/09	Newb	2m3f Cls4 Nov Hdl 4-6yo soft		£3,578
	11/09	Tntn	2m1f Cls4 Mdn Hdl gd-sft		£4,554

Generally progressive in novice chases last season and finished with two easy wins in small fields following good effort when 50-1 fifth behind Sir Des Champs in Jewson Chase; jumping fell apart on only run in handicap company but could be on a fair mark.

1105 Dunguib (Ire)

9 b g Presenting - Edermine Berry (Durgam)

Philip Fenton (Ir)   Daniel Harnett

PLACINGS: 2/111/1d111136/18/

Starts	1st	2nd	3rd	4th	Win & Pl
13	8	1	1	-	£210,389
	2/11	Gowr	2m Gd2 Hdl sft-hvy		£22,414
	2/10	Leop	2m2f Nov Gd1 Hdl soft		£46,018
	12/09	Fair	2m Nov Gd1 Hdl heavy		£53,641
	11/09	Punc	2m Hdl heavy		£9,392
	10/09	Gway	2m Mdn Hdl heavy		£8,386
	3/09	Chel	2m1¹/₂f Cls1 Gd1 NHF 4-6yo gd-sft		£34,206
	12/08	Navn	2m Gd2 NHF 4-7yo heavy		£16,754
	11/08	Punc	2m NHF 5-6yo heavy		£5,589

Once seen as next jumping superstar having hacked up in 2009 Champion Bumper and won first four starts over hurdles; could still scale those heights having run only three times since odds-on third in 2010 Supreme Novices' Hurdle due to injury; likely to go novice chasing.

1106 Dynaste (Fr)

6 gr g Martaline - Bellissima De Mai (Pistolet Bleu)

David Pipe   A J White

PLACINGS: 445/3216/1428-   RPR **162h**

Starts	1st	2nd	3rd	4th	Win & Pl
11	2	2	1	3	£80,541
141	11/11	Hayd	3m Cls1 Gd3 131-151 Hdl Hcap gd-sft		£42,713
130	12/10	Tntn	2m3¹/₂f Cls2 122-147 Cond Hdl Hcap gd-sft		£12,674

Terrific long-term chasing prospect who was kept to hurdles last season after easy win over fixed brush obstacles at Haydock; produced best subsequent effort when second to Big Buck's in Cleeve Hurdle at Cheltenham; set to go over fences.

1107 Edgardo Sol (Fr)

5 ch g Kapgarde - Tikiti Dancer (Fabulous Dancer)

Paul Nicholls   Axom XXXII

PLACINGS: 530/762311435216-   RPR **160+c**

Starts	1st	2nd	3rd	4th	Win & Pl
16	3	2	3	1	£84,931
143	4/12	Aint	2m Cls1 Gd3 135-155 Ch Hcap gd-sft		£34,170
122	11/11	Chel	2m¹/₂f Cls3 Nov 108-122 Hdl Hcap gd-sft		£6,256
127	10/11	Aint	2m Cls3 Nov 116-130 Ch Hcap good		£6,963

Raced largely over hurdles last season following move from France but produced by far his best performance when running away with major 2m handicap chase at Aintree; 14lb rise looks fair on that evidence and could find hurdles mark still workable.

1108 Emmaslegend

7 b m Midnight Legend - Cherrygayle (Strong Gale)

Suzy Smith   Mrs Emma Stewart

PLACINGS: /4P01180/30114922-11   RPR **148+c**

Starts	1st	2nd	3rd	4th	Win & Pl
22	6	2	2	2	£33,753
132	7/12	Uttx	3m2f Cls1 List 116-142 Ch Hcap good		£11,390
127	6/12	Strf	3m3f Cls3 109-135 Hdl Hcap good		£4,549
	12/11	Folk	3m1f Cls4 Ch good		£1,916
110	11/11	Asct	2m6f Cls3 105-125 Hdl Hcap good		£5,630
95	3/11	Hntg	2m5¹/₂f Cls5 62-95 Hdl Hcap good		£2,055
88	3/11	Winc	2m4f Cls5 70-90 Hdl Hcap gd-fm		£1,952

Maintained decent level of form in novice chases after winning on debut over fences last season; really blossomed this summer and looked particularly impressive when landing Listed chase at Uttoxeter; stays very well but needs to defy much higher mark.

1109 Empire Levant (USA)

5 rg g Empire Maker - Orellana (With Approval)

Paul Nicholls   Sir A Ferguson,G Mason,R Wood & P Done

PLACINGS: 312/41200-   RPR **141+h**

Starts	1st	2nd	3rd	4th	Win & Pl
8	2	2	1	1	£17,997
128	11/11	Newb	2m¹/₂f Cls3 120-128 Cond Hdl Hcap gd-sft		£3,806
	1/11	Donc	2m1¹/₂f Cls3 Hdl 4yo good		£4,228

Began last season very well handicapped and

took advantage with easy win at Newbury before chasing home Rock On Ruby two days later; well beaten in major handicaps next twice but badly hampered both times; should be even better over fences.

1110 Eradicate (Ire) (above)

8 b g Montjeu - Coyote (Indian Ridge)

Nicky Henderson   A D Spence

PLACINGS: 22/104/14667/12141P-   RPR 149+c

Starts	1st	2nd	3rd	4th	Win & Pl
18	6	4	-	3	£114,784

	1/12	Sthl	2m Cls4 Nov Ch gd-sft	£3,054
	11/11	Donc	2m3f Cls4 Nov Ch gd-fm	£4,549
141	5/11	Hayd	2m Cls1 Gd3 123-141 Hdl Hcap good	£28,505
132	5/10	Hayd	2m¹/₂f Cls1 Gd3 127-150 Hdl Hcap good	£42,758
129	2/10	Muss	2m Cls2 116-142 Hdl Hcap gd-sft	£18,786
	1/09	Tntn	2m1f Cls4 Nov Hdl gd-sft	£4,066

Dual winner of the Swinton Hurdle; didn't quite

make the grade over fences last season despite winning twice; had nothing go right when pulled up in Grand Annual (badly hampered and rider lost irons) and potentially very well handicapped.

1111 Exmoor Ranger (Ire)

10 ch g Grand Plaisir - Slyguff Torus (Torus)

Victor Dartnall   The Rangers Partnership

PLACINGS: 7712B4/439U6P/15F3F-   RPR 149+c

Starts	1st	2nd	3rd	4th	Win & Pl
28	6	1	2	3	£124,097

137	10/11	Asct	3m Cls1 Gd3 127-153 Ch Hcap good	£56,270
135	11/09	Newb	2m6¹/₂f Cls3 109-135 Ch Hcap gd-sft	£9,393
	12/08	Extr	2m3¹/₂f Cls2 Nov Ch soft	£14,636
	10/08	Extr	3m Cls4 Ch gd-sft	£5,204
114	3/08	Newb	2m3f Cls3 Nov 96-114 Hdl Hcap soft	£6,506
105	2/08	Sand	2m4f Cls4 Nov 97-113 Hdl Hcap good	£4,554

Useful staying handicap chaser who bounced

back to form last season when winning at Ascot on return; ran another cracker when third in Kim Muir at Cheltenham but blotted copybook by falling either side of that, including when going well four out on final start.

1112 Fair Along (Ger)

10 b g Alkalde - Fairy Tango (Acatenango)

Philip Hobbs   Alan Peterson

PLACINGS: /71570/1934/U26345-3   RPR **149**hc

Starts	1st	2nd	3rd	4th	Win & Pl
43	11	5	9	4	£369,649
	10/10	Weth	3m1f Cls1 Gd2 Hdl good		£18,528
	10/09	Weth	3m1f Cls1 Gd2 Hdl good		£24,514
152	12/08	Chel	3m Cls2 126-152 Hdl Hcap gd-sft		£13,776
144	11/08	Chel	3m1¹/₂f Cls1 List 124-150 Hdl Hcap soft		£28,505
	12/06	Newb	2m2¹/₂f Cls3 Nov Ch gd-sft		£7,998
	12/06	Sand	2m Cls1 Nov Gd2 Ch soft		£19,957
	11/06	Chel	2m Cls1 Nov Gd2 Ch gd-sft		£25,780
	11/05	Aint	2m²/₂f Cls2 Nov Hdl 3yo gd-sft		£10,146
	11/05	Aint	2m¹/₂f Cls1 Nov Hdl 3yo gd-sft		£17,106
	8/05	Bang	2m1f Cls4 Nov Hdl 3yo good		£3,034
	7/05	Bang	2m1f Cls4 Nov Hdl 3yo gd-sft		£3,414

Very useful stayer over hurdles and fences, particularly early in the season, and nearly exploited much lower chase mark when third to Carruthers in last season's Hennessy Gold Cup; has slipped again in handicap and may still be good enough to take advantage.

1113 Felix Yonger (Ire)

6 b g Oscar - Marble Sound (Be My Native)

Willie Mullins (Ir)   Graham Wylie

PLACINGS: 210/21125-   RPR **153**h

Starts	1st	2nd	3rd	4th	Win & Pl
8	3	3	-	-	£59,232
	2/12	Naas	2m Nov Gd2 Hdl soft		£22,479
	12/11	Dpat	2m2f Mdn Hdl 4-5yo sft-hvy		£6,841
	1/11	Muss	2m Cls6 NHF 4-6yo good		£1,626

Made quiet progress over hurdles last season, gaining biggest win in Grade 2 at Naas, before fine second to Simonsig in Neptune Hurdle on good ground when stepped up to 2m5f; yet to prove as effective in slower conditions after disappointing fifth at Punchestown.

1114 Fiendish Flame (Ire)

8 ch g Beneficial - Deenish (Callernish)

Jennie Candlish   Mr & Mrs R N C Hall

PLACINGS: 63/72136P3P7/71517-P   RPR **153**+c

Starts	1st	2nd	3rd	4th	Win & Pl
27	7	3	6	-	£75,806
140	1/12	Muss	2m4f Cls3 118-140 Ch Hcap good		£12,996
125	12/11	Leic	2m4f¹/₂f Cls3 112-129 Hdl Hcap good		£4,549
	11/10	Bang	2m1¹/₂f Cls2 Ch soft		£16,041
	2/10	Muss	2m4f Cls3 Nov Ch gd-sft		£7,806
	10/09	Carl	2m Cls3 Nov Ch good		£6,505
	2/09	Uttx	2m4¹/₂f Cls4 Nov Hdl heavy		£3,253
	1/09	Sedg	2m1f Cls4 Nov Hdl soft		£2,537

Gained wide-margin wins over hurdles and fences last season but disappointed when stepped into better company, seeming to struggle when

taken on for the lead; still on a fair chase mark and may be capable of winning good races in small fields.

1115 Final Approach

6 b g Pivotal - College Fund Girl (Kahyasi)

Willie Mullins (Ir)   Douglas Taylor

PLACINGS: 13/511/654100-   RPR **150**+h

Starts	1st	2nd	3rd	4th	Win & Pl
11	4	-	1	1	£129,549
	1/12	Cork	2m Hdl heavy		£8,050
139	3/11	Chel	2m1f Cls1 Gd3 129-153 Hdl Hcap good		£39,907
123	1/11	Leop	2m 108-134 Hdl Hcap soft		£51,724
	3/10	Dpat	2m2¹/₂f Mdn Hdl 4yo yld-sft		£4,580

Completed a major handicap double in the County Hurdle in 2011 but found life much tougher last season, coming up short in top company and rated too high to repeat handicap success; only win came at 3-10 at Cork; may need more help from assessor.

1116 Fingal Bay (Ire)

6 b g King's Theatre - Lady Marguerrite (Blakeney)

Philip Hobbs   Mrs R J Skan

PLACINGS: 1/11112-   RPR **156**+h

Starts	1st	2nd	3rd	4th	Win & Pl
6	5	1	-	-	£78,141
	12/11	Newb	2m5f Cls1 Nov Gd1 Hdl soft		£17,085
	12/11	Sand	2m4f Cls1 Nov Gd2 Hdl gd-sft		£12,073
	11/11	Chel	2m4f Cls1 Nov Gd2 Hdl gd-sft		£12,244
	10/11	Chep	2m4f Cls1 Nov Gd2 Hdl good		£14,238
	2/11	Extr	2m1f Cls5 NHF 4-6yo heavy		£1,301

Outstanding novice hurdler of first half of last season, gaining best win over Simonsig at Sandown and following up in Grade 1 Challow Hurdle; missed Cheltenham through injury and possibly not at best when second to Lovcen at Aintree; top-class chasing prospect.

1117 Finian's Rainbow (Ire)

9 b g Tiraaz - Trinity Gale (Strong Gale)

Nicky Henderson   Michael Buckley

PLACINGS: F/1/1315/11121/1211-   RPR **175**+c

Starts	1st	2nd	3rd	4th	Win & Pl
14	10	2	1	-	£461,479
	4/12	Aint	2m4f Cls1 Gd1 Ch good		£98,558
	3/12	Chel	2m Cls1 Gd1 Ch good		£182,240
	12/11	Kemp	2m Cls1 Gd2 Ch good		£25,628
	4/11	Aint	2m Cls1 Nov Gd1 Ch good		£56,632
	2/11	Wwck	2m Cls1 Nov Gd2 Ch gd-sft		£17,637
	1/11	Newb	2m1f Cls3 Nov Ch soft		£4,190
	11/10	Newb	2m1f Cls3 Nov Ch gd-sft		£6,262
	2/10	Asct	2m3¹/₂f Cls3 Nov Hdl gd-sft		£5,010
	11/09	Newb	2m¹/₂f Cls3 Nov Hdl gd-sft		£6,262
	3/09	Kemp	2m Cls6 NHF 4-6yo good		£1,713

Took form to new heights when winning at Cheltenham and Aintree last season; just wore down Sizing Europe to claim 2m crown in Champion Chase and stepped up in trip in hugely impressive fashion to add Melling Chase; should have plenty of options.

1118 First Lieutenant (Ire)

7 ch g Presenting - Fourstargale (Fourstars Allstar)

Mouse Morris (Ir)　　　　　Gigginstown House Stud

PLACINGS: 11/41311/3121P223-　　　　**RPR 164+c**

Starts	1st	2nd	3rd	4th	Win & Pl
14	6	3	3	1	£208,420

11/11	Cork	2m4f Nov Gd3 Ch soft	£19,612
10/11	Tipp	2m4f Nov Gd4 Ch soft	£15,409
3/11	Chel	2m5f Cls1 Nov Gd1 Hdl good	£57,010
12/10	Leop	2m Nov Gd1 Hdl heavy	£46,018
10/10	Punc	2m4f Mdn Hdl good	£6,412
3/10	Gowr	2m2f NHF 4-7yo yld-sft	£5,190

Won Neptune Novices' Hurdle at Cheltenham in 2011 but slightly disappointing overall over fences last season, winning twice at odds-on but losing four times as favourite; still ran a cracker back at Cheltenham when second to Bobs Worth in RSA Chase.

1119 Fistral Beach (Ire)

9 b g Definite Article - Empress Of Light (Emperor Jones)

Paul Nicholls　　　　　　　　　　　　C G Roach

PLACINGS: 3222/221U5/1P0/1P33-　　　　**RPR 151c**

Starts	1st	2nd	3rd	4th	Win & Pl
19	4	7	3	-	£58,873

138	10/11	Weth	2m4½f Cls1 List 119-145 Ch Hcap good	£11,390
131	1/11	Winc	2m5f Cls2 116-142 Ch Hcap soft	£12,524
125	1/10	Kemp	2m4½f Cls3 110-135 Ch Hcap soft	£7,514
	4/08	NAbb	2m1f Cls6 Am NHF 4-6yo gd-sft	£1,370

Hugely frustrating for much of his career (beaten favourite 12 times) but was much more consistent last season following wind operation, disappointing only once; outstayed having

---

travelled best in Topham Chase and could win more races dropped back to 2m4f.

1120 Five Dream (Fr)

8 b g Take Risks - Jenny Pous (Kaid Pous)

Paul Nicholls　　Scott-Macdonald, Kilduff, Donlon & Doyle

PLACINGS: 422/6220636/922260-0　　　　**RPR 152h**

Starts	1st	2nd	3rd	4th	Win & Pl
38	5	8	6	4	£142,438

	10/09	Aint	2m Cls3 Nov Ch gd-sft	£7,039
	5/09	Font	2m2f Cls4 Ch good	£5,070
137	1/08	Chel	2m1f Cls2 114-140 Hdl Hcap gd-sft	£16,265
128	1/08	Sand	2m1½f Cls2 115-136 Hdl Hcap soft	£18,789
	5/07	Autl	2m1½f Hdl 3yo v soft	£14,270

Without a win since landing first two novice chases in 2009 but showed much-improved form over hurdles in first half of last season, twice finishing second to Big Buck's; below-par later in campaign but could exploit much lower chasing mark.

1121 Flat Out (Fr)

7 gr g Sagamix - Divine Rodney (Kendor)

Willie Mullins (Ir)　　　　　　Michael A O'Riordan

PLACINGS: 3211152/11U/

Starts	1st	2nd	3rd	4th	Win & Pl
10	5	2	1	-	£56,273

1/11	Punc	2m4f Ch heavy	£7,138
5/10	Slig	2m Hdl gd-yld	£8,854
2/10	Punc	2m Mdn Hdl soft	£4,580
9/09	List	2m NHF 4-7yo good	£10,063
8/09	Gway	2m NHF 4yo good	£6,709

Smart novice hurdler three seasons ago (fifth in Supreme Novices' Hurdle) before winning

first two starts over fences; in front in Grade 1 at Leopardstown in February 2011 before unseating two out and hasn't run since; reportedly back from injury and remains full of potential.

1122 Flemenstar (Ire)

7 b g Flemensfirth - Different Dee (Beau Sher)

Peter Casey (Ir)   Stephen Curran

PLACINGS: U1/41/4211111-   RPR **164**+c

Starts	1st	2nd	3rd	4th	Win & Pl
9	6	1	-	2	£137,878
	4/12	Fair	2m4f Gd1 Ch good		£48,750
	3/12	Naas	2m4f Nov Gd3 Ch soft		£14,896
	1/12	Leop	2m1f Nov Gd1 Ch sft-hvy		£43,333
	1/12	Naas	2m Nov Ch sft-hvy		£11,917
	11/11	Navn	2m1f Ch sft-hvy		£9,517
	3/11	Navn	2m Mdn Hdl sft-hvy		£5,948

Won five in a row following defeat on chasing debut last season, including twice at Grade 1 level; ran away with Irish Arkle over 2m but expected to improve over further and duly landed Powers Gold Cup easily, proving ability on good ground; big Gold Cup hope.

1123 Foildubh (Ire)

8 b g Woods Of Windsor - Bushey Glen (Roselier)

John Patrick Ryan (Ir)   John Patrick Ryan

PLACINGS: 703411/U3231372621-U   RPR **151**+c

Starts	1st	2nd	3rd	4th	Win & Pl
21	5	4	4	1	£107,946
137	4/12	Punc	2m4f 126-154 Ch Hcap heavy		£41,333
	12/11	Navn	2m1f Nov Ch sft-hvy		£12,328
	12/10	Tram	2m Nov Hdl heavy		£6,412
	12/10	Cork	2m Mdn Hdl soft		£6,412
	3/10	Dpat	2m2f NHF 4-7yo yld-sft		£4,274

Highly tried in novice chases for much of last season, finishing third to Blackstairmountain in Grade 1, but flourished when switched to handicap company in spring; won good prize at Punchestown and ran well until unseating rider at the last soon after.

1124 Follow The Plan (Ire)

9 b g Accordion - Royal Rosy (Dominion Royale)

Oliver McKiernan (Ir)   Redgap Partnership

PLACINGS: 37/FU915F3/1624412-P   RPR **168**c

Starts	1st	2nd	3rd	4th	Win & Pl
32	7	3	4	2	£338,905
	4/12	Aint	3m1f Cls1 Gd-sft		£84,405
	5/11	Punc	3m1f Gd1 Ch good		£82,759
	1/11	Thur	2m4f Gd2 Ch soft		£25,216
	12/08	Leop	2m1f Nov Gd1 Ch soft		£57,353
	11/08	Gowr	2m4f Nov Ch sft-hvy		£12,446
	10/08	Clon	2m1f Ch heavy		£7,113
	3/08	Thur	2m Mdn Hdl 5yo yield		£4,319

Big-priced Grade 1 winner in each of last two seasons, most recently when landing Betfred Bowl at Aintree at 50-1; seems to come alive in the spring but acts on heavy ground (second to China Rock at Punchestown on that surface) and shouldn't be underestimated.

1125 Folsom Blue (Ire)

5 b g Old Vic - Spirit Leader (Supreme Leader)

Conor O'Dwyer (Ir)   Gigginstown House Stud

PLACINGS: 223/211124-   RPR **154**+h

Starts	1st	2nd	3rd	4th	Win & Pl
8	3	3	1	1	£37,674
	2/12	Clon	2m6f Nov List Hdl heavy		£14,354
	1/12	Thur	2m6f Nov Hdl soft		£8,050
	12/11	Limk	2m Mdn Hdl 4yo heavy		£5,948

Looked a very smart novice hurdler when easily completing hat-trick in Listed contest at Clonmel but bubble burst when beaten next twice, though ran well when second to Lyreen Legend; may not have enough size for fences but may progress over hurdles.

1126 For Non Stop (Ire)

7 b g Alderbrook - Lost Link (Shernazar)

Nick Williams   Chris Giles & Jared Sullivan

PLACINGS: 1/6643/124F0/F22213-   RPR **154**c

Starts	1st	2nd	3rd	4th	Win & Pl
15	4	4	2	2	£64,820
	2/12	Newb	2m4f Cls1 Nov Gd1 Ch gd-sft		£14,305
112	10/10	Chep	2m4f Cls3 104-130 Hdl Hcap gd-sft		£5,204

Produced a succession of fine efforts in top novice chases and secured deserved Grade 1 win at Newbury; probably ran even better when third behind Sir Des Champs at Cheltenham; well beaten on only attempt at 3m but seems a strong stayer.

1127 Forpadydeplasterer (Ire)

10 b g Moscow Society - Run Artiste (Deep Run)

Thomas Cooper (Ir)   Goat Racing Syndicate

PLACINGS: 21/222222/2P/233464-   RPR **160**c

Starts	1st	2nd	3rd	4th	Win & Pl
24	5	12	2	3	£454,822
	3/09	Chel	2m Cls1 Gd1 Ch gd-sft		£96,917
	10/08	Punc	2m Ch sft-hvy		£6,351
	2/08	Leop	2m2f Nov Gd1 Hdl yld-sft		£47,794
	12/07	Navn	2m Mdn Hdl heavy		£7,470
	10/07	Gway	2m NHF 4-7yo soft		£5,136

Highly talented chaser who won 2009 Arkle Trophy but found it hard to win even in his heyday (had run of finishing second in ten out of 11 races) and below his best last season; still ran to a fair level of form in four Grade 1 races and may benefit from drop in class.

1128 Four Commanders (Ire)

6 b g Old Vic - Fairy Blaze (Good Thyne)

Mouse Morris (Ir)   Gigginstown House Stud

PLACINGS: 1/3371537/2122423P-   RPR **149**+c

Starts	1st	2nd	3rd	4th	Win & Pl
15	2	4	4	1	£42,106
	11/11	DRoy	2m4f Ch soft		£7,435
	2/11	Thur	2m Mdn Hdl 5yo heavy		£4,461

Took to fences well last season, finishing second three times at Grade 2 level after win at Down

Royal; seemed to improve for step up to 4m when third in National Hunt Chase at Cheltenham but pulled up when favourite for Irish Grand National.

1129 Frascati Park (Ire)

8 b g Bach - Hot Curry (Beau Sher)

Nigel Twiston-Davies   Barry Connell

PLACINGS: /24322/3118/011315F-   RPR **146**c

Starts	1st	2nd	3rd	4th	Win & Pl
20	8	4	3	1	£61,431
	1/12	Wwck	3m^1/$_2$f Cls2 Nov Ch gd-sft		£10,128
	11/11	Carl	2m Cls3 Nov Ch soft		£6,368
	10/11	Carl	2m Cls4 Ch soft		£3,054
	1/11	Leic	2m Cls4 Nov Hdl soft		£1,886
	11/09	Asct	2m3^1/$_2$f Cls3 Nov Hdl gd-sft		£5,010
	3/09	Strf	2m^1/$_2$f Cls6 NHF 4-6yo good		£1,838
	9/08	MRas	2m1^1/$_2$f Cls6 NHF 4-6yo good		£1,713
	7/08	MRas	2m1^1/$_2$f Cls6 NHF 4-6yo gd-sft		£1,713

Took well to fences last season when winning three of first four chases and finishing third to Zaynar (co-favourite) in Grade 2 at Ascot; jumped moderately but still in front, though hard pressed, when falling four out on final start at Cheltenham.

1130 French Opera

9 b g Bering - On Fair Stage (Sadler's Wells)

Nicky Henderson   Mrs Judy Wilson & Martin Landau

PLACINGS: 356/11121/91651/2F4-   RPR **162**c

Starts	1st	2nd	3rd	4th	Win & Pl
24	8	7	1	1	£194,242
	4/11	Sand	2m Cls1 Gd2 Ch gd-fm		£28,505
	2/11	Newb	2m1f Cls1 Gd2 Ch gd-sft		£17,103
	4/10	Ayr	2m4f Cls1 Nov Gd2 Ch good		£23,072
147	12/09	Chel	2m^1/$_2$f Cls2 123-149 Ch Hcap soft		£14,090
138	11/09	Chel	2m Cls2 120-144 Ch Hcap gd-sft		£25,048
	10/09	Asct	2m3f Cls3 Ch good		£7,542
132	10/08	Aint	2m1f Cls2 115-136 Hdl Hcap gd-sft		£12,524
	3/07	Tntn	2m1f Cls4 Mdn Hdl 4yo good		£1,952

Has found life tough since rapid rise in the handicap three seasons ago but won pair of Grade 2 chases in following campaign and ran to similar level when chasing home Sprinter Sacre on return at Newbury last season; may need help from handicapper.

1131 Fruity O'Rooney

9 b g Kahyasi - Recipe (Bustino)

Gary Moore   Heart Of The South Racing

PLACINGS: 154/10222121/621325-   RPR **151**c

Starts	1st	2nd	3rd	4th	Win & Pl
27	6	8	3	1	£84,271
134	12/11	Kemp	3m Cls3 121-139 Ch Hcap good		£12,512
	4/11	Font	2m6f Cls4 Nov Ch good		£2,602
	2/11	Font	2m6f Cls4 Nov Ch soft		£9,625
	10/10	Font	2m4f Cls4 Ch good		£2,862
125	2/10	Ling	2m7f Cls3 125-125 Hdl Hcap heavy		£6,505
	1/09	Folk	2m6^1/$_2$f Cls4 Nov Hdl heavy		£3,253

Steadily progressive throughout last season but paid price for his consistency, climbing in handicap despite winning just once; ran best ever race when just touched off by Alfie Sherrin at Cheltenham

1132 Galaxy Rock (Ire)

8 b g Heron Island - Blue Pool (Saddlers' Hall)

Jonjo O'Neill   Michael & John O'Flynn

PLACINGS: 25/F45U1141/31P43P9-   RPR **153**+c

Starts	1st	2nd	3rd	4th	Win & Pl
31	8	2	2	4	£68,952
135	11/11	Chel	3m3^1/$_2$f Cls1 Gd3 125-151 Ch Hcap gd-sft		£22,780
124	4/11	Chel	3m4^1/$_2$f Cls3 116-129 Ch Hcap good		£6,320
	3/11	Leic	2m7^1/$_2$f Cls3 Nov Ch heavy		£5,055
	1/11	Ffos	3m Cls4 Ch soft		£3,253
118	12/09	Ffos	2m4f Cls3 107-129 Hdl Hcap gd-sft		£5,006
111	4/09	NAbb	2m6f Cls4 103-115 Hdl Hcap good		£3,578
95	3/09	Sthl	2m Cls4 83-105 Hdl Hcap good		£4,554
95	3/09	MRas	2m3^1/$_2$f Cls4 77-103 Cond Hdl Hcap gd-sft		£3,253

Easily won a red-hot handicap chase at Cheltenham early last season but slightly disappointing later in the campaign; travelled well for a long way before failing to stay 4m1f when well fancied in Scottish National and could win a major handicap over slightly shorter.

1133 Galileo's Choice (Ire)

6 b g Galileo - Sevi's Choice (Sir Ivor)

Dermot Weld (Ir)   Dr R Lambe, Dr M Smurfit, D Keough & Newtown Anner

PLACINGS: 1217-   RPR **151**+h

Starts	1st	2nd	3rd	4th	Win & Pl
4	2	1	-	-	£27,194
	2/12	Fair	2m Nov Hdl soft		£7,475
	7/11	Gway	2m Mdn Hdl good		£7,435

Won twice over hurdles last season before finishing disappointing seventh when favourite for Supreme Novices' Hurdle; has since gone from strength to strength on the Flat and may find hurdling opportunities limited, but full of potential if returning to jumps.

1134 Gauvain (Ger)

10 b g Sternkoenig - Gamina (Dominion)

Nick Williams   Jared Sullivan & Simon Brown

PLACINGS: 16P11/15528/1F1F346-   RPR **166**c

Starts	1st	2nd	3rd	4th	Win & Pl
29	8	5	3	1	£220,478
	12/11	Hntg	2m4^1/$_2$f Cls1 Gd2 Ch gd-sft		£31,323
	11/11	Chel	2m Cls2 Ch gd-sft		£28,412
	11/10	Chel	2m Cls2 Ch gd-sft		£31,310
	4/09	Chel	2m^1/$_2$f Cls2 Nov Ch gd-sft		£13,150
	4/09	Plum	2m1f Cls4 Nov Ch good		£3,444
	2/09	Sand	2m Cls1 Nov Gd2 Ch gd-sft		£19,954
	11/08	Ling	2m Cls4 Ch soft		£3,578
119	12/07	Extr	2m1f Cls3 97-123 Hdl Hcap gd-sft		£5,205

Highly tried in recent campaigns, finishing out of the frame on all five runs at Grade 1 level at around 2m but twice getting placed in Ascot Chase over 2m5f; has a good record at slightly lower level, including winning three times at Cheltenham.

Festival but not as fluent when fifth in Scottish National.

1135 General Miller

7 b g Karinga Bay - Millers Action (Fearless Action)

Nicky Henderson   W H Ponsonby

PLACINGS: 11/12U14/0/2-

Starts	1st	2nd	3rd	4th	Win & Pl
9	4	2	-	1	£60,990

4/10	Aint	2m¹/₂f Cls1 Nov Gd2 Hdl good	£34,206
12/09	Chel	2m1f Cls3 Nov Hdl 4-6yo soft	£6,262
4/09	Prth	2m¹/₂f Cls4 NHF 4-6yo good	£3,426
1/09	Kemp	2m Cls6 NHF 4-6yo soft	£1,713

Very smart novice hurdler three seasons ago, beating Menorah at Aintree; ran only once in each of two subsequent campaigns due to injury problems but did well when second to Overturn at Ayr last season; failed to stay when stepped up to 2m4f for only time.

1136 Get Me Out Of Here (Ire) (above)

8 b g Accordion - Home At Last (Mandalus)

Jonjo O'Neill   John P McManus

PLACINGS: 111112/7682P/52221-   RPR **159**h

Starts	1st	2nd	3rd	4th	Win & Pl
16	6	5	-	-	£213,512

	4/12	Fair	2m4f Gd2 Hdl gd-sft	£21,667
135	2/10	Newb	2m¹/₂f Cls1 Gd3 129-155 Hdl Hcap gd-sft	£85,515
123	11/09	Newb	2m¹/₂f Cls3 106-128 Cond Hdl Hcap soft	£6,262
	11/09	Ffos	2m Cls4 Nov Hdl good	£3,253
	10/09	Worc	2m Cls4 Nov Hdl 4-6yo gd-sft	£3,448
	5/09	Uttx	2m Cls6 NHF 4-6yo good	£1,561

Standing dish in top handicap hurdles in recent years and unlucky to finish second in Betfair Hurdle and Coral Cup last season before well-deserved win in Grade 2 at Fairyhouse; expected to stay 3m by trainer and has plenty of options with chasing a possibility.

1137 Ghizao (Ger)

8 b g Tiger Hill - Glorosia (Bering)

Paul Nicholls   The Johnson & Stewart Families

PLACINGS: 112108/21152/468-   RPR **155**+c

Starts	1st	2nd	3rd	4th	Win & Pl
14	5	3	-	1	£71,455

12/10	Newb	2m2¹/₂f Cls3 Nov Ch gd-sft	£5,855
11/10	Chel	2m Cls1 Nov Gd2 Ch gd-sft	£17,103
1/10	Tntn	2m1f Cls4 Nov Hdl soft	£3,903
11/09	Chel	2m¹/₂f Cls1 List NHF 4-6yo soft	£9,122
8/09	NAbb	2m1f Cls6 NHF 4-6yo gd-fm	£1,370

High-class novice chaser two seasons ago when unlucky not to beat Finian's Rainbow at Aintree; failed to build on that last season when disappointing on all three starts before suffering a setback; trainer still sure he has more to come but may be best in small fields.

1138 Gibb River (Ire)

6 ch g Mr Greeley - Laurentine (Private Account)

Nicky Henderson   Corbett Stud

PLACINGS: 1110/30231-   RPR **147**h

Starts	1st	2nd	3rd	4th	Win & Pl
9	4	1	2	-	£33,840

144	4/12	Sand	2m3¹/₂f Cls2 118-144 Hdl Hcap soft	£15,640
	2/11	Winc	2m Cls3 Nov Hdl gd-sft	£4,119
	1/11	Plum	2m Cls4 Nov Hdl soft	£2,055
	11/10	Hntg	2m¹/₂f Cls4 Nov Hdl gd-sft	£2,602

Had lost his way prior to a breathing operation midway through last season and made a big impression after return, staying on well to finish third in handicap hurdle at Aintree and defying top weight when stepped up to 2m3¹/₂f at Sandown; good chasing prospect.

1139 Giles Cross (Ire)

10 b g Saddlers' Hall - Mystockings (Idiots Delight)

Victor Dartnall   Mrs Kay Birchenhough

PLACINGS: 11P/P2F123/P22/121P-   RPR **149+c**

Starts	1st	2nd	3rd	4th	Win & Pl
17	5	5	2		£122,481
138	2/12	Hayd	3m4f Cls1 Gd3 133-159 Ch Hcap heavy		£42,713
132	11/11	Font	3m4f Cls3 106-132 Ch Hcap soft		£8,133
	1/10	Chep	3m Cls3 Nov Ch heavy		£6,571
	3/09	Extr	2m7¹/₂f Cls4 Nov Hdl gd-sft		£3,903
	12/08	Chep	3m Cls4 Mdn Hdl heavy		£2,927

Has a fine record in top staying handicap chases and gained much-deserved win when pipping Neptune Collonges in last season's Grand National Trial at Haydock; goes particularly well at Chepstow, finishing second in last two renewals of Welsh National.

1140 Giorgio Quercus (Fr)

7 b g Starborough - Winter Breeze (Kaldoun)

Nicky Henderson   Seasons Holidays

PLACINGS: 1615P102/F1165/2100-   RPR **156+c**

Starts	1st	2nd	3rd	4th	Win & Pl
19	6	3		1	£70,585
	1/12	Hayd	2m5f Cls2 Ch heavy		£12,660
	2/11	Sand	2m Cls3 Nov Ch soft		£7,828
	1/11	Leic	2m Cls3 Nov Ch good		£4,554
	12/10	Kemp	2m Cls4 NHF std-slw		£2,277
	2/09	Muss	2m Cls2 Nov Hdl 4yo good		£12,524
	11/08	Hrfd	2m1f Cls4 Nov Hdl 3yo soft		£3,253
	5/08	Autl	2m2f Hdl 3yo v soft		£16,235

Has plenty of ability but only seems to produce best form in small fields, such as when running out a wide-margin winner at Haydock last season; ran well for a long way in Topham Chase over National fences before appearing to run out of stamina.

1141 Go All The Way (Ire)

7 b g Milan - Kings Rose (King's Ride)

Jim Dreaper (Ir)   Ann & Alan Potts Partnership

PLACINGS: 2/4/8516-11   RPR **146+c**

Starts	1st	2nd	3rd	4th	Win & Pl
8	3	1	-	1	£22,556
	8/12	Klny	2m4¹/₂f Nov Ch soft		£6,613
	7/12	Klny	2m4¹/₂f Ch gd-yld		£4,888
	3/12	Navn	2m4f Mdn Hdl soft		£5,750

Finished fourth in Champion Bumper at Cheltenham in 2011 before missing much of last season, finishing sixth behind Simonsig at Aintree on stiffest hurdling test; began to realise early promise with sparkling chasing debut at Killarney in July; smart prospect.

1142 Go Native (Ire) (below)

9 br g Double Eclipse - Native Idea (Be My Native)

Noel Meade (Ir)   Docado Syndicate

PLACINGS: 921/121211/412110/

Starts	1st	2nd	3rd	4th	Win & Pl
15	8	4	-	1	£310,254
	12/09	Kemp	2m Cls1 Gd1 Hdl gd-sft		£57,010
	11/09	Newc	2m Cls1 Gd1 Hdl gd-sft		£56,330
	10/09	Tipp	2m Gd2 Hdl gd-fm		£34,762
	3/09	Chel	2m¹/₂f Cls1 Nov Gd1 Hdl gd-sft		£68,412
	2/09	Naas	2m Nov Gd2 Hdl soft		£31,602
	12/08	Punc	2m Nov List Hdl heavy		£19,147
	7/08	Kbgn	2m Mdn Hdl 4-5yo good		£5,081
	4/08	Punc	2m NHF 4-7yo good		£9,574

Won 2009 Supreme Novices' Hurdle and took form

to another level the following season, winning the Fighting Fifth and Christmas Hurdles; injured when favourite for the Champion Hurdle and not seen since but reportedly fit again this summer.

1143 Going Wrong
9 b g Bob Back - Lucy Glitters (Ardross)

Ferdy Murphy   Universal Recycling Company

PLACINGS: 5/445/12/4110-   RPR 138c

Starts	1st	2nd	3rd	4th	Win & Pl
10	3	1	-	3	£14,804
127	1/12	Sedg	2m¹/₂f Cls4 Nov Ch soft	£3,119
	11/11	Sedg	2m4f Cls3 Nov 113-127 Ch gd-sft................	£4,595
	11/09	Carl	2m4f Cls4 Nov Hdl soft..................................	£3,083

Did well in novice chases last season following nearly two years out through injury; gained both wins at Sedgefield, looking best suited by 2m4f, though disappointed over that trip next time at Cheltenham after early mistakes; likely to improve again.

1144 Golden Call (Ire)
8 b g Goldmark - Call Me Countess (Aristocracy)

Donald McCain   M M Allen

PLACINGS: FO/15P1/12321411F2-1   RPR 145+c

Starts	1st	2nd	3rd	4th	Win & Pl
11	5	3	1	1	£26,202
	5/12	Bang	2m4¹/₂f Cls4 Nov Ch gd-sft..........................	£3,899
128	3/12	Bang	3m Cls3 110-135 Hdl Hcap good.........................	£5,697
119	2/12	Bang	3m Cls3 111-127 Hdl Hcap good.........................	£4,549
	11/11	Sthl	3m¹/₂f Cls4 Nov Hdl good................................	£2,669
	5/11	Tipp	2m2f NHF 4-7yo good.....................................	£4,461

Developed into a useful staying hurdler last season, winning back-to-back handicaps at Bangor; looked even better on his chasing debut back at that track, making all to win by 25 lengths; could rack up plenty more wins in novice chases.

1145 Grand Vision (Ire)
6 gr g Old Vic - West Hill Rose (Roselier)

Colin Tizzard   Terry Warner

PLACINGS: 22/232113-   RPR 151+h

Starts	1st	2nd	3rd	4th	Win & Pl
8	2	4	2	-	£29,370
122	2/12	Hayd	3m Cls2 120-145 Hdl Hcap heavy......................	£11,696
114	1/12	Hntg	2m5¹/₂f Cls4 99-115 Hdl Hcap gd-sft	£3,574

Improved rapidly once sent handicapping last season, going up 22lb for wins at Huntingdon and Haydock; balloted out of Pertemps Final at Cheltenham but showed he was ready for Grade 1 company with fine third in Albert Bartlett Hurdle; top novice chase prospect.

1146 Grandouet (Fr)
5 b/br g Al Namix - Virginia River (Indian River)

Nicky Henderson   Simon Munir

PLACINGS: 331/52113B/1F11-   RPR 166+h

Starts	1st	2nd	3rd	4th	Win & Pl
13	6	1	3	-	£198,973
	12/11	Chel	2m1f Cls1 Gd2 Hdl good..................................	£74,035
	11/11	Hayd	2m Cls2 Hdl 4yo gd-sft..................................	£25,024
	5/11	Punc	2m Gd1 Hdl 4yo good....................................	£42,759
	1/11	Asct	2m Cls3 Hdl 4yo gd-sft..................................	£4,383
	12/10	Newb	2m1f Cls3 Hdl 3yo gd-sft................................	£4,879
	4/10	Engh	2m¹/₂f Hdl 3yo v soft...................................	£19,540

Much improved last season when putting himself firmly in the Champion Hurdle picture with impressive win in Boylesports International; ruled out of Cheltenham with minor setback but could still become a leading contender again.

1147 Grands Crus (Fr)
7 gr g Dom Alco - Fee Magic (Phantom Breeze)

David Pipe   Roger Stanley & Yvonne Reynolds III

PLACINGS: 97212/11122/61114-   RPR 168+c

Starts	1st	2nd	3rd	4th	Win & Pl
15	7	4	-	1	£226,434
	12/11	Kemp	3m Cls1 Nov Gd1 Ch gd-sft............................	£22,887
	11/11	Newb	3m Cls1 Nov Gd2 Ch good.............................	£13,668
	11/11	Chel	2m4¹/₂f Cls2 Nov Ch good............................	£10,675
	1/11	Chel	3m Cls1 Gd2 Hdl gd-sft................................	£22,804
132	11/10	Hayd	3m Cls5 List 125-148 Hdl Hcap gd-sft...............	£42,758
126	11/10	Chel	2m5f Cls2 113-139 Hdl Hcap gd-sft..................	£12,524
	1/10	Plum	2m5f Cls4 Nov Hdl soft.................................	£3,253

High-class staying hurdler who made brilliant start over fences last season when winning first three chases, most notably with scintillating triumph in Feltham Chase at Kempton; disappointing fourth when favourite in RSA Chase but found to be wrong later.

1148 Groody Hill (Ire)
6 gr g Alderbrook - Secret Leave (Long Leave)

Christy Roche (Ir)   John P McManus

PLACINGS: 4/6559/5361113P-   RPR 141c

Starts	1st	2nd	3rd	4th	Win & Pl
13	3	-	2	1	£76,412
124	11/11	Navn	3m 115-143 Ch Hcap sft-hvy..........................	£44,828
111	10/11	Wxfd	2m3f 95-111 Ch Hcap soft.............................	£9,815
105	10/11	Punc	2m4f 85-115 Ch Hcap heavy..........................	£5,948

Made rapid improvement last autumn when gradually stepping up in trip to win three successive handicap chases; again ran well off much higher mark when third in Paddy Power Chase at Leopardstown but pulled up when fancied for Irish Grand National.

1149 Grumeti (below, 6)

4 b g Sakhee - Tetravella (Groom Dancer)

Alan King   Mcneill Family

PLACINGS: 1F1131-   RPR **148+**h

Starts	1st	2nd	3rd	4th	Win & Pl
6	4	-	1	-	£96,759

4/12	Aint	2m¹/₂f Cls1 Gd1 Hdl 4yo gd-sft	£56,270
2/12	Kemp	2m Cls1 Nov Gd2 Hdl good	£12,130
1/12	Chel	2m1f Cls1 Gd2 Hdl 4yo gd-sft	£14,238
12/11	Tntn	2m1f Cls4 Nov Hdl gd-sft	£3,422

Arguably the leading juvenile hurdler of last season having suffered from an interrupted preparation when third at Cheltenham and then beaten Triumph Hurdle winner Countrywide Flame at Aintree; takes his racing well and could be underrated.

1150 Gullinbursti (Ire)

6 b g Milan - D'Ygrande (Good Thyne)

Emma Lavelle   N Mustoe

PLACINGS: 721/11220-   RPR **143+**h

Starts	1st	2nd	3rd	4th	Win & Pl
8	3	3	-	-	£18,588

11/11	Hrfd	2m6¹/₂f Cls4 Nov Hdl gd-sft	£2,534
11/11	Extr	2m5¹/₂f Cls4 Nov Hdl gd-sft	£2,274
3/11	Cork	2m2f NHF 5-7yo yld-sft	£5,651

Smart staying novice hurdler last season, winning twice before two good seconds in Grade 2 at Doncaster (behind Rocky Creek) and competitive handicap hurdle at Newbury; well below best at Aintree on final start; could be a good novice chaser.

1151 Harry The Viking

7 ch g Sir Harry Lewis - Viking Flame (Viking)

Paul Nicholls   Sir A Ferguson, G Mason, R Wood & P Done

PLACINGS: PU/12/11112P-   RPR **149+**c

Starts	1st	2nd	3rd	4th	Win & Pl
7	4	2	-	-	£29,875

129	12/11	Donc	3m2f Cls3 Nov 120-131 Ch Hcap gd-sft	£5,848
	12/11	Donc	3m Cls4 Nov Ch gd-sft	£3,899
	11/11	Towc	3m Cls4 Nov Hdl good	£3,249
	10/11	Chep	3m Cls5 Mdn Hdl good	£2,144

Sent over fences following two novice hurdle wins last season and soon won twice more; stayed 4m well when second in National Hunt Chase at Cheltenham, staying on having been outpaced, but always in rear when pulled up as favourite in Scottish National.

1152 Havingotascoobydo (Ire)

7 b g Witness Box - In Blue (Executive Perk)

Martin Keighley   D Bishop, C Bowkley, M Parker & M Thornton

PLACINGS: 241/1431215/1F123F2-   RPR **141+**c

Starts	1st	2nd	3rd	4th	Win & Pl
14	5	3	2	1	£32,797

	10/11	Weth	2m Cls4 Nov Ch good	£4,549
	10/11	Ffos	2m Cls4 Nov Ch good	£3,444
115	3/11	Ludl	2m5f Cls3 94-127 Hdl Hcap good	£4,619
104	3/11	Ludl	2m5f Cls3 Nov 100-116 Hdl Hcap good	£4,436
	8/10	NAbb	2m1f Cls6 NHF 4-6yo gd-sft	£1,541

Showed promise over fences last season, winning twice and getting placed in two 2m handicap chases at Cheltenham before missing end of season through injury; should improve again over further having won twice beyond 2m4f over hurdles.

1153 He'llberemembered (Ire)

9 ch g Blue Ocean - Remember Rob (Deep Society)

Paul Fahey (Ir)   Mrs Mary Lett

PLACINGS: 053312/3164/1324423-   RPR **146**h

Starts	1st	2nd	3rd	4th	Win & Pl
17	3	3	5	3	£50,457

117	10/11	Naas	2m4f 109-137 Hdl Hcap heavy	£15,409
	8/10	Gway	2m Mdn Hdl gd-fm	£7,938
	9/09	Navn	2m NHF 4-7yo gd-fm	£5,702

Improved steadily throughout last season despite failing to follow up victory in a handicap hurdle at Naas last October, running a string of good races despite climbing in the handicap; handles all types of ground and capable of winning good races.

1154 Hector's Choice (Fr)

8 b/br g Grey Risk - The Voice (Ski Chief)

Richard Lee   James And Jean Potter

PLACINGS: 442/4V/031P/1323201-   RPR **154**c

Starts	1st	2nd	3rd	4th	Win & Pl
19	5	4	3	3	£91,375

146	4/12	Chel	2m5f Cls1 Gd2 135-155 Ch Hcap gd-sft	£23,048
132	10/11	Aint	2m4f Cls3 117-135 Ch Hcap good	£6,963
	3/11	Ludl	2m4f Cls3 Nov Ch good	£5,596
129	11/08	Newb	2m1/2f Cls3 111-129 Cond Hdl Hcap gd-sft	£6,262
	4/08	Nant	2m1½f Hdl 4yo gd-sft	£4,941

Placed in a number of top handicap chases last season before gaining deserved win on final start at Cheltenham; likely to return to Prestbury Park for Paddy Power Gold Cup and may well find sufficient improvement to bag a big one.

1155 Helpston

8 b g Sir Harry Lewis - Chichell's Hurst (Oats)

Pam Sly   Mrs P M Sly

PLACINGS: 2123/0628/32/2112U1-   RPR **147**c

Starts	1st	2nd	3rd	4th	Win & Pl
18	4	6	3	-	£44,641

	2/12	Newc	3m Cls2 Nov Ch good	£7,757
	11/11	Fknm	3m1/2f Cls3 Nov Ch good	£5,848
	10/11	Weth	3m1f Cls3 Nov Ch good	£5,198
	11/08	Leic	2m4½f Cls3 Nov Hdl soft	£6,337

Benefited from failing to win in his first season over fences when winning three novice chases during the last campaign, improving steadily throughout; second in Rowland Meyrick Chase when stepping up to handicaps and could do well in staying chases.

1156 Hey Big Spender (Ire)

9 b g Rudimentary - Jim's Monkey (Monksfield)

Colin Tizzard   Brocade Racing

PLACINGS: 2121UF/1F8149P/41F1-   RPR **164**+c

Starts	1st	2nd	3rd	4th	Win & Pl
25	7	2	4	3	£118,649

156	1/12	Wwck	3m5f Cls1 Gd3 130-156 Ch Hcap gd-sft	£31,323
150	11/11	Newc	3m Cls1 List 124-150 Ch Hcap gd-sft	£14,238
150	2/11	Wwck	2m4½f Cls2 129-150 Ch Hcap gd-sft	£12,524
	11/10	Carl	3m½f Cls2 Ch heavy	£15,799
138	1/10	Chel	2m5f Cls2 Nov 120-138 Ch Hcap soft	£14,090
130	11/09	Newb	2m6½f Cls3 Nov 108-130 Ch Hcap gd-sft	£11,272
	2/09	Chep	2m4f Cls4 Mdn Hdl soft	£2,927

Comes up short at top level but has done well under big weights in staying handicaps, gaining biggest win last season in Classic Chase at Warwick;

remains on a similar mark; has finished no better than ninth in five starts on ground quicker than good to soft.

1157 Hidden Cyclone (Ire) (above)

7 b g Stowaway - Hurricane Debbie (Shahanndeh)

John Joseph Hanlon (Ir)   Mrs A F Mee

PLACINGS: 1/113111/13-   RPR **141**+c

Starts	1st	2nd	3rd	4th	Win & Pl
9	7	-	2	-	£95,132

12/11	Leop	2m3f Ch gd-yld	£7,733
3/11	Navn	2m7f Nov Hdl sft-hvy	£10,112
2/11	Thur	2m4f Nov Gd2 Hdl soft	£21,013
1/11	Leop	2m4f Nov Gd2 Hdl soft	£22,134
11/10	Navn	2m Nov Gd3 Hdl soft	£16,394
10/10	Tipp	2m Mdn Hdl 4-5yo yield	£3,186
4/10	Gowr	2m NHF 4-7yo good	£5,190

Showed vast potential in novice hurdles two seasons ago, twice winning at Grade 2 level before completing a hat-trick over 2m7f at Navan; restricted to just two runs over fences last season and no match for Sir Des Champs at Leopardstown; could do better when back up in trip.

1158 Highland Lodge (Ire)

6 b g Flemensfirth - Supreme Von Pres (Presenting)

Emma Lavelle   The Unusual Suspects

PLACINGS: 1/114-   RPR **137**+h

Starts	1st	2nd	3rd	4th	Win & Pl
3	2	-	-	1	£8,480

12/11	Hayd	2m4f Cls4 Nov Hdl heavy	£4,874
11/11	Extr	2m5¹/₂f Cls4 Nov Hdl gd-sft	£2,274

Point-to-point winner who made a big impression when winning first two starts over hurdles last

season; not right when disappointing fourth behind Cotton Mill at Warwick last time having been sent off odds-on; sure to progress again and could do well in novice chases.

1159 Hisaabaat (Ire)

4 b g Dubawi - Phariseek (Rainbow Quest)

Dermot Weld (Ir)   Dr R Lambe & D Glennane

PLACINGS: U222121-9   RPR **142**h

Starts	1st	2nd	3rd	4th	Win & Pl
8	2	4	-	-	£107,640

4/12	Punc	2m Gd1 Hdl 4yo heavy	£41,333
2/12	Leop	2m Gd1 Hdl 4yo gd-sft	£37,917

Initially found it hard to win last season but eventually proved himself the best juvenile hurdler in Ireland with two Grade 1 wins either side of terrific second in Triumph Hurdle at Cheltenham; seen by trainer as a long-term Champion Hurdle hope.

1160 Hold On Julio (Ire)

9 br g Blueprint - Eileens Native (Be My Native)

Alan King   Mr & Mrs F Bell, N Farrell & A Marsh

PLACINGS: PP/P/121111/110-   RPR **150**+c

Starts	1st	2nd	3rd	4th	Win & Pl
6	3	-	-	-	£40,035

133	1/12	Sand	3m1¹/₂f Cls2 133-159 Ch Hcap gd-sft	£31,280
117	11/11	Sand	3m1¹/₂f Cls3 104-125 Ch Hcap gd-sft	£6,882
	4/11	Kels	3m1f Cls5 Am Mdn Hunt Ch gd-sft	£1,874

Went straight into handicap chases last season after winning a maiden hunter previous April and exploited lenient mark to win twice at Sandown; found life much tougher when disappointing favourite at Cheltenham, finishing tenth; something to prove.

1161 Hollow Tree

4 b g Beat Hollow - Hesperia (Slip Anchor)

Donald McCain   Brannon Dennis & Dick Holden

PLACINGS: 121137-   **RPR 140h**

Starts	1st	2nd	3rd	4th	Win & Pl
6	3	1	1	-	£30,609

12/11	Chep	2m¹/₂f Cls1 Gd1 Hdl 3yo heavy	£17,939
11/11	Ffos	2m Cls4 Hdl 3yo soft	£2,663
9/11	Bang	2m1f Cls4 Hdl 3yo good	£2,738

Flattered by Grade 1 victory over Triumph winner Countrywide Flame (unsuited by heavy ground) at Chepstow; still performed well twice subsequently at Cheltenham, including when seventh in Triumph, and could make mark in handicaps.

1162 Houblon Des Obeaux (Fr)

5 b g Panoramic - Harkosa (Nikos)

Venetia Williams   Mrs Julian Blackwell

PLACINGS: /139B222103/9671046-   **RPR 145h**

Starts	1st	2nd	3rd	4th	Win & Pl
18	3	3	3	1	£64,431

135	1/12	Chel	3m Cls2 134-160 Hdl Hcap gd-sft	£12,512
	2/11	Chel	2m Cls2 Hdl 4yo heavy	£6,895
	5/10	Seno	1m7f Hdl 3yo good	£5,522

Showed huge improvement when stepped up in trip to 3m midway through last season, winning at Cheltenham and flying up the hill to finish excellent fourth in Pertemps Final; should find more opportunities over marathon trips when switched to fences.

1163 Hunt Ball (Ire)

7 b g Winged Love - La Fandango (Taufan)

Keiran Burke   Anthony Knott

PLACINGS: /25U1P344/111211113-   **RPR 165c**

Starts	1st	2nd	3rd	4th	Win & Pl
13	7	1	1	1	£73,928

142	3/12	Chel	2m4¹/₂f Cls1 Nov List 132-142 Ch Hcap good	£28,475
127	2/12	Kemp	2m4¹/₂f Cls3 108-128 Ch Hcap good	£7,148
117	2/12	Winc	2m5f Cls3 117-130 Ch Hcap soft	£7,148
108	1/12	Winc	2m5f Cls3 105-128 Ch Hcap gd-sft	£7,913
85	12/11	Folk	2m5f Cls5 76-95 Ch Hcap good	£1,916
75	12/11	Font	2m4f Cls5 68-94 Ch Hcap soft	£1,819
69	11/11	Folk	2m5f Cls5 Nov 69-95 Ch Hcap gd-fm	£1,916

Became the fairytale horse of last season when landing novice handicap chase at Cheltenham Festival having climbed 73lb in handicap for winning six of previous seven races; showed he belongs at top level when brilliant third in Betfred Bowl.

1164 Hurricane Fly (Ire)

8 b g Montjeu - Scandisk (Kenmare)

Willie Mullins (Ir)   George Creighton

PLACINGS: 11211/131/1111/1131-   **RPR 173+h**

Starts	1st	2nd	3rd	4th	Win & Pl
16	13	1	2	-	£967,095

4/12	Punc	2m Gd1 Hdl heavy	£80,000
1/12	Leop	2m Gd1 Hdl heavy	£59,583
5/11	Punc	2m Gd1 Hdl good	£82,759
3/11	Chel	2m¹/₂f Cls1 Gd1 Hdl good	£210,937
1/11	Leop	2m Gd1 Hdl soft	£61,638
12/10	Leop	2m Gd1 Hdl heavy	£51,770
12/10	Fair	2m4f Gd1 Hdl soft	£48,894
4/10	Punc	2m Gd1 Hdl good	£90,265
4/09	Punc	2m Nov Gd1 Hdl soft	£60,194
12/08	Leop	2m Nov Gd1 Hdl yld-sft	£38,235
11/08	Fair	2m Nov Gd1 Hdl good	£43,015
5/08	Autl	2m3¹/₂f Gd3 Hdl 4yo v soft	£43,015
5/08	Punc	2m Mdn Hdl 4-5yo gd-fm	£6,097

Fragile but brilliant hurdler who won Champion Hurdle in great style in 2011; seemed to return as good as ever when running away with Irish Champion Hurdle but only third at Cheltenham and made hard work of winning at Punchestown; still sets high standard.

1165 Ikorodu Road

9 b g Double Trigger - Cerisier (Roselier)

Matt Sheppard   W J Odell

PLACINGS: /52/U23UF3/0P52211P-   **RPR 143c**

Starts	1st	2nd	3rd	4th	Win & Pl
19	3	5	3	-	£76,011

134	3/12	Newb	3m2¹/₂f Cls2 126-152 Ch Hcap good	£31,280
131	3/12	Donc	3m2f Cls2 131-157 Ch Hcap good	£29,241
	3/09	Sthl	2m Cls4 Mdn Hdl good	£3,578

Took a long time to find his feet over fences but did really well when stepped up in trip last season, just landing Grimthorpe Chase following two narrow defeats; given 7lb rise after following up in moderate race at Newbury and pulled up in Scottish National.

1166 Il Fenomeno (Ity)

6 b g Denon - Fabulous Charm (Fabulous Dancer)

Noel Meade (Ir)   Gigginstown House Stud

PLACINGS: 5411538-   **RPR 141h**

Starts	1st	2nd	3rd	4th	Win & Pl
7	2	-	1	1	£29,426

11/11	Navn	2m Nov Gd3 Hdl yld-sft	£15,409
10/11	Punc	2m Mdn Hdl yld-sft	£5,948

Won twice in novice hurdles last season, most notably in a Grade 3 at Navan, before coming up short at a higher level; still ran well when third to Beneficient at Leopardstown and could have more to come given Flat class (Group 3 winner in Italy).

1167 Immediate Response (Ire)

9 b g Strategic Choice - Rosies All The Way (Robellino)

Willie Mullins (Ir)   Kates Monkeys Syndicate

PLACINGS: 30/3187435/664/1118-   RPR **143 +h**

Starts 16		1st 4	2nd -	3rd 3	4th 2	Win & Pl £22,771
116	3/12	Limk	2m 86-116 Hdl Hcap sft-hvy			£5,750
96	2/12	Thur	2m6f 81-101 Hdl Hcap sft-hvy			£4,600
92	2/12	Clon	2m¹/₂f 80-93 Hdl Hcap heavy			£4,025
	11/08	Gowr	2m NHF 4-5yo soft			£5,589

Had shown little ability in maiden hurdles in 2009 but showed rapid improvement on return from more than two years out last season, winning three times in impressive fashion; modest eighth next time suggests handicapper may just have his measure.

1168 Imperial Commander (Ire)

11 b g Flemensfirth - Ballinlovane (Le Moss)

Nigel Twiston-Davies   Our Friends In The North

PLACINGS: 73/114/161/P251U/1P/

Starts 19		1st 8	2nd 1	3rd 1	4th 2	Win & Pl £684,697
	11/10	Hayd	3m Cls1 Gd1 Ch gd-sft			£112,660
	3/10	Chel	3m2¹/₂f Cls1 Gd1 Ch good			£270,798
	3/09	Chel	2m5f Cls1 Gd1 Ch gd-sft			£125,422
139	11/08	Chel	2m4¹/₂f Cls1 Gd3 137-158 Ch Hcap soft			£85,515
	11/07	Chel	2m4¹/₂f Cls2 Nov Ch good			£12,572
	10/07	Chel	2m4¹/₂f Cls3 Ch good			£7,858
	1/07	Newc	2m4f Cls4 Nov Hdl soft			£2,928
	10/06	Chel	2m¹/₂f Cls4 NHF 4-6yo gd-sft			£3,578

Won Cheltenham Gold Cup in 2010 but pulled up when defending his title the following year and missed last season through injury; back in training and due to return in Betfair Chase, which he won

in 2010 having previously lost by a nose to Kauto Star.

1169 Ipsos Du Berlais (Fr)

6 gr g Poliglote - Isis Du Berlais (Cadoudal)

Noel Meade (Ir)   Gigginstown House Stud

PLACINGS: 1/11231P4P-   RPR **147 +h**

Starts 8		1st 3	2nd 1	3rd 1	4th 1	Win & Pl £33,818
	1/12	Punc	2m4f Hdl sft-hvy			£7,475
	11/11	DRoy	2m6f Mdn Hdl soft			£8,328
	10/11	Gway	2m NHF 4-7yo heavy			£5,353

Highly tried last season in staying novice hurdles, producing best efforts when third to Boston Bob at Navan and fourth to Lovcen at Aintree; struggled for consistency and has looked a tricky ride (tried in blinkers last twice); may do better over fences.

1170 It's A Gimme (Ire)

5 b g Beneficial - Sorcera (Zilzal)

Jonjo O'Neill   John P McManus

PLACINGS: 414/21218-   RPR **141 +h**

Starts 8		1st 3	2nd 2	3rd -	4th 2	Win & Pl £11,719
	2/12	Sthl	2m4¹/₂f Cls4 Nov Hdl gd-sft			£2,534
	11/11	Newb	2m¹/₂f Cls3 Mdn Hdl gd-sft			£4,224
	12/10	Extr	1m5f Cls5 NHF 3yo gd-sft			£1,952

Made an extremely bright start to hurdling career, making up for near miss at Aintree with excellent win at Newbury; disappointing subsequently but clearly failed to stay 2m4f even when winning at Southwell and could do well at 2m.

1171 Jenari (Ire)

5 b g Milan - La Noire (Phardante)

Jessica Harrington (Ir)   **John P McManus**

PLACINGS: 21/3212231F-					RPR **148h**
Starts	1st	2nd	3rd	4th	Win & Pl
10	3	4	2	-	£46,401

4/12	Fair	2m4f Nov Gd2 Hdl good £21,667
11/11	Limk	2m Mdn Hdl 4-5yo soft £7,435
4/11	Gowr	2m NHF 4yo good £3,310

Third in Grade 1 bumper at Punchestown in 2011 and reached similar level in novice hurdles last season; benefited from step up to 2m4f when winning at Fairyhouse having been placed three times over shorter but fell when going well at Punchestown.

1172 Jetson (Ire)

7 b g Oscar - La Noire (Phardante)

Jessica Harrington (Ir)   **G McGrath**

PLACINGS: 12/B5322/154125-					RPR **148h**
Starts	1st	2nd	3rd	4th	Win & Pl
124	3	4	1	1	£44,118

12/11	Leop	3m 111-139 Hdl Hcap soft £13,448
11/11	Cork	2m4f Mdn Hdl soft £8,328
2/10	Navn	2m NHF 5-7yo soft £5,190

No match for top novice hurdlers early last season but won Pertemps qualifier at Leopardstown and well fancied for final before being balloted out; improved again when second at Fairyhouse before easily forgiven subsequent flop on desperate ground at Punchestown.

1173 Join Together (Ire) (above)

7 b g Old Vic - Open Cry (Montelimar)

Paul Nicholls   **Paul K Barber & Ian J Fogg**

PLACINGS: 3/21/321P/F11P3-					RPR **156+c**
Starts	1st	2nd	3rd	4th	Win & Pl
9	3	1	2	-	£41,149

12/11	Chel	3m1¹/₂f Cls2 Nov Ch good £12,628
11/11	Chel	3m¹/₂f Cls2 Nov Ch gd-sft £12,512
2/11	Chep	3m Cls4 Nov Hdl soft £2,017

Won twice at Cheltenham last season but dropped out tamely when stepped up in class in RSA Chase and again appeared to have limitations exposed when distant third at Aintree; should relish marathon distances but looks high in handicap.

1174 Joncol (Ire)

9 b g Bob's Return - Finemar Lady (Montelimar)

Paul Nolan (Ir)   **Mrs K Browne**

PLACINGS: 2/111/32131/433/127-					RPR **162+c**
Starts	1st	2nd	3rd	4th	Win & Pl
16	7	3	4	1	£289,581

11/11	Thur	2m6f List Ch sft-hvy..............................£15,409
2/10	Leop	3m Gd1 Ch soft.....................................£91,593
12/09	Punc	2m4f Gd1 Ch heavy...............................£59,417
3/09	Naas	2m4f Nov Ch soft..................................£12,411
2/09	Naas	2m4f Nov Gd2 Ch soft...........................£30,022
12/08	Punc	2m4f Ch heavy.......................................£8,129
1/08	Thur	2m2f NHF 5-7yo heavy...........................£4,319

Dual Grade 1 winner three seasons ago and placed three times at that level from just six starts since then; has had opportunities limited by need for soft ground and suffered a tendon injury when tried on good ground for first time in Lexus Chase last season.

1175 Junior

9 ch g Singspiel - For More (Sanglamore)

David Pipe   Middleham Park Racing LI

PLACINGS: 1220/43131/321/82FP-   RPR **161+c**

Starts	1st	2nd	3rd	4th	Win & Pl
26	4	8	4	1	£110,459

134	3/11	Chel	3m1½f Cls2 129-140 Am Ch Hcap good	£30,010
	4/10	Tntn	2m7½f Cls4 Nov Ch gd-sft	£5,855
	3/10	Donc	3m Cls4 Ch good	£3,903
	12/08	Sand	2m4f Cls1 Nov Gd2 Hdl soft	£17,103

Achieved rare distinction of winning at Royal Ascot and Cheltenham Festival with wide-margin victory in Kim Muir in 2011; trained for Grand National last season but fell early and perhaps still feeling effects when pulled up in Scottish National following week.

1176 Kauto Star (Fr) *(right)*

12 b g Village Star - Kauto Relka (Port Etienne)

Paul Nicholls   Clive D Smith

PLACINGS: 2/1U11/11F/133/P11P-   RPR **182+c**

Starts	1st	2nd	3rd	4th	Win & Pl
41	23	7	4	-	£2,375,883

	12/11	Kemp	3m Cls1 Gd1 Ch gd-sft	£102,992
	11/11	Hayd	3m Cls1 Gd1 Ch gd-sft	£113,072
	11/10	DRoy	3m Gd1 Ch soft	£74,336
	12/09	Kemp	3m Cls1 Gd1 Ch gd-sft	£114,020
	11/09	Hayd	3m Cls1 Gd1 Ch soft	£112,660
	3/09	Chel	3m2½f Cls1 Gd1 Ch gd-sft	£270,798
	12/08	Kemp	3m Cls1 Gd1 Ch good	£130,684
	11/08	DRoy	3m Gd1 Ch soft	£66,912
	2/08	Asct	2m5½f Cls1 Gd1 Ch good	£84,510
	12/07	Kemp	3m Cls1 Gd1 Ch gd-sft	£126,034
	11/07	Hayd	3m Cls1 Gd1 Ch soft	£114,040
	3/07	Chel	3m2½f Cls1 Gd1 Ch gd-sft	£242,335
	2/07	Newb	3m Cls1 Gd2 Ch soft	£28,510
	12/06	Kemp	3m Cls1 Gd1 Ch gd-sft	£114,040
	12/06	Sand	2m Cls1 Gd1 Ch soft	£79,828
	11/06	Hayd	3m Cls1 Gd1 Ch gd-sft	£114,040
167	10/06	Aint	2m4f Cls1 Gd2 147-167 Ch Hcap good	£28,510
	12/05	Sand	2m Cls1 Ch soft	£71,275
	12/04	Newb	2m2½f Cls3 Nov Ch gd-sft	£8,840
	5/04	Autl	2m3½f Gd3 Hdl 4yo v soft	£38,028
	9/03	Autl	2m2f List Hdl 3yo v soft	£20,260
	5/03	Autl	1m7f Hdl 3yo v soft	£12,468
	4/03	Engh	1m7f Hdl 3yo v soft	£11,221

Legendary chaser who bounced back to form last season to land his fourth Betfair Chase at Haydock and fifth King George at Kempton; has also won the Gold Cup twice but was pulled up when last seen in March; likely to follow the same schedule if pleasing trainer this autumn.

1177 Kauto Stone (Fr)

6 ch g With The Flow - Kauto Relka (Port Etienne)

Paul Nicholls   R J H Geffen

PLACINGS: 31224/1261173/127F7-   RPR **166+c**

Starts	1st	2nd	3rd	4th	Win & Pl
22	7	4	2	1	£593,211

	11/11	DRoy	2m4f Gd2 Ch soft	£28,017
	11/10	Autl	2m6f Gd1 Ch 4yo heavy	£139,381
	10/10	Autl	2m5½f Gd3 Ch 4yo v soft	£59,735
	5/10	Autl	2m4½f Ch v soft	£38,230
	10/09	Autl	2m2f Gd2 Hdl 3yo v soft	£76,456
	9/09	Autl	2m2f Hdl 3yo v soft	£21,437
	7/09	Claf	2m1f Hdl 3yo soft	£14,913

Grade 1 winner in France who made good start to

British career last season when winning at Down Royal and chasing home Sizing Europe in Tingle Creek; bitterly disappointing in both completed starts since then, falling at Cheltenham in between; plenty to prove.

1178 Kazlian (Fr)

4 b g Sinndar - Quiet Splendor (Unbridled)

David Pipe   Twelve Pipers Piping

PLACINGS: 21147-   **RPR 134+h**

Starts	1st	2nd	3rd	4th	Win & Pl
5	2	1	-	1	£9,885
1/12	Leic	2m Cls4 Nov Hdl soft			£3,249
12/11	Ffos	2m Cls4 Hdl 3yo heavy			£2,599

Listed runner-up on the Flat who twice won well in moderate juvenile hurdles last season before running a stormer in the Fred Winter at Cheltenham, going clear before fading into fourth; didn't enjoy being held up when favourite at Aintree; should do better.

1179 Kells Belle (Ire)

6 b m Alflora - Clandestine (Saddlers' Hall)

Nicky Henderson   Brian, Gwen, Terri & Kelly Griffiths

PLACINGS: 12130/324181-   **RPR 144+h**

Starts	1st	2nd	3rd	4th	Win & Pl
11	4	2	2	1	£26,633
4/12	Chel	2m5¹/₂f Cls1 List 110-134 Hdl Hcap soft			£9,966
1/12	Sand	2m4f Cls1 List Hdl soft			£8,827
2/11	Ludl	2m Cls4 Mdn Hdl good			£2,602
5/10	Worc	2m Cls6 NHF 4-6yo good			£1,370

Ran well in big-field handicap hurdles early last season before coming into her own when switched to mares' races, finishing eighth to Quevega at Cheltenham in between good Listed wins; should

again do well in that division, perhaps over fences.

1180 Khyber Kim

10 b g Mujahid - Jungle Rose (Shirley Heights)

Nigel Twiston-Davies   Mrs Caroline Mould

PLACINGS: 404/20500/51121/496/

Starts	1st	2nd	3rd	4th	Win & Pl
17	4	2	-	3	£344,333
4/10	Aint	2m4f Cls1 Gd1 Hdl good			£91,216
12/09	Chel	2m1f Cls1 Gd2 Hdl soft			£85,515
11/09	Chel	2m¹/₂f Cls1 Gd3 120-146 Hdl Hcap soft			£57,010
12/07	Newb	2m¹/₂f Cls2 Hdl soft			£12,526

143 (left of the 11/09 row)

Developed into a top-class hurdler three seasons ago, finishing second in the Champion Hurdle before successfully stepping up to 2m4f at Aintree; below form following season and out since through injury; back in training but may need help from handicapper.

1181 Kid Cassidy (Ire)

6 b g Beneficial - Shuil Na Lee (Phardante)

Nicky Henderson   John P McManus

PLACINGS: 13/132/1F1105-   **RPR 150+c**

Starts	1st	2nd	3rd	4th	Win & Pl
11	5	1	2	-	£43,196
1/12	Donc	2m1¹/₂f Cls1 Nov Gd2 Ch gd-sft			£15,575
1/12	Ludl	2m Cls4 Ch gd-sft			£3,249
5/11	Punc	2m Nov Hdl good			£12,608
11/10	Newb	2m1¹/₂f Cls3 Mdn Hdl gd-sft			£5,855
3/10	Newb	1m4¹/₂f Cls5 NHF 4yo soft			£2,055

Hard puller who didn't quite fulfil potential last season despite winning Grade 2 novice chase at Doncaster; well fancied for 2m handicap chases at Cheltenham and Aintree only for hold-up tactics to backfire; could go far if headstrong nature can be curbed.

1182 Killyglen (Ire)

10 b g Presenting - Tina Maria (Phardante)

Stuart Crawford (Ir)				D L McCammon

PLACINGS: 2PP2P/2536F/030341U- **RPR 147+c**

Starts	1st	2nd	3rd	4th	Win & Pl
26	6	5	3	1	£105,603

3/12	DRoy	3m2f Ch soft	£8,625
4/09	Aint	3m1f Cls1 Nov Gd2 Ch good	£51,309
1/09	Ayr	3m1f Cls3 Nov Ch heavy	£6,337
10/08	Carl	2m4f Cls4 Ch gd-sft	£3,578
3/08	Dpat	2m2f Hdl yld-sft	£6,097
11/07	Ayr	2m Cls6 NHF 4-6yo soft	£1,370

Laid out for last season's Grand National having fallen when going well four out in 2011, but jumped much less fluently second time and departed early; looked better than ever on previous run when winning at Down Royal and remains a smart staying chaser.

1183 Knock A Hand (Ire)

7 br g Lend A Hand - Knockcross (Lake Coniston)

Richard Lee				Alan Halsall

PLACINGS: 8P/77P411/221111P- **RPR 144+h**

Starts	1st	2nd	3rd	4th	Win & Pl
6	4	1	-	-	£12,732

134	2/12	Newb	3m1/2f Cls2 119-145 Hdl Hcap gd-sft	£5,005
	12/11	Hayd	2m4f Cls4 Nov Hdl 4-7yo heavy	£3,249
	12/11	Chep	2m4f Cls4 Nov Hdl heavy	£2,274
	11/11	Chep	2m4f Cls5 Mdn Hdl heavy	£1,689

Dual point-to-point winner in Ireland who won first four races over hurdles last season, most notably a competitive handicap at Newbury off 134, before being pulled up early with something amiss at Aintree; remains unexposed and should make a fine chaser.

1184 Knockara Beau (Ire)

9 b g Leading Counsel - Clairabell (Buckskin)

George Charlton				W F Trueman

PLACINGS: 45/P472145/026326P-0 **RPR 156c**

Starts	1st	2nd	3rd	4th	Win & Pl
33	8	8	2	3	£155,149

148	2/11	Carl	3m1f Cls2 122-148 Hdl Hcap heavy	£8,141
	12/09	Kels	2m6¹/₂f Cls2 Nov Ch soft	£12,833
	11/09	Carl	2m4f Cls3 Ch soft	£13,010
	5/09	Ctml	2m5¹/₂f Cls4 Ch good	£3,903
	2/09	Kels	2m1f Cls1 Nov Gd2 Hdl soft	£20,047
	2/09	Muss	2m4f Cls3 Nov Hdl good	£5,204
	5/08	Aint	2m1f Cls4 NHF 4-6yo good	£3,903
	1/08	Kels	2m1¹/₂f Cls4 Mdn NHF 4-6yo heavy	£2,602

Very smart stayer over hurdles and fences who was an excellent sixth in last season's Gold Cup; has won only once since 2009, though, and seems hard to place having come up short in graded company and finished placed only once in handicap chases.

1185 Knockfierna (Ire) (above, left)

7 b m Flemensfirth - Garden Town (Un Desperado)

Charles Byrnes (Ir)				Knockfierna Syndicate

PLACINGS: 307/2111/196211011- **RPR 143+c**

Starts	1st	2nd	3rd	4th	Win & Pl
16	8	2	1	-	£138,105

3/12	Limk	2m6f Nov Gd3 Ch heavy	£23,021
1/12	Thur	2m4f Nov Gd3 Ch soft	£23,021
12/11	Cork	2m4f Nov Gd3 Ch sft-hvy	£21,013
11/11	Wxfd	2m3f Ch soft	£4,759
4/11	Fair	2m4f Nov Gd2 Hdl good	£32,220
12/10	Limk	2m6f Nov Gd3 Hdl sft-hvy	£16,394
12/10	Cork	2m Nov Hdl soft	£8,549
11/10	Limk	2m3f Mdn Hdl soft	£4,580

High-class mare who has an outstanding record against her own sex, landing a hat-trick in Grade 3 novice chases last season having twice won similar contests over hurdles in 2011; held every chance

when running out at the second-last against Sir Des Champs over Christmas.

1186 Kumbeshwar

5 b g Doyen - Camp Fire (Lahib)

Alan King   Mcneill Family & Nigel Bunter

PLACINGS: 13322/2801212234F-   RPR **151+c**

Starts	1st	2nd	3rd	4th	Win & Pl
16	3	6	3	1	£91,137

1/12	Plum	2m1f Cls3 Nov Ch heavy		£6,046
11/11	Hrfd	2m Cls4 Nov Ch gd-sft		£2,794
2/11	Sand	2m¹/₂f Cls4 Hdl 4yo good		£2,602

Consistent novice chaser last season who did particularly well when third in Grand Annual Chase; failed to justify handicap mark over hurdles having twice finished second in Grade 1 races as a juvenile, though, and may again be in handicapper's grip.

1187 Lambro (Ire)

7 b g Milan - Beautiful Tune (Green Tune)

Willie Mullins (Ir)   Byerley Thoroughbred Racing

PLACINGS: C3/121/181236-1   RPR **146+c**

Starts	1st	2nd	3rd	4th	Win & Pl
11	5	2	2	-	£62,155

5/12	Punc	2m2f Ch soft		£10,063
11/11	Naas	2m3f Ch sft-hvy		£7,138
4/11	Fair	2m4f Nov Gd2 Hdl good		£22,414
3/11	Naas	3m Mdn Hdl yield		£5,948
9/10	Clon	2m4f NHF 5-7yo gd-yld		£4,274

Coped well with some stiff tasks in novice chases last season, winning twice as well as finishing placed behind Flemenstar and Last Instalment; won over 3m as a novice hurdler but seemed not to stay that far in RSA Chase, relishing drop to 2m2f on next start.

1188 Last Instalment (Ire)

7 ch g Anshan - Final Instalment (Insan)

Philip Fenton (Ir)   Gigginstown House Stud

PLACINGS: 411/11/3P1111-   RPR **154+c**

Starts	1st	2nd	3rd	4th	Win & Pl
9	7	-	1	-	£160,722

2/12	Leop	2m5f Nov Gd1 Ch gd-sft		£40,625
12/11	Leop	3m Nov Gd1 Ch good		£42,026
11/11	Punc	2m6f Nov Gd2 Ch soft		£22,414
10/11	Gway	2m6f Ch heavy		£10,112
4/11	Limk	2m4f Nov Hdl yld-sft		£7,733
2/11	Navn	2m4f Mdn Hdl heavy		£5,948
4/10	Fair	2m2f NHF 4-6yo heavy		£28,761

Hugely exciting novice chaser last season when winning all four races over fences, most notably when thrashing RSA Chase second First Lieutenant before dropping in trip to land second Leopardstown Grade 1 over 2m5f; missed Cheltenham through injury but ready to return.

1189 Le Beau Bai (Fr)

9 b g Cadoudal - Dame Blonde (Pampabird)

Richard Lee   Glass Half Full

PLACINGS: 13P/72043P/0P71130-0   RPR **145+c**

Starts	1st	2nd	3rd	4th	Win & Pl
38	7	1	7	2	£162,156

131	12/11	Chep	3m5¹/₂f Cls1 Gd3 130-156 Ch heavy	£51,255
127	12/11	Chep	3m Cls2 117-140 Ch Hcap heavy	£10,072
134	12/10	Bang	3m Cls2 117-140 Hdl Hcap gd-sft	£11,090
139	12/09	Chep	3m Cls2 122-139 Ch Hcap heavy	£13,941
	3/09	Carl	3m¹/₂f Cls3 Nov Ch heavy	£6,505
129	2/09	Wwck	3m5f Cls3 103-129 Ch Hcap soft	£7,806
	11/08	Uttx	3m Cls4 Ch soft	£5,204
	7/08	Worc	2m4f Cls4 Nov Hdl gd-sft	£3,253
97	4/08	NAbb	2m1f Cls4 Nov 85-105 Hdl Hcap gd-sft	£3,773
	2/07	Extr	2m1f Cls5 NHF 4-6yo soft	£1,627
	2/07	Towc	2m Cls6 NHF 4-6yo soft	£1,627

Dropped 21lb during barren couple of years before winning successive handicap chases at Chepstow

144

last season, culminating in the Welsh National on heavy ground; relishes such testing conditions but may again find life tough off higher marks.

1190 Lexi's Boy (Ire)

4 gr g Verglas - Jazan (Danehill)

Donald McCain   T G Leslie

PLACINGS: P132111-B   **RPR 139+h**

Starts	1st	2nd	3rd	4th	Win & Pl
8	4	1	1	-	£36,944
132	4/12	Sand	2m Cls2 117-143 Hdl 4yo Hcap soft £15,640
	4/12	Ayr	2m Cls3 Hdl 4yo good £4,549
120	4/12	Asct	2m Cls2 112-135 Hdl 4yo Hcap good £12,825
	1/12	Ayr	2m Cls5 Mdn Hdl gd-sft.....................................£1,689

Treated for a fibrillating heart after being pulled up on hurdling debut but made rapid progress after a break during a busy second half of the season, completing a hat-trick in a strong juvenile handicap hurdle at Sandown; could still be improving.

1191 Lie Forrit (Ire) *(above, right)*

8 b g Subtle Power - Ben Roseler (Beneficial)

Willie Amos   JW McNeil,I C McNeill Ms L Gillies

PLACINGS: 120/1211/U11P9/122-   **RPR 140+c**

Starts	1st	2nd	3rd	4th	Win & Pl
15	7	4	-	-	£49,346
	12/11	Kels	2m6¹/₂f Cls2 Nov Ch soft £7,849
138	11/09	Newb	3m¹/₂f Cls2 115-139 Hdl Hcap gd-sft...............£12,524
132	11/09	Chel	3m1¹/₂f Cls1 List 131-157 Hdl Hcap soft £17,103
115	2/09	Ayr	2m5¹/₂f Cls4 90-115 Hdl Hcap soft £2,797
	1/09	Ayr	2m4f Cls4 Nov Hdl soft....................................£2,472
	11/08	Hexm	2m¹/₂f Cls6 NHF 4-6yo heavy £1,644
	11/07	Carl	1m6f Cls5 NHF 3yo good...................................£1,370

Slightly disappointing on return from 18-month absence last season when twice beaten in small-field novice chases (beaten favourite both times); sort to do well handicapping off lower chase mark

and success in big fields over hurdles; needs soft ground.

1192 Lion Na Bearnai (Ire)

10 b g New Frontier - Polly Plum (Pollerton)

Thomas Gibney (Ir)   Lock Syndicate

PLACINGS: 054934F/6732/518511-   **RPR 153c**

Starts	1st	2nd	3rd	4th	Win & Pl
29	3	2	3	2	£155,361
135	4/12	Fair	3m5f 128-148 Ch Hcap gd-sft..................£117,500
	2/12	Navn	3m Nov Gd2 Ch soft..£20,313
105	5/11	Punc	3m1f 95-123 Ch Hcap good £8,625

Underwent an astonishing transformation in final two starts last season, winning a Grade 2 novice chase at Navan at 50-1 and following up in Irish National off 30lb higher mark than only previous handicap win; hit hard by assessor but still unexposed over fences.

1193 Little Josh (Ire)

10 ch g Pasternak - Miss Top (Tremblant)

Nigel Twiston-Davies   Tony Bloom

PLACINGS: 41/2F1F16/1155/6P07-   **RPR 140c**

Starts	1st	2nd	3rd	4th	Win & Pl
20	8	2	-	1	£132,704
146	11/10	Chel	2m4¹/₂f Cls1 138-164 Ch Hcap gd-sft...........£85,515
	10/10	Carl	2m4f Cls2 Ch soft..£8,415
135	2/10	Hayd	2m4f Cls2 Nov 109-135 Ch Hcap heavy...........£11,709
	11/09	Kels	2m1f Cls4 Ch heavy..£3,665
	2/09	Chep	2m4f Cls4 Nov Hdl heavy..................................£3,253
	11/08	Ling	2m3¹/₂f Cls4 Nov Hdl soft £2,946
	10/08	Hexm	2m¹/₂f Cls6 Am NHF 4-6yo gd-sft.......................£1,644
	9/08	Strf	2m¹/₂f Cls5 Am NHF 4-6yo soft...........................£2,277

Won 2010 Paddy Power Gold Cup but then ruled out for a year through injury; given some stiff tasks last season but fair seventh when favourite for Topham Chase and continues to fall in handicap.

1194 Local Hero (Ger)

5 b g Lomitas - Lolli Pop (Cagliostro)

Steve Gollings   P J Martin

PLACINGS: 111485/302-1   **RPR 146+h**

Starts	1st	2nd	3rd	4th	Win & Pl
10	4	1	1	1	£47,289

140	7/12	MRas	2m1f Cls1 List 122-148 Hdl Hcap good	£17,085
	1/11	Chel	2m1f Cls1 Gd2 Hdl 4yo gd-sft	£12,827
	1/11	Donc	2m¹/₂f Cls4 Hdl 4yo good	£2,398
	11/10	Weth	2m¹/₂f Cls5 Mdn Hdl 3yo soft	£1,713

Missed much of last season through injury and consequently kept busy on the Flat during summer; reverted to hurdles to land Listed prize at Market Rasen, building on smart effort when second in Scottish Champion Hurdle in April; sure to be a threat in 2m handicaps.

1195 Long Run (Fr) (below)

7 b/br g Cadoudal - Libertina (Balsamo)

Nicky Henderson   Robert Waley-Cohen

PLACINGS: 13/1211113/311/2213-   **RPR 181+c**

Starts	1st	2nd	3rd	4th	Win & Pl
22	13	5	4	-	£1,263,237

	2/12	Newb	3m Cls1 Gd2 Ch gd-sft	£17,085
	3/11	Chel	3m2¹/₂f Cls1 Gd1 Ch good	£285,050
	1/11	Kemp	3m Cls1 Gd1 Ch gd-sft	£102,618
	2/10	Wwck	2m Cls1 Nov Gd2 Ch gd-sft	£17,103
	12/09	Kemp	3m Cls1 Nov Gd1 Ch gd-sft	£34,809
	11/09	Autl	2m6f Gd1 Ch 4yo holding	£152,913
	10/09	Autl	2m4¹/₂f Gd3 Ch 4yo v soft	£65,534
	5/09	Autl	2m4¹/₂f List Ch 4yo v soft	£41,942
	3/09	Autl	2m2f Gd3 Hdl 4yo holding	£56,796
	11/08	Autl	2m2f Gd1 Hdl 3yo v soft	£89,338
	10/08	Autl	2m2f Gd2 Hdl 3yo v soft	£57,904
	9/08	Autl	2m2f Hdl 3yo soft	£22,941
	5/08	Autl	2m2f List Hdl 3yo v soft	£30,000

Exciting winner of the King George and Gold Cup in 2010-11 but slightly disappointing last season when winning only one of four starts; still got placed three times at Grade 1 level and should

continue to be a major force in top staying chases.

1196 Lovcen (Ger)

7 b g Tiger Hill - Lady Hawk (Grand Lodge)

Alan King   The Barbury Apes

PLACINGS: 21/41F141-   **RPR 154+h**

Starts	1st	2nd	3rd	4th	Win & Pl
6	3	-	-	2	£71,031

130	4/12	Aint	3m¹/₂f Cls1 Nov Gd1 Ch good	£56,270
	2/12	Winc	2m6f Cls3 117-135 Hdl Hcap gd-sft	£5,848
	11/11	Towc	2m5f Cls4 Nov Hdl 4-6yo good	£3,249

Point-to-point winner who went from strength to strength in novice hurdles last season, outstaying Fingal Bay at Aintree having run on well into fourth behind Brindisi Breeze at Cheltenham; set to go novice chasing and should make an impact in stamina tests.

1197 Lucky William (Ire)

8 ch g All My Dreams - Dantes Mile (Phardante)

Thomas Cooper (Ir)   Garden Kingdom Syndicate

PLACINGS: 6S/F22B569/11244U11-   **RPR 149+c**

Starts	1st	2nd	3rd	4th	Win & Pl
26	7	6	-	2	£142,208

135	4/12	Punc	2m Nov Gd1 Ch heavy	£51,667
	4/12	Fair	2m1f Nov 114-135 Ch Hcap gd-sft	£20,313
	10/11	Punc	2m2f Nov Gd3 Ch yld-sft	£15,409
	9/11	List	2m Ch heavy	£8,328
	2/10	Navn	2m Mdn Hdl soft	£6,412
	10/09	Naas	2m3f NHF 4-7yo good	£7,044
	9/09	List	2m NHF 4-7yo soft	£6,709

Relishes testing conditions and took advantage of heavy ground at Punchestown to land biggest victory in Grade 1 novice chase last April; had previously come up short at top level when twice finishing fourth, though won good handicap at Fairyhouse.

1198 Lyreen Legend (Ire)

5 b g Saint Des Saints - Bint Bladi (Garde Royale)

Dessie Hughes (Ir)   Lyreen Syndicate

PLACINGS: 9/913122133-   RPR **148h**

Starts	1st	2nd	3rd	4th	Win & Pl
10	3	2	3	-	£58,479

3/12	Thur	2m4f Nov Gd2 Hdl sft-hvy	£21,667
12/11	Navn	2m Nov Hdl 4-5yo heavy	£7,733
10/11	Naas	2m Mdn Hdl 4yo soft	£5,948

Highly tried since landing maiden hurdle last December and maintained form superbly during busy campaign, finishing off with third behind Dedigout in Grade 1 at Punchestown; acts on any going.

1199 Mae's Choice (Ire)

6 b m Presenting - Boragh Thyme (Simply Great)

Gordon Elliott (Ir)   Miceal Martin Sammon

PLACINGS: 311121-   RPR **143+h**

Starts	1st	2nd	3rd	4th	Win & Pl
4	3	1	-	-	£40,304

4/12	Punc	2m2f Gd3 Hdl heavy	£32,500
1/12	Muss	2m4f Cls4 Nov Hdl good	£2,599
12/11	Dpat	2m5¹/₂f Mdn Hdl sft-hvy	£4,461

Shock 33-1 winner of Grade 3 mares' hurdle at Punchestown but had done well at a lower level before, suffering only defeat when unsuited by drop to 2m; relished stamina test on heavy ground but will want further when getting quicker surface.

1200 Magnanimity (Ire)

8 b/br g Winged Love - Mossy Mistress (Le Moss)

Dessie Hughes (Ir)   Gigginstown House Stud

PLACINGS: 12313/51124/8746PP-5   RPR **148c**

Starts	1st	2nd	3rd	4th	Win & Pl
19	4	3	3	2	£92,721

1/11	Leop	2m5f Nov Gd2 Ch sft-hvy	£21,013
11/10	Punc	2m4f Ch sft-hvy	£7,938
4/10	Fair	2m4f Nov Gd2 Hdl heavy	£23,009
12/09	Navn	2m Mdn Hdl heavy	£9,728

Beaten only a length when fourth in 2011 RSA Chase and ran much better than form figures suggest last season; travelled well before fitness gave out in Lexus Chase and looked likely to be placed in Irish National before being pulled up after bad blunder two out.

1201 Make Your Mark (Ire)

5 b g Beneficial - Bell Star (Roselier)

Willie Mullins (Ir)   Gigginstown House Stud

PLACINGS: 11137-   RPR **137h**

Starts	1st	2nd	3rd	4th	Win & Pl
4	2	-	1	-	£14,264

12/11	Leop	2m4f Mdn Hdl 4yo good	£6,543
11/11	Punc	2m NHF 4yo soft	£4,759

Highly rated last season having won first two novice hurdles, though reputation took a knock when well beaten by Boston Bob at Leopardstown

and just seventh in Neptune Hurdle; ran like a non-stayer both times despite winning a point-to-point over 3m.

1202 Manyriverstocross (Ire)

7 b g Cape Cross - Alexandra S (Sadler's Wells)

Alan King   Mrs M C Sweeney

PLACINGS: 131737/3/

Starts	1st	2nd	3rd	4th	Win & Pl
7	2	-	3	-	£47,822

12/09	Sand	2m4f Cls1 Nov Gd2 Hdl heavy	£17,103
11/09	Chep	2m¹/₂f Cls4 Mdn Hdl soft	£2,927

Smart Flat stayer who did well when switched to hurdles three seasons ago; due to return having not run since finishing third in 2010 Greatwood Hurdle and should again be a force in major 2m handicap hurdles.

1203 Marasonnien (Fr)

6 b g Mansonnien - Maracay (Subotica)

Willie Mullins (Ir)   Mrs S Ricci

PLACINGS: 382/42/2121-   RPR **144+h**

Starts	1st	2nd	3rd	4th	Win & Pl
9	2	4	1	1	£78,272

4/12	Punc	3m Nov Gd1 Hdl heavy	£38,750
1/12	Naas	2m3f Mdn Hdl sft-hvy	£8,050

Form of Grade 1 win at Punchestown seems all but worthless given very few rivals performed on desperate ground but at least showed he stays well and acts on heavy going; future lies chasing anyway having been second over fences to Aerial in France in 2010.

1204 Marito (Ger)

6 b g Alkalde - Maratea (Fast Play)

Willie Mullins (Ir)   Mrs S Ricci

PLACINGS: 3166/22/52-   RPR **148+h**

Starts	1st	2nd	3rd	4th	Win & Pl
8	1	3	1	-	£82,986

12/09	Autl	2m2f Hdl 3yo heavy	£27,961

Dual Listed runner-up over hurdles in France in 2010 but off the track for nearly two years before making debut for Willie Mullins at end of last season; ran a cracker when second in 2m4f handicap hurdle at Punchestown on second start; could soon rate much higher.

1205 Marsh Warbler

5 ch g Barathea - Echo River (Irish River)

Brian Ellison   Dan Gilbert & Kristian Strangeway

PLACINGS: 31110/25736-   RPR **149+h**

Starts	1st	2nd	3rd	4th	Win & Pl
10	3	1	2	-	£42,466

1/11	Chep	2m¹/₂f Cls1 Gd1 Hdl 4yo soft	£19,954
11/10	Sedg	2m1f Cls4 Hdl 3yo soft	£2,472
11/10	Bang	2m1f Cls4 Mdn Hdl 3yo soft	£2,927

Won a Grade 1 juvenile hurdle two seasons ago

but generally struggled off stiff handicap mark last season; still capable of high-class form in testing conditions and nearly won Haydock Champion Hurdle Trial when third following final-flight blunder.

and took record in races with seven runners or fewer to six out of seven with two wins last season; tends to just come up short in bigger fields at higher level, though wasn't beaten far when sixth in Betfred Bowl.

1206 Massini's Maguire (Ire)

11 b g Dr Massini - Molly Maguire (Supreme Leader)

David Pipe   Alan Peterson

PLACINGS: 1U5314/12235/3/1/P1-   RPR **158**+c

Starts	1st	2nd	3rd	4th	Win & Pl
22	7	5	4	2	£259,327
148	2/12	Asct	3m Cls1 List 139-159 Ch Hcap gd-sft		£22,887
146	10/10	Asct	3m Cls1 List 129-155 Ch Hcap good		£56,330
	11/08	Asct	2m5½f Cls3 Ch good		£6,262
	3/07	Chel	2m5f Cls1 Nov Gd1 Hdl gd-sft		£68,424
	11/06	Chel	2m5f Cls2 Nov Hdl gd-sft		£12,526
	10/06	Chep	2m¹/₂f Cls4 Nov Hdl good		£3,253
	5/05	Limk	2m2f NHF 4yo soft		£4,901

Won at the Cheltenham Festival in 2007 and remains as good as ever despite a string of injury problems in recent years, winning two of his three starts since 2009, both over 3m at Ascot; still on a feasible mark after latest victory in February.

1207 Master Of The Hall (Ire)

8 b g Saddlers' Hall - Frankly Native (Be My Native)

Nicky Henderson   Martin Landau & Jonathan Duffy

PLACINGS: 1/4113/15116F/1R16-   RPR **158**+c

Starts	1st	2nd	3rd	4th	Win & Pl
14	7		1	1	£73,569
	3/12	Kels	2m6½f Cls2 Ch good		£12,512
	12/11	Aint	3m1f Cls1 List Ch heavy		£20,554
	2/11	Asct	3m Cls1 Nov Gd2 Ch soft		£14,083
	1/11	Hntg	3m Cls3 Nov Ch soft		£4,554
	11/10	Asct	2m5½f Cls3 Ch gd-sft		£7,514
	1/10	Newb	2m¹/₂f Cls4 Nov Hdl soft		£2,927
	12/09	Sand	2m¹/₂f Cls3 Nov Hdl heavy		£5,204

Often looks a potential superstar in small fields

1208 Master Overseer (Ire)

9 b g Old Vic - Crogeen Lass (Strong Gale)

David Pipe   Brocade Racing

PLACINGS: 4/61321/2111/2/16P1-   RPR **138**c

Starts	1st	2nd	3rd	4th	Win & Pl
15	6	1		1	£72,518
126	3/12	Uttx	4m1½f Cls1 List 123-149 Ch Hcap gd-sft		£37,018
121	11/11	Chep	3m Cls3 99-125 Hdl Hcap soft		£3,639
116	1/10	Plum	3m5f Cls3 103-124 Ch Hcap soft		£12,524
105	12/09	Winc	3m1½f Cls3 96-112 Ch Hcap heavy		£9,432
98	11/09	Towc	3m¹/₂f Cls4 73-99 Ch Hcap soft		£5,204
	3/07	Font	2m2¹/₂f Cls6 NHF 4-6yo heavy		£1,627

Extremely progressive staying chaser until twice disappointing at Chepstow last season but then bounced back to win Midlands National at Uttoxeter; should continue to do well in long-distance handicaps and could have a second crack at Welsh National.

1209 Medermit (Fr)

8 gr g Medaaly - Miss D'Hermite (Solicitor I)

Alan King   The Dunkley & Reilly Partnership

PLACINGS: 3174/1R12142/132234-   RPR **170**+c

Starts	1st	2nd	3rd	4th	Win & Pl
26	8	7	5	3	£306,813
154	11/11	Extr	2m1½f Cls1 Gd2 140-160 Ch Hcap good		£34,170
	2/11	Sand	2m4¹/₂f Cls1 Nov Gd1 Ch good		£21,094
	12/10	Plum	2m1f Cls3 Nov Ch gd-sft		£6,262
	10/10	Aint	2m Cls3 Nov Ch gd-sft		£6,983
	1/10	Hayd	2m¹/₂f Cls1 Gd2 Hdl soft		£25,655
	12/08	Asct	2m Cls1 Nov Gd2 Hdl gd-sft		£17,103
	11/08	Folk	2m1¹/₂f Cls4 Nov Hdl 4-6yo soft		£3,253
	5/08	Nant	2m1¹/₂f Hdl 4yo holding		£5,294

Progressed into a genuine Grade 1 performer last

season without following up Haldon Gold Cup success; twice placed behind Riverside Theatre at Ascot and Cheltenham before staying on well on in fourth on first attempt at 3m at Aintree; rock-solid performer.

1210 Meister Eckhart (Ire)

6 b/br g Flemensfirth - Carrabawn (Buckskin)

Philip Hobbs   Carters Of Baltimore

PLACINGS: 11135-   **RPR 144h**

Starts	1st	2nd	3rd	4th	Win & Pl
5	3	-	1	-	£17,659
	12/11	Ffos	2m4f Cls4 Nov Hdl heavy	£2,599
	10/11	Naas	2m3f NHF 4-7yo yield	£5,948
	9/11	Slig	2m2f NHF 4-7yo soft	£4,164

Smart staying novice hurdler last season, suffering both defeats behind Brindisi Breeze and beaten by less than ten lengths at Cheltenham having travelled well (yet to prove he truly stays 3m); seems to have a touch of class and should do well chasing.

1211 Melodic Rendezvous

6 ch g Where Or When - Vic Melody (Old Vic)

Jeremy Scott   Cash For Honours

PLACINGS: 12-   **RPR 135b**

Starts	1st	2nd	3rd	4th	Win & Pl
2	1	1	-	-	£13,239
	3/12	Chep	2m¹/₂f Cls6 NHF 4-6yo gd-sft	£1,365

Flat-bred gelding who did well in bumpers last season, winning nicely on a sound surface at Chepstow and doing even better to chase home Cheltenham winner Champagne Fever in desperate conditions at Punchestown; seems to have a bright future.

1212 Menorah (Ire)

7 b g King's Theatre - Maid For Adventure (Strong Gale)

Philip Hobbs   Mrs Diana L Whateley

PLACINGS: 21212/115/4U411F314-   **RPR 164+c**

Starts	1st	2nd	3rd	4th	Win & Pl
19	9	3	1	3	£330,758
	4/12	Aint	2m4f Cls1 Nov Gd1 Ch gd-sft	£42,713
	1/12	Kemp	2m Cls2 Nov Ch good	£13,436
	12/11	Tntn	2m3f Cls4 Nov Ch gd-sft	£3,764
	12/10	Chel	2m1f Cls1 Gd2 Hdl gd-sft	£85,515
151	11/10	Chel	2m¹/₂f Cls1 Gd3 127-151 Hdl Hcap gd-sft	£57,010
	3/10	Chel	2m¹/₂f Cls1 Nov Gd1 Hdl gd-sft	£57,010
	12/09	Kemp	2m Cls2 Nov Hdl gd-sft	£10,019
	11/09	Wwck	2m Cls4 Nov Hdl good	£2,927
	8/09	Naas	2m3f NHF 4-7yo soft	£5,702

High-class hurdler (second favourite for Champion Hurdle in 2011) but struggled over fences last season until landing soft Grade 1 at Aintree when step up in trip seemed to help suspect jumping; unsuited by heavy ground when fourth at Punchestown.

1213 Merigo (Fr) (below, left)

11 ch g Pistolet Bleu - Muleta (Air De Cour)

Andrew Parker   Mr & Mrs Raymond Anderson Green

PLACINGS: 21/72d61/8F82/708011-   **RPR 149c**

Starts	1st	2nd	3rd	4th	Win & Pl
27	7	3	1	3	£342,637
134	4/12	Ayr	4m¹/₂f Cls1 Gd3 132-158 Ch good	£102,510
129	3/12	Ayr	3m1f Cls3 112-129 Ch heavy	£5,653
127	4/10	Ayr	4m¹/₂f Cls1 Gd3 127-153 Ch good	£114,020
125	2/09	Newc	4m1f Cls2 110-136 Ch heavy	£31,182
121	12/08	Donc	3m Cls2 121-143 Ch soft	£26,020
113	4/08	Ayr	3m1f Cls2 Nov 113-132 Ch good	£12,698
100	3/08	Ayr	3m1f Cls3 100-124 Ch heavy	£5,999

Remarkably won his second Scottish National in three years last season, having finished second in the race in between; tends to be out of form through the winter, though, having won only one other race since February 2009, leaving him on a good mark.

1214 Micheal Flips (Ire)

8 b g Kayf Tara - Pianissimo (Shernazar)

Andy Turnell   M Tedham

PLACINGS: 6194F/2404/62147124-   RPR **151+c**

Starts	1st	2nd	3rd	4th	Win & Pl
23	5	4	1	5	£80,580
137	1/12	Tntn	2m3f Cls2 122-145 Ch Hcap gd-sft		£12,027
	10/11	Asct	2m3f Cls3 Ch good		£6,882
137	1/10	Kemp	2m5f Cls2 126-152 Hdl Hcap soft		£18,786
	12/08	Kemp	2m Cls2 Nov Hdl good		£10,019
	10/08	Strf	2m¹/₂f Cls3 Mdn Hdl gd-fm		£6,337

Former Lanzarote Hurdle winner who soon reached similar standard over fences last season, finishing second to For Non Stop and fourth to Sir Des Champs in Grade 1 novice chases; no surprise to see him pick up a decent handicap chase prize.

1215 Michel Le Bon (Fr)

9 b g Villez - Rosacotte (Rose Laurel)

Paul Nicholls   C G Roach

PLACINGS: 3/131/1/0P1-   RPR **140+h**

Starts	1st	2nd	3rd	4th	Win & Pl
8	4	-	2	-	£36,803
134	4/12	Chel	3m Cls2 120-140 Hdl Hcap soft		£7,507
	11/09	Newb	3m Cls1 Nov Gd2 Ch gd-sft		£21,462
	3/09	Newb	3m¹/₂f Cls4 Nov Hdl good		£3,253
	12/08	Chep	2m4f Cls4 Mdn Hdl soft		£3,903

Made a huge impression when landing a Grade 2 on his chasing debut in 2009 but missed next two years through injury; twice disappointed on return but won a handicap hurdle at Cheltenham and on a good mark if recovering form over fences.

1216 Midnight Chase (above)

10 b g Midnight Legend - Yamrah (Milford)

Neil Mulholland   Lady Clarke

PLACINGS: /332311/411115/F317-   RPR **168c**

Starts	1st	2nd	3rd	4th	Win & Pl
25	12	2	4	1	£198,960
	1/12	Chel	3m1¹/₂f Gd2 Ch gd-sft		£56,950
155	12/10	Chel	3m1¹/₂f Cls1 List 138-164 Ch Hcap good		£22,804
146	11/10	Chel	3m3¹/₂f Cls1 Gd3 126-149 Ch Hcap gd-sft		£28,505
137	10/10	Chel	3m¹/₂f Cls2 125-149 Ch Hcap good		£14,090
	5/10	Hexm	3m1f Cls4 Nov Ch gd-fm		£4,665
125	4/10	Chel	2m5f Cls3 Nov 111-127 Ch Hcap good		£6,262
	3/10	Font	2m4f Cls4 Ch gd sft		£3,998
125	2/09	Font	2m4f Cls3 113-130 Hdl Hcap heavy		£6,337
118	1/09	Fknm	2m4f Cls3 95-118 Hdl Hcap good		£6,505
112	12/08	Leic	2m4¹/₂f Cls3 95-119 Hdl Hcap heavy		£6,337
105	12/08	Folk	2m6¹/₂f Cls4 79-105 Hdl Hcap heavy		£3,253
	4/07	Prth	2m¹/₂f Cls4 Mdn Hdl gd-sft		£3,904

High-class staying chaser who has gained all but two of his wins over fences at Cheltenham, landing fifth victory there in Argento Chase last season; again came up short in Gold Cup when only seventh but could continue to excel at slightly lower level.

1217 Midnight Game

5 b g Montjeu - Midnight Angel (Acatenango)

Willie Mullins (Ir)   Gigginstown House Stud

PLACINGS: 2411064-   RPR **146+h**

Starts	1st	2nd	3rd	4th	Win & Pl
7	2	1		2	£23,084
	1/12	Naas	2m Nov Hdl sft-hvy		£10,925
	12/11	Leop	2m Mdn Hdl 4yo yld-sft		£6,841

Dual Listed runner-up on the Flat who initially

made steady improvement over hurdles last season, beating a couple of useful rivals at Naas; well beaten in Supreme Novices' Hurdle and season went downhill subsequently; remains capable of better.

1218 Mikael D'Haguenet (Fr)

8 b g Lavirco - Fleur D'Haguenet (Dark Stone)

Willie Mullins (Ir)   Mrs S Ricci

PLACINGS: 1/1/F53F/4831112P5-0   RPR **159+h**

Starts	1st	2nd	3rd	4th	Win & Pl
24	9	3	2	1	£312,588

1/12	Naas	2m3f Gd3 Hdl sft-hvy	£14,896
12/11	Punc	2m4f Hdl heavy	£11,207
12/11	Fair	2m Hdl sft-hvy	£11,767
5/09	Punc	2m4f Nov Gd1 Hdl sft-hvy	£54,175
3/09	Chel	2m5f Cls1 Nov Gd1 Hdl gd-sft	£68,412
2/09	Punc	2m Nov Gd2 Hdl soft	£28,126
1/09	Naas	2m4f Nov Gd1 Hdl soft	£33,182
12/08	Navn	2m4f Nov Gd1 Hdl heavy	£45,662
11/08	Navn	2m Mdn Hdl heavy	£8,129

Brilliant unbeaten novice hurdler four seasons ago but largely out of sorts since; still a novice over fences having lost confidence after debut fall on return from 18-month layoff; won three times back over hurdles last season but flopped in higher grade.

1219 Minella Class (Ire)

7 br g Oscar - Louisas Dream (Supreme Leader)

Nicky Henderson   Deal, George, Kelvin-Hughes & Nicolson

PLACINGS: 4/24012/1126/2UPP-   RPR **143c**

Starts	1st	2nd	3rd	4th	Win & Pl
11	3	3	-	-	£35,818

1/11	Sand	2m¹/₂f Cls1 Nov Gd1 Hdl heavy	£17,103
12/10	Newb	2m¹/₂f Cls4 Mdn Hdl good	£3,903
2/10	Naas	2m3f NHF 4-7yo heavy	£7,022

Very smart novice hurdler two seasons ago, winning Tolworth Hurdle at Sandown before finishing sixth at Cheltenham Festival; suffered jumping problems over fences last season and disappointed when returned to hurdles; talented but has plenty to prove.

1220 Minsk (Ire)

4 b g Dalakhani - Penza (Soviet Star)

Dessie Hughes (Ir)   Barry Connell

PLACINGS: 2-   RPR **129h**

Starts	1st	2nd	3rd	4th	Win & Pl
1	-	1	-	-	£5,937

Long-time favourite for last season's Triumph Hurdle following brilliant win in 2011 Irish Cesarewitch but had hurdling debut held up by injuries and missed Cheltenham after narrow defeat at Fairyhouse; remains a top-class prospect for novice hurdles.

1221 Module (Fr)

5 b g Panoramic - Before Royale (Dauphin Du Bourg)

Tom George   Simon W Clarke

PLACINGS: 1/5B1-   RPR **140+h**

Starts	1st	2nd	3rd	4th	Win & Pl
4	2	-	-	-	£35,292

130	1/12	Chel	2m1f Cls2 119-145 Hdl Hcap gd-sft	£13,646
	4/11	Engh	2m1¹/₂f Hdl 4yo soft	£19,862

Made light of an opening handicap mark of 130 on British debut at Cheltenham last season (had run three times in France) when winning well; missed spring targets due to lack of experience and should reward connections' patience over fences.

1222 Mon Parrain (Fr)

6 b g Trempolino - Kadaina (Kadalko)

Paul Nicholls   Mr & Mrs J D Cotton

PLACINGS: P1P1316112/5312/734-   RPR **160c**

Starts	1st	2nd	3rd	4th	Win & Pl
17	6	2	3	1	£117,145

133	3/11	Sand	3m1¹/₂f Cls3 113-135 Ch Hcap good	£6,505
	12/09	Autl	2m1¹/₂f Ch 3yo heavy	£23,301
	11/09	Nanc	2m1f Ch v soft	£7,922
	10/09	Toul	2m1¹/₂f Ch 3yo gd-sft	£10,252
	8/09	Vich	2m¹/₂f Hdl 3yo	£7,922
	5/09	Roya	2m Hdl 3yo	£6,058

Proved rather frustrating last season having started out with major aspirations; struggled to keep up with early pace when seventh in Paddy Power Gold Cup yet finished weakly when stepped up beyond 3m on final two starts; out until new year.

1223 Monksland (Ire)

5 b g Beneficial - Cush Jewel (Executive Perk)

Noel Meade (Ir)   Mrs Patricia Hunt

PLACINGS: 01113-   RPR **148+h**

Starts	1st	2nd	3rd	4th	Win & Pl
4	3	-	1	-	£42,016

1/12	Naas	2m4f Nov Gd2 Hdl sft-hvy	£20,313
12/11	Navn	2m Mdn Hdl sft-hvy	£5,948
11/11	DRoy	2m NHF 4-7yo soft	£5,056

Suffered only defeat under rules when suffering bad interference in the Neptune Hurdle at Cheltenham before finishing third, though hard to say he would have troubled Simonsig; had looked very smart in winning a Grade 2 at Naas; good chasing prospect.

1224 Montbazon (Fr)

5 b/br g Alberto Giacometti - Duchesse Pierji (Cadoudal)

Alan King   David Sewell

PLACINGS: 212/32114-   RPR **148h**

Starts	1st	2nd	3rd	4th	Win & Pl
8	3	3	1	1	£53,937

2/12	Newb	2m1¹/₂f Cls4 Nov Hdl gd-sft	£3,249
1/12	Plum	2m Cls5 Mdn Hdl gd-sft	£1,916
3/11	Donc	2m1¹/₂f Cls2 NHF 4-5yo good	£34,585

Not far off the best in bumpers and novice hurdles, finishing last season with a career-best effort when fourth in Supreme Novices' Hurdle at Cheltenham; still not the finished article according to his trainer and on a workable handicap mark; more to come.

1225 Moscow Mannon (Ire)

6 b g Moscow Society - Unfaithful Thought (Mind Games)

Brian Hamilton (Ir)   Jonathan Flanagan

PLACINGS: 31114-   RPR **137b**

Starts	1st	2nd	3rd	4th	Win & Pl
5	3	-	1	1	£23,208
	1/12	Gowr	2m NHF 4-7yo sft-hvy		£7,479
	12/11	Fair	2m NHF 4-7yo sft-hvy		£6,246
	7/11	Gway	2m NHF 4-7yo good		£5,948

Won three times in bumpers last season, looking particularly impressive in testing conditions at Fairyhouse and Gowran Park; coped well with good ground when fourth in Champion Bumper at Cheltenham but should do better on softer surface.

1226 Mossley (Ire)

6 b g Old Vic - Sorivera (Irish River)

Robbie Hennessy (Ir)

PLACINGS: F/11152P/12PP-   RPR **143+c**

Starts	1st	2nd	3rd	4th	Win & Pl
10	4	2	-	-	£47,826
	11/11	Kemp	3m Cls4 Ch good		£3,249
	12/10	Chel	3m Cls1 Nov Gd2 Hdl gd-sft		£14,253
	10/10	Hntg	2m4¹/₂f Cls4 Nov Hdl good		£2,740
	6/10	Worc	2m Cls6 NHF 4-6yo good		£1,713

High-class novice hurdler two seasons ago (second to Bobs Worth at Cheltenham Festival) but never anywhere near as convincing over fences and pulled up last twice; since left Nicky Henderson and set to revert to hurdles for new trainer but well handicapped over fences if jumping improves.

1227 Mount Benbulben (Ire)

7 b g Beneficial - Dramatic Dame (Buckskin)

Gordon Elliott (Ir)   Barry Connell

PLACINGS: 21411/S1127-   RPR **148+h**

Starts	1st	2nd	3rd	4th	Win & Pl
8	4	1	-	1	£47,887
	11/11	Navn	2m4f Nov Gd2 Hdl sft-hvy		£21,013
	11/11	Thur	2m2f Mdn Hdl 5-6yo sft-hvy		£4,461
	3/11	Limk	2m3f NHF 5-7yo soft		£5,948
	2/11	Thur	2m NHF 5-7yo soft		£4,759

Won first two completed hurdles races in hugely impressive fashion and had excuses for subsequent defeats at Grade 1 level, jumping badly right when second to Boston Bob at Naas and not staying 3m at Cheltenham after racing keenly; could go far over fences.

1228 Mourad (Ire)

7 ch g Sinndar - Mouramara (Kahyasi)

Willie Mullins (Ir)   Teahon Consulting Limited

PLACINGS: 213/4113/24223163-04   RPR **161+h**

Starts	1st	2nd	3rd	4th	Win & Pl
25	6	7	6	4	£349,929
	2/12	Navn	2m5f Gd2 Hdl soft		£21,667
	1/11	Gowr	3m Gd2 Hdl soft		£21,013
	12/10	Leop	3m Gd2 Hdl heavy		£25,885
	4/10	Fair	2m4f Gd3 Hdl heavy		£17,832
	1/10	Punc	2m4f Hdl heavy		£8,561
	12/08	Punc	2m Mdn Hdl 3yo yld-sft		£6,097

Very smart staying hurdler who has won three times at Grade 2 level and been placed seven times in Grade 1 races; hard to see him making a breakthrough beyond that having failed to progress last season, though again ran several decent races in defeat.

1229 Mr Moonshine (Ire)

8 b g Double Eclipse - Kinross (Nearly A Hand)

Sue Smith   Mrs S Smith

PLACINGS: 1/2/16321600/113507-   RPR **154c**

Starts	1st	2nd	3rd	4th	Win & Pl
15	4	2	2	-	£49,708
	11/11	Hayd	2m6f Cls2 Nov Ch good		£16,643
	11/11	Carl	2m4f Cls2 Ch gd-sft		£11,696
120	1/11	Hntg	3m2f Cls2 113-138 Ch Hcap soft		£8,238
	5/10	Weth	2m4f Cls4 Nov Hdl good		£2,740

Capable of some very smart performances in lesser company, as when romping to victory on his first two runs over fences; yet to make a mark at a higher level and twice well beaten in Grade 1 races but has slipped back to a good mark as a result.

1230 Muirhead (Ire)

9 b g Flemensfirth - Silaoce (Nikos)

Noel Meade (Ir)   Mrs P Sloan

PLACINGS: 252425/15/6314180-61   RPR **157+c**

Starts	1st	2nd	3rd	4th	Win & Pl
26	7	4	1	3	£224,111
	9/12	Gway	2m6f Ch soft		£11,917
	10/11	Limk	3m 124-140 Ch Hcap yld-sft		£41,379
	8/11	Baln	2m4f Hdl gd-fm		£9,517
	10/10	Punc	2m4f Ch good		£7,938
	12/07	Fair	2m Nov Gd1 Hdl heavy		£39,527
132	11/07	DRoy	2m Mdn Hdl 4-6yo good		£7,003
	10/07	Gowr	2m NHF 4yo gd-fm		£5,369

Former high-class 2m hurdler (fifth in 2009 Champion Hurdle) who has been reinvented as a staying handicap chaser, winning last season's Munster National at Limerick; subsequently flopped in Hennessy Gold Cup but should do better after just seven runs over fences.

1231 My Tent Or Yours (Ire)

5 b g Desert Prince - Spartan Girl (Ela-Mana-Mou)

Nicky Henderson   The Happy Campers

PLACINGS: 122-   RPR **132+b**

Starts	1st	2nd	3rd	4th	Win & Pl
3	1	2	-	-	£17,456
	12/11	Ludl	1m6f Cls5 NHF 4-5yo gd-sft		£2,274

Won well on his bumper debut at Ludlow last season and made a big impression even in defeat on next two starts, going close despite pulling hard at Newbury and travelling best when second in Grade 2 at Aintree; should be an exciting novice hurdler at 2m.

1232 Nacarat (Fr) (above)

11 gr g Smadoun - Gerbora (Art Bleu)

Tom George   Simon W Clarke

PLACINGS: /8P423/14431/443515-   RPR **168+c**

Starts	1st	2nd	3rd	4th	Win & Pl
35	9	3	5	6	£482,718
154	2/12	Kemp	3m Cls1 Gd3 140-158 Ch Hcap good		£56,950
	4/11	Aint	3m1f Cls1 Gd1 Ch gd-sft		£84,780
	10/10	Weth	3m1f Cls1 Gd2 Ch good		£57,010
147	2/09	Kemp	3m Cls1 Gd3 135-160 Ch Hcap good		£57,010
135	1/09	Donc	2m3f Cls2 112-138 Ch Hcap soft		£16,263
118	1/08	Winc	2m5f Cls3 110-131 Ch Hcap soft		£11,711
	9/07	Autl	2m2f Hdl heavy		£14,270
	4/07	Autl	2m2f Hdl v soft		£14,270
	3/07	Autl	2m2½f Ch heavy		£15,568

High-class 3m chaser who has maintained form well in recent times, landing Totesport Bowl at Aintree in 2011 and bouncing back to form to land valuable handicap chase at Kempton last season; may be just past his best but remains capable on good ground.

1233 New Year's Eve

4 b g Motivator - Midnight Angel (Acatenango)

John Ferguson   Bloomfields

PLACINGS: 1129-   RPR **132b**

Starts	1st	2nd	3rd	4th	Win & Pl
4	2	1	-	-	£15,067
	2/12	MRas	2m1f Cls6 NHF 4-6yo gd-sft		£1,365
	1/12	Ludl	2m Cls6 NHF 4-6yo gd-sft		£1,949

Valuable Flat-bred type who unsurprisingly did very well in bumpers last season, twice winning at a modest level before chasing home Champagne Fever at Cheltenham; flopped on heavy ground at Punchestown but should make a big mark in 2m novice hurdles.

1234 Noble Prince (Ger)

8 b g Montjeu - Noble Pearl (Dashing Blade)

Paul Nolan (Ir)   D P Sharkey

PLACINGS: 1123354/1221/F1222P-   RPR **165c**

Starts	1st	2nd	3rd	4th	Win & Pl
21	6	7	2	1	£188,602
	10/11	Naas	2m Gd3 Ch heavy		£15,409
	3/11	Chel	2m4f Cls1 Nov Gd2 Ch good		£51,309
	10/10	Punc	2m Ch gd-yld		£7,938
	10/09	Naas	2m4f Hdl sft-hvy		£13,273
	5/09	Punc	2m4f Hdl heavy		£10,063
	4/09	Gowr	2m4f Mdn Hdl 4-5yo yield		£7,380

Has run over inadequate trips for much of his chasing career and looked a future star when winning Jewson Chase over 2m4f at Cheltenham in 2011; laid out for Ryanair Chase last season (second three times over 2m before then) only to be pulled up.

1235 Notus De La Tour (Fr)

6 b g Kutub - Ridiyla (Akarad)

David Pipe   D Bradshaw,J Dale,P Deal,J Smee,W Walsh

PLACINGS: 361127/4305/211323F-   **RPR 152c**

Starts	1st	2nd	3rd	4th	Win & Pl
18	4	3	4	2	£92,152

11/11	Plum	2m4f Cls3 Nov Ch gd-sft	£6,256
10/11	Carl	2m4f Cls4 Nov Ch gd-sft	£4,679
1/10	Plum	2m Cls4 Nov Hdl soft	£3,253
12/09	Autl	2m2f Hdl 3yo heavy	£10,252

Hasn't quite fulfilled early promise but did fairly well in novice chases last season, winning twice at odds-on before twice getting placed at Grade 1 level in Ireland; fell early in Byrne Group Plate but had been well fancied and could bag a big handicap.

1236 Oh Crick (Fr)

9 ch g Nikos - Other Crik (Bigstone)

Alan King   David Sewell

PLACINGS: 34574/66306/4736134-   **RPR 151+c**

Starts	1st	2nd	3rd	4th	Win & Pl
34	8	3	6	5	£201,821

137	2/12	Chep	2m¹/₂f Cls2 118-137 Ch Hcap soft	£15,825
139	4/09	Aint	2m Cls1 Gd3 129-150 Ch Hcap good	£45,608
130	3/09	Chel	2m¹/₂f Cls1 Gd3 130-156 Ch Hcap gd-sft	£51,309
	5/08	Hrfd	2m3f Cls4 Ch good	£4,436
123	2/08	Hrfd	2m1f Cls3 104-130 Hdl Hcap good	£10,141
116	2/08	Extr	2m1f Cls3 110-130 Hdl Hcap gd-sft	£5,855
111	1/08	Chel	2m1f Cls3 Nov 91-115 Hdl Hcap gd-sft	£10,334
	12/07	Plum	2m Cls4 Nov Hdl heavy	£3,904

Achieved a Cheltenham/Aintree double in 2009 and competed with great credit at Grade 1 level in following campaign; paid the price with handicap mark and didn't win again until last February; still well weighted at his best and could step up in trip.

1237 Oiseau De Nuit (Fr)

10 b g Evening World - Idylle Du Marais (Panoramic)

Colin Tizzard   Terry Warner

PLACINGS: 32/U6483124/30437B6-   **RPR 156c**

Starts	1st	2nd	3rd	4th	Win & Pl
41	6	8	5	6	£162,696

145	3/11	Chel	2m¹/₂f Cls1 Gd3 130-151 Ch Hcap good	£42,758
133	1/10	Ffos	2m Cls2 131-148 Ch Hcap soft	£15,655
120	4/09	Chel	2m¹/₂f Cls3 108-134 Cond Ch Hcap gd-sft	£6,888
109	11/08	Ling	2m Cls3 109-119 Ch Hcap heavy	£6,505
102	1/08	Hntg	2m¹/₂f Cls4 78-104 Ch Hcap heavy	£3,904
93	12/07	Hntg	2m¹/₂f Cls4 79-104 Ch Hcap gd-sft	£3,904

Landed a 40-1 victory in the Grand Annual Chase in 2011 but remained in the grip of the handicapper throughout last season when unable to add to his victories; has produced best form on good ground and could bounce back in spring if dropping in weights.

1238 On His Own (Ire) (above)

8 b g Presenting - Shuil Na Mhuire (Roselier)

Willie Mullins (Ir)   Semore Kurdi

PLACINGS: 110/414P1/B1F-   **RPR 153+c**

Starts	1st	2nd	3rd	4th	Win & Pl
10	4	-	-	2	£65,755

125	1/12	Gowr	3m 123-144 Ch Hcap sft-hvy	£43,333
116	4/11	Ayr	2m1f Cls2 Nov 104-130 Ch Hcap good	£10,408
	1/11	Muss	3m Cls4 Ch gd-sft	£3,253
	12/09	Leop	2m4f NHF 4-7yo yield	£7,044

Going well in last season's Grand National when falling at the second Becher's; had put himself among the leading fancies for the race with a breathtaking win in the Thyestes, jumping superbly and relishing big test of stamina; may well head back to Aintree.

1239 Organisedconfusion (Ire)

7 b g Laveron - Histologie (Quart De Vin)

Arthur Moore (Ir)　　　　　　　　Mrs A Dunlop

PLACINGS: 08F514/76312/133F5U-　　　　RPR **132**+h

Starts	1st	2nd	3rd	4th	Win & Pl
17	3	1	3	1	£146,573
132	4/11	Fair	3m5f 130-155 Ch Hcap good		£121,552
	2/11	Clon	2m1f Ch heavy		£6,841
	2/10	Gowr	2m2f Ch soft		£7,938

Won 2011 Irish National when racing beyond 2m5f for first time; again dropped in trip last season in apparent bid to protect handicap mark, even having first two runs over hurdles, but unseated rider before halfway in Grand National.

1240 Oscar Nominee (Ire)

5 b g Old Vic - Native Bid (Be My Native)

Nicky Henderson　　　　　　　　Michael Buckley

PLACINGS: 9/81313-　　　　　　RPR **143**+h

Starts	1st	2nd	3rd	4th	Win & Pl
6	2	-	2	-	£11,010
	2/12	Donc	2m¹/₂f Cls4 Nov Hdl 4-7yo good		£2,599
	1/12	Sthl	2m Cls5 Mdn Hdl gd-sft		£1,985

Won pair of soft 2m novice hurdles last season but relished step up to 2m5f when third in conditional jockeys' handicap hurdle at Cheltenham Festival; form looks strong and seems likely to progress.

1241 Oscar Whisky (Ire)

7 b g Oscar - Ash Baloo (Phardante)

Nicky Henderson　　　　　　　Walters Plant Hire Ltd

PLACINGS: 1/1114/1131/F1151-　　　RPR **167**+h

Starts	1st	2nd	3rd	4th	Win & Pl
14	10	-	1	1	£316,226
	4/12	Aint	2m4f Cls1 Gd1 Hdl good		£91,096
	2/12	Kemp	2m Cls6 NHF std-slw		£2,599
	1/12	Chel	2m4¹/₂f Cls2 Hdl gd-sft		£12,512
	12/11	Chel	2m4¹/₂f Cls1 Gd2 Hdl good		£17,085
	4/11	Aint	2m4f Cls1 Gd1 Hdl good		£90,432
	2/11	Ffos	2m Cls2 Hdl gd-sft		£28,179
	1/11	Chel	2m4¹/₂f Cls2 Hdl gd-sft		£12,524
	2/10	Sand	2m¹/₂f Cls3 Nov Hdl heavy		£5,204
	12/09	Newb	2m¹/₂f Cls4 Mdn Hdl soft		£3,253
	11/09	Newb	2m¹/₂f Cls5 NHF 4-6yo soft		£1,952
	3/09	Newb	1m4¹/₂f Cls5 NHF 4yo good		£2,055

Dual winner of Aintree Hurdle, confirming status as best 2m4f hurdler in training when touching off Thousand Stars for second successive year; failed to stay 3m when well beaten in World Hurdle.

1242 Oscara Dara (Ire)

7 b g Oscar - Lisa's Storm (Glacial Storm)

Nicky Henderson　　　　　　Bg Racing Partnership

PLACINGS: 2/141-　　　　　　　RPR **138**+h

Starts	1st	2nd	3rd	4th	Win & Pl
4	2	1	-	1	£18,979
	4/12	Punc	2m Nov Hdl heavy		£12,188
	3/12	Sand	2m¹/₂f Cls4 Nov Hdl gd-sft		£2,599
	12/10	Sthl	2m Cls6 NHF 3-6yo std-slw		£1,370

Off the track for more than a year before doing well

---

in a brief novice hurdle campaign at the end of last season, suffering sole defeat behind Darlan in top-class company at Aintree; won nicely next time at Punchestown and should do well over fences.

1243 Oscargo (Ire)

8 b g Oscar - Broken Rein (Orchestra)

Paul Nicholls　　　　　　　Hordle, Evans & Nicholls

PLACINGS: U1/31U6-　　　　　　RPR **141**+h

Starts	1st	2nd	3rd	4th	Win & Pl
5	2	-	1	-	£16,277
128	12/11	Chel	3m Cls7 123-141 Hdl Hcap good		£11,261
	3/11	Chep	3m Cls5 Mdn Hdl good		£2,342

Did well in handicap hurdles last season having had only one previous run, finishing third at Cheltenham in November before winning well the following month; struggled to cope with 17lb rise but has size and scope to do better over fences.

1244 Oscars Well (Ire)

7 b/br g Oscar - Placid Willow (Convinced)

Jessica Harrington (Ir)　　　　Molley Malone Syndicate

PLACINGS: 270/21114/323264-　　　RPR **164**h

Starts	1st	2nd	3rd	4th	Win & Pl
14	3	4	2	2	£151,593
	2/11	Leop	2m2f Nov Gd1 Hdl heavy		£44,828
	12/10	Navn	2m4f Nov Gd1 Hdl soft		£43,142
	11/10	Punc	2m4f Mdn Hdl sft-hvy		£8,854

Failed to win last season but ran several excellent races in defeat, including when sixth in Champion Hurdle; stays 2m4f well and might have won 2011 Neptune Hurdle but for final-flight blunder; likely to go novice chasing.

1245 Osirixamix (Ire)

9 b g Desert Prince - Osirixa (Linamix)

Tony Martin (Ir)　　　　　　　Timothy Fitzgerald

PLACINGS: 3619/83/511P/PF3PF1-　　RPR **149**+c

Starts	1st	2nd	3rd	4th	Win & Pl
19	4	-	3	2	£30,279
113	1/12	Fair	2m 100-118 Hdl Hcap sft-hvy		£8,338
	1/11	Limk	2m1f Ch heavy		£7,138
102	12/10	Cork	2m 90-116 Hdl Hcap soft		£6,412
	12/08	DRoy	2m Mdn Hdl soft		£4,319

Failed to complete in four out of five chases since an impressive debut over fences in January 2011; still showed promise last season, falling at the last when set to win Grade 2 at Cork and reverting to hurdles to easily land handicap at Fairyhouse.

1246 Our Father (Ire)

6 gr g Shantou - Rosepan (Taipan)

David Pipe　　　　　　　The Ives & Johnson Families

PLACINGS: 122/10P-　　　　　　RPR **147**+h

Starts	1st	2nd	3rd	4th	Win & Pl
6	2	2	-	-	£10,214
129	12/11	Asct	2m6f Cls3 110-130 Hdl Hcap soft		£6,256
	1/11	Chep	2m4f Cls4 Mdn Hdl soft		£2,602

Won well on handicap debut at Ascot last season

and subsequently laid out for Pertemps Final but seemed to find quicker ground against him and pulled up in similar conditions at Aintree; remains an exciting prospect on soft ground; set to go novice chasing.

1247 Our Mick (below)

6 gr g Karinga Bay - Dawn's Della (Scottish Reel)

Donald McCain   K Benson & Mrs E Benson

PLACINGS: 1/22312F/5311133-   RPR **153+c**

Starts		1st	2nd	3rd	4th	Win & Pl
14		3	3	3	-	£39,765
	1/12	Hayd	2m4f Cls1 Nov Gd2 Ch heavy			£13,326
123	12/11	Kemp	2m4½f Cls3 Nov 113-127 Ch Hcap gd-sft			£6,882
	11/11	Catt	2m3f Cls5 Ch good			£1,949
	2/11	Hrfd	2m1f Cls4 Mdn Hdl soft			£2,147
	4/10	MRas	2m1f Cls6 Am NHF 4-6yo good			£1,507

Sharply progressive in novice chases last season, following three successive wins with excellent third behind For Non Stop in Grade 1 at Newbury; coped well with move into handicap company with similarly fine effort at Cheltenham Festival on first run at 3m.

1248 Out Now (Ire)

8 br g Muroto - Raven Night (Mandalus)

Edward O'Grady (Ir)   D Cox & Nelius Hayes

PLACINGS: /9072/204/14814F22-0   RPR **144c**

Starts		1st	2nd	3rd	4th	Win & Pl
16		2	4		3	£74,993
119	11/11	Clon	2m4f 112-134 Ch Hcap soft			£8,922
	5/11	Limk	2m1f Ch good			£9,517

Unlucky to be touched off in two valuable handicap chases last season, most notably when outstayed in Irish National having travelled well; had shown best form at 2m4f prior to that so may well be capable of landing a major prize at around 3m.

1249 Overturn (Ire)

8 b g Barathea - Kristal Bridge (Kris)

Donald McCain   T G Leslie

PLACINGS: 32111/212573/111232-   RPR **167h**

Starts		1st	2nd	3rd	4th	Win & Pl
19		7	5	3	2	£474,624
	11/11	Newc	2m Cls1 Gd1 Hdl gd-sft			£58,521
	11/11	Asct	2m3½f Cls1 Gd2 Hdl good			£51,001
160	8/11	Prth	2m1½f Cls2 140-160 Hdl Hcap good			£24,760
145	7/10	Gway	2m 123-147 Hdl Hcap good			£133,186
130	4/10	Ayr	2m Cls1 Gd2 128-147 Hdl Hcap good			£45,608
	3/10	Ayr	2m Cls4 Nov Hdl gd-sft			£3,578
100	3/10	Ayr	2m Cls4 Nov 74-101 Hdl Hcap good			£2,797

Hugely popular dual-purpose performer who went from strength to strength over hurdles last season, winning the Fighting Fifth and finishing second in the Champion Hurdle; fine second in Chester Cup next time (first run on soft ground since 2009); could go novice chasing.

1250 Owen Glendower (Ire)

7 br g Anshan - Native Success (Be My Native)

Nicky Henderson   The Ten From Seven

PLACINGS: 213/11493/431413P-6   RPR **144c**

Starts		1st	2nd	3rd	4th	Win & Pl
16		5	1	4	3	£30,687
	2/12	Hntg	2m1½f Cls3 Nov Ch gd-sft			£5,653
	11/11	Ludl	2m4f Cls4 Ch good			£3,282
	10/10	Strf	2m1½f Cls3 Nov Hdl 4-6yo gd-sft			£5,070
	10/10	Worc	2m Cls4 Nov Hdl 4-6yo gd-sft			£3,253
	12/09	Tntn	2m1f Cls5 NHF 4-6yo soft			£2,227

Unable to match record in small fields when sent handicapping (yet to win after eight runs in such races) but did much better when third in novice handicap chase at Cheltenham Festival; could win good races on that form and going well when blundered and pulled up next time.

1251 Pacha Du Polder (Fr)

5 b g Muhtathir - Ambri Piotta (Caerwent)

Paul Nicholls The Stewart & Wylie Families

PLACINGS: 921/151F1- **RPR 147+c**

Starts	1st	2nd	3rd	4th	Win & Pl
8	4	1	-	-	£59,630

	4/12	Ayr	2m4f Cls1 Nov Gd2 Ch good	£17,832
	1/12	Wwck	2m4½f Cls3 Nov Ch gd-sft	£5,653
	11/11	Sand	2m Cls4 Ch gd-sft	£3,899
	3/11	Engh	2m2f Hdl 4yo v soft	£21,517

Won three times after arriving from France last season, most notably in Grade 2 at Ayr on final start; had disappointed on two previous starts in better company but expected to find plenty of improvement with age, particularly over 3m.

1252 Paint The Clouds

7 b g Muhtarram - Preening (Persian Bold)

Warren Greatrex Peter Deal & Jill & Robin Eynon

PLACINGS: 1144533/147211/111- **RPR 132+h**

Starts	1st	2nd	3rd	4th	Win & Pl
16	8	1	2	3	£33,563

130	10/11	Chel	3m Cls2 123-149 Hdl Hcap gd-fm	£8,758
	5/11	Towc	2m6f Cls4 Nov Ch gd-fm	£2,407
	5/11	Worc	2m7f Cls4 Ch good	£2,277
118	4/11	Chel	3m Cls3 Nov 100-120 Hdl Hcap good	£6,262
	3/11	Winc	2m6f Cls4 Nov Hdl gd-fm	£2,602
	10/10	Strf	2m½f Cls3 Mdn Hdl good	£4,119
	6/09	MRas	2m1½f Cls6 NHF 4-6yo good	£1,713
	6/09	Sedg	2m1f Cls6 Mdn NHF 4-6yo gd-fm	£1,561

Won five successive races from March to October 2011, including first two chase starts before reverting to hurdles to land Cheltenham handicap; set to return after missing rest of season but dependent on quick ground.

1253 Pearl Swan (Fr)

4 b g Gentlewave - Swanson (Diesis)

Paul Nicholls R J H Geffen

PLACINGS: 11dF- **RPR 143+h**

Starts	1st	2nd	3rd	4th	Win & Pl
3	1	1	-	-	£11,190

	1/12	Tntn	2m1f Cls3 Nov Hdl gd-sft	£5,848

Very useful juvenile last season who did well to pip Grumeti at Cheltenham on his second start in Britain only to lose race in stewards' room; dropped out early in the Triumph Hurdle before staying on well before falling at the last; out until the new year.

1254 Pearlysteps

9 ch g Alflora - Pearly-B (Gunner B)

Henry Daly The Glazeley Partnership

PLACINGS: 84/52114/22137/F2PP- **RPR 147c**

Starts	1st	2nd	3rd	4th	Win & Pl
17	3	5	1	2	£30,376

	1/11	Hrfd	3m1½f Cls4 Ch soft	£2,602
	3/10	Donc	2m3½f Cls3 Nov Hdl good	£5,204
	2/10	Towc	2m Cls4 Nov Hdl soft	£3,253

Finished good seventh in National Hunt Chase in 2011 and would have done well last season but for jumping problems, falling once and ruining chance with blunders last twice; second in Peter Marsh Chase on only completed start and capable of landing good prize.

1255 Peddlers Cross (Ire)

7 b g Oscar - Patscilla (Squill)

Donald McCain T G Leslie

PLACINGS: 1/11111/1127/1128- **RPR 159+c**

Starts	1st	2nd	3rd	4th	Win & Pl
13	9	2	-	-	£274,475

	11/11	Bang	2m1½f Cls3 Nov Ch gd-sft	£7,148
	11/11	Bang	2m1½f Cls4 Ch gd-sft	£3,899
	2/11	Kels	2m2f Cls2 Hdl soft	£9,758
	11/10	Newb	2m½f Cls1 Gd1 Hdl gd-sft	£51,309
	4/10	Aint	2m4f Cls1 Nov Gd2 Hdl good	£34,206
	3/10	Chel	2m5f Cls1 Nov Gd1 Hdl good	£57,010
	1/10	Hayd	2m½f Cls1 Nov Gd2 Hdl soft	£17,637
	12/09	Bang	2m1f Cls4 Nov Hdl soft	£3,415
	11/09	Hayd	2m½f Cls4 NHF 4-6yo soft	£4,879

Bitterly disappointing in novice chases last season having finished second in 2011 Champion Hurdle; jumped well when landing soft races at Bangor but no match for Sprinter Sacre at Kempton and ran even worse at Cheltenham; return to hurdles may spark revival.

1256 Penny Max (Ire)

6 b g Flemensfirth - Ballymartin Trix (Buckskin)

Emma Lavelle Highclere Thoroughbred Racing-Penny Max

PLACINGS: 2/134/311- **RPR 141+c**

Starts	1st	2nd	3rd	4th	Win & Pl
6	3	-	2	1	£15,980

	1/12	Extr	3m Cls3 Nov Ch soft	£6,368
118	12/11	Newb	3m Cls3 Nov 107-125 Ch Hcap soft	£6,498
	11/10	Folk	2m1½f Cls5 NHF 4-6yo heavy	£1,713

Potentially smart chaser who made a big impression when winning twice over fences last season, jumping notably well, but missed subsequent spring targets on quicker ground; looks very well handicapped granted soft ground and a strong test of stamina.

1257 Pepite Rose (Fr)

5 b/br m Bonbon Rose - Sambre (Turgeon)

Venetia Williams Falcons Line Ltd

PLACINGS: 4/43713314/84411114- **RPR 150+c**

Starts	1st	2nd	3rd	4th	Win & Pl
18	6	-	4	6	£61,926

135	3/12	Newb	2m6½f Cls1 Nov List 110-135 Ch Hcap good	£16,881
	3/12	Wwck	2m4½f Cls4 Nov Ch good	£3,899
118	3/12	Newb	2m2½f Cls3 Nov 109-127 Ch Hcap good	£7,148
111	2/12	Bang	2m1½f Cls4 Nov 93-115 Ch Hcap good	£3,054
	2/11	Wwck	2m Cls4 Hdl 4yo heavy	£2,602
	11/10	Folk	2m1½f Cls4 Hdl 3yo heavy	£2,602

Proved a revelation when switched to fences towards end of last season, winning four times in less than a month, including valuable mares' contest at Newbury, and rising 39lb in handicap; only fourth at Aintree but may have found that one race too many.

1258 Petit Robin (Fr)

9 b g Robin Des Pres - Joie De Cotte (Lute Antique)

Nicky Henderson   Mr & Mrs John Poynton

PLACINGS: /12237/12053/2F/39-5   RPR **147**+h

Starts	1st	2nd	3rd	4th	Win & Pl
19	5	4	3	-	£204,285

	12/09	Kemp	2m Cls1 Gd2 Ch gd-sft £34,206
132	11/08	Newb	2m1f Cls2 118-141 Ch Hcap gd-sft £18,786
	12/07	Newb	2m3f Cls4 Nov Hdl 4-6yo gd-sft £4,229
	2/07	Pau	2m3¹/₂f Ch 4yo v soft £10,378
	1/07	Pau	2m1f Ch 4yo soft £10,378

Top-class 2m chaser in his heyday (second three times at Grade 1 level) but was off the track for a year after falling in 2011 Victor Chandler Chase; retains plenty of ability judged on hurdles runs on comeback, notably when fast-finishing fifth in Swinton Hurdle.

1259 Pique Sous (Fr)

5 gr g Martaline - Six Fois Sept (Epervier Bleu)

Willie Mullins (Ir)   Supreme Horse Racing Club

PLACINGS: 313-3112   RPR **140**b

Starts	1st	2nd	3rd	4th	Win & Pl
7	3	1	3	-	£31,231

7/12	Tipp	2m NHF 4-7yo soft £6,038
7/12	Bell	2m1f NHF 4-7yo soft £4,888
2/12	Leop	2m NHF 4-7yo gd-sft £4,600

Close third in Champion Bumper at Cheltenham and continued to gain experience during summer, winning twice more and looking particularly impressive when defying double penalty at Tipperary; has plenty of speed and could be a leading novice hurdler at around 2m.

1260 Pittoni (Ire)

6 b g Peintre Celebre - Key Change (Darshaan)

Charles Byrnes (Ir)   Patrick Wilmott

PLACINGS: 11130/1/1381-   RPR **154**h

Starts	1st	2nd	3rd	4th	Win & Pl
10	6	-	2	-	£102,014

	3/12	Leop	2m2f Hdl good £10,833
	10/11	Naas	2m3f Hdl yield £8,328
131	2/11	Leop	2m 108-136 Hdl Hcap soft £12,608
	2/10	Leop	2m Gd1 Hdl 4yo soft £37,389
	1/10	Punc	2m Gd3 Hdl 4yo heavy £16,419
	12/09	Punc	2m Mdn Hdl 3yo heavy £7,044

Has an excellent strike-rate and won first four races over Flat and jumps in 2011 before coming unstuck when stepped up in class (has twice flopped at Cheltenham but unsuited by good ground both times); may still be capable of better if kept to testing conditions.

1261 Planet Of Sound

10 b g Kayf Tara - Herald The Dawn (Dubassoff)

Philip Hobbs   C G M Lloyd-Baker

PLACINGS: /41133/12F01/35/230-   RPR **161**c

Starts	1st	2nd	3rd	4th	Win & Pl
22	6	5	5	2	£296,158

	4/10	Punc	3m1f Gd1 Ch good £119,469
152	11/09	Extr	2m1¹/₂f Cls1 Gd2 147-167 Ch Hcap gd-sft ... £42,758
	1/09	Newb	2m2¹/₂f Cls3 Nov Ch soft £6,505
	12/08	Newb	2m2¹/₂f Cls3 Nov Ch gd-sft £6,505
	4/08	Newb	2m¹/₂f Cls3 Nov Hdl gd-sft £4,436
	11/07	Chep	2m¹/₂f Cls5 Mdn Hdl good £2,277

Very lightly raced since winning Grade 1 at Punchestown in 2010; produced three good efforts in major staying handicaps last season, most notably when second in Hennessy Gold Cup; jumped well when leading to four out in Grand National only to run out of stamina.

1262 Poker De Sivola (Fr)

9 b g Discover D'Auteuil - Legal Union (Law Society)

Ferdy Murphy   D A Johnson

PLACINGS: /8362F70/29511P/6U1/

Starts	1st	2nd	3rd	4th	Win & Pl
30	7	3	3	2	£168,401

136	4/11	Sand	3m5¹/₂f Cls1 Gd3 124-150 Ch Hcap gd-fm £79,814
	3/10	Chel	4m Cls2 Nov Am Ch good £45,015
	2/10	Catt	3m1¹/₂f Cls3 Nov Ch gd-sft £5,998
119	11/07	Hexm	2m4¹/₂f Cls3 105-124 Hdl Hcap soft £13,012
	4/07	Hexm	2m4¹/₂f Cls4 Nov Hdl gd-fm £3,083
	1/07	Catt	2m3f Cls4 Nov Hdl soft £3,253
	11/06	Hexm	2m1¹/₂f Cls5 Mdn Hdl 3yo soft £2,946

Missed last season through injury but had been a steady improver in staying chases; won National Hunt Chase at Cheltenham in 2010 having only broken chasing duck on previous run at 11th attempt and later added 2011 Bet365 Gold Cup after another injury-troubled season.

1263 Poole Master

7 ch g Fleetwood - Juste Belle (Mansonnien)

David Pipe   G Thompson

PLACINGS: 0/214/1110F-   RPR **144**+h

Starts	1st	2nd	3rd	4th	Win & Pl
9	4	1	-	1	£9,385

3/12	Newb	2m5f Cls4 Nov Hdl gd-sft £2,859
1/12	Ling	2m¹/₂f Cls4 Nov Hdl soft £2,738
11/11	Uttx	2m Cls5 Mdn Hdl gd-sft £1,819
11/10	Uttx	2m Cls6 NHF 4-6yo soft £1,301

Won a hat-trick of novice hurdles last season, looking particularly impressive when stepped up to 2m4f at Newbury; failed to figure in Coral Cup and out of touch when fell three out in Grade 1 at Aintree; could be a useful 3m novice chaser.

1264 Poquelin (Fr)

9 bl g Lahint - Babolna (Tropular)

Paul Nicholls   The Stewart Family

PLACINGS: 87/1212U/25141/5U26-   RPR **172c**

Starts		1st	2nd	3rd	4th	Win & Pl
30		9	4	4	2	£425,124
170	4/11	Chel	2m5f Cls1 Gd2 150-170 Ch Hcap good			£22,804
163	12/10	Chel	2m5f Cls1 Gd3 137-163 Ch Hcap gd-sft			£85,515
151	12/09	Chel	2m5f Cls1 Gd3 134-160 Ch Hcap soft			£85,515
139	10/09	Chel	2m4f Cls2 119-139 Ch Hcap gd-fm			£31,310
	10/08	Chel	2m Cls2 Nov Ch good			£13,776
	5/08	NAbb	2m¹/₂f Cls4 Nov Ch gd-fm			£3,513
	4/08	Sand	2m Cls2 Hdl good			£15,655
	4/07	Ayr	2m Cls2 Nov Hdl 4yo gd-fm			£9,395
	12/06	Kemp	2m Cls3 Nov Hdl 3yo gd-sft			£6,263

Cheltenham specialist who finds life hard off stiff official mark but proved as good as ever when second to Gold Cup runner-up The Giant Bolster last January; slightly disappointing otherwise, including when sixth in Melling Chase having raced too freely.

1265 Portrait King (Ire)

7 gr g Portrait Gallery - Storm Queen (Le Bavard)

Maurice Phelan (Ir)   Marie Davis

PLACINGS: 1343/6642F/6302110-   RPR **148+c**

Starts		1st	2nd	3rd	4th	Win & Pl
15		2	2	3	2	£45,355
131	2/12	Newc	4m1f Cls2 109-135 Ch Hcap good			£21,790
113	2/12	Punc	3m4f 102-130 Ch Hcap heavy			£14,896

Failed to win in first 12 starts under rules but found his feet when sent over long distances last season, following up Punchestown win with victory in Eider Chase at Newcastle; raised 9lb and seemed to get outpaced in Scottish National; may need softer ground.

1266 Poungach (Fr)

6 b g Daliapour - Shalaine (Double Bed)

Paul Nicholls   Donlon, Doyle, Macdonald & Webb

PLACINGS: 131/125-   RPR **154h**

Starts		1st	2nd	3rd	4th	Win & Pl
6		3	1	2	-	£23,894
137	12/11	Sand	2m6f Cls2 120-145 Hdl Hcap gd-sft			£9,697
	1/11	Asct	2m3¹/₂f Cls1 Nov Hdl 4-7yo gd-sft			£5,010
	5/10	Strf	2m¹/₂f Cls6 NHF 4-6yo good			£1,626

Lightly raced over hurdles but showed plenty to suggest he has a big future over fences, winning easily on handicap debut at Sandown and beating all bar Oscar Whisky in good conditions hurdle at Cheltenham; should do well in novice chases.

1267 Pride Ofthe Parish (Ire)

8 b g Flemensfirth - Rose Island (Jupiter Island)

Willie Mullins (Ir)   Mrs Violet O'Leary

PLACINGS: 1-   RPR **125+b**

Starts		1st	2nd	3rd	4th	Win & Pl
1		1	-	-	-	£4,758
	12/11	Limk	2m2f NHF 4-7yo heavy			£4,759

Grand chasing type who did well to win sole bumper so easily last season, quickening clear off moderate gallop to triumph by 12 lengths at Limerick; seems sure to improve over hurdles given size and scope; may well figure among top staying novices.

1268 Prince De Beauchene (Fr)

9 b g French Glory - Chipie D'Angron (Grand Tresor)

Willie Mullins (Ir)   Graham Wylie

PLACINGS: 11/321/271/U5351/51-   RPR **155+c**

Starts		1st	2nd	3rd	4th	Win & Pl
18		7	2	4	-	£130,214
	2/12	Fair	3m1f Gd2 Ch soft			£21,667
138	4/11	Aint	3m1f Cls1 List 128-154 Ch Hcap good			£34,206
132	4/10	Hayd	2m4f Cls2 120-145 Ch Hcap heavy			£31,310
	1/09	Ayr	2m4f Cls4 Nov Hdl soft			£2,472
	12/07	Pau	2m3¹/₂f Ch 4yo soft			£10,378
	11/07	Agtn	1m6f NHF 4yo soft			£8,108
	6/07	Land	1m5f NHF v soft			£3,041

Ante-post favourite for last season's Grand National until being ruled out due to a stress fracture in his hip; had won at Aintree the previous season for Howard Johnson and looked better than ever when winning Grade 2 at Fairyhouse on most recent start.

1269 Prince Of Pirates (Ire)

7 b g Milan - Call Kate (Lord Americo)

Nicky Henderson   John P McManus

PLACINGS: 1/61/8112-   RPR **143+c**

Starts		1st	2nd	3rd	4th	Win & Pl
7		3	2	1	-	£16,751
134	2/12	Leic	2m7¹/₂f Cls3 Nov 121-135 Ch Hcap good			£3,690
	12/11	Donc	2m3f Cls4 Ch gd-sft			£3,054
	12/10	Chel	2m1f Cls3 Nov Hdl 4-6yo good			£6,262
	2/10	Kemp	2m Cls6 Mdn NHF 4-6yo gd-sft			£1,713

Slightly unconvincing in novice chases last season, but clearly possesses a massive engine having overcome poor jumping to win at Doncaster and dead-heat at Leicester; much better than his handicap mark if managing to get things together.

1270 Problema Tic (Fr)

6 b g Kapgarde - Atreide (Son Of Silver)

David Pipe   Mrs Jo Tracey

PLACINGS: 1/11148/1211-   RPR **148+c**

Starts		1st	2nd	3rd	4th	Win & Pl
10		7	1	-	1	£33,263
137	4/12	Ayr	3m1f Cls2 Nov 112-138 Ch Hcap good			£12,996
	3/12	Kemp	3m Cls3 Nov Ch good			£7,323
	12/11	Font	2m4f Cls4 Ch soft			£3,054
	1/11	MRas	2m3f Cls4 Nov Hdl good			£2,602
	1/11	Sthl	2m Cls5 Mdn Hdl gd-sft			£1,541
	5/10	Aint	2m1f Cls5 NHF 4-6yo good			£1,952
	3/10	Towc	2m Cls6 NHF 4-6yo good			£1,626

Won first four starts under rules before coming unstuck in better company over hurdles; kept to a lower level when sent chasing last season and improved when stepped up to 3m for final two wins (latest after switch from Nicky Henderson); useful prospect.

1271 Prospect Wells (Fr)

7 b g Sadler's Wells - Brooklyn's Dance (Shirley Heights)

Paul Nicholls   Andrea & Graham Wylie

PLACINGS: 1214453-   **RPR 146h**

Starts	1st	2nd	3rd	4th	Win & Pl
7	1	1		2	£30,674

11/11	Newb	2m¹/₂f Cls3 Nov Hdl gd-sft	£5,630
10/11	Chep	2m¹/₂f Cls4 Nov Hdl gd-sft	£2,669

High-class Flat horse (Group 2 winner) who ran consistently well in top novice hurdles last season; given breathing operation after sole flop at Sandown and returned to finish close fifth in Supreme Novices' Hurdle; likely sort for big-field handicap hurdles.

1272 Punjabi

9 b g Komaite - Competa (Hernando)

Nicky Henderson   Raymond Tooth

PLACINGS: 21/4231/1F31/242190/

Starts	1st	2nd	3rd	4th	Win & Pl
19	7	4	2	3	£588,275

2/10	Kemp	2m Cls2 Hdl soft	£8,171
3/09	Chel	2m¹/₂f Cls1 Gd1 Hdl gd-sft	£210,937
12/08	Weth	2m¹/₂f Cls1 Gd1 Hdl soft	£33,798
4/08	Punc	2m Gd1 Hdl good	£97,059
4/07	Punc	2m Gd1 Hdl 4yo good	£46,081
2/07	Kemp	2m Cls1 Nov Gd2 Hdl 4yo soft	£14,825
1/07	Ludl	2m Cls4 Nov Hdl 4yo good	£3,578

Gutsy winner of the Champion Hurdle in 2009 but seemed to lose his sparkle in following campaign when only ninth at Cheltenham and missed last two seasons through injury; back in training this summer and likely to go novice chasing.

1273 Quantitativeeasing (Ire)

7 ch g Anshan - Mazuma (Mazaad)

Nicky Henderson   John P McManus

PLACINGS: 111257/7112/02175-   **RPR 157+c**

Starts	1st	2nd	3rd	4th	Win & Pl
15	6	3	-	-	£132,354

145			
12/11	Chel	2m5f Cls1 Gd3 138-157 Ch Hcap good	£56,950
2/11	MRas	2m6¹/₂f Cls3 Nov Ch good	£5,692
1/11	Font	2m6f Cls4 Nov Ch heavy	£2,932
12/09	Newb	2m¹/₂f Cls3 Nov Hdl heavy	£5,010
11/09	Newc	2m Cls5 Mdn Hdl 4-6yo gd-sft	£2,082
4/09	Punc	2m NHF 4yo soft	£9,392

Took advantage of good handicap mark at start of last season to win Spinal Research Gold Cup after second in Paddy Power Gold Cup; found life tougher in two subsequent starts over 3m, though not helped by heavy ground at Punchestown; should stay further.

1274 Quel Esprit (Fr) (below)

8 gr g Saint Des Saints - Jeune D'Esprit (Royal Charter)

Willie Mullins (Ir)   Red Barn Syndicate

PLACINGS: 4/1112F6/1FF/B1113-0   **RPR 160c**

Starts	1st	2nd	3rd	4th	Win & Pl
17	8	1	1	1	£178,996

2/12	Leop	3m Gd1 Ch gd-sft	£76,667
1/12	Thur	2m2f Gd3 Ch heavy	£15,438
11/11	Naas	2m3f Ch sft-hvy	£11,207
11/10	Limk	2m3¹/₂f Ch heavy	£7,938
12/09	Cork	3m Nov Gd3 Hdl sft-hvy	£18,961
11/09	Punc	2m4f Mdn Hdl heavy	£9,728
4/09	Punc	2m NHF 4-7yo sft-hvy	£10,734
12/08	Leop	2m4f NHF 4-7yo yld-sft	£6,097

Failed to complete on last three starts as a novice

chaser but had his confidence restored last season in lesser company before landing soft Hennessy Gold Cup at Leopardstown; didn't stay 3m on heavy ground at Punchestown but high-class given lesser test.

1275 Quentin Collonges (Fr)

8 gr g Dom Alco - Grace Collonges (Bayolidaan)

Henry Daly   Neville Statham & Family

PLACINGS: 7224/1514160/3/212P-   RPR **140+c**

Starts	1st	2nd	3rd	4th	Win & Pl
18	4	2		2	£40,528

	2/12	Donc	3m Cls4 Ch good	£3,249
125	3/10	Donc	3m¹/₂f Cls2 114-140 Hdl Hcap good	£11,709
	12/09	Hntg	3m2f Cls4 Nov Hdl gd-sft	£2,927
	10/09	Ludl	2m5f Cls4 Nov Hdl good	£4,228

Useful hurdler (sixth at 2010 Cheltenham Festival) who impressed over fences on return from long absence last season at around 3m; well fancied for Scottish National when making too many mistakes but could make mark in similar events this term.

1276 Quevega (Fr)

8 b m Robin Des Champs - Vega Iv (Cap Martin)

Willie Mullins (Ir)   Hammer & Trowel Syndicate

PLACINGS: 1119/311/3911/1/111-   RPR **159+h**

Starts	1st	2nd	3rd	4th	Win & Pl
20	9	-	4	1	£536,263

	4/12	Punc	3m Gd1 Hdl heavy	£82,667
	3/12	Chel	2m4f Cls1 Gd1 Hdl good	£39,389
	5/11	Punc	3m Gd1 Hdl good	£85,517
	3/11	Chel	2m4f Cls1 Gd2 Hdl good	£39,431
	4/10	Punc	3m Gd1 Hdl good	£93,274
	3/10	Chel	2m4f Cls1 Gd2 Hdl good	£50,697
	3/09	Chel	2m4f Cls2 Gd2 Hdl gd-sft	£56,330
	2/09	Punc	2m4f Hdl soft	£12,076
	4/08	Gowr	2m Nov Hdl heavy	£8,638
	2/08	Punc	2m Mdn Hdl 4yo yield	£4,319
	11/07	Drtl	1m3f NHF 3yo gd-sft	£10,135
	9/07	Vich	1m4f NHF 3yo good	£3,716
	9/07	Vich	1m4f Mdn NHF 3yo heavy	£3,378

Outstanding mare who has won mares' hurdle at Cheltenham for last four years and 3m Grade 1 hurdle at Punchestown for last three; hasn't run anywhere else since 2009, though, so very lightly raced and connections may stick to that formula again.

1277 Quiscover Fontaine (Fr)

8 b g Antarctique - Blanche Fontaine (Oakland)

Willie Mullins (Ir)   John P McManus

PLACINGS: 31119/1169/2F/4910F-   RPR **134h**

Starts	1st	2nd	3rd	4th	Win & Pl
17	7	1	1	1	£100,912

	12/11	Leop	2m Hdl good	£9,517
	2/10	Clon	2m1f Ch heavy	£7,327
	1/10	Limk	2m3¹/₂f Ch heavy	£7,950
	1/09	Limk	2m Nov Hdl heavy	£10,063
	12/08	Limk	2m Hdl 4yo soft	£12,685
	12/08	Gowr	2m Mdn Hdl 4yo heavy	£6,097
	4/08	Punc	2m NHF 4-5yo good	£32,537

Former useful 2m novice chaser (sixth in 2010 Arkle Trophy) who coped well with big step up in

trip when fourth in Irish National following year and was laid out for last season's Grand National, winning on second of three hurdles runs only to fall when in rear at Aintree.

1278 Quito De La Roque (Fr)

8 b g Saint Des Saints - Moody Cloud (Cyborg)

Colm Murphy (Ir)   Gigginstown House Stud

PLACINGS: 122141/12111/113-   RPR **167+c**

Starts	1st	2nd	3rd	4th	Win & Pl
13	8	3	1	1	£289,845

	11/11	DRoy	3m Gd1 Ch soft	£72,414
	5/11	Punc	3m1f Nov Gd1 Ch gd-yld	£42,759
	4/11	Aint	3m1f Cls1 Nov Gd2 Ch good	£42,959
	2/11	Navn	3m Nov Gd2 Ch heavy	£21,013
	1/11	Naas	3m Nov Gd2 Ch sft-hvy	£22,414
	12/10	Clon	2m4f Ch sft-hvy	£5,190
123	4/10	Fair	3m Nov 102-127 Hdl Hcap heavy	£34,513
	2/10	Clon	2m6f Nov List Hdl heavy	£15,819

High-class novice chaser two seasons ago and began last campaign by outstaying Sizing Europe at Punchestown before one-paced third behind Synchronised in Lexus Chase; kept out of spring targets after several setbacks; may need stiff stamina test to fulfil potential.

1279 Ranjaan (Fr)

4 b g Dubai Destination - Ridafa (Darshaan)

Paul Nicholls   Highclere Thoroughbred Racing – Ranjaan

PLACINGS: 2F11-   RPR **137+h**

Starts	1st	2nd	3rd	4th	Win & Pl
4	2	1	-	-	£17,693

132	1/12	Tntn	2m1f Cls2 116-142 Hdl Hcap gd-sft	£10,128
	12/11	Kemp	2m Cls3 Hdl 3yo gd-sft	£5,848

Useful Flat performer who overcame difficult start to hurdling career (fell heavily on second run) to win twice, most notably in open handicap company at Taunton; being prepared for Triumph Hurdle when suffered setback; has potential to be a Champion Hurdle horse.

1280 Rathlin

7 b g Kayf Tara - Princess Timon (Terimon)

Mouse Morris (Ir)   Gigginstown House Stud

PLACINGS: 2/13/216/257231112-   RPR **154+c**

Starts	1st	2nd	3rd	4th	Win & Pl
13	4	4	2	-	£73,750

	2/12	Naas	2m4f Nov Gd2 Ch soft	£21,667
	2/12	Fair	2m5¹/₂f Nov Ch heavy	£9,200
	1/12	Fair	2m5¹/₂f Ch sft-hvy	£6,900
	3/11	Gowr	2m Mdn Hdl yld-sft	£5,948

Initially disappointing over fences last season but much improved following a wind operation; completed a hat-trick in a Grade 2 at Naas in impressive fashion and beat all bar brilliant Flemenstar in Powers Gold Cup; trainer convinced he will stay 3m.

1281 Raya Star (Ire)

6 b g Milan - Garden City (Shernazar)

Alan King   Simon Munir

PLACINGS: 1/2F1F4/2131301-   RPR **149+h**

Starts	1st	2nd	3rd	4th	Win & Pl
13	5	2	2	1	£135,605

143	4/12	Ayr	2m Cls1 Gd2 129-147 Hdl Hcap good	£22,780
134	12/11	Asct	2m Cls1 List 133-159 Hdl Hcap soft	£84,405
120	10/11	Weth	2m¹/₂f Cls3 100-121 Hdl Hcap good	£4,224
	2/11	Donc	2m¹/₂f Cls4 Nov Hdl gd-sft	£2,055
	3/10	Uttx	2m Cls6 NHF 4-6yo soft	£1,561

Showed remarkable consistency last season given he was running in big-field handicap hurdles, disappointing just once at Cheltenham; won Ladbroke Hurdle at Ascot and produced career-best effort on final start in Scottish Champion Hurdle; set to go novice chasing.

1282 Realt Dubh (Ire)

8 b g Beneficial - Suez Canal (Exit To Nowhere)

Noel Meade (Ir)   D J Sharkey

PLACINGS: 217/3/1F12113/1252-0   RPR **169+c**

Starts	1st	2nd	3rd	4th	Win & Pl
21	8	6	3	-	£289,061

	4/11	Fair	2m4f Gd1 Ch good	£50,431
	1/11	Leop	2m1f Nov Gd1 Ch soft	£44,828
	12/10	Leop	2m1f Nov Gd1 Ch heavy	£51,770
	11/10	Punc	2m Nov Gd2 Ch sft-hvy	£23,009
	9/10	Navn	2m4f Ch yield	£7,938
	2/09	Punc	2m Hdl soft	£12,076
	12/08	Leop	2m Mdn Hdl 4yo yld-sft	£7,113
	11/08	Thur	2m NHF 4yo soft	£4,319

Triple Grade 1 winner as a novice chaser two seasons ago, though twice no match for Captain Chris; restricted to just two starts last season following injury but produced a career-best when chasing home Sizing Europe at Punchestown; should win good races.

1283 Realt Mor (Ire)

7 b g Beneficial - Suez Canal (Exit To Nowhere)

Nicky Richards   Mrs Pat Sloan

PLACINGS: 1/F1/F2-   RPR **141+c**

Starts	1st	2nd	3rd	4th	Win & Pl
4	1	1	-	-	£2,867

	4/11	Kels	2m2f Cls4 Nov Hdl gd-sft	£1,952

Won Irish point-to-point and would have a strong record under rules but for twice falling when in front, including when clear at the last on chasing debut last season; remains good chase prospect.

1284 Rebel Du Maquis (Fr)

7 b g Brier Creek - Jade De Chalamont (Royal Charter)

Paul Nicholls   Mrs Kathy Stuart & P F Nicholls

PLACINGS: 22/21F021/113541/19-

Starts	1st	2nd	3rd	4th	Win & Pl
16	6	4	1	1	£54,929

142	5/11	Strf	2m5¹/₂f Cls2 120-142 Ch Hcap good	£7,765
	4/11	Extr	2m3¹/₂f Cls3 Nov Ch gd-fm	£5,334
	11/10	Tntn	2m3f Cls4 Nov Ch good	£5,204
	10/10	Chel	2m4¹/₂f Cls3 Nov Ch good	£7,514
	4/10	Winc	2m4f Cls5 Nov Hdl gd-fm	£2,927
	10/09	Extr	2m1f Cls5 Nov Hdl gd-sft	£3,253

Found out at the top level as a novice chaser two seasons ago despite three wins but seemed much improved when winning a summer chase at Stratford; only seen once since then due to series of niggles but should be back for major 2m5f handicap chases at Cheltenham.

1285 Rebel Fitz (Fr)

7 b g Agent Bleu - Gesse Parade (Dress Parade)

Michael Winters (Ir)   Brian Sweetnam

PLACINGS: 114/2121124-111   RPR **161+h**

Starts	1st	2nd	3rd	4th	Win & Pl
13	8	3	-	2	£223,961

	8/12	Cork	2m2f Hdl yld-sft	£11,917
145	8/12	Gway	2m 131-150 Hdl Hcap soft	£130,500
	7/12	Tipp	2m Gd3 Hdl soft	£33,854
	10/11	Cork	2m Nov Hdl yield	£10,112
	9/11	Clon	2m¹/₂f Nov Hdl good	£5,948
	8/11	Cork	2m Mdn Hdl good	£5,948
	10/10	Gway	2m NHF 4-7yo gd-yld	£7,022
	9/10	List	2m NHF 5yo good	£6,106

Not far off last season's leading novice hurdlers (won three times and fourth in Grade 1 at Punchestown) and improved again this summer; won well at Tipperary before defying mark of 145 in Galway Hurdle; needs to progress again to become Champion Hurdle contender.

1286 Restless Harry

8 b g Sir Harry Lewis - Restless Native (Be My Native)

Robin Dickin   R G Whitehead

PLACINGS: 1F1/337339/1323410F-   RPR **156+h**

Starts	1st	2nd	3rd	4th	Win & Pl
21	5	3	6	1	£112,532

	2/12	Hayd	3m Cls1 Gd2 Hdl heavy	£18,509
	10/11	Weth	3m1f Cls1 Gd2 Hdl good	£18,310
	4/10	Chel	2m5¹/₂f Cls2 Nov Hdl good	£8,532
	1/10	Chel	2m4¹/₂f Cls1 Nov Gd2 Hdl soft	£15,393
	11/09	Towc	2m5f Cls3 Nov Hdl 4-6yo heavy	£6,337

High-class staying hurdler who has won three

Grade 2 races and been placed three times at Grade 1 level in last three seasons; further success may depend on going back over fences having reverted to hurdles after two defeats last term.

1287 Reve De Sivola (Fr)

7 b g Assessor - Eva De Chalamont (Iron Duke)

Nick Williams   Paul Duffy Diamond Partnership

PLACINGS: 6/12121/413733/4753-   **RPR 144 + c**

Starts	1st	2nd	3rd	4th	Win & Pl
20	4	3	6	2	£167,482

12/10	Chel	2m5f Cls2 Nov Ch good	£9,798
4/10	Punc	2m4f Nov Gd1 Hdl good	£46,637
12/09	Newb	2m5f Cls1 Nov Gd1 Hdl heavy	£24,229
10/09	Chep	2m4f Cls1 Nov Gd2 Hdl soft	£17,103

Top-class novice hurdler three seasons ago, winning Grade 1 at Punchestown after chasing home Peddlers Cross at Cheltenham; nowhere near as fluent over fences but seemed to be steadily improving (third in three major handicaps) until missing second half of last season.

1288 Rigour Back Bob (Ire)

7 ch g Bob Back - Rigorous (Generous)

Edward O'Grady (Ir)   Gaticoma Syndicate

PLACINGS: 14111241/1461325/F2-   **RPR 144h**

Starts	1st	2nd	3rd	4th	Win & Pl
19	7	3	2	4	£119,745

12/10	Navn	2m4f Gd2 Hdl soft	£24,159
5/10	DRoy	2m6f Hdl gd-fm	£10,075
4/10	Punc	3m Nov Gd3 Hdl good	£20,133
12/09	Limk	2m Hdl 4yo heavy	£13,589
12/09	Thur	2m Nov Hdl 4yo sft-hvy	£7,044
11/09	Limk	2m Mdn Hdl 4yo heavy	£5,032
5/09	Baln	2m NHF 4yo soft	£5,367

Progressive staying hurdler two seasons ago, beaten less than six lengths when fifth in World Hurdle; suffered a leg injury when second at Thurles last October and missed rest of season; likely to go novice chasing.

1289 Riverside Theatre

8 b g King's Theatre - Disallowed (Distinctly North)

Nicky Henderson   Jimmy Nesbitt Partnership

PLACINGS: 12114/3115F/121/11P-   **RPR 172 + c**

Starts	1st	2nd	3rd	4th	Win & Pl
18	10	2	2	1	£431,498

3/12	Chel	2m5f Cls1 Gd1 Ch good	£148,070
2/12	Asct	2m5¹/₂f Cls1 Gd1 Ch gd-sft	£84,478
2/11	Asct	2m5¹/₂f Cls1 Ch soft	£84,660
11/10	Kemp	2m4¹/₂f Cls2 Ch good	£15,655
12/09	Kemp	2m Cls1 Nov Gd2 Ch gd-sft	£18,813
11/09	Newb	2m1f Cls3 Ch gd-sft	£6,285
3/09	Newb	2m¹/₂f Cls4 Nov Hdl good	£2,927
1/09	Kemp	2m Cls4 Nov Hdl soft	£2,927
11/08	Asct	2m Cls4 NHF 4-6yo good	£3,131
2/08	Kemp	2m Cls4 NHF 4-6yo good	£3,253

Landed Grade 1 double over 2m4f last season, most notably with gutsy win in Ryanair Chase; pulled up in Melling Chase next time and likely to be kept fresh with just two outings, with King George run determining Cheltenham Festival target.

1290 Roalco De Farges (Fr)

7 gr g Dom Alco - Vonaria (Vorias)

Philip Hobbs   The Brushmakers

PLACINGS: 3F/235331/001362512-   **RPR 143 + c**

Starts	1st	2nd	3rd	4th	Win & Pl
14	3	2	4	-	£52,191

4/12	Chep	3m Cls3 Nov Ch gd-sft	£4,549
11/11	Newb	2m6¹/₂f Cls3 Nov 107-130 Ch Hcap good	£6,882
4/11	Chep	2m4f Cls3 109-132 Hdl Hcap gd-sft	£3,643

Not always very fluent with his jumping in novice chases last season but steadily improved, helped by stepping up in trip when second in Bet365 Gold Cup at Sandown; likely to be aimed at Welsh National and has already won twice at Chepstow.

1291 Rock On Ruby (Ire)

7 b g Oscar - Stony View (Tirol)

Harry Fry   The Festival Goers

PLACINGS: 411/11223/1213-   **RPR 171 + h**

Starts	1st	2nd	3rd	4th	Win & Pl
12	6	3	2	1	£302,905

3/12	Chel	2m1f Cls1 Gd1 Hdl good	£210,715
11/11	Newb	2m¹/₂f Cls1 List 125-145 Hdl Hcap gd-sft	£11,390
12/10	Newb	2m¹/₂f Cls3 Hdl gd-sft	£5,010
11/10	Chel	2m¹/₂f Cls1 List NHF 4-6yo gd-sft	£6,841
3/10	Newb	2m¹/₂f Cls5 NHF 4-6yo gd-sft	£2,055
2/10	Tntn	2m1f Cls5 Mdn NHF 4-6yo soft	£2,192

Relished a furious gallop when winning Champion Hurdle at Cheltenham from Overturn; unlikely to enjoy speed tests as much (narrow second to Binocular in Christmas Hurdle) but should be a major threat at Cheltenham again.

1292 Rocky Creek (Ire)

6 b g Dr Massini - Kissantell (Broken Hearted)

Paul Nicholls   The Johnson & Stewart Families

PLACINGS: 1/218-   **RPR 142 + h**

Starts	1st	2nd	3rd	4th	Win & Pl
3	1	1	-	-	£15,640

1/12	Donc	3m¹/₂f Cls1 Nov Gd2 Hdl gd-sft	£14,305

Seemed to find 2m6f too sharp when beaten on hurdling debut but did well to land a fair Grade 2 next time before finishing eighth in Grade 1 novice hurdle at Cheltenham; set to go chasing and could do well given an extreme test of stamina.

1293 Roi Du Mee (Fr)

7 b g Lavirco - British Nellerie (Le Pontet)

Gordon Elliott (Ir)   Gigginstown House Stud

PLACINGS: 7/6F321117/512F5358-   **RPR 156 + c**

Starts	1st	2nd	3rd	4th	Win & Pl
25	6	5	3	1	£96,163

10/11	Punc	2m7f Gd3 Ch yld-sft	£16,810
2/11	Naas	2m5f Ch sft-hvy	£22,414
2/11	Punc	2m6f Nov Ch heavy	£9,517
12/10	Limk	2m6f Ch sft-hvy	£8,243
12/09	Gowr	2m Mdn Hdl 4yo heavy	£7,044
9/09	Sabl	1m5¹/₂f NHF 4yo v soft	£10,680

Began last season well with Grade 3 win over 2m7f

before dropping in trip to run fine second to Kauto Stone at Down Royal; failed to convince he stays 3m strongly enough to win good races at that trip when disappointing subsequently but becoming well handicapped.

1294 Ronaldo Des Mottes (Fr)

7 b g Rifapour - Gemma (Djarvis)

David Pipe   K & D Ives

PLACINGS: 12211120/0127/3F6/

Starts	1st	2nd	3rd	4th	Win & Pl
15	5	4	1	-	£85,394
131	12/09 Kemp	2m Cls3 111-133 Hdl Hcap gd-sft................£6,262			
	2/09 Sand	2m¹/₂f Cls3 Nov Hdl soft.........................£5,204			
	1/09 Folk	2m1¹/₂f Cls4 Mdn Hdl 4yo soft..............£3,426			
	11/08 Nant	1m4f NHF 3yo heavy.............................£15,074			
	7/08 Sabl	1m5¹/₂f NHF 3yo v soft...........................£4,044			

Progressed rapidly in handicap hurdles three seasons ago, finishing second in Totesport Trophy, and has since run well in top company, including when just running out of stamina when last seen in 2011 Aintree Hurdle; back in training after subsequent injury.

1295 Roudoudou Ville (Fr)

7 b/br g Winning Smile - Jadoudy Ville (Cadoudal)

Victor Dartnall   Mrs S De Wilde

PLACINGS: 1/1366834/P11/213-   RPR **154+c**

Starts	1st	2nd	3rd	4th	Win & Pl
14	5	1	3	1	£40,879
137	11/11 Sand	2m4¹/₂f Cls3 124-153 Ch Hcap gd-sft........£7,507			
114	3/11 Chep	2m3¹/₂f Cls4 99-114 Ch Hcap good............£3,253			
102	3/11 Winc	2m Cls4 87-105 Ch Hcap gd-fm................£2,700			
	5/09 Rost	1m3f NHF 4-5yo good............................£3,884			
	9/08 Chat	1m5f NHF 3yo gd-sft...............................£5,147			

Missed much of last season through injury having looked an unlucky third in December Gold Cup at Cheltenham (collared close home) but due to return after Christmas; has made sharp rate of progress having won three of previous four starts; could be top-class.

1296 Rubi Light (Fr)

7 b g Network - Genny Lights (Lights Out)

Robbie Hennessy (Ir)   W Hennessy

PLACINGS: 12294/117213/312154-   RPR **169+c**

Starts	1st	2nd	3rd	4th	Win & Pl
24	7	6	3	2	£213,364
	2/12 Gowr	2m4f Gd2 Ch soft...................................£21,667			
	12/11 Punc	2m4f Gd1 Ch heavy..............................£44,828			
	2/11 Gowr	2m4f Gd2 Ch heavy...............................£22,414			
130	11/10 Punc	2m 107-130 Ch Hcap sft-hvy..................£13,518			
	9/10 Slig	2m4f Ch yield..£7,785			
	12/09 Limk	2m3f Hdl heavy..£9,728			
	4/09 Fntb	2m2f Ch 4yo v soft..................................£6,990			

Has gained several major wins over 2m4f, most notably in Grade 1 at Punchestown last season, as well as running well in last two renewals of Ryanair Chase; best on heavy ground but failed to stay 3m in those conditions when fourth behind China Rock last time.

1297 Sadler's Risk (Ire)

4 b g Sadler's Wells - Riskaverse (Dynaformer)

Philip Hobbs   R S Brookhouse

PLACINGS: 12632-   RPR **145h**

Starts	1st	2nd	3rd	4th	Win & Pl
5	1	2	1	-	£24,349
	1/12 Kemp	2m Cls4 Hdl 4yo good............................£3,249			

A 13-2 shot for last season's Triumph Hurdle but only sixth there before being beaten much further at Aintree; bounced back with good second at Sandown and may be better right-handed given all wins (Flat and jumps) have come that way around.

1298 Sailors Warn (Ire)

5 b g Redback - Coral Dawn (Trempolino)

Edward O'Grady (Ir)   Patrick Wilmott

PLACINGS: 34126/7122763-53   RPR **149+h**

Starts	1st	2nd	3rd	4th	Win & Pl
14	2	3	3	1	£83,642
	10/11 Limk	2m2f Hdl 4yo yld-sft..............................£11,487			
	12/10 Leop	2m Gd2 Hdl 3yo sft-hvy.........................£28,761			

Likeable hurdler who was sixth in red-hot Triumph Hurdle in 2011 and bounced back to that form when third in last season's County Hurdle (both on good ground); slightly below that level in more testing conditions but still rarely runs a bad race.

1299 Saint Are (Fr)

6 b/br g Network - Fortanea (Video Rock)

Tim Vaughan   D W Fox

PLACINGS: 7/53172F31/02524U01-   RPR **148+c**

Starts	1st	2nd	3rd	4th	Win & Pl
17	3	3	2	1	£109,174
137	4/12 Aint	3m1f Cls1 List 124-150 Ch Hcap good........£34,170			
	4/11 Aint	3m¹/₂f Cls1 Nov Gd1 Hdl good...................£56,570			
	6/10 Sabl	2m1f Hdl 4yo gd-sft................................£8,920			

Has won at Aintree for last two seasons, following up Grade 1 novice hurdle win in 2011 with narrow handicap chase success last April; had been left on a good mark due to largely disappointing form over fences in between when stable was struggling.

1300 Salden Licht

8 b g Fantastic Light - Salde (Alkalde)

Alan King   Dai Griffiths

PLACINGS: 1132/1B53/

Starts	1st	2nd	3rd	4th	Win & Pl
8	3	2	1	-	£38,795
142	1/11 Extr	2m1f Cls2 119-142 Hdl Hcap soft...............£8,238			
	1/10 Plum	2m Cls4 Nov Hdl soft...............................£2,927			
	12/09 Newb	2m¹/₂f Cls4 Mdn Hdl soft..........................£3,253			

Much improved over hurdles two seasons ago, finishing fifth under a big weight in the County Hurdle and third when stepped up to 2m4f for first time in Aintree Hurdle; missed last season through injury but likely to return in novice chases and could go far.

1301 Salsify (Ire)

7 b g Beneficial - Our Deadly (Phardante)

Rodger Sweeney (Ir)   Mrs J B Sweeney

PLACINGS: 633/1F172U/112P11F-1   **RPR 148+c**

Starts	1st	2nd	3rd	4th	Win & Pl
16	6	1	2		£68,140
	6/12 Strf	3m4f Cls2 Am Hunt Ch good			£14,990
	3/12 Chel	3m2¹/₂f Cls2 Hunt Ch good			£20,986
	2/12 Leop	3m Hunt Ch gd-sft			£8,625
	5/11 Punc	3m1f Hunt Ch yield			£12,328
	4/11 Fair	3m1f Hunt Ch good			£4,759
	2/11 Clon	2m4f Mdn Hunt Ch sft-hvy			£4,164

Won several major hunter chases last season following victories at Fairyhouse and Punchestown the previous spring, most notably outstaying Chapoturgeon at Cheltenham; good enough to make mark in open races.

1302 Salut Flo (Fr)

7 b g Saint Des Saints - Royale Marie (Garde Royale)

David Pipe   Allan Stennett

PLACINGS: 7F3913/1528112/01-   **RPR 151+c**

Starts	1st	2nd	3rd	4th	Win & Pl
16	5	2	2		£121,843
137	3/12 Chel	2m5f Cls1 Gd3 127-153 Ch Hcap good			£42,713
118	3/10 Donc	2m3f Cls3 115-124 Ch Hcap good			£6,505
	1/10 Cagn	2m3f Ch holding			£13,593
	5/09 Autl	2m3¹/₂f Hdl 4yo Hcap heavy			£18,641
	3/09 Pari	2m1f Hdl 4yo gd-sft			£6,943

Patiently handled when returning from 18-month absence last season, winning Byrne Group Plate having blundered when in contention for similar handicap chase at Cheltenham; raised 11lb but still capable of much better if jumping improves.

1303 Sam Winner (Fr)

5 b g Okawango - Noche (Night Shift)

Paul Nicholls   Mrs Angela Yeoman

PLACINGS: 22/211446/FF-   **RPR 127+c**

Starts	1st	2nd	3rd	4th	Win & Pl
10		2	3	2	£65,170
	12/10 Chel	2m1f Cls2 Hdl 3yo gd-sft			£8,141
	11/10 Chel	2m¹/₂f Cls1 Gd2 Hdl 3yo gd-sft			£14,253

Very smart juvenile hurdler two seasons ago when fourth in Triumph Hurdle; fell on both runs in novice chases last season but going well when departing three out on second occasion in strong contest at Cheltenham; has recovered from subsequent knee injury.

1304 Samain (Ger)

6 b g Black Sam Bellamy - Selva (Darshaan)

Willie Mullins (Ir)   Gigginstown House Stud

PLACINGS: 2/111/

Starts	1st	2nd	3rd	4th	Win & Pl
4	3	1	-	-	£29,401
	4/11 Curr	2m NHF 4-7yo gd-sft			£15,409
	2/11 Naas	2m NHF 4-7yo sft-hvy			£8,030
	1/11 Punc	2m NHF 5-7yo heavy			£4,759

Had been Ireland's shortest-priced contender for 2011 Champion Bumper before connections opted to miss that race, keeping his bumper campaign low-key with third successive win coming at the Curragh; missed last season through injury but should be top novice hurdler.

1305 Sanctuaire (Fr)

6 b/br g Kendor - Biblique (Saint Cyrien)

Paul Nicholls   Jared Sullivan

PLACINGS: 53113/F371P/855111-   **RPR 168+c**

Starts	1st	2nd	3rd	4th	Win & Pl
16	6	-	3	-	£154,575
	4/12 Sand	2m Cls1 Gd2 Ch soft			£42,713
	3/12 Sand	2m Cls4 Nov Ch good			£5,198
	1/12 Tntn	2m3f Cls4 Nov Ch gd-sft			£5,198
144	4/11 Ayr	2m Cls1 Gd2 140-160 Hdl Hcap good			£28,505
127	3/10 Chel	2m¹/₂f Cls1 Nov Gd3 122-135 Hdl 4yo Hcap good			£42,758
	2/10 Tntn	2m1f Cls4 Nov Hdl soft			£3,903

Failed to build on rich juvenile promise over hurdles but has already scaled much greater heights as a chaser, stepping up in class to land a third front-running win in the Grade 2 Celebration Chase at Sandown; looks an ideal Tingle Creek type.

1306 Sea Of Thunder (Ire)

7 b g Old Vic - Snob's Supreme (Supreme Leader)

Charles Byrnes (Ir)   Gigginstown House Stud

PLACINGS: 2116/704/312F50P-   **RPR 141+h**

Starts	1st	2nd	3rd	4th	Win & Pl
11	1	1	1	1	£5,877
	10/11 Thur	2m Mdn Hdl 5-6yo good			£4,461

Gained only win out of ten races under rules over 2m but proved a revelation when stepped up to 3m at Cheltenham last season, falling at the last when well clear; bitterly disappointing back there in March but remains a fine prospect for staying novice chases.

1307 Seabass (Ire)

9 b g Turtle Island - Muscovy Duck (Moscow Society)

Ted Walsh (Ir)   Gunners Syndicate

PLACINGS: 90/47/523F11/111113-   **RPR 158c**

Starts	1st	2nd	3rd	4th	Win & Pl
15	6	1	2	1	£220,285
	2/12 Naas	2m Gd2 Ch soft			£25,188
131	1/12 Leop	2m5f 120-148 Ch Hcap yield			£40,625
122	12/11 Limk	2m3¹/₂f 112-140 Ch Hcap heavy			£22,414
114	12/11 Punc	2m6f 99-127 Ch Hcap heavy			£13,168
104	2/10 Fair	2m5f Nov 88-106 Ch Hcap sft-hvy			£6,412
95	1/10 Punc	2m4f 88-115 Ch Hcap heavy			£6,421

Massive improver last season, winning four out of four before gallant third in Grand National; showed improved stamina at Aintree given he had never won beyond 2m6f and had enough speed to win 2m Grade 2 on previous start; may progress again.

1308 Shakalakaboomboom (Ire)

8 b g Anshan - Tia Maria (Supreme Leader)

Nicky Henderson   Liam Breslin

PLACINGS: 0252/311797/11229-   RPR **153c**

Starts	1st	2nd	3rd	4th	Win & Pl
15	4	4	1	-	£80,571

140	12/11	Chel	3m1¹/₂f Cls1 Gd3 131-152 Ch Hcap good	£20,787
131	5/11	Punc	3m1f 118-139 Ch Hcap yield	£25,216
128	1/11	Tntn	2m7¹/₂f Cls3 Nov 118-132 Ch Hcap gd-sft	£6,851
119	11/10	Kemp	2m4¹/₂f Cls3 111-130 Ch Hcap good	£5,855

Progressive handicap chaser who won at Punchestown in 2011 and returned from a break to follow up at Cheltenham on return; laid out for the Grand National after that and ran well until stamina faded from two out; still well handicapped on that evidence.

1309 Shutthefrontdoor (Ire)

5 b/br g Accordion - Hurricane Girl (Strong Gale)

Jonjo O'Neill   John P McManus

PLACINGS: 111-   RPR **125+b**

Starts	1st	2nd	3rd	4th	Win & Pl
3	3	-	-	-	£14,490

2/12	Newb	2m¹/₂f Cls1 List NHF 4-6yo gd-sft	£5,695
12/11	Asct	2m Cls1 List NHF 4-6yo soft	£7,290
11/11	Ffos	2m Cls6 NHF 4-5yo soft	£1,506

Unbeaten in three bumpers last season, including twice at Listed level at Ascot and Newbury; got up late on final occasion to pip Village Vic and seems sure to be suited by longer trips when sent over hurdles; should make a fine staying chaser in time.

1310 Silver By Nature

10 gr g Silver Patriarch - Gale (Strong Gale)

Lucinda Russell   G S Brown

PLACINGS: 5/24F13FU/5121/0710/

Starts	1st	2nd	3rd	4th	Win & Pl
25	7	2	3	2	£167,381

149	2/11	Hayd	3m4f Cls1 Gd3 125-149 Ch Hcap heavy	£43,511
143	2/10	Hayd	3m4f Cls1 Gd3 132-158 Ch Hcap heavy	£57,010
123	11/09	Carl	3m2f Cls3 121-135 Ch Hcap soft	£26,020
	2/09	Ayr	2m4f Cls3 Nov Ch soft	£6,440
	2/08	Ayr	2m Cls4 Nov Hdl soft	£3,123
	12/07	Kels	2m¹/₂f Cls4 Mdn Hdl soft	£3,426
	4/07	Prth	2m¹/₂f Cls5 NHF 4-6yo gd-sft	£2,056

Top-class staying chaser on heavy ground, twice winning Grand National Trial at Haydock by 15 lengths, but flopped at Aintree following latest victory in 2011 and missed last season through

injury; hasn't won on ground quicker than soft since bumper days.

1311 Silviniaco Conti (Fr)

6 ch g Dom Alco - Gazelle Lulu (Altayan)

Paul Nicholls   Potensis Limited & Chris Giles

PLACINGS: 11/11134/31241-   RPR **166+c**

Starts	1st	2nd	3rd	4th	Win & Pl
12	7	1	2	2	£181,406

	4/12	Aint	3m1f Cls1 Nov Gd2 Ch good	£42,713
	11/11	Winc	2m5f Cls1 Nov Gd2 Ch gd-sft	£20,093
	11/10	Asct	2m3¹/₂f Cls1 Gd2 Hdl gd-sft	£50,697
	10/10	Chep	2m1f Nov Gd2 Hdl soft	£14,253
	10/10	Bang	2m1f Cls3 Nov Hdl good	£4,879
	4/10	Nanc	2m1f Hdl 4yo good	£12,743
	3/10	Seno	2m2f Hdl 4yo gd-sft	£5,097

High-class hurdler who steadily improved over fences last season and produced best effort when easily winning at Aintree on final start; had also shown promise behind Grands Crus before poor effort at Ascot when trainer's horses were wrong; top prospect.

1312 Simenon (Ire)

5 b g Marju - Epistoliere (Alzao)

Willie Mullins (Ir)   Wicklow Bloodstock Limited

PLACINGS: 51203-1   RPR **148+h**

Starts	1st	2nd	3rd	4th	Win & Pl
6	2	1	1	-	£26,341

| | 5/12 | Cork | 2m Hdl good | £8,050 |
| | 1/12 | Cork | 2m Mdn Hdl 4-5yo heavy | £6,038 |

Dual Royal Ascot winner this summer who improved steadily over hurdles prior to that, finishing third in Grade 1 at Punchestown and winning well at Cork after poor effort in Supreme Novices' Hurdle; has potential to do much better.

1313 Simonsig

6 gr g Fair Mix - Dusty Too (Terimon)

Nicky Henderson   R A Bartlett

PLACINGS: 1F1/112111-   RPR **162+h**

Starts	1st	2nd	3rd	4th	Win & Pl
6	5	1	-	-	£130,353

	4/12	Aint	2m4f Cls1 Nov Gd2 Hdl good	£28,475
	3/12	Chel	2m5f Cls1 Nov Gd1 Hdl good	£56,950
	2/12	Kels	2m3¹/₂f Cls1 Gd2 Hdl gd-sft	£9,747
	11/11	Asct	2m3¹/₂f Cls3 Nov Hdl good	£5,005
	4/11	Fair	2m2f NHF 4-6yo good	£25,647

Hugely exciting talent who won well at Cheltenham and Aintree last season, seemingly

improving following earlier second behind Fingal Bay even though key rivals departed in both races; good enough to make big mark over hurdles but may well go novice chasing.

1314 Sir Des Champs (Fr)

6 b g Robin Des Champs - Liste En Tete (Video Rock)

Willie Mullins (Ir)   Gigginstown House Stud

PLACINGS: 1/11/11111-   RPR **168+c**

Starts		1st	2nd	3rd	4th	Win & Pl
8		8	-	-	-	£197,007
	4/12	Punc	3m1f Nov Gd1 Ch sft-hvy			£41,333
	3/12	Chel	2m4f Cls1 Nov Gd2 Ch good			£51,255
	1/12	Leop	2m5f Nov Gd2 Ch yield			£21,667
	12/11	Limk	2m3¹/₂f Nov Gd2 Ch heavy			£21,013
	12/11	Fair	2m5¹/₂f Ch sft-hvy			£7,138
134	3/11	Chel	2m4¹/₂f Cls2 127-140 Cond Hdl Hcap good			£28,179
	1/11	Navn	2m Hdl soft			£7,733
	3/10	Autl	2m1¹/₂f Hdl 4yo soft			£18,690

Unbeaten in eight starts under rules and looked particularly good when switched to fences last season, winning five times; most impressive in Jewson Chase at Cheltenham when routing classy field before stepping up to 3m at Punchestown; potential superstar.

1315 Sire De Grugy (Fr)

6 ch g My Risk - Hirlish (Passing Sale)

Gary Moore   The Preston Family & Friends

PLACINGS: 221113/64138-   RPR **149h**

Starts		1st	2nd	3rd	4th	Win & Pl
11		4	2	2	1	£50,152
141	2/12	Tntn	2m1f Cls2 121-147 Hdl Hcap gd-sft			£12,660
	2/11	Kemp	2m Cls1 Nov Gd2 Hdl gd-sft			£12,086
	2/11	Folk	2m1¹/₂f Cls4 Nov Hdl gd-sft			£1,918
	1/11	Fknm	2m Cls5 Mdn Hdl soft			£1,713

Won a Grade 2 novice hurdle two seasons ago and unlucky not to land a major handicap last season when close fourth in Betfair Hurdle and third in Imperial Cup after 6lb rise for winning at Taunton; has the build to do even better over fences.

1316 Sizing Europe (Ire)

10 b g Pistolet Bleu - Jennie Dun (Mandalus)

Henry De Bromhead (Ir)   Ann & Alan Potts Partnership

PLACINGS: 111113/2231/2121121-   RPR **174+c**

Starts		1st	2nd	3rd	4th	Win & Pl
31		15	7	3	1	£897,597
	4/12	Punc	2m Gd1 Ch sft-hvy			£72,333
	2/12	Punc	2m Gd2 Ch soft			£21,667
	12/11	Sand	2m Cls1 Gd1 Ch gd-sft			£68,340
	10/11	Gowr	2m4f Gd2 Ch soft			£21,853
	3/11	Chel	2m Cls1 Gd1 Ch good			£182,432
	3/10	Chel	2m Cls1 Gd1 Ch gd-sft			£85,515
	12/09	Leop	2m1f Nov Gd1 Ch yield			£56,796
	11/09	Punc	2m Nov Gd2 Ch heavy			£25,282
	10/09	Punc	2m2f Nov Gd3 Ch gd-yld			£18,013
	5/09	Punc	2m4f Ch heavy			£9,057
	1/08	Leop	2m Gd1 Hdl yield			£73,529
137	11/07	Chel	2m1¹/₂f Cls1 Gd3 124-143 Hdl Hcap soft			£57,020
	4/07	Punc	2m Nov Hdl good			£13,196
	11/06	Newb	2m1¹/₂f Cls3 Mdn Hdl gd-sft			£6,506
	10/06	Naas	2m NHF 4yo soft			£4,289

Outstanding 2m chaser who was just pipped by

Finian's Rainbow when defending Champion Chase crown last season but went on to take tally of Grade 1 wins to six at Punchestown; may attempt 3m again despite losing all three races beyond 2m4f.

1317 Smad Place (Fr)

5 gr g Smadoun - Bienna Star (Village Star)

Alan King   Mrs Peter Andrews

PLACINGS: 621310/123U-   RPR **164h**

Starts		1st	2nd	3rd	4th	Win & Pl
10		3	2	2	-	£75,317
144	1/12	Asct	2m3¹/₂f Cls1 Gd2 125-145 Hdl Hcap gd-sft			£22,780
	2/11	Winc	2m Cls4 Nov Hdl gd-sft			£2,439
	11/10	Newb	2m¹/₂f Cls3 Hdl 3yo gd-sft			£6,505

Made rapid progress in staying hurdles after missing first half of last season, finishing fine third in World Hurdle, but unseated rider four out when still going well at Aintree; set to go novice chasing and could develop into leading candidate for RSA Chase.

1318 Snap Tie (Ire)

10 b g Pistolet Bleu - Aries Girl (Valiyar)

Philip Hobbs   Mrs Diana L Whateley

PLACINGS: 1262/1223/12376/1/1-   RPR **158h**

Starts		1st	2nd	3rd	4th	Win & Pl
15		5	5	2	-	£114,435
137	4/12	Punc	2m 110-137 Hdl Hcap sft-hvy			£16,250
	10/09	Chel	2m Cls2 Nov Ch gd-fm			£12,640
	10/08	Kemp	2m Cls2 Hdl good			£18,786
	10/07	Chel	2m¹/₂f Cls3 Mdn Hdl good			£6,263
	5/06	Limk	2m NHF 4yo good			£5,007

Returned from two-and-a-half-year absence to win handicap hurdle at Punchestown at end of last season and reportedly came out of that race well; had been very smart at his peak (seventh in 2009 Champion Hurdle) and won only start over fences later that year.

1319 So Young (Fr)

6 b g Lavirco - Honey (Highlanders)

Willie Mullins (Ir)   Mrs M McMahon

PLACINGS: 51211/113/61119-   RPR **155h**

Starts		1st	2nd	3rd	4th	Win & Pl
13		8	1	1	-	£97,831
	1/12	Navn	2m Hdl sft-hvy			£10,833
	12/11	Thur	2m List Hdl heavy			£15,409
	11/11	Punc	2m Hdl soft			£11,207
	2/11	Punc	2m Nov Hdl heavy			£7,733
	12/10	Leop	2m4f Mdn Hdl 4yo sft-hvy			£7,022
	4/10	StCl	1m4f NHF 4yo gd-sft			£13,274
	3/10	Nant	1m4f NHF 4-5yo gd-sft			£7,080
	10/09	Mlns	1m3f NHF 3yo v soft			£5,825

Has won all five starts below Grade 1 level in impressive fashion but beaten on three most serious tests, though would have gone close in 2011 Neptune Hurdle but for mistake at last; expected to stay 3m and could rack up more wins in staying novice chases.

1320 Solix (Fr)

6 b/br g Al Namix - Solimade (Loup Solitaire)

Ian Williams

PLACINGS: 1162/2571475/11264-   RPR **156c**

Starts	1st	2nd	3rd	4th	Win & Pl
16	5	3	-	2	£217,489

12/11	Chel	2m5f Cls2 Nov Ch good	£10,897
11/11	Asct	2m5¹/₂f Cls3 Ch good	£7,692
10/10	Autl	2m3¹/₂f Gd3 Hdl 4yo heavy	£51,770
2/10	Pau	2m1¹/₂f List Hdl 4yo heavy	£25,487
1/10	Pau	2m1f Hdl 4yo heavy	£12,743

Made a big impression when winning first two novice chases last season and ran a cracker when close second to Champion Court at Cheltenham but jumping fell apart when disappointing on his final two starts; subsequently sold out of Nicky Henderson's yard but remains capable of better.

1321 Soll

7 ch g Presenting - Montelfolene (Montelimar)

Willie Mullins (Ir)   Derrick Mossop

PLACINGS: 21/1/21B-   RPR **142c**

Starts	1st	2nd	3rd	4th	Win & Pl
4	2	1	-	-	£9,897

2/12	DRoy	2m4f Ch heavy	£4,600
1/11	Newc	3m Cls3 Nov Hdl soft	£3,643

Showed huge promise in just two completed starts over fences last season, including when showing good speed to win easily over 2m4f considering he was subsequently aimed at 4m National Hunt Chase; in rear but still going well when brought down at Cheltenham.

1322 Solwhit (Fr)

8 b g Solon - Toowhit Towhee (Lucky North)

Charles Byrnes (Ir)   Top Of The Hill Syndicate

PLACINGS: 1/1211/1131162/1222/

Starts		1st	2nd	3rd	4th	Win & Pl
18		10	5	1	-	£616,666

	11/10	Punc	2m Gd1 Hdl sft-hvy	£48,894
	1/10	Leop	2m Gd1 Hdl sft-hvy	£63,274
	12/09	Leop	2m Gd1 Hdl soft	£56,796
	11/09	Punc	2m Gd1 Hdl heavy	£53,641
	5/09	Punc	2m Gd1 Hdl sft-hvy	£116,505
	4/09	Aint	2m4f Cls1 Gd1 Hdl gd-sft	£96,917
	2/09	Gowr	2m Gd2 Hdl soft	£36,342
127	11/08	Fair	2m 117-145 Hdl Hcap soft	£19,147
	4/08	Punc	2m Hdl 4yo gd-yld	£14,360
	11/07	Engh	2m1¹/₂f Hdl 3yo heavy	£14,270

Prolific Grade 1 hurdler in Ireland from 2m to 2m4f, winning six times at the top level and finishing second four times to Hurricane Fly, though only sixth in 2010 Champion Hurdle; set to go novice chasing before missing last season through injury but due to return over fences.

1323 Some Target (Ire)

8 b g Witness Box - Bayloughbess (Lancastrian)

Willie Mullins (Ir)   Captain Conflict Syndicate

PLACINGS: 2115/23515/PP24U64P-   RPR **142+h**

Starts		1st	2nd	3rd	4th	Win & Pl
18		3	4	1	2	£41,666

125	1/11	Punc	3m4f 110-138 Ch Hcap soft	£16,250
	2/10	Clon	2m4f Mdn Hdl heavy	£4,580
	1/10	Limk	2m NHF 5-7yo soft	£4,281

Pulled up in Irish National for second successive year last season but ran several good races in top staying handicap chases in between, including

when fourth in Haydock Grand National Trial; creeping down handicap and could land good prize.

1324 Somersby (Ire)

8 b g Second Empire - Back To Roost (Presenting)

Mick Channon · Mrs T P Radford

PLACINGS: /1122/33253/1224172- · RPR **169**c

Starts	1st	2nd	3rd	4th	Win & Pl
22	6	6	6	2	£285,812
	1/12	Asct	2m1f Cls1 Gd1 Ch gd-sft		£59,135
	10/11	Kemp	2m4¹/₂f Cls2 Ch good		£12,512
	12/09	Sand	2m Cls1 Nov Gd2 Ch soft		£18,813
	11/09	Wwck	2m Cls3 Nov Ch good		£6,505
	11/08	Kemp	2m Cls4 Nov Hdl 4-6yo good		£4,554
	3/08	Hntg	2m¹/₂f Cls5 NHF 4-6yo soft		£1,713

Finally landed a Grade 1 at the eighth attempt when outstaying subsequent improver Finian's Rainbow in the Victor Chandler Chase; two previous best performances had also come at Ascot but slightly disappointing otherwise; didn't stay 3m in King George.

1325 Son Amix (Fr)

6 gr g Fragrant Mix - Immage (Bad Conduct)

Thomas Cooper (Ir) · Whitechurch Stud Syndicate

PLACINGS: 26144/22422/92922U1- · RPR **142**+c

Starts	1st	2nd	3rd	4th	Win & Pl
20	3	9	-	4	£87,625
	12/11	Punc	3m Ch heavy		£7,138
	2/10	Navn	2m Mdn Hdl 4yo sft-hvy		£6,412
	8/09	Stma	1m4f NHF 3yo gd-sft		£7,767

Useful staying handicap hurdler (second in 2011 Pertemps Final) who was a steady improver when

sent chasing in first half of last season; managed first win at fourth attempt from Soll before missing end of season through injury; could be an interesting handicapper.

1326 Son Of Flicka (orange cap)

8 b g Groom Dancer - Calendula (Be My Guest)

Donald McCain · Twenty Four Seven Recruitment

PLACINGS: 6/191825322F/90901F- · RPR **142**+h

Starts	1st	2nd	3rd	4th	Win & Pl
31	5	9	3	-	£87,584
135	3/12	Chel	2m5f Cls1 Gd3 134-155 Hdl Hcap good	£39,865
129	6/10	Worc	2m4f Cls3 120-135 Hdl Hcap good	£4,879
125	4/10	Bang	2m1f Cls3 113-127 Hdl Hcap soft	£6,971
	12/08	Bang	2m1f Cls4 Nov Hdl soft	£3,578
	3/08	Newb	1m4¹/₂f Cls5 NHF 4yo soft	£2,056

Seems a Cheltenham Festival specialist, winning last season's Coral Cup after a string of moderate runs since finishing second to Sir Des Champs at the meeting in 2011; clearly best on good ground and revised mark still 6lb below highest.

1327 Sous Les Cieux (Fr)

6 ch g Robin Des Champs - Joie De La Vie (Quart De Vin)

Willie Mullins (Ir) · Mrs S Ricci

PLACINGS: 31443/2/113253- · RPR **153**+h

Starts	1st	2nd	3rd	4th	Win & Pl
12	3	2	4	2	£99,070
	12/11	Fair	2m Nov Gd1 Hdl sft-hvy		£42,026
	11/11	Fair	2m4f Mdn Hdl soft		£5,948
	10/09	Fntb	1m7f NHF 3yo v soft		£6,796

Won a Grade 1 novice hurdle at Leopardstown early last season but form wasn't as strong as it seemed at the time and beaten favourite next twice; shaped well when stepped up to longer trips at Cheltenham and Punchestown and could do well over 3m.

1328 Spirit River (Fr)

7 b g Poliglote - Love River (Epervier Bleu)

Nicky Henderson   Michael Buckley

PLACINGS: 51/5101/FF0/4FP-   **RPR 146h**

Starts	1st	2nd	3rd	4th	Win & Pl
12	3	-	-	1	£72,755
141	3/10	Chel	2m5f Cls1 Gd3 126-151 Hdl Hcap good		£42,758
128	12/09	Chel	2m1f Cls3 108-128 Hdl Hcap good		£6,262
	3/09	Autl	2m2f Hdl 4yo holding		£20,505

Has completed only twice since winning 2010 Coral Cup at Cheltenham, falling on both runs over fences; retains plenty of ability judged on run in last season's Coral Cup when close up only to fall at the last; got loose before being pulled up at Aintree.

1329 Sprinter Sacre (Fr)

6 b/br g Network - Fatima III (Bayolidaan)

Nicky Henderson   Mrs Caroline Mould

PLACINGS: 11/2113/11111-   **RPR 176+c**

Starts	1st	2nd	3rd	4th	Win & Pl
11	9	1	1	-	£194,971
	4/12	Aint	2m Cls1 Nov Gd1 Ch good		£56,270
	3/12	Chel	2m Cls1 Gd1 Ch good		£74,035
	2/12	Newb	2m1f Cls1 Gd2 Ch gd-sft		£17,085
	12/11	Kemp	2m Cls1 Nov Gd2 Ch good		£13,326
	12/11	Donc	2m²/₂f Cls4 Nov Ch good		£3,444
	2/11	Asct	2m Cls2 Nov Hdl soft		£6,262
	2/11	Ffos	2m Cls4 Nov Hdl gd-sft		£2,602
	4/10	Ayr	2m Cls4 NHF 4-6yo good		£4,554
	2/10	Asct	2m Cls3 NHF 4-6yo gd-sft		£5,204

Unbeaten in five races over fences last season,

earning reputation as the best novice chaser seen for many years; looked particularly brilliant when routing his rivals in the Arkle Trophy at Cheltenham; will be tough to beat.

1330 Stagecoach Pearl (below)

8 gr g Classic Cliche - Linwood (Ardross)

Sue Smith   John Conroy Jaqueline Conroy

PLACINGS: 1/82221131129F/1532-   **RPR 156c**

Starts	1st	2nd	3rd	4th	Win & Pl
23	8	6	3	-	£74,923
146	11/11	Kels	2m1f Cls2 146-166 Ch Hcap good		£10,072
140	11/10	Hayd	2m Cls2 123-140 Ch Hcap gd-sft		£16,263
128	10/10	Aint	2m Cls2 120-138 Ch Hcap gd-sft		£9,428
118	7/10	Worc	2m Cls3 118-135 Ch Hcap good		£5,386
	7/10	Ctml	2m1¹/₂f Cls4 Ch gd-sft		£3,253
108	12/09	Donc	2m¹/₂f Cls4 Nov 90-110 Hdl Hcap good		£3,253
	9/09	Sedg	2m1f Cls4 Mdn Hdl gd-fm		£2,537
	12/08	Catt	2m Cls5 NHF 4-6yo good		£1,953

Front-running chaser who seems at his best in small fields and won well at Kelso on his return last season; twice ran well under big weights to be placed in subsequent handicaps, including when tried on soft ground for first time in nearly three years.

1331 Starluck (Ire)

7 gr g Key Of Luck - Sarifa (Kahyasi)

David Arbuthnot   A T A Wates

PLACINGS: 11143/1225/23134/30-   **RPR 144h**

Starts	1st	2nd	3rd	4th	Win & Pl
16	5	3	4	2	£150,947
	2/11	Hntg	2m¹/₂f Cls3 Nov Ch soft		£4,554
	10/09	Chel	2m¹/₂f Cls2 Hdl 4yo gd-fm		£31,310
	12/08	Kemp	2m Cls3 Nov Hdl 3yo good		£6,262
	11/08	Fknm	2m Cls4 Nov Hdl 3yo gd-sft		£4,554
	10/08	Hntg	2m¹/₂f Cls4 Nov Hdl 3yo good		£3,578

A high-class hurdler at his peak (twice second

at Grade 1 level) but disappointed over fences two seasons ago and missed most of last term through injury; still retains plenty of ability judged on unlucky handicap debut in County Hurdle.

1332 Staying Article (Ire)

7 b g Definite Article - Sejour (Bob Back)

Edward O'Grady (Ir)   Thomas Barr

PLACINGS: 11/213-   RPR **155**h

Starts	1st	2nd	3rd	4th	Win & Pl
5	3	1	1	-	£41,907
130	12/11	Fair	2m 104-130 Hdl Hcap sft-hvy		£21,013
	11/10	Naas	2m Mdn Hdl sft-hvy		£6,412
	10/10	Punc	2m NHF 4-7yo good		£5,190

Missed most of novice season but swiftly made strides in handicaps last term, going close under a big weight despite racing keenly in the Boylesports Hurdle at Leopardstown; met with a setback subsequently but already looks better than a handicapper.

1333 Steps To Freedom (Ire)

6 b g Statue Of Liberty - Dhakhirah (Sadler's Wells)

Jessica Harrington (Ir)   Mrs Sean Hussey

PLACINGS: 1F1/011105-   RPR **141**h

Starts	1st	2nd	3rd	4th	Win & Pl
9	5	-	-	-	£58,517
	11/11	Chel	2m¹/₂f Cls1 Nov Gd2 Hdl good		£12,244
	10/11	Punc	2m Gd3 Hdl yld-sft		£16,810
	9/11	Fair	2m Mdn Hdl 4-5yo good		£5,948
	4/11	Aint	2m1f Cls1 Gd2 Hdl 4-6yo good		£17,103
	6/10	Tipp	2m NHF 4yo gd-fm		£6,412

Winter options likely to be limited by preference for quick ground (unraced between November and March last season) though did well to beat Sailors Warn at Punchestown on ground softer than ideal; reported to be coughing after disappointing in Supreme Novices' Hurdle.

1334 Sunnyhillboy (Ire)

9 b g Old Vic - Sizzle (High Line)

Jonjo O'Neill   John P McManus

PLACINGS: 1/415312/73F/37P912-   RPR **154**c

Starts	1st	2nd	3rd	4th	Win & Pl
23	8	2	4	2	£382,473
142	3/12	Chel	3m1¹/₂f Cls2 126-143 Am Ch Hcap good		£29,980
127	2/10	Ludl	2m4f Cls3 107-130 Ch Hcap good		£7,828
	11/09	Ling	2m Cls4 Ch soft		£3,383
133	4/09	Aint	2m4f Cls1 List 127-145 Hdl Hcap good		£34,206
128	12/08	Sand	2m¹/₂f Cls1 List 116-142 Hdl Hcap soft		£28,505
118	11/08	Chel	2m¹/₂f Cls3 Nov 107-123 Hdl Hcap soft		£9,393
108	10/08	Extr	2m3f Cls4 95-115 Hdl Hcap gd-sft		£5,139
	11/07	Hntg	2m¹/₂f Cls5 NHF 4-6yo good		£2,056

Well fancied for a number of major handicap chases in his time and finally began to realise potential towards end of last season when running away with Kim Muir at Cheltenham and getting touched off by a nose in the Grand National; has shot up in the weights.

1335 Super Duty (Ire)

6 b g Shantou - Sarah's Cottage (Topanoora)

Donald McCain   Brannon, Dick, Hernon & Holden

PLACINGS: 1/11F12-   RPR **142**+h

Starts	1st	2nd	3rd	4th	Win & Pl
6	4	1	-	-	£29,026
	2/12	Asct	2m3¹/₂f Cls2 Nov Hdl gd-sft		£10,010
	11/11	Hayd	2m4f Cls4 Nov Hdl 4-7yo gd-sft		£4,224
	10/11	Carl	2m3¹/₂f Cls4 Nov Hdl good		£2,738
	4/11	Bang	2m1f Cls5 NHF 4-6yo good		£1,370

Beaten only once when completing last season and lost no caste when unable to keep tabs with Simonsig at Aintree, doing well to finish second despite bad mistake two out; fine chasing prospect.

1336 Sweet My Lord (Fr)

6 b g Johann Quatz - Hasta Manana (Useful)

Willie Mullins (Ir)   Aiden Devaney

PLACINGS: 1F1F/210/0144-91   RPR **152**h

Starts	1st	2nd	3rd	4th	Win & Pl
13	5	1	-	2	£47,751
	8/12	Tram	2m Ch soft		£4,600
128	11/11	Cork	2m4f 108-136 Hdl Hcap sft-hvy		£15,409
	12/10	Limk	2m3f Hdl sft-hvy		£8,854
	4/10	Cork	2m Mdn Hdl 4yo heavy		£6,412
	10/09	Nant	1m4f NHF 3yo soft		£5,825

Winning juvenile hurdler three seasons ago and has since made steady progress in handicap company; fine fourth in Boylesports Hurdle over inadequate 2m (previous fourth over 3m) and looked leading candidate for Coral Cup prior to injury.

1337 Sword Of Destiny (Ire)

6 gr g Shantou - Sparkling Sword (Broadsword)

Noel Meade (Ir)   Gigginstown House Stud

PLACINGS: 01/911-   RPR **146**+h

Starts	1st	2nd	3rd	4th	Win & Pl
4	3	-	-	-	£33,552
	11/11	Cork	3m Nov Gd3 Hdl soft		£22,414
	10/11	Punc	2m4f Mdn Hdl yld-sft		£5,948
	11/10	Gowr	2m NHF 4-5yo sft-hvy		£5,190

Missed much of last season through injury but had shown himself to be a very smart novice hurdler when winning twice, most notably in a Grade 3 at Cork; strong stayer who has a big future over fences but could have more to offer over hurdles.

1338 Tanks For That (Ire)

9 br g Beneficial - Lady Jurado (Jurado)

Nicky Henderson   Mrs Christopher Hanbury

PLACINGS: 6212PP/342003/1F32P-   RPR **159**c

Starts	1st	2nd	3rd	4th	Win & Pl
21	3	5	4	2	£63,533
140	11/11	Chel	2m Cls2 119-146 Ch Hcap good		£25,024
	2/10	Plum	2m1f Cls4 Ch gd-sft		£3,444
	3/09	Sand	2m1¹/₂f Cls3 Ch Nov Hdl gd-sft		£5,204

Has a fair record in succession of top 2m handicap chases during last two seasons, winning well at Cheltenham last November and running a cracker when second in Grand Annual Chase; ran flat when pulled up at Aintree but climbing up handicap anyway.

1339 Tap Night (USA)

5 ch g Pleasant Tap - Day Mate (Dayjur)

Lucinda Russell — Miss Jane Buchanan

PLACINGS: 2231116-					RPR **140h**
Starts	1st	2nd	3rd	4th	Win & Pl
7	3	2	1	-	£24,587

	3/12	Kels	2m2f Cls1 Gd2 Hdl good	£17,085
	2/12	Newc	2m4f Cls4 Nov Hdl soft	£2,014
110	11/11	Carl	2m3¹/₂f Cls4 Nov 84-110 Hdl Hcap gd-sft	£2,738

Completed a hat-trick in a Grade 2 novice hurdle at Kelso last season, beating Tolworth winner Captain Conan; seemed sure to appreciate a much longer trip but failed to stay 3m when sixth in Grade 1 at Aintree; has more to come over 2m4f.

1340 Tarla (Fr)

6 b m Lavirco - Targerine (Gairloch)

Willie Mullins (Ir) — Mrs S Ricci

PLACINGS: 11/4221521/1					RPR **150+h**
Starts	1st	2nd	3rd	4th	Win & Pl
10	5	3	-	1	£195,948

	8/12	Rosc	2m4¹/₂f Hdl yield	£5,750
	4/10	Punc	2m2f Gd3 Hdl good	£39,403
	9/09	Autl	2m2f Hdl 3yo v soft	£30,291
	4/09	Autl	1m7f Hdl 3yo v soft	£24,233
	3/09	Autl	1m7f Hdl 3yo holding	£24,233

Smart juvenile hurdler in France three seasons ago when second at Grade 2 level and won on debut for Willie Mullins in Grade 3 at Punchestown at end of last season; out through injury before returning on

the Flat this summer and easily won first hurdle at Roscommon in August.

1341 Tartak (Fr)

9 b g Akhdari - Tartamuda (Tyrnavos)

Tim Vaughan — Power Panels Electrical Systems Ltd

PLACINGS: 27554/311574/586050-					RPR **152c**
Starts	1st	2nd	3rd	4th	Win & Pl
33	7	7	2	2	£243,611

149	1/11	Chel	2m5f Cls3 Gd3 127-153 Ch Hcap gd-sft	£22,804
	12/10	Newb	2m4f Cls1 Gd2 Ch good	£17,405
	4/09	Aint	2m4f Cls1 Nov Gd2 Ch good	£45,822
	2/09	Kemp	2m4¹/₂f Cls2 Ch gd-sft	£18,786
	11/08	Hntg	2m4¹/₂f Cls3 Nov Ch gd-sft	£6,505
	6/08	NAbb	2m5¹/₂f Cls5 Ch soft	£2,277
	11/07	Autl	2m2f Hdl 4yo heavy	£14,270

Generally out of sorts last season, though showed signs of old ability with 50-1 fifth in Byrne Group Plate; had done well in previous campaign, winning big handicap chase at Cheltenham, and dropped to same mark after below-par effort in Topham Chase.

1342 Tataniano (Fr) (below)

8 b g Sassanian - Rosa Carola (Rose Laurel)

Paul Nicholls — The Stewart Family

PLACINGS: 1/12141/1121/35/1-					RPR **167+c**
Starts	1st	2nd	3rd	4th	Win & Pl
12	7	2	1	1	£132,080

160	10/11	Chep	2m¹/₂f Cls2 139-165 Ch Hcap good	£16,245
	4/10	Aint	2m Cls1 Nov Gd1 Ch good	£62,711
	11/09	Chel	2m Cls1 Nov Gd2 Ch soft	£20,577
	10/09	Extr	2m1¹/₂f Cls3 Ch good	£6,505
	4/09	Chel	2m1f Cls2 Nov Hdl good	£10,645
	1/09	Extr	2m3f Cls4 Nov Hdl good	£3,253
	10/08	Chep	2m¹/₂f Cls6 NHF 4-6yo good	£1,713

Top-class 2m novice chaser three seasons ago but

has struggled with injuries since then, running only three times in last two campaigns; produced a career-best effort at Chepstow last October prior to latest setback and remains a fine prospect; likely to step up in trip.

1343 Tatenen (Fr)

8 b g Lost World - Tamaziya (Law Society)

Richard Rowe				The Stewart Family

PLACINGS: 5U369UP/363170/715U-　　**RPR 150c**

Starts	1st	2nd	3rd	4th	Win & Pl
26	6	3	3	1	£333,595

143	1/12	Asct	2m5¹/₂f Cls2 126-152 Ch Hcap gd-sft	£43,792
137	1/11	Asct	2m5¹/₂f Cls2 125-150 Ch Hcap gd-sft	£43,834
	11/08	Chel	2m Cls1 Nov Gd2 Ch soft	£22,804
	10/08	Aint	2m Cls1 Nov List Ch gd-sft	£12,690
	10/07	Autl	2m2f Gd2 Hdl 3-5yo v soft	£120,777
	9/07	Autl	2m2f List Hdl 3yo v soft	£18,811

Failed to justify early promise when trained by Paul Nicholls but has done well for new yard and landed same handicap chase at Ascot for last two seasons; had moderate record over 3m earlier in career but could be worth returning to slightly longer trips.

1344 Teaforthree (Ire)

8 b g Oscar - Ethel's Bay (Strong Gale)

Rebecca Curtis				T437

PLACINGS: 32213/421328/321P11-　　**RPR 153+c**

Starts	1st	2nd	3rd	4th	Win & Pl
13	4	3	3	1	£63,953

	3/12	Chel	4m Cls2 Nov Am Ch good	£44,970
	2/12	Chep	3m Cls4 Nov Ch soft	£2,599
	12/11	Chep	3m Cls3 Nov Ch heavy	£4,549
	11/10	Ffos	3m Cls4 Nov Hdl gd-sft	£2,602

Won pair of novice chases at Chepstow last season following close second to Join Together; set the standard in National Hunt Chase at Cheltenham on that form and duly coped with step up to 4m to grind out victory; likely sort for Welsh National given course form.

1345 Tetlami (Ire)

6 ch g Daylami - Tetou (Peintre Celebre)

Nicky Henderson				Mrs Susan Roy

PLACINGS: 1210/1198-　　**RPR 142+h**

Starts	1st	2nd	3rd	4th	Win & Pl
8	4	1	-	-	£25,386

	2/12	Kemp	2m Cls6 NHF std-slw	£2,599
	12/11	Kemp	2m Cls2 Nov Hdl gd-sft	£9,697
	12/11	Sand	2m¹/₂f Cls4 Nov Hdl gd-sft	£3,249
	1/10	Chel	1m6¹/₂f Cls1 List NHF 4yo soft	£10,115
	10/09	Extr	1m5f Cls6 NHF 3yo gd-sft	£1,626

Made bright start to hurdling career last season following 18-month absence, though form took some knocks; fair ninth in Supreme Novices' Hurdle when beaten only 12 lengths; pulled too hard on handicap debut when eighth in Scottish Champion Hurdle.

1346 Texas Jack (Ire)

6 b g Curtain Time - Sailors Run (Roselier)

Noel Meade (Ir)				Robert Watson

PLACINGS: 11146476-　　**RPR 143+h**

Starts	1st	2nd	3rd	4th	Win & Pl
8	3	-	-	2	£67,145

	11/11	Clon	2m4f Nov Hdl soft	£8,328
	10/11	Fair	2m4f Mdn Hdl good	£5,948
	5/11	Punc	2m NHF 4-5yo gd-yld	£50,862

Won his first two hurdles impressively but failed to live up to that promise and yet to prove he finds much off the bridle; faced tough tasks, though, and regarded highly enough to be very well backed at Fairyhouse; could leave form behind.

1347 The Cockney Mackem (Ire)

6 b g Milan - Divine Prospect (Namaqualand)

Nigel Twiston-Davies				Mills & Mason Partnership

PLACINGS: 1223/F22U32223-　　**RPR 136c**

Starts	1st	2nd	3rd	4th	Win & Pl
13	1	7	3	-	£32,343

	9/10	Prth	2m¹/₂f Cls6 NHF 4-6yo soft	£1,713

Without a win since his bumper debut but ran some fine races in defeat last season, most notably when chasing home Salut Flo in Byrne Group Plate; didn't stay 3m on only attempt at Doncaster but should continue to run well over slightly shorter.

1348 The Giant Bolster

7 b g Black Sam Bellamy - Divisa (Lomitas)

David Bridgwater				Simon Hunt

PLACINGS: 52365/1F1UF/4U72142-　　**RPR 172c**

Starts	1st	2nd	3rd	4th	Win & Pl
20	4	4	1	2	£163,079

145	1/12	Chel	2m5f Cls1 Gd3 142-168 Ch Hcap gd-sft	£22,780
140	1/11	Chel	2m5f Cls2 Nov 121-140 Ch Hcap gd-sft	£12,524
	10/10	Worc	2m7f Cls3 Nov Ch good	£4,861
	11/09	MRas	2m3f Cls4 Nov Hdl soft	£2,737

Plagued by jumping problems early in chasing career but came of age once putting those right last season; ran away with competitive Cheltenham handicap and nearly pulled off major upset when fine second in Gold Cup; set to be aimed at top staying chases.

1349 The Knoxs (Ire)

9 b g Close Conflict - Nicola Marie (Cardinal Flower)

Paul Nicholls				Andrea & Graham Wylie

PLACINGS: F1/1105/FF11/15771-　　**RPR 152+h**

Starts	1st	2nd	3rd	4th	Win & Pl
13	6	-	-	-	£38,475

137	4/12	Ayr	2m4f Cls2 116-142 Ch Hcap good	£15,640
132	11/11	Extr	2m7¹/₂f Cls2 124-150 Hdl Hcap soft	£8,133
	3/11	Carl	2m Cls4 Nov Ch gd-sft	£2,602
	2/11	Sedg	2m Cls4 Nov Ch soft	£3,295
	1/10	Newc	3m Cls3 Nov Hdl soft	£5,204
	11/09	Newc	2m Cls4 Nov Hdl gd-sft	£2,797

Let down by his jumping as a novice chaser but showed plenty of talent and again hinted at much more to come last season, notably when winning handicap chase at Ayr on final start; had failed to stay 3m previously and needs to go left-handed over fences.

1350 The Minack (Ire)

8 b g King's Theatre - Ebony Jane (Roselier)

Paul Nicholls   C G Roach

PLACINGS: 3116117/113P/11F-   RPR **161**+c

Starts	1st	2nd	3rd	4th	Win & Pl
12	7	-	1	-	£89,482

150	12/11	Asct	3m Cls1 List 135-161 Ch Hcap soft	£22,527
141	11/11	Winc	3m1¹/₂f Cls1 List 123-146 Ch Hcap gd-sft	£34,170
	1/11	Wwck	2m4¹/₂f Cls3 Nov Ch gd-sft	£4,554
	1/11	Winc	2m5f Cls3 Nov Ch soft	£5,855
	2/10	Hntg	2m4¹/₂f Cls2 Nov Hdl soft	£11,384
	1/10	Kemp	2m5f Cls3 Nov Hdl soft	£4,684
	11/09	Extr	2m5¹/₂f Cls4 Nov Hdl soft	£3,253

Rose through the handicap in staying chases last season, winning twice under big weights at Wincanton and Ascot before suffering a heavy fall on final start; unlikely to be seen before Christmas but lightly raced enough to maintain progress in graded chases once back.

1351 The New One (Ire)

4 b g King's Theatre - Thuringe (Turgeon)

Nigel Twiston-Davies   Mrs S Such

PLACINGS: 1161-   RPR **128**+b

Starts	1st	2nd	3rd	4th	Win & Pl
4	3	-	-	-	£24,160

4/12	Aint	2m1f Cls1 Gd2 NHF 4-6yo good	£14,238
1/12	Chel	1m6¹/₂f Cls1 NHF 4yo gd-sft	£7,133
11/11	Wwck	1m6f Cls6 NHF 3yo good	£2,053

Won his first two bumpers last season in good style before running well in sixth (second best of the four-year-olds) in Champion Bumper at

Cheltenham; did even better when winning Grade 2 at Aintree next time; set to step up in trip when sent hurdling.

1352 The Package

9 br g Kayf Tara - Ardent Bride (Ardross)

David Pipe   D A Johnson

PLACINGS: /362203/92312U5/5/4-   RPR **145**c

Starts	1st	2nd	3rd	4th	Win & Pl
21	3	6	3	1	£91,822

132	12/09	Chel	3m1¹/₂f Cls1 List 132-158 Ch Hcap soft	£28,505
	11/07	Newb	2m¹/₂f Cls3 Mdn Hdl gd-sft	£6,506
	4/07	Towc	2m Cls5 Mdn NHF 4-6yo gd-fm	£2,277

Progressive handicapper chaser three seasons ago and returned from nearly 18 months out to finish fourth in 3m handicap chase at last season's Cheltenham Festival (sent off just 6-1); remains fragile but clearly regarded as much better than his handicap mark.

1353 The Tracey Shuffle

6 br g Kapgarde - Gaspaisie (Beyssac)

David Pipe   Mrs Jo Tracey

PLACINGS: 110/213-0   RPR **140**h

Starts	1st	2nd	3rd	4th	Win & Pl
7	3	1	1	-	£7,877

2/12	Ayr	2m4f Cls4 Mdn Hdl soft	£2,534
2/11	Newc	2m Cls6 NHF 4-6yo heavy	£1,431
2/11	Muss	2m Cls5 NHF 4-6yo soft	£1,626

Dual bumper winner who was slightly disappointing over hurdles last season, with wide-margin odds-on win at Ayr in between two defeats as favourite, though could improve after just four runs over jumps; looked a non-stayer when stepped up to 3m at Haydock.

1354 Third Intention (Ire)

5 b g Azamour - Third Dimension (Suave Dancer)

Colin Tizzard   Robert & Sarah Tizzard

PLACINGS: 12271/6720184-   RPR **151+h**

Starts	1st	2nd	3rd	4th	Win & Pl
12	3	3	-	1	£47,003

2/12	Font	2m4f Cls1 Gd2 Hdl gd-sft	£16,800
4/11	Chel	2m1f Cls2 Nov Hdl good	£6,262
12/10	Newb	2m¹/₂f Cls4 Hdl 3yo good	£3,903

Useful juvenile hurdler two seasons ago but found handicap mark just too high last season; still ran well in string of top handicap hurdles before landing weak Grade 2 at Fontwell on first attempt at 2m4f; likely to find more opportunities when sent chasing.

1355 Thousand Stars (Fr)

8 gr g Grey Risk - Livaniana (Saint Estephe)

Willie Mullins (Ir)   Hammer & Trowel Syndicate

PLACINGS: 3/74342/221123423-11   RPR **165h**

Starts	1st	2nd	3rd	4th	Win & Pl
32	8	5	5	5	£701,246

	6/12	Autl	3m1¹/₂f Gd1 Hdl v soft	£138,750
	5/12	Autl	2m5¹/₂f Gd2 Hdl v soft	£65,625
	11/11	Punc	2m Gd1 Hdl soft	£41,379
	6/11	Autl	3m1¹/₂f Gd1 Hdl v soft	£143,534
134	3/10	Chel	2m1f Cls1 Gd3 129-152 Hdl Hcap good	£42,758
125	11/09	Fair	2m 121-149 Hdl Hcap heavy	£18,645
107	10/09	Naas	2m3f 103-150 Hdl Hcap good	£16,433
	5/08	Klny	2m1f Mdn Hdl 4yo good	£4,827

Consistent hurdler at Grade 1 level, winning from 2m to 3m2f last season and retaining French Champion Hurdle crown over longer trip despite appearing not to stay that far when fourth in World Hurdle at Cheltenham; seems best at 2m4f (twice second in Aintree Hurdle).

1356 Tidal Bay (Ire)

11 b g Flemensfirth - June's Bride (Le Moss)

Paul Nicholls   Andrea & Graham Wylie

PLACINGS: 5/24174/3226U/32541-   RPR **170+c**

Starts	1st	2nd	3rd	4th	Win & Pl
35	12	11	3	4	£622,863

154	4/12	Sand	3m5¹/₂f Cls1 Gd3 128-154 Ch Hcap soft	£85,425
	1/10	Chel	3m Cls1 Gd2 Hdl soft	£28,505
	11/08	Carl	2m4f Cls2 Ch soft	£13,010
	4/08	Aint	2m Cls1 Nov Gd1 Ch good	£71,598
	3/08	Chel	2m Cls1 Gd1 Ch good	£96,934
	12/07	Chel	2m5f Cls2 Nov Ch good	£12,526
	11/07	Carl	2m4f Cls3 Nov Ch gd-sft	£9,759
	10/07	Aint	2m4f Cls3 Nov Ch good	£9,759
	4/07	Aint	2m4f Cls1 Nov Gd2 Hdl good	£31,361
	12/06	Chel	2m1f Cls2 Nov Hdl 4-6yo soft	£9,395
	11/06	Carl	2m4f Cls4 Nov Hdl heavy	£3,426
	10/06	Weth	2m4¹/₂f Cls4 Nov Hdl soft	£3,426

Frustrating character who has largely failed to fulfil his immense potential since winning the Arkle Trophy in 2008; still proved willing enough to land Bet365 Gold Cup at Sandown last season in impressive fashion, relishing an extreme test of stamina on heavy ground.

1357 Time For Rupert (Ire) (below, left)

8 ch g Flemensfirth - Bell Walks Run (Commanche Run)

Paul Webber   Littlecote Racing Partnership

PLACINGS: 1101/7122/115/25145-   RPR **164c**

Starts	1st	2nd	3rd	4th	Win & Pl
19	8	3	-	1	£213,504

	12/11	Newb	3m Cls2 Ch soft	£12,996
	12/10	Chel	3m1¹/₂f Cls2 Nov Ch gd-sft	£9,393
	11/10	Chel	2m4¹/₂f Cls2 Nov Ch gd-sft	£9,393
145	12/09	Chel	3m Cls2 124-150 Hdl Hcap soft	£12,524
134	4/09	Aint	3m1¹/₂f Cls1 List 132-150 Hdl Hcap good	£34,206
	2/09	Hntg	2m4¹/₂f Cls2 Nov Hdl gd-sft	£13,010
	1/09	Catt	2m3f Cls4 Nov Hdl 4-7yo soft	£3,253
	4/08	Ludl	2m Cls5 NHF 4-6yo good	£2,277

Didn't quite live up to lofty expectations last

season, though win over The Giant Bolster at Newbury reads well and threatened for a long way when fifth in Gold Cup (finished exhausted); could move to handicaps with chase mark lower than hurdles rating.

1358 Tocca Ferro (Fr)

7 gr g April Night - La Pelode (Dress Parade)

Emma Lavelle   Mrs Sarah Prior & Tim Syder

PLACINGS: 1/3147/11/

Starts	1st	2nd	3rd	4th	Win & Pl
7	4	-	1	1	£32,631
134	11/10	Newb	2m¹/₂f Cls1 List 125-145 Hdl Hcap gd-sft		£14,253
126	10/10	Asct	2m Cls1 List 124-150 Hdl Hcap good		£12,393
	1/10	Sthl	2m Cls4 Nov Hdl gd-sft		£2,472
	3/09	Winc	2m Cls5 Mdn NHF gd-sft		£1,952

Developed into an exciting handicap hurdler in first half of 2010-11 season when winning Listed races at Ascot and Newbury; favourite for Totesport Trophy before suffering setback and missed last season through injury; likely to return in top 2m handicap hurdles.

1359 Tofino Bay (Ire)

9 br g Bishop Of Cashel - Boyne View (Buckskin)

Dessie Hughes (Ir)   Gigginstown House Stud

PLACINGS: 7/2211/41/42321-   RPR 150+h

Starts	1st	2nd	3rd	4th	Win & Pl
8	3	2	1	2	£52,834
	4/12	Punc	2m4f Hdl heavy		£12,188
	2/11	Punc	2m Mdn Hdl heavy		£5,948
	4/09	Fair	2m2f NHF 4-6yo good		£25,282

Extremely fragile but proved very smart on return from second lengthy absence last season; improved for first three runs when good second to Get Me

Out Of Here in Grade 2 at Fairyhouse and won soft contest at Punchestown; good chasing prospect.

1360 Toner D'Oudairies (Fr)

5 b g Polish Summer - Iroise D'Oudairies (Passing Sale)

Gordon Elliott (Ir)   Gigginstown House Stud

PLACINGS: 3171146/54U627-   RPR 145+h

Starts	1st	2nd	3rd	4th	Win & Pl
13	3	1	1	2	£48,794
	12/10	Fair	2m Gd3 Hdl 3yo soft		£17,257
	11/10	DRoy	2m Mdn Hdl 3yo soft		£8,549
	7/10	Le L	1m3¹/₂f NHF 3yo gd-sft		£11,504

Took a long time to live up to promise of Grade 3 win as a juvenile in 2010 but ran a blinder when seemingly laid out for conditional jockeys' handicap hurdle at Cheltenham Festival, just getting pipped by Attaglance; has a big handicap in him.

1361 Toubab (Fr) (above)

6 gr g Martaline - Tabachines (Art Francais)

Paul Nicholls   Hills Of Ledbury (Aga)

PLACINGS: 352/4134/2F1B2-   RPR 150+c

Starts	1st	2nd	3rd	4th	Win & Pl
12	2	3	2	2	£63,808
	2/12	Sand	2m Cls2 Nov Ch good		£8,123
	11/10	Hayd	2m Cls1 Nov List Hdl gd-sft		£10,413

Has often hinted at rich potential despite winning only twice; sent novice chasing last season and brought down when still going well in Grand Annual before blundering two out when set to challenge Sprinter Sacre at Aintree; could be very well handicapped.

1362 Tranquil Sea (Ire)

10 b g Sea Raven - Silver Valley (Henbit)

Edward O'Grady (Ir)   Nelius Hayes

PLACINGS: 12196/117/U1P23415-2   RPR **163**+c

Starts		1st	2nd	3rd	4th	Win & Pl
32		12	6	2	1	£404,093
	3/12	Navn	2m4f Gd2 Ch good			£20,313
	11/11	Clon	2m4f Gd2 Ch soft			£25,216
	12/10	Fair	2m4f Gd1 Ch soft			£48,894
	11/10	Clon	2m4f Gd2 Ch heavy			£25,885
	2/10	Leop	2m1f Gd2 Ch heavy			£23,009
148	11/09	Chel	2m4¹/₂f Cls1 Gd3 135-161 Ch Hcap soft			£85,515
	10/09	Naas	2m Gd3 Ch sft-hvy			£18,013
	11/08	Cork	2m4f Nov List Ch heavy			£19,147
	4/08	Punc	2m4f Nov Gd1 Hdl good			£50,147
	4/08	Limk	2m4f Nov Hdl yld-sft			£12,446
	12/07	Leop	2m2f Mdn Hdl good			£6,770
	2/07	Leop	2m NHF 4-6yo heavy			£6,070

Hasn't reached the heights that seemed likely in 2010 when sent off 11-2 for Ryanair Chase and winning a Grade 1; still managed to win twice at Grade 2 level during a consistent campaign last season and has dropped to a fair handicap mark; best over 2m4f.

1363 Treacle (Ire)

11 ch g Zaffaran - Current Liability (Caribo)

Tom Taaffe (Ir)   B E Nielsen

PLACINGS: 1/3F/116PP/P/51423F-   RPR **151**+c

Starts		1st	2nd	3rd	4th	Win & Pl
24		5	4	3	2	£149,905
119	10/11	Gowr	3m 101-119 Ch Hcap soft			£8,625
122	10/09	Limk	3m 120-144 Ch Hcap yld-sft			£66,320
112	6/09	List	2m6f 100-130 Ch Hcap yield			£11,405
	10/07	Fair	3m Ch good			£5,836
	12/06	Cork	2m Mdn Hdl 4-5yo heavy			£6,195

Has struggled with injuries but finally got chance to realise potential last season; excellent second

in Paddy Power Chase at Leopardstown before finishing third in Hennessy Gold Cup; well fancied for Grand National but fell on first circuit.

1364 Triangular (USA)

7 b g Diesis - Salchow (Nijinsky)

Tom George   Mrs Henrietta Charlet

PLACINGS: 924152529/P1721P-   RPR **145**+c

Starts		1st	2nd	3rd	4th	Win & Pl
20		3	4	1	1	£62,373
127	3/12	Newb	2m6¹/₂f Cls3 104-130 Ch Hcap good			£6,330
112	12/11	Wwck	2m Cls4 101-120 Ch Hcap good			£4,549
	12/10	Pau	2m4f Ch 5yo v soft			£13,593

Took advantage of very lenient initial handicap mark following move from France last season, looking particularly impressive when landing second victory at Newbury; didn't take to Grand National fences when pulled up in Topham Chase after 13lb rise.

1365 Trifolium (Fr)

5 b g Goldneyev - Opium Des Mottes (April Night)

Charles Byrnes (Ir)   Gigginstown House Stud

PLACINGS: 521P23/123112132-   RPR **147**h

Starts		1st	2nd	3rd	4th	Win & Pl
15		5	5	3	-	£96,867
	2/12	Punc	2m Nov Gd2 Hdl heavy			£21,396
	12/11	Limk	2m Hdl 4yo heavy			£11,487
	12/11	Cork	2m Mdn Hdl 4-5yo sft-hvy			£5,948
	5/11	Fntb	1m4¹/₂f NHF 4yo soft			£12,069
	11/10	Ange	1m6¹/₂f NHF 3yo v soft			£7,522

Maintained high level of form during busy novice campaign last season, often racing against more experienced rivals; produced best effort when encountering quickest ground in Supreme Novices'

Hurdle at Cheltenham, finishing close third; should improve.

1366 Triolo D'Alene (Fr)

5 ch g Epalo - Joliette D'Alene (Garde Royale)

Nicky Henderson   Mr & Mrs Sandy Orr

PLACINGS: 4541110-2   RPR **139**c

Starts	1st	2nd	3rd	4th	Win & Pl
8	3	1	-	2	£36,497
127	1/12	Asct	2m3f Cls3 Nov 120-134 Ch Hcap gd-sft............£9,495
	11/11	Fntb	2m2f Cls4 Ch v soft............£9,103
	10/11	Mlns	2m2f Ch 4yo soft............£6,621

Dual chase winner in France who was let in lightly for his handicap debut at Ascot but then let down by jumping errors when flopping behind Hunt Ball at Cheltenham Festival; jumped better in defeat next time at Market Rasen and capable of big improvement.

1367 Tullamore Dew (Ire)

10 ch g Pistolet Bleu - Heather Point (Pollerton)

Nick Gifford   Give Every Man His Due

PLACINGS: 72/912123/5F94U20PP-   RPR **147**c

Starts	1st	2nd	3rd	4th	Win & Pl
26	4	6	1	1	£56,550
	1/11	Plum	2m1f Cls3 Nov Ch soft............£6,320
	11/10	Font	2m2f Cls4 Ch heavy............£2,992
	2/09	Font	2m2¹/₂f Cls4 Nov Hdl 4-7yo soft............£3,903
	10/08	Plum	2m5f Cls4 Nov Hdl gd-fm............£3,253

Slightly lost his way last season, not being helped by jumping problems, but came close to landing good handicap chase at Ascot when beaten by a head and has already slipped back to lower mark; goes particularly well at Cheltenham (twice placed at festival).

1368 Turban (Fr)

5 b g Dom Alco - Indianabelle (Useful)

Willie Mullins (Ir)   Edward O'Connell

PLACINGS: 152402-   RPR **146**+h

Starts	1st	2nd	3rd	4th	Win & Pl
6	1	2		1	£9,736
	11/11	Thur	2m Mdn Hdl 4yo sft-hvy............£4,461

Largely disappointing after debut win last season (beaten favourite twice) but produced best run on desperate ground at Punchestown when second having travelled strongly and made a mistake at the last; may well be capable of much better.

1369 Un Atout (Fr)

4 br g Robin Des Champs - Badrapette (Bad Conduct)

Willie Mullins (Ir)   Gigginstown House Stud

PLACINGS: 1-   RPR **128**+b

Starts	1st	2nd	3rd	4th	Win & Pl
1	1	-	-	-	£4,600
	1/12	Naas	2m NHF 4yo sft-hvy............£4,600

Sensational 24-length winner of only bumper start last season at Naas when effortlessly justifying odds of 2-7; not felt to be ready for Cheltenham and could go for one or two more bumpers before being sent novice hurdling; top-class prospect.

1370 Unaccompanied (Ire)

5 b m Danehill Dancer - Legend Has It (Sadler's Wells)

Dermot Weld (Ir)   Moyglare Stud Farm

PLACINGS: 112/4114-   RPR **153**+h

Starts	1st	2nd	3rd	4th	Win & Pl
7	4	1	-	2	£133,482
	12/11	Leop	2m Gd1 Hdl soft............£47,629
	11/11	Naas	2m List Hdl 4yo sft-hvy............£14,009
	2/11	Leop	2m Gd1 Hdl 4yo heavy............£39,224
	12/10	Punc	2m Mdn Hdl 3yo sft-hvy............£6,412

Very smart dual-purpose mare who has continued improvement on the Flat since landing second Grade 1 over hurdles in Festival Hurdle at Leopardstown last season; has done most winning on soft ground but finished second on good in 2011 Triumph Hurdle.

1371 Uncle Junior (Ire)

11 b g Saddlers' Hall - Caslain Nua (Seymour Hicks)

Willie Mullins (Ir)   Mrs M McMahon

PLACINGS: 4/223611/14731781-64   RPR **146**c

Starts	1st	2nd	3rd	4th	Win & Pl
30	10	5	3	3	£115,734
	4/12	Punc	4m1f Ch heavy............£13,542
	11/11	Chel	3m7f Cls2 Ch firm............£13,763
	5/11	Punc	3m6f 112-140 Ch Hcap yield............£14,009
130	4/11	Tram	2m6f Ch good............£6,841
	3/11	Gowr	2m4f Ch sft-hvy............£7,138
	11/07	Thur	2m6¹/₂f Hdl yield............£3,454
	11/07	Clon	2m4f Nov Hdl gd-yld............£8,797
	11/07	DRoy	2m6f Mdn Hdl good............£7,003
	7/07	Bell	2m1f NHF 4-7yo yield............£4,435
	6/07	Kbgn	2m3f NHF 5-7yo yield............£3,969

Did well two seasons ago on return from more than two years off the track but took form to a new level when switched to cross-country chases last term, winning at Cheltenham and just landing La Touche Cup; should continue to be a force in that sphere.

1372 Une Artiste (Fr)

4 b f Alberto Giacometti - Castagnette III (Tin Soldier)

Nicky Henderson   Simon Munir

PLACINGS: 931111411R-   **RPR 133+h**

Starts	1st	2nd	3rd	4th	Win & Pl
10	6	-	1	1	£86,439

4/12	Chel	2m1f Cls1 Nov List Hdl soft	£11,888
127 3/12	Chel	2m¹/₂f Cls1 Gd3 125-138 Hdl 4yo gd-good	£34,170
2/12	Hayd	2m Cls2 Hdl 4yo soft	£10,072
1/12	Pau	2m1¹/₂f Hdl 4yo heavy	£12,800
12/11	Pau	1m4f NHF 3yo v soft	£6,466
10/11	Fntb	1m4¹/₂f NHF 3yo v soft	£6,034

Three-time winner in France who made a big impression following switch to Britain earlier this year, twice winning at Cheltenham, including Fred Winter Hurdle in March; has her quirks, though, and refused to race when favourite for mares' hurdle at Punchestown.

1373 Universal Soldier (Ire)

7 b g Winged Love - Waterland Gale (Fourstars Allstar)

Charlie Longsdon   Lindie Donaldson & Regan King

PLACINGS: 513/1/2P17-   **RPR 146+c**

Starts	1st	2nd	3rd	4th	Win & Pl
8	3	1	1	-	£11,932

1/12	Towc	3m¹/₂f Cls4 Ch gd-sft	£2,599
125 1/11	Chep	3m Cls3 115-130 Hdl Hcap soft	£4,554
2/10	Ffos	2m4f Cls4 Nov Hdl 4-7yo gd-sft	£3,578

Quietly campaigned during last two seasons but has shown plenty of promise, easily winning a novice chase at Towcester before a good seventh in National Hunt Chase (given too much to do in race dominated by front-runners); still a top prospect.

1374 Up The Beat

7 b/br g Beat All - Everything's Rosy (Ardross)

Willie Mullins (Ir)   Mrs A M Varmen & R J D Varmen

PLACINGS: 4/4266/3124-   **RPR 147c**

Starts	1st	2nd	3rd	4th	Win & Pl
9	1	2	1	3	£17,114

12/11	Fair	2m5¹/₂f Ch sft-hvy	£7,138

Boldly stepped up into handicap company with just two runs over fences behind him last season, finishing a fine second to Portrait King at Fairyhouse and fourth behind Sunnyhillboy in the Kim Muir; should progress further and could be a fine staying chaser.

1375 Ut De Sivola (Fr)

4 b g Robin Des Champs - Kerrana (Cadoudal)

Willie Mullins (Ir)   Philip J Reynolds

PLACINGS: 2117P2-5   **RPR 140h**

Starts	1st	2nd	3rd	4th	Win & Pl
7	2	2	-	-	£45,859

1/12	Punc	2m Gd3 Hdl 4yo sft-hvy	£14,896
12/11	Clon	2m¹/₂f Mdn Hdl 3yo heavy	£4,461

Earned a big reputation with impressive win on hurdling debut but only seventh when favourite

---

for Grade 1 at Leopardstown and then pulled up in Triumph Hurdle; did much better back in testing conditions when second at Punchestown.

1376 Vendor (Fr)

4 gr g Kendor - Village Rainbow (Village Star)

Alan King   Thurloe 52

PLACINGS: U2/F42F131-   **RPR 133h**

Starts	1st	2nd	3rd	4th	Win & Pl
9	2	2	1	1	£31,714

4/12	Towc	2m Cls4 Nov Hdl good	£2,274
12/11	Newb	2m¹/₂f Cls3 Hdl 3yo soft	£5,848

Ran well in top juvenile hurdles in France before making successful British debut at Newbury; held back for Fred Winter Hurdle to exploit favourable mark but just came up short in third before winning at 1-7 at Towcester; could make mark in top handicap hurdles.

1377 Victors Serenade (Ire)

7 b g Old Vic - Dantes Serenade (Phardante)

Anthony Honeyball   Michael & Angela Bone

PLACINGS: 5739/13212/R11-   **RPR 150+c**

Starts	1st	2nd	3rd	4th	Win & Pl
12	4	2	2	-	£19,454

128 3/12	Ffos	3m Cls3 112-132 Ch Hcap soft	£7,027
120 2/12	Ffos	2m5f Cls4 103-120 Ch Hcap soft	£3,899
1/11	Towc	3m Cls4 Nov Hdl soft	£2,602
104 11/10	Extr	2m7¹/₂f Cls4 97-114 Hdl Hcap soft	£3,253

Has had opportunities limited by need for soft ground but sharply progressive in those conditions last season, winning two handicap chases at Ffos Las; should improve again having run just four times over fences.

1378 Viking Blond (Fr)

7 ch g Varese - Sweet Jaune (Le Nain Jaune)

Nigel Twiston-Davies   Mrs Caroline Mould

PLACINGS: 12/P623070/143P5FP-0   **RPR 145c**

Starts	1st	2nd	3rd	4th	Win & Pl
23	3	3	3	2	£26,413

10/11	Chep	3m Cls4 Nov Ch gd-sft	£3,217
114 3/10	Chep	3m Cls3 105-124 Hdl Hcap heavy	£4,879
102 2/10	Extr	2m7¹/₂f Cls4 89-115 Hdl Hcap soft	£3,253

Moved into handicap company after winning on chasing debut last October but season tailed off after initial promise; pulled up when favourite for Welsh National and fell at first in Grand National; stays well and could be smart if allowed to lead.

1379 Village Vic (Ire)

5 b g Old Vic - Etoile Margot (Garde Royale)

Philip Hobbs   Alan Peterson

PLACINGS: F/11205-   **RPR 125+b**

Starts	1st	2nd	3rd	4th	Win & Pl
4	1	1	-	-	£3,501

12/11	Chep	2m1¹/₂f Cls6 NHF 4-6yo heavy	£1,365

Point-to-point winner who initially did very well

in bumpers last season, winning well in heavy ground at Chepstow and just getting pipped by Shutthefrontdoor at Newbury; may have found ground too quick in Champion Bumper at Cheltenham; capable of better.

1380 Voler La Vedette (Ire)

8 b m King's Theatre - Steel Grey Lady (Roselier)

Colm Murphy (Ir)   Mrs M Brophy

PLACINGS: 1139/12341/14111222-   RPR 163+h

Starts	1st	2nd	3rd	4th	Win & Pl
24	13	4	3	2	£411,098
12/11	Leop	3m Gd2 Hdl good			£22,414
12/11	Fair	2m4f Gd1 Hdl sft-hvy			£44,828
11/11	Navn	2m4f Gd2 Hdl yld-sft			£21,013
4/11	Fair	2m4f Gd2 Hdl good			£22,414
2/11	Navn	2m5f Gd2 Hdl heavy			£23,254
10/10	Punc	2m2f List Hdl good			£14,956
12/09	Leop	2m4f List Hdl yield			£25,282
11/09	DRoy	2m Gd3 Hdl soft			£31,602
10/09	Punc	2m2f List Hdl gd-yld			£16,433
5/09	Punc	2m2f Gd3 Hdl soft			£44,243
12/08	Leop	2m2f Mdn Hdl 4yo soft			£7,367
10/08	DRoy	2m NHF 4-7yo soft			£7,621
10/08	Fair	2m NHF 4-7yo sft-hvy			£4,319

High-class mare who produced best ever run when second to Big Buck's in World Hurdle; has been prolific at around 2m4f but seemed well suited by stiff test of stamina and may not have enjoyed slower gallop when no match for Quevega at Punchestown.

1381 Waaheb (USA)

5 b g Elusive Quality - Nafisah (Lahib)

Dermot Weld (Ir)   John P McManus

PLACINGS: 111/2-

Starts	1st	2nd	3rd	4th	Win & Pl
4	3	1	-	-	£37,000
4/11	Limk	2m List NHF 4yo yld-sft			£14,009
2/11	Leop	2m NHF 4yo soft			£5,948
1/11	Leop	2m NHF 4yo soft			£4,759

Won first three bumpers early in 2011, and was most impressive when stepped up to Listed level at Limerick; lost little in defeat when surrendering unbeaten record at Punchestown by a short-head; missed last season through injury but should still be a top-class novice hurdler.

1382 Walkon (Fr)

7 gr g Take Risks - La Tirana (Akarad)

Alan King   Mcneill Family

PLACINGS: 121121/207/1345P-   RPR 156+c

Starts	1st	2nd	3rd	4th	Win & Pl
14	5	3	1	1	£184,878
12/11	Extr	2m3¹/₂f Cls2 Nov Ch gd-sft			£10,860
4/09	Aint	2m¹/₂f Cls1 Nov Gd1 Hdl 4yo good			£74,113
1/09	Chel	2m1f Cls1 Nov Gd2 Hdl 4yo heavy			£17,103
12/08	Chep	2m¹/₂f Cls1 Gd1 Hdl 3yo soft			£28,505
11/08	Hntg	2m¹/₂f Cls2 Nov Hdl 3yo good			£13,010

Let down by his jumping after winning on his chasing debut last season but ran much better for

a long way before fading into fifth in RSA Chase; blatant non-stayer when stepped up to 4m in Scottish National; remains on a lower chase mark than over hurdles.

1383 Wayward Prince

8 b g Alflora - Bellino Spirit (Robellino)

Ian Williams   T J & Mrs H Parrott

PLACINGS: 61/22121/11134/P47P-   RPR 146c

Starts	1st	2nd	3rd	4th	Win & Pl
14	5	3	1	2	£116,557
2/11	Weth	3m1f Cls1 Nov Gd2 Ch gd-sft			£13,397
11/10	Chel	3m¹/₂f Cls2 Nov Ch gd-sft			£9,393
10/10	Hntg	3m Cls3 Nov Ch good			£5,529
4/10	Aint	3m¹/₂f Cls1 Nov Gd1 Hdl good			£57,010
2/10	Donc	3m¹/₂f Cls4 Mdn Hdl gd-sft			£2,602

Smart stayer over hurdles and fences, winning Grade 1 novice hurdle at Aintree in 2010 and third in RSA Chase the following year; endured a miserable campaign last season and pulled up when reverted to hurdles last time; has dropped sharply in handicap.

1384 Weapon's Amnesty (Ire)

9 ch g Presenting - Victoria Theatre (Old Vic)

Charles Byrnes (Ir)   Gigginstown House Stud

PLACINGS: 25/511215/3F1221/

Starts	1st	2nd	3rd	4th	Win & Pl
14	5	4	1	-	£216,848
3/10	Chel	3m¹/₂f Cls1 Gd1 Ch good			£85,515
11/09	Newc	3m Cls3 Nov Ch gd-sft			£6,262
3/09	Chel	3m Cls1 Nov Gd1 Hdl gd-sft			£57,010
12/08	Limk	2m6f Nov Gd3 Hdl soft			£19,147
12/08	Gowr	3m Mdn Hdl heavy			£6,097

Has missed last two seasons through injury but remains a potential Gold Cup winner having thrashed Burton Port and Long Run when last seen in 2010 RSA Chase; had also won at Cheltenham Festival in 2009 over hurdles; very classy chaser if staying sound.

1385 Weird Al (Ire)

9 b g Accordion - Bucks Gift (Buckley)

Donald McCain   Brannon Dick Holden

PLACINGS: 2/1/111/18P/13PF-   RPR 170c

Starts	1st	2nd	3rd	4th	Win & Pl
12	6	1	1	-	£133,600
10/11	Weth	3m1f Cls1 Gd2 Ch good			£56,950
10/10	Carl	2m4f Cls2 Ch soft			£8,415
2/10	Weth	3m1f Cls1 Nov Gd2 Ch soft			£17,637
12/09	Chel	2m5f Cls2 Nov Ch soft			£12,524
11/09	Chel	2m4¹/₂f Cls2 Nov Ch gd-sft			£12,570
11/08	Wwck	2m5f Nov Hdl soft			£3,253

Has shown high-class form in small fields, winning Charlie Hall Chase last season before good third in Betfair Chase; broke blood vessels for third time when pulled up for second year running in Gold Cup but was running well when late faller in Grand National.

1386 West End Rocker (Ire)

10 b/br g Grand Plaisir - Slyguff Lord (Lord Americo)

Alan King — Barry Winfield & Tim Leadbeater

PLACINGS: 23212P/07/11PB/P1FP-   RPR **155+c**

Starts	1st	2nd	3rd	4th	Win & Pl
22	5	6	2	-	£113,362

137	12/11	Aint	3m2f Cls1 List 127-151 Ch Hcap heavy	£56,437
133	1/11	Wwck	3m5f Cls1 Gd3 122-148 Ch Hcap heavy	£34,206
129	12/10	Newb	3m2½f Cls3 112-130 Ch Hcap good	£5,855
	2/09	Donc	3m Cls4 Ch good	£3,903
	3/08	Chep	3m Cls4 Mdn Hdl soft	£2,114

Failed to complete five of last six starts but easily won Becher Chase over Grand National fences last season; fell early when well fancied for National itself and never travelled in Bet365 Gold Cup.

1387 Western Leader (Ire)

8 b g Stowaway - Western Whisper (Supreme Leader)

John Joseph Hanlon (Ir) — Barry Connell

PLACINGS: 52121/23112/22P-   RPR **144h**

Starts	1st	2nd	3rd	4th	Win & Pl
13	4	6	1	-	£76,069

2/10	Thur	2m4f Nov Gd2 Hdl soft	£23,009
12/09	Leop	2m4f Mdn Hdl yield	£7,715
3/09	Limk	2m3f NHF 5-7yo sft-hvy	£7,715
12/08	Limk	2m NHF 4-5yo soft	£5,335

Looked a top-class prospect in novice hurdles three seasons ago when set to complete a hat-trick in Grade 1 at Aintree until breaking down; missed nearly two years before returning last season, twice showing useful form before being pulled up on final start.

1388 What A Friend

9 b g Alflora - Friendly Lady (New Member)

Paul Nicholls — Ged Mason & Sir Alex Ferguson

PLACINGS: /1161/211/524P/33F7-   RPR **167c**

Starts	1st	2nd	3rd	4th	Win & Pl
20	7	3	3	1	£301,708

4/10	Aint	3m1f Cls1 Gd1 Ch good	£86,520
12/09	Leop	3m Gd1 Ch soft	£90,291
4/09	Strf	2m7f Cls4 Nov Ch good	£5,844
12/08	Chel	3m1½f Cls2 Nov Ch gd-sft	£13,776
10/08	Uttx	3m Cls4 Ch good	£5,529
12/07	Chep	2m4f Cls4 Mdn Hdl soft	£3,253
5/07	NAbb	2m1f Cls6 NHF 4-6yo gd-fm	£1,370

Dual Grade 1 winner three seasons ago but without a win in two fairly quiet campaigns since and has had his attitude questioned; finished good fourth in 2011 Gold Cup but fell in last season's race and moderate seventh in Betfred Bowl at Aintree.

1389 White Star Line (Ire)

8 b g Saddlers' Hall - Fairly Deep (Deep Run)

Dessie Hughes (Ir) — P A Byrne

PLACINGS: 5/262127/4U326-2   RPR **142c**

Starts	1st	2nd	3rd	4th	Win & Pl
13	1	5	1	1	£24,000

1/11	Naas	2m3f Mdn Hdl soft	£5,948

Remains a novice over fences having failed to win last season but ran much his best race when second to Hunt Ball in novice handicap chase at Cheltenham Festival; seemed to benefit from strong gallop and well handicapped on that form.

1390 William's Wishes (Ire)

7 b g Oscar - Strong Wishes (Strong Gale)

Evan Williams — Mrs D E Cheshire

PLACINGS: 3/2312211/7111/   RPR

Starts	1st	2nd	3rd	4th	Win & Pl
12	6	3	2	-	£26,896

1/11	Hrfd	2m Cls3 Nov Ch soft	£4,554
11/10	Leic	2m Cls3 Nov Ch good	£4,816
10/10	Ludl	2m Cls4 Ch good	£3,757
4/10	Sthl	2m Cls4 Nov Hdl good	£3,426
3/10	Hrfd	2m1f Cls4 Nov Cond Hdl gd-sft	£3,253
9/09	Worc	2m4f Cls4 Mdn Hdl good	£2,602

Missed last season through injury but had been much improved to win five of last six starts prior to that, including all three runs over fences; among leading Grand Annual fancies before suffering setback; could be a contender for top 2m handicap chases upon return.

1391 Wise Old Owl (Ire)

8 b g Beneficial - Mother Superior (Camden Town)

John Kiely (Ir) — John P McManus

PLACINGS: 5222112/22-9   RPR **124c**

Starts	1st	2nd	3rd	4th	Win & Pl
10	2	6	-	-	£67,244

9/10	Clon	3m Nov Ch good	£12,655
9/10	List	2m6f Ch gd-yld	£8,854

Out of the first two for only the second time over fences when ninth in Galway Plate, though faced stiff task on first run for a year after injury; had looked on the upgrade when second in that race in 2011 when last seen; potential contender for major handicap chases.

1392 Wishfull Thinking

9 ch g Alflora - Poussetiere Deux (Garde Royale)

Philip Hobbs — Mrs Diana L Whateley

PLACINGS: 1F0/F12121/16526F25-   RPR **168c**

Starts	1st	2nd	3rd	4th	Win & Pl
20	7	5	-	-	£214,755

159	5/11	Punc	2m5f Nov 138-159 Ch Hcap yield	£40,086
	4/11	Aint	2m4f Cls1 Nov Gd2 Ch gd-sft	£42,959
148	1/11	Chel	2m5f Cls1 Gd3 131-157 Ch Hcap gd-sft	£22,804
	11/10	Winc	2m5f Cls1 Nov Gd2 Ch good	£18,458
	2/10	Extr	2m3f Cls4 Nov Hdl gd-sft	£2,897
	1/10	Tntn	2m3½f Cls3 Nov Hdl 4-7yo soft	£5,529
	12/09	Hrfd	2m4f Cls4 Mdn Hdl soft	£3,578

Very disappointing last season when failing to follow up impressive novice campaign; did best when second to Finian's Rainbow at Aintree when possibly helped by longer trip (had most runs at 2m despite never winning below 2m3f); struggles on soft ground.

1393 Wymott (Ire)

8 b g Witness Box - Tanya Thyne (Good Thyne)

Donald McCain   Trevor Hemmings

PLACINGS: 210/2121/111P/6P60-   RPR 143c

Starts	1st	2nd	3rd	4th	Win & Pl
15	6	3	-	-	£42,854

2/11	Bang	2m4¹/₂f Cls3 Nov Ch gd-sft	£6,337
12/10	Extr	3m Cls4 Nov Ch gd-sft	£5,204
11/10	Bang	2m4¹/₂f Cls4 Ch soft	£3,903
2/10	Hayd	3m1f Cls1 Nov Gd2 Hdl soft	£17,103
11/09	Kels	2m6¹/₂f Cls4 Mdn Hdl heavy	£2,927
3/09	Bang	2m1f Cls6 NHF 4-6yo soft	£1,884

Grade 2 winner over hurdles who looked to hold bright future when winning first three chases but lost his way last season; dropped to 11lb below highest mark and interesting if trainer can bring him back to form.

1394 Wyse Hill Teabags

7 b g Theatrical Charmer - Mrs Tea (First Trump)

Jim Goldie   Mr & Mrs Philip C Smith

PLACINGS: 751/31313/2P-   RPR 140+h

Starts	1st	2nd	3rd	4th	Win & Pl
10	3	1	3	-	£22,935

3/11	Kels	2m2f Cls4 Nov Hdl gd-sft	£2,602
2/11	Muss	2m4f Cls3 Nov Hdl gd-sft	£4,228
3/10	Ayr	2m Cls6 NHF 4-6yo good	£1,644

Progressive novice hurdler two seasons ago and improved again when second to Any Given Day on return last term; missed rest of season after being pulled up next time but fit again and could resume upward curve.

1395 You Must Know Me (Ire)

6 ch g Snurge - Waterloo Park (Alphabatim)

Henry de Brodhead (Ir)   Peter O'Dwyer

PLACINGS: 1221-   RPR 131+h

Starts	1st	2nd	3rd	4th	Win & Pl
3	1	2	-	-	£6,445

4/12	Tipp	3m Mdn Hdl soft	£4,313

Twice beaten in bumpers last season but showed much improved form when back over jumps to win on hurdling debut in April, easing home by 11 lengths at Tipperary; looks a very exciting prospect for staying novice chases.

1396 Zaidpour (Fr)

6 b g Red Ransom - Zainta (Kahyasi)

Willie Mullins (Ir)   Mrs S Ricci

PLACINGS: 11227/111182-25   RPR 166h

Starts	1st	2nd	3rd	4th	Win & Pl
13	6	4	-	-	£222,111

2/12	Gowr	2m Gd2 Hdl soft	£21,667
1/12	Gowr	3m Gd2 Hdl sft-hvy	£21,667
12/11	Navn	2m4f Gd2 Hdl sft-hvy	£21,013
11/11	Thur	2m6¹/₂f Hdl heavy	£5,948
12/10	Fair	2m Nov Gd1 Hdl soft	£46,018
11/10	Punc	2m4f Mdn Hdl 4yo soft	£6,412

Slightly disappointing as a novice hurdler but

fulfilled his potential last season, winning four times before running two fine races in top company over 2m; could be better over further and has already won over 3m, although that came in a very slowly-run race.

1397 Zarkandar (Ire)

5 b g Azamour - Zarkasha (Kahyasi)

Paul Nicholls   Potensis Limited & Chris Giles

PLACINGS: 111/15F-   RPR 164c

Starts	1st	2nd	3rd	4th	Win & Pl
6	4	-	-	-	£222,492

151	2/12	Newb	2m¹/₂f Cls1 Gd3 136-162 Hdl Hcap gd-sft	£86,849
	4/11	Aint	2m¹/₂f Cls1 Gd1 Hdl 4yo gd-sft	£56,632
	3/11	Chel	2m1f Cls1 Gd1 Hdl 4yo good	£57,010
	2/11	Kemp	2m Cls1 Gd2 Hdl 4yo gd-sft	£12,086

Won a red-hot Triumph Hurdle in 2011 and thrown in for belated return last season when getting up late to win Betfair Hurdle at Newbury; again looked in need of further than 2m when fifth in Champion Hurdle but fell when favourite for Aintree Hurdle.

1398 Zarrafakt (Ire)

8 b g Rudimentary - Carrick Glen (Orchestra)

Emma Lavelle   G P Macintosh

PLACINGS: 12F5/1545/1PP/21P-   RPR 155+c

Starts	1st	2nd	3rd	4th	Win & Pl
14	4	2	-	1	£29,509

133	1/12	Winc	3m1¹/₂f Cls3 108-134 Ch Hcap gd-sft	£9,384
117	11/10	Folk	2m5f Cls3 98-121 Ch Hcap soft	£9,393
114	11/09	Newb	2m5f Cls3 Nov 94-118 Hdl Hcap soft	£5,204
	11/08	Folk	2m1¹/₂f Cls6 NHF 4-6yo soft	£1,713

Looked a major improver when winning by 12 lengths at Wincanton but jumped badly right when pulled up at Cheltenham; goes well fresh; was beaten a head last season when going for fourth successive win first time out.

1399 Zaynar (Fr) *(right)*

7 gr g Daylami - Zainta (Kahyasi)

David Pipe   Men In Our Position

PLACINGS: 1233/440/37332144U7-   RPR 156+c

Starts	1st	2nd	3rd	4th	Win & Pl
21	6	2	5	4	£263,698

12/11	Asct	2m3f Cls1 Nov Gd2 Ch soft	£16,881
12/09	Chel	2m4¹/₂f Cls2 Gd2 Hdl soft	£24,343
11/09	Asct	2m3¹/₂f Cls1 Gd2 Hdl good	£56,379
3/09	Chel	2m1f Cls1 Gd1 Hdl 4yo gd-sft	£68,412
1/09	Asct	2m Cls3 Nov Hdl 4yo gd-sft	£6,575
12/08	Newb	2m¹/₂f Cls4 Nov Hdl 3yo soft	£3,253

Former Triumph Hurdle winner who has become increasingly mulish since then and ended last season running for third different trainer in little over a year in bid to rekindle enthusiasm; won good novice chase last season to show he retains plenty of ability.

Pen portraits written by Dylan Hill

TEN TO FOLLOW HORSES LISTED BY TRAINER

William Amos
1191 Lie Forrit (Ire)

David Arbuthnot
1331 Starluck (Ire)

Kim Bailey
1091 Darna

Mark Bradstock
1066 Carruthers

David Bridgwater
1348 The Giant Bolster

Keiran Burke
1163 Hunt Ball (Ire)

Charles Byrnes
1185 Knockfierna (Ire)
1260 Pittoni (Ire)
1306 Sea Of Thunder (Ire)
1322 Solwhit (Fr)
1365 Trifolium (Fr)
1384 Weapon's Amnesty (Ire)

Jennie Candlish
1114 Fiendish Flame (Ire)

Peter Casey
1122 Flemenstar (Ire)

Mick Channon
1054 Calgary Bay (Ire)
1324 Somersby (Ire)

George Charlton
1184 Knockara Beau (Ire)

Thomas Cooper
1127 Forpadydeplasterer (Ire)
1197 Lucky William (Ire)
1325 Son Amix (Fr)

Stuart Crawford
1182 Killyglen (Ire)

Rebecca Curtis
1344 Teaforthree (Ire)

Luke Dace
1011 American Spin

Henry Daly
1254 Pearlysteps
1275 Quentin Collonges (Fr)

Victor Dartnall
1010 Ambion Wood (Ire)
1111 Exmoor Ranger (Ire)
1139 Giles Cross (Ire)
1295 Roudoudou Ville (Fr)

Henry De Bromhead
1034 Berties Dream (Ire)
1052 Buckers Bridge (Ire)
1092 Days Hotel (Ire)
1316 Sizing Europe (Ire)
1395 You Must Know Me (Ire)

Robin Dickin
1286 Restless Harry

Jim Dreaper
1141 Go All The Way (Ire

Gordon Elliott
1064 Carlito Brigante (Ire)

1069 Cause Of Causes (USA)
1075 Chicago Grey (Ire)
1099 Don Cossack (Ger)
1199 Mae's Choice (Ire)
1227 Mount Benbulben (Ire)
1293 Roi Du Mee (Fr)
1360 Toner D'Oudairies (Fr)

Brian Ellison
1205 Marsh Warbler

Pat Fahey
1153 He'llberemembered (Ire)

Seamus Fahey
1058 Caolaneoin (Ire)

Philip Fenton
1105 Dunguib (Ire)
1188 Last Instalment (Ire)

John Ferguson
1084 Cotton Mill
1233 New Year's Eve

Harry Fry
1291 Rock On Ruby (Ire)

Mrs Pauline Gavin
1001 Ad Idem

Tom George
1021 Baby Mix (Fr)
1087 Crack Away Jack
1221 Module (Fr)
1232 Nacarat (Fr)
1364 Triangular (USA)

Thomas Gibney
1192 Lion Na Bearnai (Ire)

Nick Gifford
1367 Tullamore Dew (Ire)

Noel Glynn
1031 Becauseicouldntsee (Ire)

Jim Goldie
1394 Wyse Hill Teabags

Steve Gollings
1194 Local Hero (Ger)

Warren Greatrex
1252 Paint The Clouds

Brian Hamilton
1225 Moscow Mannon (Ire)

John Joseph Hanlon
1157 Hidden Cyclone (Ire)
1387 Western Leader (Ire)

Jessica Harrington
1047 Bostons Angel (Ire)
1078 Citizenship
1171 Jenari (Ire)
1172 Jetson (Ire)
1244 Oscars Well (Ire)
1333 Steps To Freedom (Ire)

Nicky Henderson
1038 Binocular (Fr)
1043 Bobs Worth (Ire)
1051 Broadbackbob (Ire)
1053 Burton Port (Ire)
1062 Captain Conan (Fr)

1090 Darlan
1110 Eradicate (Ire)
1117 Finian's Rainbow (Ire)
1130 French Opera
1135 General Miller
1138 Gibb River (Ire)
1140 Giorgio Quercus (Fr)
1146 Grandouet (Fr)
1179 Kells Belle (Ire)
1181 Kid Cassidy (Ire)
1195 Long Run (Fr)
1207 Master Of The Hall (Ire)
1219 Minella Class (Ire)
1231 My Tent Or Yours (Ire)
1240 Oscar Nominee (Ire)
1241 Oscar Whisky (Ire)
1242 Oscara Dara (Ire)
1250 Owen Glendower (Ire)
1258 Petit Robin (Fr)
1269 Prince Of Pirates (Ire)
1272 Punjabi
1273 Quantitativeeasing (Ire)
1289 Riverside Theatre
1308 Shakalakaboomboom (Ire)
1313 Simonsig
1328 Spirit River (Fr)
1329 Sprinter Sacre (Fr)
1338 Tanks For That (Ire)
1345 Tetlami (Ire)
1366 Triolo D'Alene (Fr)
1372 Une Artiste (Fr)

Robert Alan Hennessy
1226 Mossley (Ire)
1296 Rubi Light (Fr)

Philip Hobbs
1028 Balthazar King (Ire)
1061 Captain Chris (Ire)
1073 Chance Du Roy (Fr)
1074 Cheltenian (Fr)
1082 Colour Squadron (Ire)
1104 Duke Of Lucca (Ire)
1112 Fair Along (Ger)
1116 Fingal Bay (Ire)
1210 Meister Eckhart (Ire)
1212 Menorah (Ire)
1261 Planet Of Sound
1290 Roalco De Farges (Fr)
1297 Sadler's Risk (Ire)
1318 Snap Tie (Ire)
1379 Village Vic (Ire)
1392 Wishfull Thinking

Anthony Honeyball
1016 As De Fer (Fr)
1377 Victors Serenade (Ire)

Dessie Hughes
1198 Lyreen Legend (Ire)
1200 Magnanimity (Ire)
1220 Minsk (Ire)
1359 Tofino Bay (Ire)
1389 White Star Line (Ire)

Malcolm Jefferson
1019 Attaglance
1059 Cape Tribulation

Martin Keighley
1072 Champion Court (Ire)
1152 Havingotascoobydo (Ire)

John F Kiely
1063 Carlingford Lough (Ire)
1391 Wise Old Owl (Ire)

Alan King
1014 Araldur (Fr)
1024 Balder Succes (Fr)
1041 Bless The Wings (Ire)
1149 Grumeti
1160 Hold On Julio (Ire)
1186 Kumbeshwar
1196 Lovcen (Ger)
1202 Manyriverstocross (Ire)
1209 Medermit (Fr)
1224 Montbazon (Fr)
1236 Oh Crick (Fr)
1281 Raya Star (Fr)
1300 Salden Licht
1317 Smad Place (Fr)
1376 Vendor (Fr)
1382 Walkon (Fr)
1386 West End Rocker (Fr)

Emma Lavelle
1086 Court In Motion (Ire)
1150 Gullinbursti (Ire)
1158 Highland Lodge (Ire)
1256 Penny Max (Fr)
1358 Tocca Ferro (Fr)
1398 Zarrafakt (Fr)

Richard Lee
1154 Hector's Choice (Fr)
1183 Knock A Hand (Ire)
1189 Le Beau Bai (Fr)

Charlie Longsdon
1373 Universal Soldier (Ire)

Tony Martin
1032 Benefficient (Ire)
1044 Bog Warrior (Ire)
1094 Dedigout (Ire)
1245 Osirixamix (Ire)

Donald McCain
1012 Any Given Day (Ire)
1026 Ballabriggs (Ire)
1077 Cinders And Ashes
1144 Golden Call (Ire)
1161 Hollow Tree
1190 Lexi's Boy (Ire)
1247 Our Mick
1249 Overturn (Ire)
1255 Peddlers Cross (Ire)
1326 Son Of Flicka
1335 Super Duty (Ire)
1385 Weird Al (Ire)
1393 Wymott (Ire)

Oliver McKiernan
1124 Follow The Plan (Ire)

Noel Meade
1100 Donnas Palm (Ire)
1142 Go Native (Ire)
1166 Il Fenomeno (Ity)

1169 Ipsos Du Berlais (Fr)
1223 Monksland (Ire)
1230 Muirhead (Ire)
1282 Realt Dubh (Ire)
1337 Sword Of Destiny (Ire)
1346 Texas Jack (Ire)

Arthur Moore
1239 Organisedconfusion (Ire)

Gary Moore
1131 Fruity O'Rooney
1315 Sire De Grugy (Fr)

Mouse Morris
1023 Baily Green (Ire)
1076 China Rock (Ire)
1118 First Lieutenant (Ire)
1128 Four Commanders (Ire)
1280 Rathlin

Neil Mulholland
1216 Midnight Chase

Anthony Mullins
1050 Bridgets Pet (Ire)

Margaret Mullins
1101 Down In Neworleans (Ire)

Thomas Mullins
1005 Alderwood (Ire)
1042 Bob Lingo (Ire)

Willie Mullins
1008 Allee Garde (Fr)
1009 Allure Of Illusion (Ire)
1013 Apt Approach (Ire)
1015 Arvika Ligeonniere (Fr)
1039 Bishopsfurze (Ire)
1040 Blackstairmountain (Ire)
1046 Boston Bob (Ire)
1055 Call The Police (Ire)
1071 Champagne Fever (Ire)
1103 Drive Time (USA)
1113 Felix Yonger (Ire)
1115 Final Approach
1121 Flat Out (Fr)
1164 Hurricane Fly (Ire)
1167 Immediate Response (Ire)
1187 Lambro (Ire)
1201 Make Your Mark (Ire)
1203 Marasonnien (Fr)
1204 Marito (Ger)
1217 Midnight Game
1218 Mikael D'Haguenet (Fr)
1228 Mourad (Ire)
1238 On His Own (Ire)
1259 Pique Sous (Fr)
1267 Pride Ofthe Parish (Ire)
1268 Prince De Beauchene (Fr)
1274 Quel Esprit (Fr)
1276 Quevega (Fr)
1277 Quiscover Fontaine (Fr)
1304 Samain (Ger)
1312 Simenon (Ire)
1314 Sir Des Champs (Fr)
1319 So Young (Fr)
1321 Soll
1323 Some Target (Ire)
1327 Sous Les Cieux (Fr)
1336 Sweet My Lord (Fr)
1340 Tarla (Fr)
1355 Thousand Stars (Fr)

1368 Turban (Fr)
1369 Un Atout (Fr)
1371 Uncle Junior (Ire)
1374 Up The Beat
1375 Ut De Sivola (Fr)
1396 Zaidpour (Fr)

Colm Murphy
1036 Big Zeb (Ire)
1278 Quito De La Roque (Fr)
1380 Voler La Vedette (Ire)

Ferdy Murphy
1093 De Boitron (Fr)
1096 Divers (Fr)
1143 Going Wrong
1262 Poker De Sivola (Fr)

Paul Nicholls
1002 Aerial (Fr)
1003 Al Ferof (Fr)
1035 Big Buck's (Fr)
1049 Brampour (Ire)
1070 Celestial Halo (Ire)
1088 Cristal Bonus (Fr)
1095 Definity (Ire)
1097 Dodging Bullets
1098 Doeslessthanme (Ire)
1107 Edgardo Sol (Fr)
1109 Empire Levant (USA)
1119 Fistral Beach (Ire)
1120 Five Dream (Fr)
1137 Ghizao (Ger)
1151 Harry The Viking
1173 Join Together (Ire)
1176 Kauto Star (Fr)
1177 Kauto Stone (Fr)
1215 Michel Le Bon (Fr)
1222 Mon Parrain (Fr)
1243 Oscargo (Ire)
1251 Pacha Du Polder (Fr)
1253 Pearl Swan (Fr)
1264 Poquelin (Fr)
1266 Poungach (Fr)
1271 Prospect Wells (Fr)
1279 Ranjaan (Fr)
1284 Rebel Du Maquis (Fr)
1292 Rocky Creek (Ire)
1303 Sam Winner (Fr)
1305 Sanctuaire (Fr)
1311 Silviniaco Conti (Fr)
1342 Tataniano (Fr)
1349 The Knoxs (Ire)
1350 The Minack (Ire)
1356 Tidal Bay (Ire)
1361 Toubab (Fr)
1388 What A Friend
1397 Zarkandar (Ire)

Paul Nolan
1174 Joncol (Ire)
1234 Noble Prince (Ger)

Fergal O'Brien
1048 Bradley

Michael John O'Connor
1080 Clonbanan Lad (Ire)

Conor O'Dwyer
1125 Folsom Blue (Ire)

Edward O'Grady
1067 Cash And Go (Ire)

1068 Catch Me (Ger)
1248 Out Now (Ire)
1288 Rigour Back Bob (Ire)
1298 Sailors Warn (Ire)
1332 Staying Article (Ire)
1362 Tranquil Sea (Ire)

Jonjo O'Neill
1004 Albertas Run (Ire)
1006 Alfie Sherrin
1132 Galaxy Rock (Ire)
1136 Get Me Out Of Here (Ire)
1170 It's A Gimme (Ire)
1309 Shutthefrontdoor (Ire)
1334 Sunnyhillboy (Ire)

Andrew Parker
1213 Merigo (Fr)

Maurice Phelan
1265 Portrait King (Ire)

David Pipe
1017 Ashkazar (Fr)
1025 Balgarry (Fr)
1030 Battle Group
1081 Close House
1102 Dream Esteem
1106 Dynaste (Fr)
1147 Grands Crus (Fr)
1175 Junior
1178 Kazlian (Fr)
1206 Massini's Maguire (Ire)
1208 Master Overseer (Ire)
1235 Notus De La Tour (Fr)
1246 Our Father (Ire)
1263 Poole Master
1270 Problema Tic (Fr)
1294 Ronaldo Des Mottes (Fr)
1302 Salut Flo (Fr)
1352 The Package
1353 The Tracey Shuffle
1399 Zaynar (Fr)

John Quinn
1085 Countrywide Flame

Keith Reveley
1033 Benny Be Good

Nicky Richards
1283 Realt Mor (Ire)

Christy Roche
1148 Groody Hill (Ire)

Richard Rowe
1343 Tatenen (Fr)

Lucinda Russell
1045 Bold Sir Brian (Ire)
1310 Silver By Nature
1339 Tap Night (USA)

John Patrick Ryan
1123 Foildubh (Ire)

Jeremy Scott
1211 Melodic Rendezvous

Matt Sheppard
1165 Ikorodu Road

Oliver Sherwood
1079 Clerk's Choice (Ire)

Pam Sly
1155 Helpston

Sue Smith
1020 Auroras Encore (Ire)
1229 Mr Moonshine (Ire)
1330 Stagecoach Pearl

Suzy Smith
1108 Emmaslegend

Rodger Sweeney
1301 Salsify (Ire)

Tom Taaffe
1363 Treacle (Ire)

Colin Tizzard
1056 Cannington Brook (Ire)
1089 Cue Card
1145 Grand Vision (Ire)
1156 Hey Big Spender (Ire)
1237 Oiseau De Nuit (Fr)
1354 Third Intention (Ire)

Andy Turnell
1214 Micheal Flips (Ire)

Nigel Twiston-Davies
1000 Ackertac (Fr)
1018 Astracad (Fr)
1037 Billie Magern
1129 Frascati Park (Ire)
1168 Imperial Commander (Ire)
1180 Khyber Kim
1193 Little Josh (Ire)
1347 The Cockney Mackem (Ire)
1351 The New One (Ire)
1378 Viking Blond (Fr)

Tim Vaughan
1027 Ballyrock (Ire)
1299 Saint Are (Fr)
1341 Tartak (Fr)

Ted Walsh
1307 Seabass (Ire)

Paul Webber
1057 Cantlow (Ire)
1357 Time For Rupert (Ire)

Dermot Weld
1133 Galileo's Choice (Ire)
1159 Hisaabaat (Ire)
1370 Unaccompanied (Ire)
1381 Waaheb (USA)

Evan Williams
1060 Cappa Bleu (Ire)
1390 William's Wishes (Ire)

Ian Williams
1022 Baile Anrai (Ire)
1029 Barbatos (Fr)
1320 Solix (Fr)
1383 Wayward Prince

Nick Williams
1007 Alfie Spinner (Ire)
1083 Cornas (NZ)
1126 For Non Stop (Ire)
1134 Gauvain (Ger)
1287 Reve De Sivola (Fr)

Venetia Williams
1065 Carrickboy (Ire)
1162 Houblon Des Obeaux (Fr)
1257 Pepite Rose (Fr)

Michael Winters
1285 Rebel Fitz (Fr)

LEADING BRITISH JUMP TRAINERS: 2011-12

Trainer	Wins-runs	Wins (%)	2nd	3rd	4th	Win prize	Total prize	Profit/loss (£)
Paul Nicholls	138–598	23	97	75	54	£2,577,195	£3,297,804	-61.12
Nicky Henderson	167–627	27	108	49	67	£2,073,910	£2,741,455	-5.94
Donald McCain	153–717	21	120	87	63	£849,027	£1,248,262	+17.65
Jonjo O'Neill	97–649	15	81	53	54	£685,165	£1,144,902	-109.52
Alan King	82–523	16	82	71	59	£726,399	£1,135,082	-134.10
David Pipe	101–632	16	74	70	75	£686,358	£996,492	-149.28
Philip Hobbs	73–512	14	74	57	58	£492,420	£959,802	-145.80
Nigel Twiston-Davies	70–579	12	96	67	52	£324,111	£666,758	-185.66
Evan Williams	88–579	15	74	78	59	£342,144	£588,367	-112.79
Tim Vaughan	102–592	17	104	72	62	£341,776	£547,817	-100.97
Colin Tizzard	46–320	14	38	45	41	£240,385	£413,389	-82.69
Lucinda Russell	57–454	13	69	66	53	£270,174	£397,826	-123.17
Charlie Longsdon	69–349	20	50	31	24	£278,105	£382,762	+56.70
Tom George	40–247	16	43	29	18	£216,541	£356,575	-24.52
Sue Smith	45–337	13	37	49	38	£220,503	£356,412	-38.12
Venetia Williams	52–401	13	46	29	38	£220,611	£344,274	-70.94
Nick Williams	20–132	15	20	21	9	£167,192	£342,708	-53.54
Peter Bowen	53–413	13	47	38	37	£219,333	£340,140	-112.25
Brian Ellison	37–230	16	34	41	17	£211,263	£327,817	-56.64
W P Mullins	5–52	10	3	4	4	£149,967	£327,673	-15.43
Victor Dartnall	24–154	16	25	19	14	£223,617	£307,347	+10.53
Malcolm Jefferson	26–178	15	13	27	24	£241,760	£304,945	+82.88
Emma Lavelle	42–219	19	26	28	21	£178,962	£275,656	+23.58
Martin Keighley	34–251	14	40	35	27	£121,193	£271,330	-16.50
Gary Moore	29–314	9	39	45	27	£102,832	£254,257	-159.22
Paul Webber	31–209	15	19	21	27	£137,551	£246,661	-67.35
Keith Reveley	31–199	16	37	26	27	£139,683	£229,405	-15.06
Henrietta Knight	9–124	7	17	14	14	£152,084	£227,530	-72.50
Rebecca Curtis	39–180	22	25	22	16	£164,039	£217,485	-21.86
Richard Lee	17–150	11	13	15	21	£142,228	£215,218	-33.79
David Bridgwater	13–70	19	10	2	10	£61,658	£186,464	+24.63
John Quinn	17–74	23	17	9	7	£131,217	£180,783	+35.28
Ferdy Murphy	23–333	7	31	48	38	£75,765	£180,393	-170.63
Henry Daly	26–186	14	26	31	19	£111,157	£174,504	-9.52
Kim Bailey	32–211	15	30	26	19	£111,983	£171,075	+17.38
Ian Williams	29–229	13	26	25	21	£97,623	£166,756	-94.49
Gordon Elliott	32–149	21	28	15	7	£99,681	£162,762	-49.02
James Ewart	23–153	15	22	21	19	£104,647	£160,597	-24.12
Henry De Bromhead	3–18	17	1	1	3	£80,520	£159,890	-8.38
Brendan Powell	31–268	12	28	31	24	£89,955	£142,000	-66.57
Andrew Parker	9–60	15	11	4	2	£126,340	£138,196	+18.41
Nicky Richards	29–170	17	28	23	16	£85,717	£136,405	-18.65
Charlie Mann	22–203	11	25	23	23	£78,077	£136,291	-12.61
Neil Mulholland	16–181	9	20	27	15	£97,334	£130,615	-42.25
Jamie Snowden	19–120	16	19	16	12	£93,465	£127,016	-1.02
Jeremy Scott	24–138	17	18	15	18	£86,704	£125,357	+22.80
Dr Richard Newland	21–139	15	14	24	18	£74,519	£119,930	-31.09
Jim Goldie	16–150	11	25	19	10	£63,042	£118,482	-47.00
Tony Carroll	23–237	10	29	23	31	£62,017	£113,754	-56.25
Chris Grant	23–235	10	25	25	20	£66,695	£112,490	-56.82

LEADING BRITISH JUMP JOCKEYS: 2011-12

Trainer	Wins-runs	Wins (%)	2nd	3rd	4th	Win prize	Total prize	Profit/loss (£)
A P McCoy	199–727	27	128	77	61	£1,062,898	£1,473,738	-62.83
Richard Johnson	153–834	18	152	115	98	£727,950	£1,296,402	-104.85
Jason Maguire	144–625	23	115	69	53	£731,451	£1,095,248	-6.46
Tom O'Brien	83–536	15	57	51	74	£400,414	£577,086	-31.41
Daryl Jacob	83–455	18	77	48	49	£1,146,752	£1,391,366	-70.19
Paddy Brennan	82–477	17	74	53	34	£372,273	£568,807	-11.56
Sam Twiston-Davies	81–598	14	91	68	63	£329,174	£629,580	-150.63
Paul Moloney	70–547	13	65	56	59	£259,667	£473,899	-111.47
Tom Scudamore	65–450	14	53	53	50	£389,347	£701,472	-129.29
Barry Geraghty	63–220	29	37	17	23	£1,465,352	£1,735,426	-15.17
Aidan Coleman	58–381	15	53	39	36	£290,360	£458,292	-53.81
Denis O'Regan	55–428	13	46	40	54	£352,005	£509,502	-61.98
R Walsh	55–221	25	30	24	16	£1,141,004	£1,497,668	-45.89
Brian Hughes	53–492	11	50	60	63	£177,441	£314,865	-153.67
James Reveley	53–414	13	62	59	54	£219,007	£419,645	-107.24
Robert Thornton	51–353	14	49	47	41	£375,535	£683,903	-127.01
Noel Fehily	49–351	14	56	46	26	£471,828	£713,324	-116.51
Nick Scholfield	48–381	13	39	43	51	£208,734	£335,804	+8.27
Andrew Tinkler	48–287	17	46	18	36	£157,707	£290,602	-96.47
Felix De Giles	44–299	15	38	27	25	£173,357	£259,363	+24.70
Wayne Hutchinson	43–316	14	55	39	32	£390,371	£511,979	-84.50
Jamie Moore	42–460	9	53	50	41	£170,992	£366,349	-153.72
Dougie Costello	42–378	11	56	51	43	£282,104	£438,608	-100.43
Henry Brooke	42–355	12	40	36	27	£160,191	£232,250	-75.62
Timmy Murphy	42–302	14	45	30	38	£417,100	£562,217	-99.39
Leighton Aspell	41–377	11	47	48	51	£107,461	£223,931	-129.84
Andrew Thornton	39–449	9	38	53	53	£149,143	£224,799	-212.35
Lucy Alexander	38–332	11	32	37	45	£126,601	£188,780	+19.55
Peter Buchanan	38–307	12	46	39	29	£145,669	£229,626	-103.96
Campbell Gillies	38–300	13	38	34	33	£190,864	£253,040	-37.05
Dominic Elsworth	36–292	12	38	43	28	£257,324	£403,940	-90.69
C O'Farrell	35–258	14	38	39	28	£166,158	£271,554	-63.62
Richie McGrath	32–327	10	35	35	24	£124,599	£189,905	-107.18
Tom Cannon	32–281	11	35	38	26	£92,796	£167,482	-64.88
Adam Wedge	32–239	13	20	35	29	£108,415	£158,819	-34.50
David Bass	32–220	15	28	25	28	£131,141	£198,297	-46.28
Graham Lee	31–299	10	40	38	24	£117,806	£206,676	-120.71
Sam Thomas	30–306	10	24	26	23	£87,224	£142,130	-63.29
Brendan Powell	29–222	13	22	30	30	£72,929	£123,254	-49.50
Jack Quinlan	27–133	20	19	12	13	£87,608	£117,267	+13.89
Joe Tizzard	26–215	12	25	30	24	£147,998	£260,041	-74.03
Richard Killoran	26–139	19	11	17	16	£70,374	£94,034	+33.20
Will Kennedy	25–274	9	20	30	28	£102,769	£177,127	-76.63
Lee Edwards	25–212	12	24	19	33	£70,912	£109,934	+16.88
Jack Doyle	25–207	12	21	26	23	£96,540	£158,245	-38.83
Wilson Renwick	24–309	8	30	41	29	£81,119	£136,094	-120.68
Kielan Woods	23–132	17	15	14	12	£55,375	£79,521	+16.27
Jeremiah McGrath	22–133	17	16	19	10	£128,473	£159,921	+22.74
Ryan Mania	21–168	13	28	25	12	£98,774	£199,780	+22.25
Rachael Green	21–80	26	9	11	6	£68,289	£90,152	+46.38

LEADING BRITISH JUMP OWNERS: 2011-12

Trainer	Wins-runs	Wins (%)	2nd	3rd	4th	Win prize	Total prize
John P McManus	99–534	19%	75	38	49	£911,139	£1,393,422
J Hales	3–21	14%	4	3	2	£581,722	£639,044
The Stewart Family	16–59	27%	8	6	4	£460,873	£525,282
Michael Buckley	17–59	29%	10	5	9	£358,774	£423,966
T G Leslie	25–96	26%	21	8	7	£257,817	£410,232
Andrea & Graham Wylie	18–76	24%	15	8	9	£217,438	£345,554
Trevor Hemmings	22–186	12%	26	23	22	£115,262	£338,194
Simon Munir	12–50	24%	7	4	4	£299,673	£334,543
The Festival Goers	3–8	38%	1	1	0	£224,811	£256,742
Clive D Smith	3–8	38%	0	1	0	£244,673	£250,023
Jimmy Nesbitt Partnership	2–3	67%	0	0	0	£232,548	£232,548
John Wade	20–224	9%	37	28	21	£120,977	£216,720
Mrs Diana L Whateley	9–57	16%	7	8	9	£83,935	£206,552
Mrs T P Radford	6–35	17%	7	4	2	£142,760	£202,415
Walters Plant Hire Ltd	17–76	22%	9	9	11	£166,800	£192,165
Potensis Ltd & Chris Giles	4–15	27%	4	1	1	£161,898	£188,415
Mr & Mrs Raymond Green	14–88	16%	16	7	7	£150,960	£183,425
Mrs Caroline Mould	7–28	25%	3	2	3	£171,276	£181,372
Robert Waley-Cohen	1–22	5%	3	5	2	£17,085	£163,394
D A Johnson	11–42	26%	7	3	5	£126,814	£155,136
Mrs S Smith	27–156	17%	16	17	16	£118,861	£153,983
Gigginstown House Stud	2–27	7%	5	2	4	£53,854	£140,877
Ann & Alan Potts Ptnrship	1–7	14%	1	0	1	£68,340	£140,582
Simon Hunt	1–7	14%	2	0	2	£22,780	£136,777
Dunkley & Reilly Ptnrship	1–13	8%	4	4	2	£34,170	£135,707
Mr & Mrs William Rucker	10–53	19%	9	11	5	£54,347	£135,707
Brocade Racing	11–48	23%	3	7	6	£113,421	£129,070
Terry Warner	10–70	14%	5	12	10	£64,110	£126,365
Mrs Jo Tracey	7–35	20%	4	5	6	£74,590	£124,807
McNeill Family	5–16	31%	1	3	2	£96,920	£119,133
R A Bartlett	5–10	50%	2	0	1	£102,126	£116,057
Bran'n Dennis Dick Hold'n	4–13	31%	1	2	0	£80,290	£109,311
C G Roach	7–29	24%	4	4	1	£83,735	£104,601
J Sullivan & S Brown	2–10	20%	0	3	1	£59,734	£104,220
Gunners Syndicate	0–1	—	0	1	0	£0	£102,863
Jared Sullivan	4–11	36%	3	0	0	£67,414	£102,152
Banks, Blackshaw,Gann'n	2–6	33%	0	1	0	£85,085	£98,995
Estio Pinnacle Racing	4–7	57%	3	0	0	£67,282	£98,419
The Not Afraid Ptnrship	2–4	50%	1	1	0	£87,703	£97,490
Simon W Clarke	3–18	17%	4	2	1	£73,198	£97,324
H R Mould	8–51	16%	10	4	6	£54,520	£90,845
The Brushmakers	4–14	29%	2	1	0	£52,152	£90,775

INDEX OF HORSES

NOTES